BRITISH RAILWAYS
EASTERN REGION

B.R. 32402/3
BRITISH TRANSPORT COMMISSION
MOTIVE POWER DEPARTMENT
Staveley STATION

Date 17th June, 1958

Ext.   Ref.   Reference

To Mr Walker,

Dear Sir,

Thanks for your letter of the 14th instant.

I will arrange for your request to be carried out for a week commencing next Monday, 23rd June and will get the Engine cleaned up as much as possible with the staff available.

I would inform you, regarding your proposed visit to Staveley which you say will have to be on a Saturday that the Engine leaves Loco at 11.15am S.O. to work 12/3pm Chesterfield – Sheffield, arrive at 12/47, shunt there, depart 5/49pm E.W.D working.

TRAIN SERVICE

NOTTINGHAM and RUGBY CENTRAL

On and from 5th September 1966 the following service will operate

						SO				SX
NOTTINGHAM Victoria	dep.	07.50	08.22	12.27	13.55	16.17	17.34	18.52
EAST LEAKE	dep.	08.05	08.37	12.42	14.10	16.32	17.49	19.07
LOUGHBORO' CENTRAL	arr.	08.12	08.44	12.49	14.17	16.39	17.56	19.14
" "	dep.	08.13	08.45	12.50	14.18	16.40	17.57	19.15
LEICESTER CENTRAL	arr.	08.26	08.58	13.03	14.31	16.53	18.10	19.28
" "	dep.	08.28	09.00	13.05	14.33	16.55	18.12	19.30
ASHBY MAGNA	dep.	08.39	09.11	13.16	14.44	17.06	18.23	19.41
LUTTERWORTH	dep.	08.46	09.18	13.23	14.51	17.13	18.30	19.48
RUGBY CENTRAL	arr.	08.55	09.27	13.32	15.00	17.22	18.39	19.57

				SO			SX	
RUGBY CENTRAL	dep.	—	07.11	10.30	12.30	15.05	16.20	17.37	18.55
LUTTERWORTH	dep.	—	07.20	10.39	12.39	15.14	16.29	17.46	19.04
ASHBY MAGNA	dep.	—	07.28	10.47	12.47	15.22	16.37	17.54	19.12
LEICESTER CENTRAL	arr.	—	07.41	11.00	13.00	15.35	16.50	18.07	19.25
" "	dep.	07.10	07.43	11.02	13.05	15.37	16.55	18.12	19.30
LOUGHBORO' CENTRAL	arr.	07.21	07.54	11.13	13.16	15.48	17.06	18.23	19.41
" "	dep.	07.22	07.55	11.14	13.17	15.49	17.07	18.24	19.42
EAST LEAKE	dep.	07.30	08.03	11.22	13.25	15.57	17.15	18.32	19.50
NOTTINGHAM Victoria	arr.	07.44	08.17	11.36	13.39	16.11	17.29	18.46	20.04

Notes— SO—Saturday Only.   SX—Saturdays excepted.

This service will provide accommodation for SECOND CLASS passengers only.

Passengers will be able to obtain tickets, **between stations served by this Service only**, from the Guard in charge of the train.

Accommodation will be provided for the conveyance of cycles, perambulators, etc., accompanied by passengers, who will be responsible for the removal of these articles from the stations.

Unaccompanied traffic will not be conveyed.

Season tickets, **between stations served by the Service only**, will be issued at Nottingham Midland, Leicester Midland and Rugby Midland Stations.

From:	Notting-ham		East Leake		Lough-boro Cen.		Leicester Central		Ashby Magna		Lutter-worth		Rugby Central	
To:	S	R	S	R	S	R	S	R	S	R	S	R	S	R
Nottingham	—	—	2/9	3/3	4/–	4/6	6/6	6/6	9/–	10/6	10/3	12/6	12/–	14/6
East Leake	2/9	3/3	—	—	1/4	2/3	4/3	5/–	6/6	9/3	7/9	11/–	9/6	13/3
Loughboro Cen.	4/–	4/6	1/4	2/3	—	—	2/9	4/3	5/6	8/3	6/3	10/3	8/3	13/–
Leicester Central	6/6	6/6	4/3	5/–	2/9	4/3	—	—	2/9	4/3	4/–	5/9	5/3*	8/3
Ashby Magna	9/–	10/6	6/6	9/3	5/6	8/3	2/9	4/3	—	—	1/2	2/3	3/–	5/–
Lutterworth	10/3	12/6	7/9	11/–	6/3	10/3	4/–	5/9	1/2	2/3	—	—	2/–	3/6
Rugby Central	12/–	14/6	9/6	13/3	8/3	13/–	5/3*	8/3	3/–	5/–	2/–	3/6	—	—

The return fare quoted above is that for Cheap Day Return.   *Cheap Single Fare.

 **British Rail**
London Midland Region

Issued by British Railways
Divisional Manager, Furlong House,
Middle Furlong Road, Nottingham.

AD 36   BR 35000   August 1966

GREAT CENTRAL TWILIGHT FINALE

1. The 'South Yorkshireman' running between Bradford and Marylebone was one of the Great Central route's two named expresses. Here, after an engine change a V2 2-6-2 No 60842 still wearing its Eastern Region shed code makes an exhibitionist start from Leicester Central with the southbound express.

GREAT CENTRAL TWILIGHT FINALE

by

Colin Walker

PENDYKE PUBLICATIONS

In an age when large chunks of the railway network are struggling against massive odds to provide an even adequate service it is salutory to look back to times when the system afforded a more comprehensive, complete and confident capability.

Like its locomotives and rolling stock, a remarkable amount of railway fabric and structure combined functional effectiveness and durability with a certain elegance of style and it is therefore a matter of genuine regret that so many fine urban and rural stations have been reduced to crumbling, bricked-up, graffiti-covered, unstaffed halts or have been demolished altogether to be replaced by bus-stop style shelters.

Stations, large and small, were designed and constructed to accommodate a 'family' of staff who besides serving the public and feeding the trains also tended the buildings' upkeep. Through its staff/customer relations a station's reputation was influenced for good or ill.

As with any family relationship this staff 'atmosphere' varied considerably from station to station and to a regular rail user or observer was something that could be distinctly 'felt'.

My previous books on the Great Central have been dedicated in general to the staff of the line and particularly to those who have featured more prominently in their pages. This, my last book to be devoted to the line, offers the same dedication but with an important and specific inclusion.

With hindsight it is now possible to appreciate the remarkably high quality of service offered not only by the train crews at Leicester Central but also by individual members of the station staff. In the 1950s, before negative policies began to take effect, their calibre and motivation was impressively high.

I am referring to the 'resident' staff rather than the hierarchy because in the 1950s station masters at the larger stations on the Great Central tended to be 'in passage' and brief in their tenure. Remembered with regard and real respect were people like the diminutive and affable Station Inspector Frank Pole whose occasional bursts of fire when under stress were more than compensated for by a warm and helpful manner which bred cooperation from platform staff and train crews as well as appreciation from passengers.

Then there was Jack Frith the bespectacled, breezy ticket collector whose fresh, crisp greetings welcomed rail customers at the stair-top platform barrier or, alternatively, chilled the blood of potential fare dodgers. His clear-voiced train announcements over the platform loud speaker system would herald the arrival of the expresses and conclude with that unforgettable flourish, "This train is provided with a restaurant car".

Downstairs at street level, Harry Sales, the chief booking clerk, with his juniors, Clive Berry, Len Rudkin and Derek Powell ran a large booking office of high professionalism. They revelled in their membership of the railway service and the Great Central line in particular and there was no take-it-or-leave-it indifference in their attitude to customers but a genuine desire to advise, inform and assist.

And what of those whose lot it was to work amongst the grease and grime? The station shunters like big Bert Naylor and his colleagues, the Toone brothers who played a key role in the ritual of engine change. Wearing their enormous red rubber gloves glistening with oil they would squeeze themselves between coach and locomotive tender alongside those lethal buffers and disconnect and connect the brake hoses and train heating pipes and swing-lift the massive chains and buck-eye couplings with an easy-action rhythm which made their task a skill rather than a crude labour. After a contorted climb back onto the safety of the platform their shout of 'blow up' would announce the task complete and in true Great Central fashion if urgency demanded it they could have an express on its way again in less than four minutes after its arrival.

Finally, there was Miss Piggott and her industrious assistant in the station refreshment room. Here one could still sit in relaxing green upholstered chairs with mahogany backs inlaid with the brass insignia GCR and in their comfort relish one of the best cups of coffee in Leicester. The room was a perfect period setting with huge mirrors and an ornamental fireplace incorporated into walls of decorative glazed tiles. The floor was mosaic and behind the mahogany and marble topped counter climbed rows of shelves also in mahogany. They were surmounted by a clock over the central opening into the back kitchen. The whole was kept in immaculate order by an equally immaculate Miss Piggott. Apart from the chairs and perhaps the clock the whole was ruthlessly destroyed by the demolition gangs when they moved in in the 1970s.

This high quality of station service on the Great Central was, I am sure, not confined to Leicester Central and no doubt other stations on the line could equally claim their own special brand of 'family' excellence. However, it was exceptional for such a large station to work so compatibly and the fact that most of its activity was contained on an island platform was no doubt a factor in its fine reputation. But, it was still essentially people who made it work so well and as with Great Central enginemen, both passenger and freight, such motivated staff were ever a privilege to know. This book salutes their memory.

ISBN 0 904318 15 X

© Colin Walker 1993

Published by:-Pendyke Publications,
'Gorffwysfa',
Methodist Hill,
Froncysyllte,
Llangollen,
Clwyd.
LL20 7SN.

Photoset in North Wales by
Derek Doyle & Associates, Mold, Clwyd.

Printed by The Amadeus Press Ltd.,
Huddersfield, West Yorkshire.

INTRODUCTION

Great Central Twilight Finale concludes my trio of books devoted to the last years of the Great Central main Line to London and it effectively exhausts the photographs I took of the line and its trains. Inevitably perhaps, as the choices become narrowed, so it concentrates more and more on those parts of the line that I frequented most and as a result it stresses even more than the earlier books, the London Extension through the city and county of Leicester.

Though the photographs have not appeared in the earlier titles some may have been taken on the same occasions. Also, the settings of some of my favourite spots are repeated because compared with the diesels and electrics, when all the variables of light, wind and weather were combined with an engine's exhaust, its effort and its boiler pressure no two steam displays were ever the same.

At the risk of some repetition it is necessary to put the photographs into their context.

Before the Second World War the Great Central had been a highly effective mover of coal from the Nottinghamshire, Derbyshire and South Yorkshire pits to the south and south-west of England. It was also a major linking route for a variety of mixed freight between the north and north east of England and the south and west. Its high profile in the country's freight network was heavily emphasised during the war when vast tonnages travelled its tracks and its simplicity of operation and efficiency ensured that traffic was kept flowing in a way that was not so noticeable on some other lines where junctions and bottlenecks created a logjam.

Under a lively and enterprising L.N.E.R. management the Great Central section's passenger services and particularly its cross-country and Marylebone expresses had been growing in popularity and loading well. With the electrification of the Sheffield-Manchester section through the Pennines well in hand the future of the line looked very optimistic indeed.

After the war, like much of the railway network, the Great Central main line was faced with an enormous backlog of maintenance and repair but there was every prospect that this would be undertaken and that a programme of rapid recovery would be pursued. As a token of this intent the L.N.E.R. bestowed titles upon two of the line's expresses – 'The Master Cutler' and 'The South Yorkshireman'. They were the first officially named services to run over the route and in catching the attention of the travelling public they also gave a lift to staff morale.

On the freight side, the L.N.E.R., in a final gesture before being nationalised, had reorganised the operation of traffic running between the marshalling yards at Annesley and Woodford thereby creating a freight service that was to have no parallel anywhere in the country. The new out-and-home service worked by one engine and crew between the two yards meant that the 'windcutters' or 'runners', as they were to be dubbed by the railwaymen themselves, became a model of efficiency and economy.

With the nationalisation of the railways the whole line's future was immediately cast into doubt because, under the new regional structure, the Great Central route became a geographical misfit and it lost its unified management. Instead, it was placed under the control of three different regions though its operation was retained by the Eastern Region which was successor to the old L.N.E.R. This ridiculous arrangement ensured that there would be no incentive to promote the line and the London Midland Region, which now controlled the major part of it, only viewed it as a continuing impediment and threat to its own struggling services.

The result was predictable. The recovery, revival and gradual accelerations which were taking place elsewhere were denied to the Great Central which was left to languish so that a spirit of creeping indifference began to replace the former optimism. By the mid 1950s this indifference had developed into an active policy of obstruction designed to discourage use of its services so that passenger numbers could be reduced and the line brought to its knees and to ultimate closure. The appointment of Dr. Richard Beeching to the chair of the Railways Board on June 1st 1961 only confirmed and accelerated the process.

With such an absurdly divided and often hostile management the strategy of reducing revenue while increasing costs posed no problem at all and the ploys that were used seemed to embrace just about every dirty trick in the book. Indeed, the amount of negative energy that went into the run-down was quite shameful as was the complete lack of concern that hard won traffic and custom, far from being neatly transferred to alternative rail routes, (as we were assured they would be), were instead almost completely lost to the railway.

The closure was effected in stages. It began in earnest during the mid 1950s with the vigorous promotion of services and accelerations on competing lines and particularly over the Midland route. This was done at the expense of the Great Central where speed restrictions were kept in force over formerly favourable stretches of the line thus hampering the running of its expresses. Other pin pricks then followed which started the flow of life blood. They included the depopularisation and ultimate transfer to the East Coast route of the highly successful 'Master Cutler' express which had become an almost exclusive first class club train with business men from Sheffield, Nottingham and Leicester. Then, on January 4th 1960, although they were still covering their costs after years of commercial 'dissuasion', all the through daytime expresses from Manchester, Bradford and Sheffield to Marylebone were hastily withdrawn.

The nine and ten coach expresses with their restaurant cars were replaced by a grudging semi-fast service of three trains each way daily between Marylebone and Nottingham only. With six or seven carriages they ran at unattractive times and, because of their frequent stops, to lengthy schedules. To reduce their convenience further particularly for anyone from the north wishing to travel to Oxford and beyond connections at Woodford and Banbury were either broken or deliberately missed by a matter of minutes.

A suggestion that a new revised service should be introduced operated by diesel sets was instantly dismissed because, it was claimed, there were no facilities for servicing and maintaining diesels on the Great Central. This flimsy excuse however, had not deterred the Eastern Region at Sheffield from sending one of their new English Electric 2000 hp locomotives to Leicester Central during 1958 on a regular Summer Saturday filling in turn with the Newcastle–Bournemouth through train and back with the 12.15 pm down Marylebone–Manchester express. Nor did it prevent the same depot in 1962 from employing one of their Type 3 diesels right through to Banbury and back with the York–Bournemouth and Bournemouth–York trains. Equally, as any nocturnal visit to Leicester Central would prove, the Western Region seemed to have no qualms about running their Hymek and 'Warship' hydraulic diesels over the Great Central with the night mail from Swindon.

Typically, once the rundown of the line was well advanced and irreversible the lack of diesel servicing facilities suddenly no longer mattered and the first semi-fast out of Marylebone in the morning and its return from Nottingham at 12.25 pm became the daily task of a four coach diesel set.

Together with all the Sunday passenger services, the local trains which had served the expresses were axed in 1963. The first to go were those between Nottingham and Sheffield and between Aylesbury and Rugby to be followed by those linking Woodford and Banbury. The service between Rugby and Nottingham was retained only on the recommendations of the area Transport User's Consultative Committee after strenuous opposition to its loss was registered by a large number of local objectors in the East Midlands. The recast service however did ensure that some of the better used and most profitable trains were withdrawn and that the closure of the smaller stations included those contributing the most passengers! The country stations had of course all been kept staffed until their closure which helped to keep up the costs. Equally there was no economising on permanent way maintenance by the introduction of mobile gangs as was happening elsewhere. Oh no, the time-honoured, labour intensive, fixed length gangs were retained almost to the end.

Alongside these permanent, major withdrawals and closures went the removal of many signal boxes and the elimination of supporting facilities such as car parking, refreshment rooms and newsagencies at the larger stations. There was also a constant 'drip' of short term obstructions, not all intentional perhaps, but nevertheless cynically fortuitous to those promoting the closure process. These ranged from an increasing number of engine failures, shortage of staff and crews, stock, turntable, water and coaling plant failures to the occasional use of suburban, non-corridor stock on some of the semi-fasts so that passengers were denied even basic bladder comfort on their journeys. Then there were the timetable and advertising omissions and lapses when stations were prematurely announced as having closed and their services axed before approval for such action had even been sought from the various Transport Users' Consultative Committees.

By such tactics was the confidence of the travelling public undermined and, as if to celebrate the achievement, the formation of the semi-fasts was reduced to four coaches in March 1963 when the trains were incorporated into the Nottingham–Rugby commuter service with additional stops.

One of the most self-destructive weapons to be employed had been the actual closure of sections of the line on Sundays for engineering work to be undertaken. No other double track main line resorted to such a drastic measure and cancelled or interrupted its popular Sunday services as happened on the Great Central.

The Sheffield–Marylebone and Sheffield–Swansea (later Swindon) Sunday trains were, on the whole, extremely well patronised and were good revenue earners. If they were going to be prepared for withdrawal a prolonged but intermittent programme of engineering work lasting several years was an ideal weapon and within this strategy the *pièce de résistance* was surely the closure of Catesby tunnel.

Nothing was more likely to deter a regular passenger from using a service than to have to leave a cosy and comfortable train on a raw winter evening at Woodford and to descend the station steps to board a cramped, unheated bus of questionable vintage for a ¾ hour switchback journey through the Northamptonshire/Warwickshire border country to Rugby where the rail journey was then resumed in another barely heated train.

The Sunday engineering line closures were most effective nails in the line's coffin. Apart from the inconvenience and disruption to passengers' journeys they also required the doubling of train sets, engines, crews and guards; the hire of coaches and of course the gathering of an army of men paid at double time rates to undertake the engineering and permanent way work.

Similar engineering tasks on other parts of the railway system were expedited in a fraction of the time but such was the lack of urgency on the Great Central that during the closures of Catesby tunnel some elements of the workforce had time to ferment and indulge in brawls and fights. These further delayed the site clearance and also disrupted the early Monday morning train services. For a short time the Great Central Sunday closures became a *cause célèbre* in parliament with some penetrating questions to Minister Marples from Sheffield M.P. George Darling and Leicester's Sir Barnet Janner but to no avail.

When it came to words and statistics some astounding comments and assertions were made both in parliament and at meetings of the various Transport Users' Consultative Committees. In April 1961 Mr. John Albert Hay, a Joint Parliamentary Secretary to the Minister of Transport, was stressing to the house that, "there was no intention of closing the Great Central line but to use it for freight and parcels traffic". He also assured the house that, "not all passenger facilities would be withdrawn".

As for Mr. G.B. Gray, the London Midland Region's area manager at Nottingham his performances at meetings of the local T.U.C.C. were hardly convincing either particularly when confronted with some well worked out plans for a revival of Great Central passenger services. These included an enterprising and economical timetable drawn up by a well informed group of objectors who anticipated the current trends of today by offering to run their own charter diesel trains. That proposal was very swiftly nipped in the bud.

The claimed savings from the withdrawal of traffic were riddled with contradictions and obfuscations as were the returns quoted on traffic receipts. For instance in 1961 the revenue earned on parcels and allied traffic was said to be only £3350 for the whole line while it was revealed by the National Homing Union that the pigeon traffic contributed by them alone in the area between Sheffield and Nottingham over only a five month period in that year amounted to £24,000.

Also, at another T.U.C.C. meeting on January 9th 1962, though no such accusation had actually been levelled by any of the objecting parties, Mr. Gray heatedly declared in an attack on the opposition that, "there is no proposal to close Nottingham Victoria and Sheffield Victoria stations". What he should perhaps have added were the words, "at this meeting" because we all know what happened to those two stations. Only a conscience consumed by guilt and some seriously disturbed nights could have provoked such an outburst because secret negotiations about the site of the former station and its development as a shopping centre were probably even then well under way.

At another crucial meeting where counter proposals were to be made he employed the familiar fillibustering technique of waffling for 1¼ hours so that time ran out for the main objectors who were unable to fully state their cases.

It became clear to everybody at the time that the decisions of the Transport Minister and the recommendations and proposals of British Railways regional and area managers could never be challenged however shallow, fatuous, evasive or down right misleading their arguments. The minister could always claim that "he had 'no responsibility for rail closures or adjustments to the timing of trains", while the toothless, impotent and partial T.U.C.C.s could always aver that a particular matter was, "beyond the scope of their enquiry or terms of reference" and should be directed to British Railways or to the Transport Commission with the inevitable consequences.

In truth the London Midland Region of British Railways was given almost a free hand and either ignored or took liberties with any minor, temporary restraints that were placed upon it. It was also interesting that none of the large city councils at Leicester, Nottingham, Sheffield or Manchester put up any resistance to the loss of such useful rail services and amenities. Mindful of the prime land that would be released for all kinds of development no doubt they stood to do well out of the closure and one can only imagine what concealed palliatives, placibos and perks were exchanged for their stoic silence. Certainly, one was aware of attempts to 'buy off in kind' individual resistance and it did not pass unnoticed that one influential objector was treated to a day out over the Great Central on the restored Midland Compound.

The final public enquiry that was convened by the East Midlands T.U.C.C. to discuss the London Midland Region's sparsely advertised proposals to withdraw all the semi-fast and through passenger services, and to close the Great Central line north of Nottingham Arkwright Street and south of Rugby was arranged with only 10 days notice on Friday, October 22nd 1965. A 10am start ensured that a great many individual and corporate objectors would not be able to attend nor were they given the time to prepare their cases.

At various stages in the line's run-down, correspondence was aired in both the national press and in provincial newspapers throughout the length of the line. With the most minor exceptions the views expressed were in favour of the line's retention and opposed to its decline. However, at a small town near Nottingham where a lively debate was conducted in the local press, a notable advocate and supporter of the London Midland Region's plans to close the local station turned out to be none other than the incumbent station master. Such seemingly suicidal tendencies were, of course, quite prevalent at that time and fully consistent with a climate which saw many a railwayman's promotion prospects enhanced by his contribution to the contraction of the railway system rather than his advancement of it. One trusts that the gentleman concerned was rewarded with a suitably 'plum' job for his 'loyalty'.

The through trains, including the York–Bournemouth, ran for the last time on Saturday, September 3rd 1966 leaving an even more grudging diesel multiple unit service running between Rugby and Nottingham Arkwright Street. Some of the trains became notoriously popular because the volume of passengers using them was such that the guard was unable to collect all the fares and free travel for some became a precarious bonus. This pathetic remnant of the Great Central line's services was itself finally withdrawn on 3rd May 1969 after which the elimination of the 'London Extension' was complete and it was erased from the railway network, apart from short lengths south of Loughborough where the Main Line Steam Trust began the long slog of reclaiming the line back to Birstall, and north of the town where track was retained to serve the gypsum mines in the wolds near Gotham.

Since their inception railways have been the subject of a long and continuing evolution influenced not only by technological developments and social and industrial change but also by the numerous mergers that swallowed up and combined the early companies. It is necessary to say this because as one who was born after the formation of the big four companies the personal memories I have of the Great Central main line began when it was already a part of the L.N.E.R.

Exciting railway though it certainly was, it only required references to Bradshaw's Timetables of the early years of the century and to numerous reminders by Cecil Allen in magazine articles to realise that the really dynamic period in the line's story took place long before I was even conceived when it was locked in unfettered competition with the company it directly challenged, namely the Midland Railway.

Those were the days when the Great Central set about winning passengers to its services from London, Leicester, Nottingham, Sheffield and, (not so easily), Manchester by running short, tightly timed expresses hauled by robust Gorton-built locomotives that combined workmanlike reliability with Edwardian elegance. A train like the 3.15 pm down 'Sheffield Special' covering the 163¾ mile trip in 2 hours and 57 minutes at an average speed of 55.85 mph was never subsequently bettered.

Such was the average Great Central engine crew's pride in the engines of their company that the 'foreign' locomotives that appeared after the 1923 grouping were often viewed with suspicion, disdain and even contempt. One was frequently reminded by some of the older drivers that on the formation of the L.N.E.R. the locomotive stud contributed by the Great Central was, on the whole, more solidly contructed than many of the products of Doncaster and gave a better ride. The Great Central Atlantics and 'Director' 4-4-0s, for instance, were extremely well proportioned engines and very good runners, though it must be admitted that neither possessed the flamboyant, buccaneering flair of the G.N. Ivatt large boilered Atlantics nor their ebullient riding qualities!

The continuing preference for things Great Central was therefore well justified and quickly recognised by the newly formed grouped company which virtually left the Great Central section undisturbed for over twelve years before introducing any new permanent express passenger engines to it in the shape of the B17 4-6-0s. Though puissant in performance they too fell far short of the cab standards enjoyed on the Great Central classes and only reinforced the view that improvements in locomotive power, speed and efficiency were only made at the cost of the old Great Central virtues of steady, civilised riding.

Even the regular appearance of the Gresley Pacifics in 1938 was only grudgingly accepted as an advance by some of the Great Central diehards for were they not also of Great Northern lineage? Certainly one had to be very careful about effusing too strongly about them to Percy Banyard. Percy was the local Locomotive Inspector at Leicester Central and a more staunch champion of the old company it would be difficult to find. He was an incredible mine of information and anecdote and in his partisan view the big Gresley engines could do nothing that a Great Central Atlantic was not capable of doing. With the nine and ten coach loads running to some of the easier post-war-decline schedules he was probably right but whereas the Pacifics and V2s were able to do it well within their capacity one feels that the gracious G.C. 4-4-2s would have been quite fully stretched.

It was perhaps the more pragmatic drivers of Great Central origin who declared the real truth like Leicester driver Jack Webb who, towards the end of his career, climbed down from No 60107 'Royal Lancer' after an impressive trip from Marylebone and announced that the A3 was the finest engine he had ever driven. This was some accolade from a man who had been reared on the comfortable, rolling gait of the Gorton Atlantics and who entered the annals of professional fame when, on July 8th 1939 with Fireman Bob Hayes, he worked up from Leicester Central to Marylebone with B17 4-6-0 No 2848 'Arsenal' on an express that had been loaded up to 13 coaches because of the inclusion of a boat portion from Immingham. With 465 tons of train he reached London in only 109 minutes.

If it is easy for someone born in the 1930s to overlook the early dynamic history of the Great Central it would be equally wrong for an even younger generation to gain the impression that the line in its final years was in any way typical of its real ethos. Compared with the preceeding eras of the L.N.E.R. and the Eastern Region of the nationalised British Railways when plans for the route were still imbued with some optimistic and progressive thinking, the Great Central section's transfer into London Midland control was like the injection of a slow, debilitating virus which was depressing to watch in action. As such it could quite reasonably be asserted that the appearance of the 'Royal Scots', 'Black 5s' and even 'Britannia' Pacifics on the ludicrous six and four coach semi-fasts were ominous symbols of rapid decay and terminal decline. Indeed many of these engines were run-down rejects from depots where they were surplus to requirements.

The big London Midland engines also exposed some of the appalling hypocrisy that surrounded the decision to close the route. In 1963 when the late Dr. Richard Beeching released a television documentary film 'The Reshaping of Britain's Railways' in support of the drastic cuts he was proposing the opportunity was eagerly taken to show one of Neasden's V2s arriving at Brackley with the 1.15 pm all stations passenger train from Nottingham Victoria to Marylebone. This train also served a very useful operating function by including in its make-up the empty newspaper vans returning to London. Though it had obviously been filmed some years earlier the big engine, long train and dearth of passengers at 3.50 in the afternoon made for a perfect spectacle of waste and inefficiency.

What viewers were not to know was that the V2 was returning home after working the 10 am down Manchester express from Marylebone to Leicester which was always a well filled and popular train and that the engine had in reality earned its keep that day. This was more than could be said later of the more than ample power like the coal-hungry 'Royal Scots' which ambled around on trains of trivial tonnage in the years that followed. Obviously when the Great Central's future closure was ensured such deliberate waste no longer mattered though dubious and dishonest practices of this kind also helped to keep the costs up.

As I have already described the tactics employed in the run down of the services embraced a deliberate policy of discouragement and less than concealed hostility on the part of the London Midland Region management. Faced with a route that was not actually failing; which had a freight service that was a national showpiece and was moving over 2,400 wagons and vans daily, and whose expresses, on the region's own admission, were not unremunerative perhaps only a strategy of slow sabotage was possible. Certainly as the arguments for the run-down were advanced so it was impossible not to sense that behind the scenes some old scores were being settled.

There is no doubt that the Great Central had been a chronic irritant to the Midland Railway and later the L.M.S. not just as a successful poacher of traffic but also, one suggests, psychologically. Almost from the outset the Great Central's express locomotive stud was quite the equal of anything the Midland possessed while on the freight side the introduction of the sturdy 'Pom Pom' 0-6-0 in 1901 and later the remarkable Great Central 'Tiny' 2-8-0 in 1911 eclipsed every Midland freight design.

Then there was the question of 'topographical' psychology. As the younger route the Great Central's crossings over the Midland main line at places where competition was keenest like Loughborough, Nottingham and Sheffield and also over the London and North Western's West Coast main line at South Hampstead, Harrow and Rugby were all 'over the top'. That it put this literal 'one upmanship' to effective use there is no question and in particular its crossing of the Midland stations at Loughborough and Nottingham seemed strategically sited to exert the most potent and acute demoralisation.

Any passenger standing on Nottingham's Midland station awaiting a train to St. Pancras or Sheffield and hearing a Great Central line

Following page.
The Marylebone Expresses
The A3 Pacifics.
2. A sombre industrial morning in March 1957 finds A3 Pacific No 60111 'Enterprise' blowing away the cobwebs as she gains speed over the fine Braunstone Gate bowstring girder bridge in Leicester. The train is the 8.30am up from Manchester and the photograph was taken from the rear roof of Kirby and West's 1930s model dairy which possessed a street facade of white, green and blue glazed tiles.

express pounding through the girders above him would be forgiven if he began to entertain doubts about his choice of route. If he was bound for Leicester such doubts would be more than justified as there was nearly a ten minute difference in the journey times. Similarly at Loughborough where the two stations were a mile apart any northbound Great Central express that had called at the Central station would be up to 40 miles an hour and in full cry by the time it crossed over the Midland platform ends. As for the non-stops like the 'Master Cutler' which would be well in the 80s at the bottom of the Loughborough 'dip' and preparing to rush Barnston bank their crossing would be both fleeting and furious.

Even at Rugby where the Great Central made a prolonged crossing of the North Oxford Canal, River Avon and the West coast main line the way in which Great Central expresses 'hit' the birdcage bridge in both directions could never be ignored. Nor for that matter could the Annesley–Woodford 'windcutters' which rattled through the steelwork with a nonchalance that was in marked contrast to the sluggish pace of most of the freight traffic down below where the usual queues and tail backs were the order of the day.

My collection of Great Central line photographs might have been very much greater had it not been for a certain K3! In the summer of 1955 my wife-to-be and I were searching for our first home and inspecting the numerous small estates of semis that were springing up on many sites on the Leicester fringes.

One such development was taking place on Greengate Lane at Birstall, a road that crossed over the Great Central north of Belgrave and Birstall station and, as it happened, the last house was in the course of construction right next to the railway cutting and close to the overbridge!

As we wandered over the site and what would become the garden I remember putting forward a most plausible and convincing suggestion that a neighbouring railway had distinct advantages offering a high degree of privacy and that from previous personal experience passing trains were never any problem. (I had indeed once lived in a house where the garden backed onto the busy Midland branch from Leicester to Burton on Trent.)

The idea was thoughtfully if not eagerly received and we made our way onto the bridge to look down onto the line. As the reconnoitre was concluding a sound drifted onto the ear and arrested our departure. To me it was thrilling but in the circumstances distinctly alarming.

It was a Saturday afternoon and into view came a K3 going absolutely all out up the climb from Rothley with a holiday extra loaded to 14 coaches. The exhaust from its chimney was being hurled well above the top of the cutting and it was very, very black. As it passed beneath us we were showered with sparks, ash and soot and enveloped in a cloud of smoke laced with the pungent aroma of hard coal combustion.

As my partner was something of a perfectionist when it came to matters of laundry I knew that a home within two miles of that spot was instantly eliminated. My curses were silent as we left the bridge without a word being spoken.

My residence in Leicester, however, was extremely fortuitous because it was a key staging point for engines and crews on the Great Central line Marylebone–Manchester expresses. The fine reputation and loyal public support commanded by them almost to the end was inextricably wrapped up with the attitude and lively professionalism of the Leicester enginemen.

They were a fascinating group of men to know and so often an inspiration after travelling with crews elsewhere whose running was conditioned and inhibited by loadings, regulations and restrictions or the inertia born of traditions, habits and practices that sapped initiative and sparkle. That contemptuous rejoinder voiced by Leicester Central driver Len Woodhead, "We do our best with what we've got", when quizzed about train loadings was not only a succinct and unequivocal put-down to an alien, self-important but bewildered locomotive inspector from another railway, it was also a declaration of a completely different outlook and philosophy which, alas, was to be stifled and extinguished by the regional changes of 1958.

When I started photographing on the Great Central in 1957 Leicester still had eight A3s Pacifics which, thanks to Leslie Warren the shedmaster of the day, were, for a time, kept in a very creditable condition in spite of an appalling labour shortage which was to get worse. They were Nos 60039 'Sandwich' (which only stayed six months), 60049 'Galtee More', 60059 'Tracery', 60102 'Sir Frederick Banbury', 60104 'Solario', 60106 'Flying Fox', 60107 'Royal Lancer', and 60111 'Enterprise'. They were supplemented by two V2s Nos 60863 and 60878. Then came nine B1 4-6-0s Nos 1008 'Kudu', 61063, 61269, 61298, 61299, 61369, 61376, 61380 and 61381. Leicester Central's allocation of engines was completed by J11 0-6-0s Nos 64375 and 64453 and the humble, essential, not-to-be-forgotten J52 shunting tank No 68839.

One does not have to analyse this list of engines to appreciate that Leicester Central shed was almost totally committed to express passenger work and after the electrification of the Manchester–Sheffield section over the Pennines through Woodhead tunnel in 1956 the main burden of responsibility for running the expresses over the remaining steam section between Sheffield and Marylebone fell to the depot. The contribution of Neasden and Sheffield, though important, was secondary.

The pleasures of adventure, challenge, vigilant responsibility, professional rivalry and even mischief that helped to shape the Great Central spirit undoubtedly drew inspiration from the line itself. It was a spirit that was available for export or absorption by newcomers but it was never imported. Where it infiltrated other parts of the L.N.E.R. it manifested itself among engine crews in several and diverse ways. With many of them it was expressed by a healthy professional arrogance which averred that no one knew how to run trains like they did and woe betide anyone who suggested otherwise.

It also embraced a driver's gut dislike of running double headed unless, of course, it was ordered by Control for convenience of operating. Indeed, it was almost an admission of failure to seek the assistance of a second engine. This was perhaps why Leicester driver Sid Parker (then in No 2 link), after finding himself coupling up to the 10 o'clock mail to Manchester and Liverpool well beyond the platform end at Marylebone one night in July 1958 and warned by the guard that his load was 15 instead of the normal 8 or 9 nevertheless elected to remain in sole charge of his train and to go it alone. He arrived in Leicester 5 minutes late with B1 No 61381.

This particular episode demonstrated how well most Great Central men rose to the occasion when faced with adversity provided of course, the conditions leading to the difficulty were not repeated because of a lack of remedial action on the part of those responsible for its correction or repair.

Among my own personal experiences I relish the memory of a fascinating run with Leicester Driver Albert Chafer who had limped into Marylebone with B1 No 61111 on the the 8.30 am from Manchester and promptly failed it. The date was Saturday, 6th September 1958 and it happened that I was returning from a West Country family holiday on the 3.20 pm down which was Albert's return working.

Walking up the platform I found Albert, the train but no engine and there was only five minutes to go before departure time. Having exchanged greetings and learned of his difficulties I entered into what I considered to be some very safe jocularity by suggesting he might be provided with a 'bloodspitter' by way of a replacement. A 'bloodspitter' was the lurid name given by Leicester men to the former North Eastern Railway Raven 4-6-0s and their Thompson rebuilds of Class B16 which were mostly shedded at York and which quite often worked through to Banbury on the express freights but were not commonly seen in London. They were a competent mixed traffic engine but were not really cut out for express work.

The improbability of my suggestion allowed us to share the joke until at 3.20 the tender of a locomotive emerged from the tunnel mouth and approached No 4 platform. It was not a familiar one and as the smiles faded and facial muscles hardened 'bloodspitter' No 61449 looking very care worn backed onto the train and coupled up.

Now Albert Chafer was a man of somewhat rugged temperament and he possessed an even more rugged vocabulary which was by now extremely audible. So, after taking a furtive photograph I deemed it prudent to keep well clear and quietly joined the family in the first coach of the train.

We left Marylebone at 3.24 and I prepared myself for a depressing trip home behind a morose and sullen driver who could justifiably claim that his engine was not a suitable instrument for the job. Not so. "We do our best with what we've got" was obviously part of Albert's philosophy too because by dint of some fine enginemanship he contrived to reach Leicester just over one minute early on what was admittedly an easy Saturday schedule.

There were some very memorable features of this trip like the drama of 'catching the water' when we attacked the climb to Amersham. After passing through Rickmansworth at a much reduced 15 mph No 61449 began to prime and we were treated to an amazing display of mixed water and fireworks. The roar from the engine's chimney was quite fearsome as a veritable cocktail of hot ashes and blackened water rained down upon our carriage roof and streamed down the carriage windows but, in spite of being rather winded, the B16 made it and we topped the climb at a steady 30mph.

At Aylesbury the stop was prolonged to nearly 4½ minutes while the bag was frantically inserted into the tender tank in the hope of recouping some of the water deposited over the Chilterns. The lesson having been learned the rest of the run was characterised by steady accelerations from station stops after which the 'bloodspitter' was prodded along in the mid 60s with 70mph touched at Culworth Junction.

The last stage between Rugby and Leicester was quite a gallant effort no doubt made with a feeling that there was not much to lose in having a go. The 25 minute timing for the 19¾ miles was cut to 20 minutes and 42 seconds. With a maximum of 76 at Whetstone the B16 was pounded into Leicester with the usual abandon that brought up a time of 75 seconds from passing Leicester South Goods to a stand in the Central station. One of the locally perfected single brake application stops was no doubt employed.

This endeavour by one of Leicester's less conspicuous performers was fairly typical of the positive outlook one could find anywhere on the Great Central but if exception rather than the rule was sought then one had to draw upon amazing episodes like the triumph of Driver Fred Birtwhistle and his fireman Norman Buswell who on 27th October 1949 failed at Marylebone with lubricator trouble on A3 No 60061 'Pretty Polly' after bringing in the up 'Master Cutler'. For their return with the 12.15 down Manchester express which took the long route through Wycombe and Princes Risborough, Neasden had nothing better to offer them than a former Great Central A5 4-6-2 tank used for local suburban workings. With a load of 10 coaches they took on the challenge and with stops at Wycombe and Woodford for water they arrived in Leicester only 11 minutes late. The amount of coal left in the bunker was not recorded but what an engine, what a crew and what guts!

Other heroic efforts by Leicester men arising from engine failures involved the uncouth L1 tanks, another remarkably strong Thompson design which was so scimped in its construction that, like the B1s, it suffered from the most rapid, self-inflicted mechanical wear and tear.

On 13th November 1950, almost a year following the A5 tank triumph the anxiety levels must have been raised again at Marylebone when the A3 working the down 'Master Cutler' failed and L1 tank No 67785 was hooked on to the 12 coaches and dispatched 45 minutes late from the terminus. Statistically, in terms of tractive effort the L1 was nearly the equal of the A3 Pacific and the weight of the train would have posed no problem but its riding qualities were somewhat different and in description perhaps more close to a nightmare. It was eventually removed from the train at Woodford having lost another 45 minutes on the way.

Even my friends Messrs Durrington and Cassie found themselves sharing the discomforts of one of the L1 2-6-4 tanks on the up 'South Yorkshireman' in 1955 when their A3, No 60104 'Solario' ground to a halt in a cloud of dust while departing from Aylesbury. Climbing down they were confronted with a broken left hand connecting rod which had momentarily lifted up their engine as it dug itself into the ballast. The local shed could only offer an L1 tank which was duly flogged up the Chiltern climb through Stoke Mandeville and Wendover to Amersham and then down to London where their much delayed arrival in Marylebone included only some 15 minutes extra on their scheduled time from Aylesbury.

These sample heroic efforts are but a confirmation of the remarkable attitude displayed by most G.C. line engine crews when things went wrong. Even when presented with the most unlikely replacement for their failed engine they did not resort to refusal or limp along in surly defeat but instead would rise to the challenge and even extract some masochistic pleasure and entertainment from their predicament.

One of the worst insults that could be offered to a Great Central line driver was to suggest that he needed advice, or worse, tutorial assistance in driving a 'foreign' engine. This did occasionally occur as when George Evinson's B1 No 61380 became derailed at Old Oak Common after working an excursion from Leicester to Marlow in Buckinghamshire on Saturday, June 14th 1958. George was offered No 6920 'Kingstone Grange' to take the train back together with a spare Old Oak driver who would show him how to handle a Western engine. George took the 'Grange' but not the driver saying, "he didn't need any bloody tuition, thank you". He had an uneventful trip back to Leicester with 25 inches of vaccuum for his brake instead of the usual 21 inches and his comment on arrival was that "there was nothing special about those engines".

Then, of a different order, there was the keen eyed vigilance of top link driver Tommy Chamberlain who dashing into Leicester and approaching Rowley Fields with the Sunday 3.30 pm express from Marylebone to Manchester spotted that while his colour lights for Leicester South Goods gave him a clear green on the main line the points it guarded were switched into the South Goods loop! That he managed to get his train down to a speed low enough to take the swerve without derailing was a miracle. Such were the hazardous results of Sunday signal and track repairs when not carried out correctly.

My early footplate trips over the Great Central were with Driver Durrington and his fireman Ron Cassie. Behind a highly developed cavalier facade they were a good crew with an excellent working relationship. They also possessed a deadly blend of mischievous humour that did not always go down too well with 'authority'.

My very first run with them was probably the only serious one I ever had and is etched deeply into the memory. The engine was B1 No 61066 heading the down 'Master Cutler' non stop between Leicester and Nottingham.

Even in the 'comfort' of the fireman's seat I was quite unprepared for the first B1 buffetting I was to endure and at the height of my initiation as we were heading to pass beneath the overbridges announcing Loughborough I became aware of a voice shouting in my left ear above the clamour and din. It was Albert who, after checking his signals, had left his seat and crossed over to counsel me with the following advice- "If ever anything 'appens always stick to your engine. Never jump. The engine'll always look after you. A fireman once jumped here from a 'Sam Fay' on an express and he hit the bridge wall. It killed him. You've never seen such a mess".

With speed in the 80s and striving to keep my seat on a temporarily driverless and tortured engine this homely piece of advice fed an imagination that was already barely functioning as a calming influence. When Albert withdrew to regain his seat and resume control the lips literally had to be tongue moistened as one would do in the aftermath of some acute crisis. It took not a few trips with Mr. Durrington before I got used to his colourful brand of description.

As for their wit and pranks both on and off the footplate I never really did get used to them and was caught out on many, many occasions and perhaps one of the most embarrassing episodes occurred one school lunch time when I ventured out to photograph their departure through the Leicester outskirts near Rowley Fields with the up 'South Yorkshireman'. I was honoured on this occasion to have the company of Leslie Warren, the Leicester shedmaster who I had recently got to know.

When the express appeared and B1 No 61380 passed by, a facetious voice shouted from the engine, "Why don't you take some real photos like these?" At the same moment a soft missile landed in the grass beside us and as its pages wafted over in the breeze the contents of a particularly ripe girlie magazine were revealed which had been discovered in the engine's locker.

Now, this high risk crew had obviously not reckoned on the appearance of the shedmaster as well and for all I knew Leslie was, outside his professional calling, a devoutly religious man with the severest of puritanical ideals and strict moral views. So, respectability and pure mindedness obviously had to be displayed and the publication was left severely untouched and uninspected while a series of chronic coughs accompanied our hurried departure from the scene.

Even worse experiences befell other representatives of 'authority'. In 1957 when the Eastern Region A3 Pacifics were still in command of the expresses and the groundwork was being prepared for the London Midland Region to take over the operating of the Great Central line a number of locomotive inspectors from the Midland depots were instructed to ride over and acquaint themselves with this anticipated addition to their territory and power. To observe and hear of some of their experiences caused no small amusement and they must have been a salutory eye opener to a quite different attitude and tradition. Characters like Durrington and Cassie seized such opportunities with the most evil relish and concealed some deliberately nail biting driving and firing practices behind a facade of calm indifference. I seem to recall that during one of these episodes I found myself in the role of 'double agent'.

One winter evening I was present on the platform at Leicester Central station to watch the 3.20 pm down from Marylebone make its engine change. Slightly before time the express's headlamps appeared out on the West Bridge viaduct before swinging into the platform road and A3 No 60049 'Galteemore' dashed in with a more than usual swagger and came to an abrupt halt.

There were three figures on the footplate and in addition to Messrs Durrington and Cassie I recognised an inspector from the Midland shed at Leicester. Now I happened to meet this gentleman in a completely different social context over a pint of beer in the 'Welcome Inn' on a Friday evening. He was a competent church organist and an amiable character whose railway career had been mostly spent at the Midland's Spital depot at Peterborough. His promotion had brought him to Leicester Midland where he was made a firing instructor before becoming a fully fledged locomotive inspector. His enthusiasm for his work and the railway in general was not of the highest and whenever we met he was always reluctant to discuss his job. When he did so it was invariably condemnatory and he found it difficult to understand anyone who found railways, and particularly steam locomotives, interesting.

This being the case I decided to keep discreetly out of the way but I did notice that after collecting his bag from 'Galteemore's' tender locker he stepped from the engine in what could only be described as a state of dazed shock. With the grimmest of countenances he made straight for the 'Gents' and I was also aware that as the A3 moved off its train to retire to the shed peals of previously suppressed mirth floated from the engine's cab.

Later that week when we met up in the 'Welcome' I risked asking my inspector friend how he had got on and was treated to an erruption that suggested that the experience was not open for discussion but that "That lot over there are completely mad".

How I chuckled internally. No doubt he had been treated to the complete works which included some of the infamous Leicester Central single brake application stops from 70 mph plus and he had also suffered the notorious Catesby 'drop' which I too had first hand experience of.

The Catesby 'drop' was a piece of bad rail inside Catesby tunnel which, if one was unprepared for it, could be extremely disorientating to say the least. It came at a particularly critical moment when one was adjusting to the change of light and space. The sinister strategy was to have the firedoor closed and to ensure that the 'victim' was free standing somewhere near the middle of the cab when the engine plunged into the darkness of the tunnel. Then, in the event of a loss of balance or vertical posture when the engine gave its lurch a fullsome show of sham concern and sympathy would be unstintingly offered by the culprits sitting securely in their seats.

My favourite run over the Great Central was on the 4.5 pm from Manchester which changed engines at Leicester and left soon after ten minutes to seven. It was a leisurely run calling at Rugby, Woodford, Brackley, Aylesbury and Harrow with an arrival in Marylebone at 9.20 pm. There then followed a 4½ hour break before returning to Leicester with the 1.45 am early morning 'Newspaper' express.

Neither Albert Durrington nor his fireman were avid consumers of ale and were more than content to fortify themselves with a good brew of tea in the spartan enginemen's cabin beside the Marylebone turntable. I personally found this most convenient because while they studied those early tabloid stalwarts the 'Mirror' and 'Reveille' which were of course essential reading in any railway messroom, I was able to set up my tripod in the dark and take long experimental exposures of our engine standing proudly and massively on the turntable. They were extremely memorable occasions that are still relished.

Things were rather different if I travelled up with Driver George Evinson. George enjoyed his pint and so the chance of calling into the Boston Arms near the Rossmore Road overbridge before closing time at 10 o'clock was always the incentive for a prompt arrival in Marylebone. The moment the empty stock had been removed our engine would be urged across to the turntable, placed in mid gear and then abandoned while we hurried across to the pub. Here, while George lined up his pints and collected a reserve supply in his Corona bottles I would find myself sharing light conversation with some of the ladies of the night who collected there in the course of their profession. "Do you want anything, love" one might quietly enquire but scruffy overalls and a shortage of time was always acceptable as a polite but firm refusal. Perhaps some things just wouldn't mix anyway.

George Evinson also possessed a rare brand of humour. It was he who on one occasion as our V2 climbed from Rickmansworth through the Chilterns with the down 'Newspaper' fumbled in his jacket pocket and withdrew a rather large torch and shone it from the cab window at an angle that was distinctly at right angles from the engine. As its beam stabbed the night and lit up passing tree trunks, branches, leaves, fences, greenhouses, gardens and the odd bedroom window he was asked what he was doing. "I'm trying to see where we're bloody going" was his shouted reply.

At depots like Leicester there was always a long, distinguished and continuous tradition which men like George Evinson were very much a part of. George had once fired for Percy Banyard before Percy was promoted to Locomotive Inspector while, in his time, Percy had fired on Great Central Atlantics and the Gresley 'Footballers' with Driver Tetlow, a cantankerous man with a formidable reputation for hard running way back in Great Central and L.N.E.R. days. Similarly Sid Lees, another thoroughly conscientious and thinking driver had in his young days fired on the Robinson Atlantics for another Leicester Central driving celebrity Tommy Newall. They were splendid men.

During the last years of the expresses the frustration of many engine crews with the restrictions imposed on their running could be quite tangibly felt and there was much straining at the leash. True, in spite of an official overall 75 mph speed limit over the route the sprint between Leicester and Nottingham was still largely unhindered and gave an inspired crew the chance to ignore the restriction and run the 23½ miles in 22 minutes or less if they had a suitable engine and the urge to do so. However, this was offset by the colliery subsidence checks between Nottingham and Sheffield and the curb on speed down the long bank from Catesby where, before the war, expresses had displayed some joi de vivre that carried them well into the 80s. Also, south of Aylesbury the problems of finding a path through the intensive Metropolitan line services remained a serious handicap. How ironic it was that the quadrupling of the section between Harrow on the Hill and Watford South Junction just short of Rickmansworth, which promised to relieve the pressure and give Great Central expresses a much freer run into and out of the capital was only completed to coincide with their withdrawal. The improvement was therefore never exploited.

When additional, if temporary, obstacles were added to the regular restrictions the frustration could become quite acute and even the down early morning 'newspaper' was not exempt from such delaying devices. The London Midland Region, whose record of time keeping on its own main line from St. Pancras in the late 1950s was sometimes quite shameful, was quite prepared to put this lucrative traffic at risk by routing the train at very short notice over the 'new line' through Northolt, Wycombe, Risborough and Ashendon instead of by the direct Aylesbury route. Not only was it a longer mileage for a vitally important train of 'perishable' print but instead of being given a clear run, it was turned through all the platform roads between Neasden South and Northolt Junctions, which meant a severe braking to 15 mph at each station, and then opening up again on regaining the main line. Such an obstructed path could add nearly half an hour to the run to Leicester.

Even in such dispiriting circumstances many engine crews refused to admit defeat and once they had a clear road some tremendous running followed. Perhaps no better proof of this could be provided than the thrilling sound recording made by Peter Handford at around 3 am that concludes his record 'The Great Central'. It captures Leicester V2 No 60831 as it surmounts Saunderton summit with the down 'newspaper' and then racing down through Princes Risborough and the Vale of Aylesbury in a furious attempt to regain the lost time. No 60831 was not the freeest running of V2s but Albert Durrington certainly made her run that night as I well remember.

As already remarked, when the Great Central line expresses were withdrawn on January 2nd 1960 they were replaced by a temporary and token semi-fast service between Marylebone and Nottingham. The working of the service was spread between the depots at Annesley, Leicester, Woodford and Neasden and the contraction immediately threatened the careers of engine crews so that many took redundancy or scanned the lists of vacancies elsewhere.

Some, like Albert Durrington who was the senior driver at Leicester Central when the expresses finished managed to retire with unruffled dignity to dig two allotment gardens and nurse an invalid wife. Like many men of his generation he was a tremendous family man and his G.P. declared that his devoted care gave her an extra five years of life. He himself died in December 1989 aged 95.

Other, younger drivers like Ken Davies, George Evinson and Len Woodhead transferred to the Midland depot at Leicester where their professional quality and commitment rapidly enabled them to master the new diesels and in a very short time they had leapt into the main line links, incurring no little resentment from the aboriginals in the process. Wherever they went the 'invaders' took with them their Great Central pride and disdain while rapidly making the grade and seeking top link responsibilities.

I recall visiting Crewe with a party of schoolboys in 1963 and while waiting for the DMU back to Derby a steamy hoot drew my attention to Stanier Pacific No 46239 'City of Chester' which was waiting in one of the middle roads to take over an express to Euston. On closer study of the man at the regulator I recognised former Leicester Central driver Len Royston who had transferred to the West Coast main line in the face of his dwindling prospects on the Great Central. I was intrigued to learn that in spite of his illustrious charge he would have preferred a V2!

The Great Central spirit was not only carried abroad by the express passenger men but it was also exported from the freight depots at Woodford and Annesley. Nearly two decades after the end of the 'windcutters' when collecting information as part of my research I called into the London Midland diesel depot at Toton in the hope of finding some former Annesley men. When I enquired at the crew supervisers office I was met with the jocular reply, "Oh yes, there's quite a few men from Annesley here and they're still telling us how to run our bloody railway". When the word was passed round two crewmen presented themselves and within seconds they launched into memories of their days on the 'windcutters'. Their assertions that "With those 9Fs we were down through Leicester before they'd even left the yard here" was greeted with good natured but long suffering groans of, "Here we go again", from their assembled colleagues. Somehow one suspects that their claims were not far short of the truth.

In addition to its unique spirit and because its links with other lines were so few there was also a strong family atmosphere about the Great Central. Apart from some of the cross country trains and latterly the 'Starlight Specials' the locomotives that headed the expresses, semi-fasts and the 'windcutters' appeared repeatedly and their very familiarity exuded a sense of 'belonging'. There was also a much closer link between train crews and station staff than pertained on many other main lines while the dependence of both passenger and freight trains on the same pair of tracks ensured that a considerable amount of mutual respect was cultivated among the enginemen involved in the running of both kinds of traffic.

This family atmosphere was perhaps nowhere more strongly felt than at Woodford Halse – that railway village set in the rolling uplands of south east Northamptonshire which served and serviced a junction station, a large engine shed and extensive marshalling yards. The railway at Woodford belonged to its people. It was their livelihood and a major topic in any conversation or gossip. In such a rare, specialised, industrial community set in a rural fastness any visit by a new or interesting 'foreign' engine brought out the local residents in force to make their way to the station or the engine shed to cast a critical eye over the intruder.

The closure of the railway had a prolonged and devastating effect on the village and for many years it was in a collective state of concealed mourning. This profound sadness found a deeply moving release in a flower festival that was organised in June 1976. It lasted three days and included a poignant exhibition of railway memorabilia in both the parish church and the church hall.

On the second day of the festival on a golden Sunday morning the village turned out and from the one time Railwaymen's Club and Institute they paraded beneath the forlorn station arches to St. Mary's church which had been lovingly decorated with a mixture of delicate flower arrangements and collections of railway souvenirs and relics. In one of the deserted top floor rooms of the Railwaymen's club the old N.U.R. local branch banner had been discovered. It was lifted out, unfurled, raised again and carried at the head of the procession to the church and in the service that followed which was attended by a packed congregation, Derek Thornton who had once been a fireman on the 'windcutters' and later a passed fireman, read one of the lessons.

Possibly the vicar, the Reverend Haydn Christopher Smart, did suffer some misgivings and fears that the spiritual purpose of his service was in danger of being swamped by a wave of temporal nostalgia but one did feel that Woodford church that morning fulfilled quite splendidly the function of enabling its village to release some profoundly sad emotions and memories that still lingered from the destruction of its whole way of life. The service and festival seemed to signal the end of a long period of genuine corporate grief and to what more appropriate purpose could the proceeds of the service and festival have been put than the restoration of Woodford's church bells.

And finally, what of the future? The closure of the Great Central main line has by now been generally accepted as a 'fate' accompli that can never be undone. However, times change and already plans have been discussed to re-open the route north of Aylesbury to a point near Rugby where freight could be transferred to the M1 and M6 motorways having bypassed and avoided the London orbital congestion.

More interesting though, will be the enormous pressures that will build when the Channel Tunnel comes into operation and our railway facilities and fabric are revealed to be so desperately inferior to those of France and our European partners. In a country like England with such a high density of population and where land is so scarce what course will a high speed rail route linking the Channel Tunnel and London with the North, North West and North East of England have to take if one has to be built that is unimpeded by junctions, level crossings, gauge restrictions and slower moving traffic.

Political folly and crass short sightedness has abandoned such a potential railway but the course of the Great Central is still very much in place and with some necessary re-alignment and compulsory repurchase much of it could be reinstated and incorporated into a 200mph railway. Many of the old handicaps to ultra high speed like its island platforms and mining subsidence will by then no longer be a problem and the whole route could be considerably upgraded.

Should such a rebirth ever occur one hopes the authorities would respect the line's historic past and show some imagination and even wry humour by naming its crack train 'The Windcutter'. As for the Great Central Railway 1976 PLC and its splendid preservation achievements perhaps it should keep its eyes open and its ears close to the ground! After all, official assurances were once made that the Great Central main line would not be closed and it was. By the same token any fresh vigorous denials could ensure its reopening. Who knows?

3. Engine change at Leicester Central. On a hazy Spring morning in 1957 another A3 No 60106 'Flying Fox' having brought in the up 'Master Cutler' from Sheffield makes a snappy dash for the shed. The Pacific's crew Driver Durrington and Fireman Cassie are a familiar pair and the photograph was taken somewhat hurriedly to foil an attempt to beat the photographer's camera preparations as the passing shouts of derision from the engine's cab made clear.

4. A3 No 60106 'Flying Fox' again approaching the signal gantry on the West Bridge viaduct at Leicester with the up 'South Yorkshireman'.

5. A3 No 60107 'Royal Lancer' pulls out of Leicester Central onto the West Bridge viaduct with the up 'Master Cutler' from Sheffield. Labour shortages were having a marked effect on the cleanliness of engines at this time and No 60107 is looking very neglected externally but was in good shape within. Her driver was Sid Lees and it is interesting to see that he has chosen to place the headboard on the buffer beam instead of at its more customary position below the chimney. Sid Lees was a 'thinking' driver and he averred that hanging the headboard at the top of the smoke box was detrimental to the engine's draughting and steaming.

6. No 60107 'Royal Lancer' again heading the up 'Master Cutler' takes the curve into the short Ashby Magna tunnel at the top of the climb out of Leicester.

7. A3 No 60104 'Solario' in very respectable condition gets into its stride past Leicester South Goods with the 8.30am express from Manchester to Marylebone. Her driver is George Taylor who was rather 'heavy handed' with his engines and notable for making a quite a lot of noise.

8. Driver Albert Durrington and his regular fireman Ronald Cassie of Leicester Central's top link on A3 No 60104 'Solario' waiting to work the up 'Master Cutler'. They were an excellent partnership but a deadly mix for those who were unaware of their mischievous brand of laid-back humour.

9. Home and dry. Driver Cyril Chamberlain with A3 Pacific No 60104 'Solario' heading the 3.20pm down express from Marylebone to Manchester bustles into Leicester over the West Bridge viaduct and prepares to give up the train to a fresh crew.

10. Another photograph from the rooftop of Kirby and West's dairy in Leicester's Braunstone Gate shows A3 No 60104 'Solario' storming over the girder bridge with the 8.30 am from Manchester to Marylebone. What an incredible sense of thrust and impetus is conveyed by the engine's exhaust which so wonderfully echoes the curve of the bridge. There must surely be few machines that could produce a dynamic spectacle like this.

11. A night portrait of No 60104 'Solario' standing on the turntable at Marylebone. It was not always possible to pitch a tripod in a position where a full side view was presented as indeed was the case here so that the loss of a buffer was a price that had to be paid. 23.2.57

12. The same combination of obstruction and confined space also exerted restrictions on this long exposure shot of No 60104 'Solario' standing on the Marylebone turntable in the first hour of the morning on February 23rd 1957 before its return to Leicester with the 1.45am down 'Newspaper'.

Following page.
13. A3 Valette. The last Leicester A3 to be given a major overhaul at Doncaster works was No 60111 'Enterprise'. She was taken into the works on 9th July 1957 having run 79,253 miles and she returned on 15th August. Only five weeks later 'Enterprise' was recalled back to the East Coast Main line and transferred to Grantham where she ended her days. Here, shortly after her return from shopping and still gleaming from a repaint she stands vigorously raising steam at 1.30 in the morning at the head of the 1.45 am down 'Newspaper'. Her crew that night was Driver Ken Davies and Fireman Jack Freer. September 1957

14. A fresh brew of tea in the enginemen's cabin at Marylebone obviously took priority over turning the engine on this occasion because No 60107 'Royal Lancer' has been temporarily abandoned and left on the turntable approach road. Her next assignment will be to work the 1.45 early morning down 'Newspaper' express back to Leicester Central.

15. Messrs Durrington and Cassie take A3 No 60107 'Royal Lancer' onto the West Bridge viaduct over the River Soar navigation in Leicester on a Summer evening in 1957. Their train is the 4.5pm express from Manchester to Marylebone.

Two photographs taken on a glorious summer evening on a footplate trip to Marylebone on A3 No 60107 'Royal Lancer' heading the 4.5 pm express from Manchester to Marylebone.

16. A blackbird plays a risky game of 'chicken' in front of 'Royal Lancer' as it approaches an overbridge near the top of Ashby Magna bank. 17.5.57.

17. Albert. The evening sun shafts into the cab as 'Royal Lancer' climbs away round 'Cosby Corner' and catches Driver Durrington in a relaxed but vigilant posture as he grasps a wide open regulator to provide a study in sunshine, shadow and serenity. 17.5.57

18. I was not sure whether to include this photograph but it does make a significant point about Great Central line running. The style of entry into Leicester by expresses in both directions with local crews was the source of no small amusement to me and logs of engines still nudging 70 mph while only a mile from the station stop did appear in print from time to time in the railway enthusiast press. Against many of the correct procedures a number of Leicester men excelled in the single brake application stop and to see and feel this put into practice on the footplate was usually accompanied by a rise in the pulse.

This shot of No 60106 'Flying Fox' arriving back with the down 'South Yorkshireman' on a June evening in 1957 with Ernie Warren driving perhaps sums it up. My intention was to catch the engine in the short length of open steel lattice work above the water before it reached the brickwork. Alas, the 25mph limit numerals displayed on the bridge might well not have been there and the engine must still have

The V2s. With the transfer of the A3 Pacifics back to the East Coast Main Line the Great Central section collected a number of V2 2-6-2s at Leicester as replacements including a small clutch from the G.N. main line. There were eight of them: 60828, 60831, 60842, 60854, 60863, 60878, 60879, and 60911 and these highly competent engines took over the working of the expresses. Though maintenance problems eventually overtook them particularly after control of the line had passed to the London Midland Region, they were still accorded a more dignified status on the Great Central expresses than they received on the G.N. main line where they were usually relegated to fast freight work or used as substitutes for the Pacifics.

19. Gathering speed alongside the North Goods loop at Leicester is No 60842 with the up 'Master Cutler'. Looking out is Driver Ken Davies who after nationalisation transferred to Leicester Central from the North Wales freight depot at Mold Junction. His admiration for the Gresley Pacifics and V2s was well known and he thrived on hard running. He was a fine 'import' and became a great asset to the Great Central section.

20. Driver Ernie Warren is at the regulator of V2 No 60911 which is pulling out of Leicester Central with the up 'South Yorkshireman'. In No 4 bay a 9F 2-10-0 No 92178

21. Running off the Leicester viaduct and approaching the North Goods loop No 60878 heads for London with the up 'Cutler'. Top link driver Tommy Chamberlain is

22. No 60911 which was well overdue for a shopping when this photograph was taken quickens its syncopated roar as it bounds through the girders of the Braunstone Gate bowstring bridge with the up 'South Yorkshireman'. February 1958.

23. A V2 swap at the North end of Leicester Central. No 60828 arrives in Platform 5 at Leicester Central with the 3.20 pm down express from Marylebone to Manchester and prepares to hand over the train to sister engine No 60863 which stands alongside raising steam for the run to Sheffield. These Leicester Central engine changes were quite legendary and when time was short could be accomplished in under 4 minutes

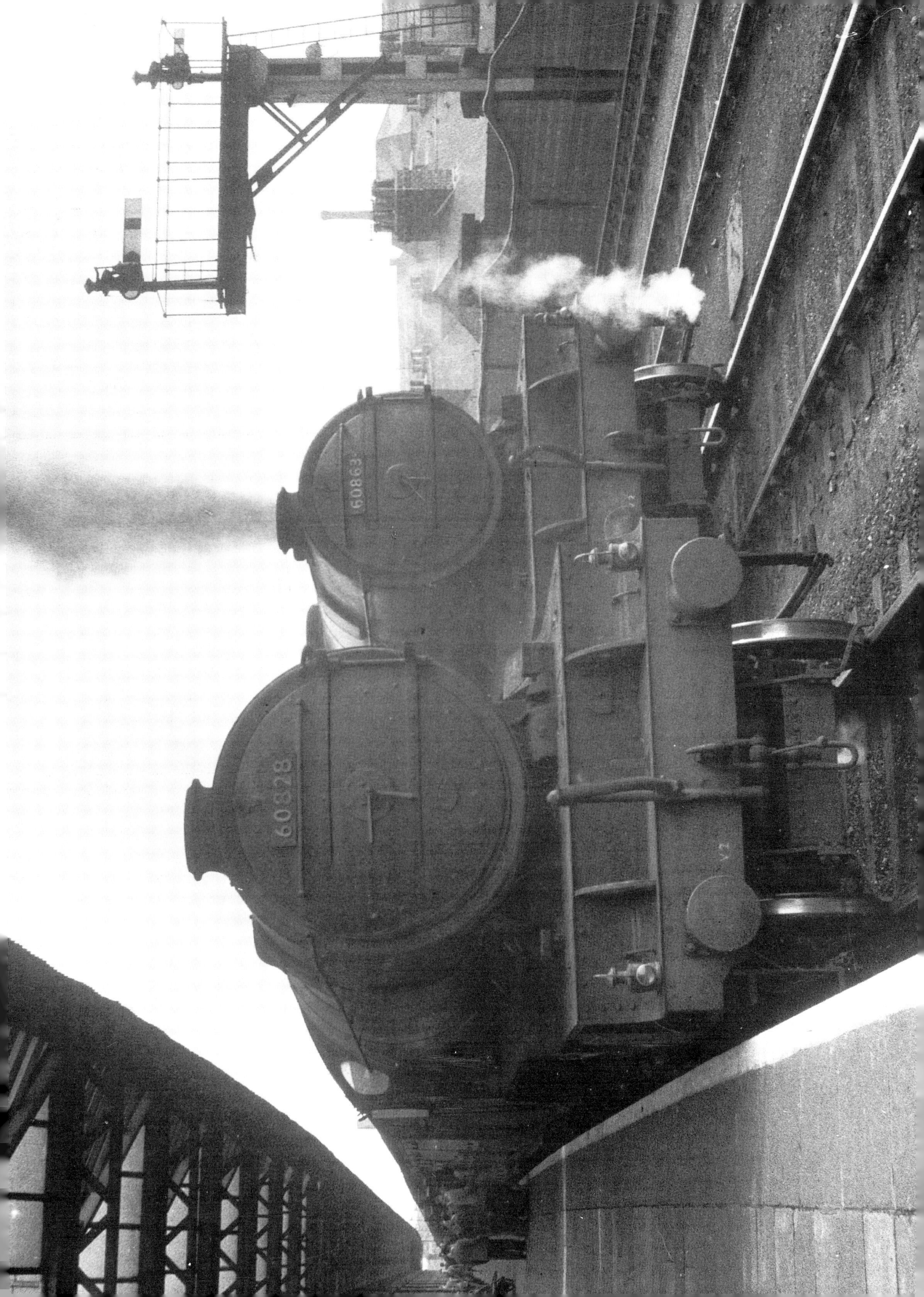
60863
60828

24. Driver Sid Lees brings No 60911 round 'Cosby Corner' on the climb to Ashby Magna with the 8.30 am Manchester- Marylebone express.

25. After begging a brief sprint to Rugby Central with Messrs Durrington and Cassie I managed to secure a shot of No 60842 as she set off for Marylebone with the up 'South Yorkshireman'. It was something of a relief that the photograph wasn't sabotaged by an opening of the cylinder drains! 16.8.58.

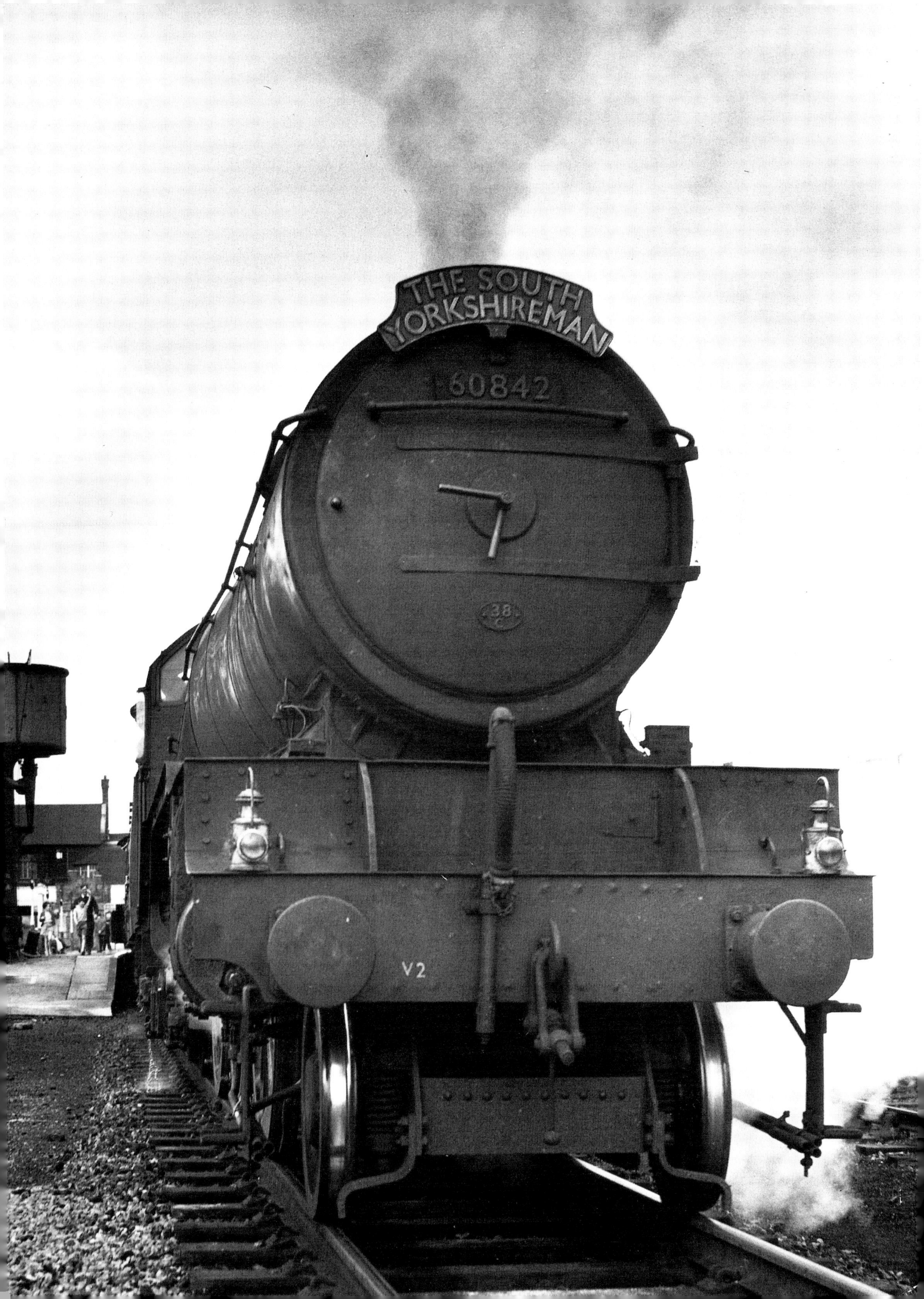
THE SOUTH YORKSHIREMAN
60842
V2

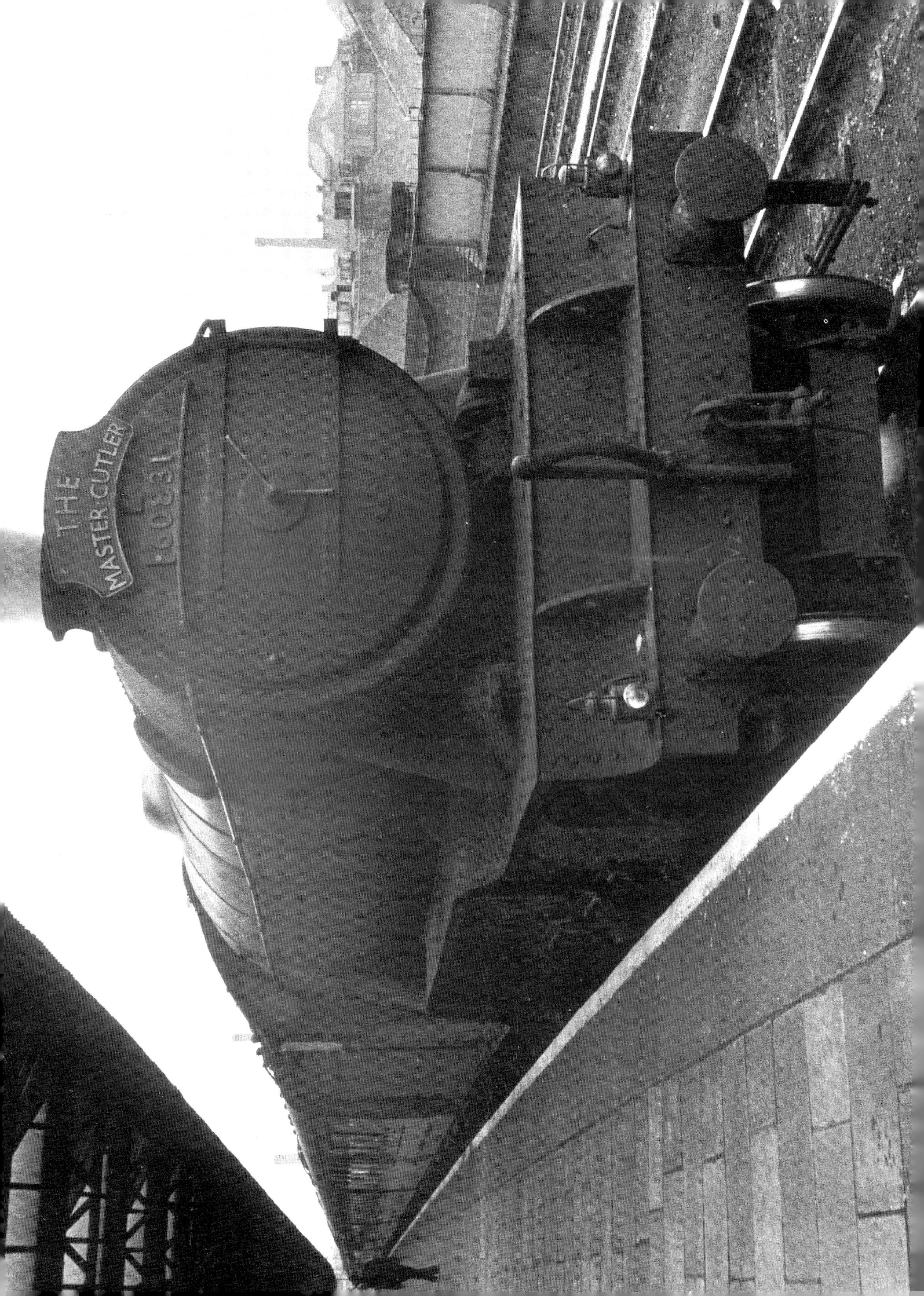
THE
MASTER-CUTLER
60831

21. An every day view of the Great Central enjoyed by passengers using Leicester's public transport to reach the west and south west of the city as their buses (and at one time trams) negotiated the tortuous mediaeval road arrangements around the West Bridge area. At this spot river, road and rail all crossed at different levels. In this picture Driver Sid Lees and Fireman Ted Jones are taking No 60831 to London with the up 'South Yorkshireman' on a grey day in May 1958.

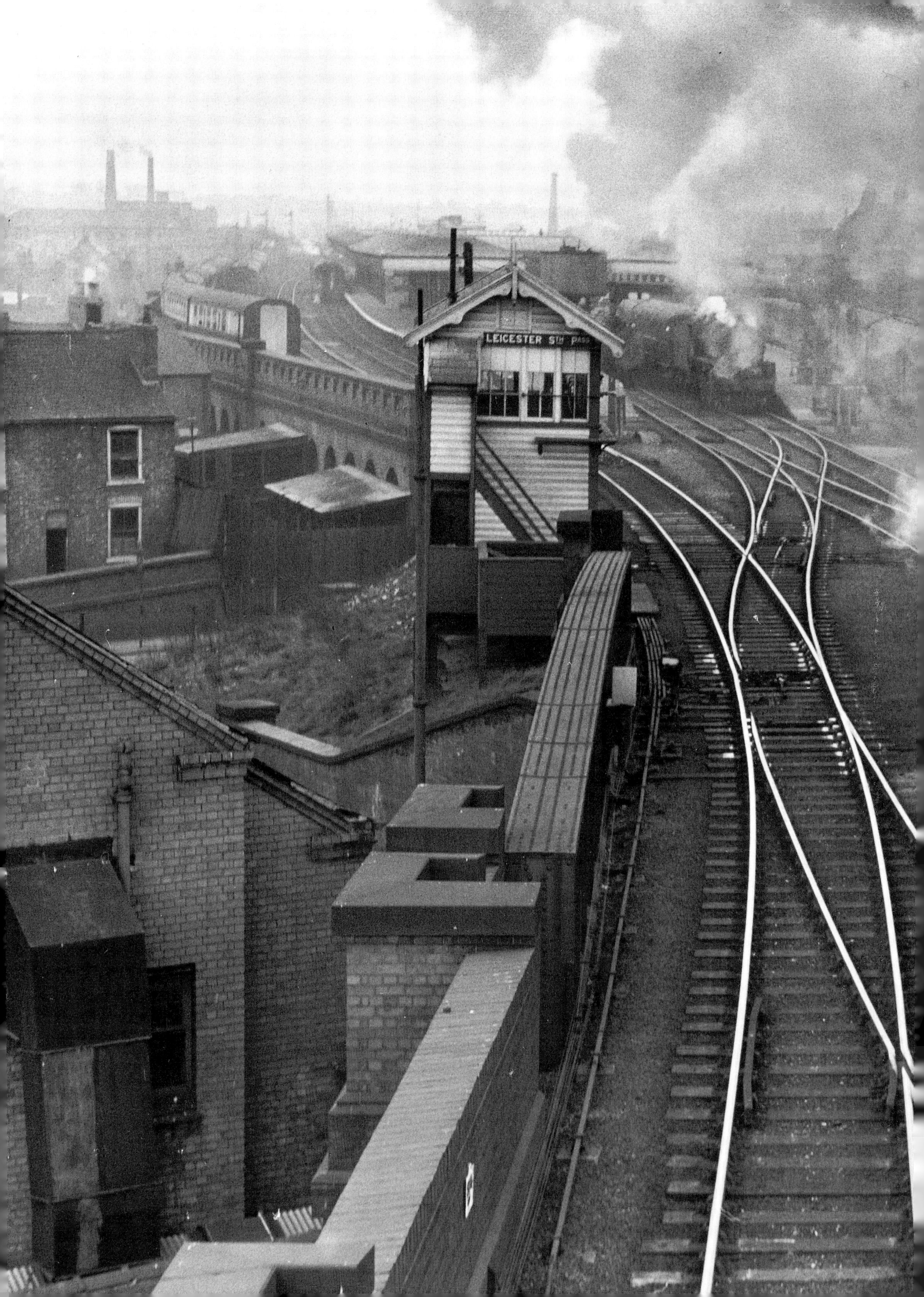
LEICESTER

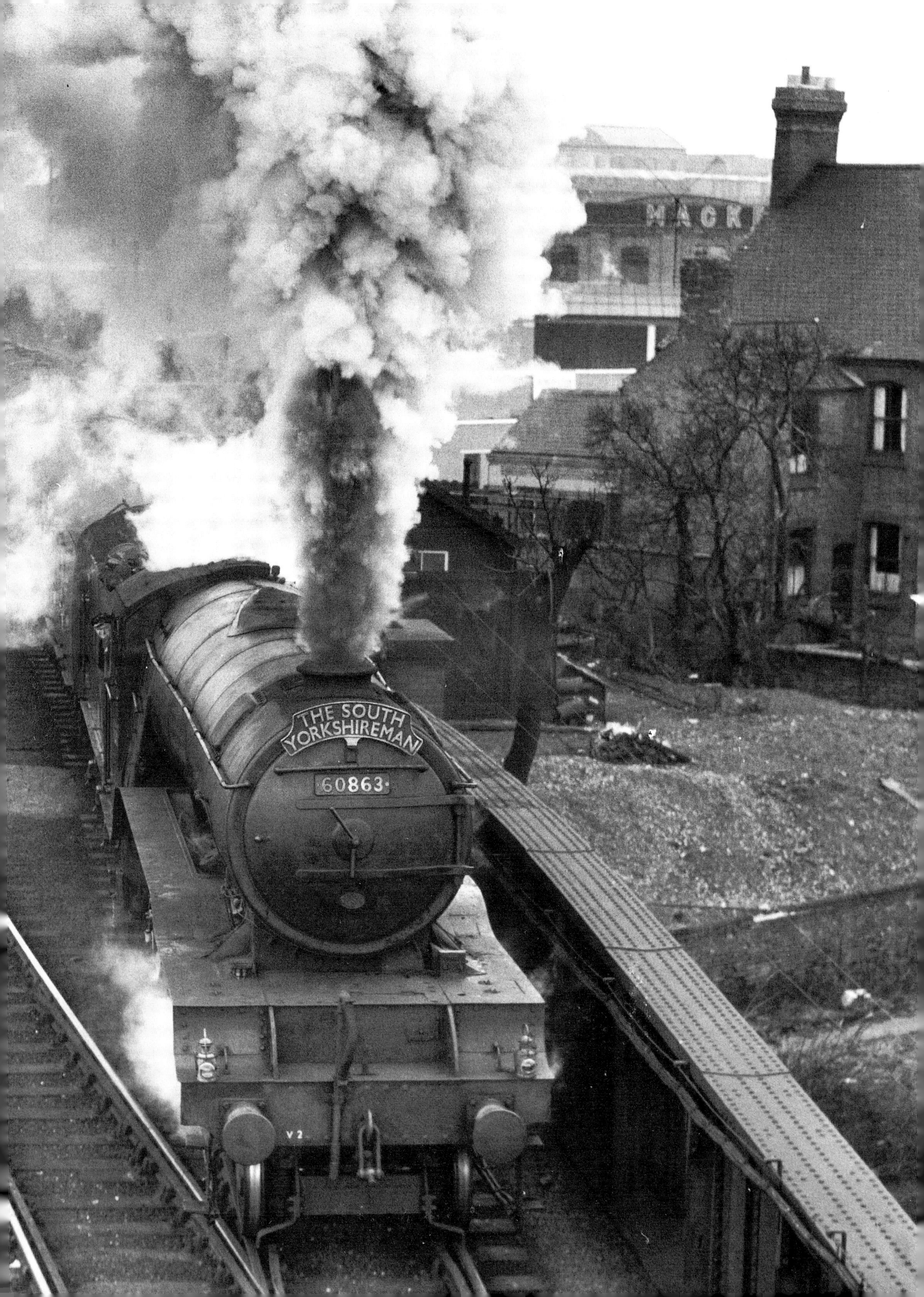

MACK
THE SOUTH YORKSHIREMAN
60863
V2

Previous page.

28. One of a number of photographs I took of V2 No 60863 in the school lunchtime during a week in May 1958 when it was heading the up 'South Yorkshireman'. Inspector Frow who was in charge of the area Signals and Telegraph Department who was a near neighbour of mine at the time kindly accompanied me onto the gantry on the West Bridge viaduct while I took my photographs. He was a rather portly gentleman and I seem to remember that he had some difficulty in maneouvring his bulk around the ladders, wires, arms and posts on the gantry. 19.5.58.

29. An exhibitionist display is provided by V2 No 60911 as she backs onto the nine coaches of the 8.30am express from Manchester to Marylebone at Leicester Central. 15.3.58.

30. No 60842 is in back gear having just entered No 4 bay ready to take over the 2.10 pm express from Manchester to Marylebone. This train was dubbed the 'Teatime Fast' by the enginemen and was a Leicester Number Two link duty. The return working was the 9pm York parcels from Marylebone and the engine allocated to this duty was not always in prime condition. Certainly 60842 shows all the signs of high mileage and neglect.

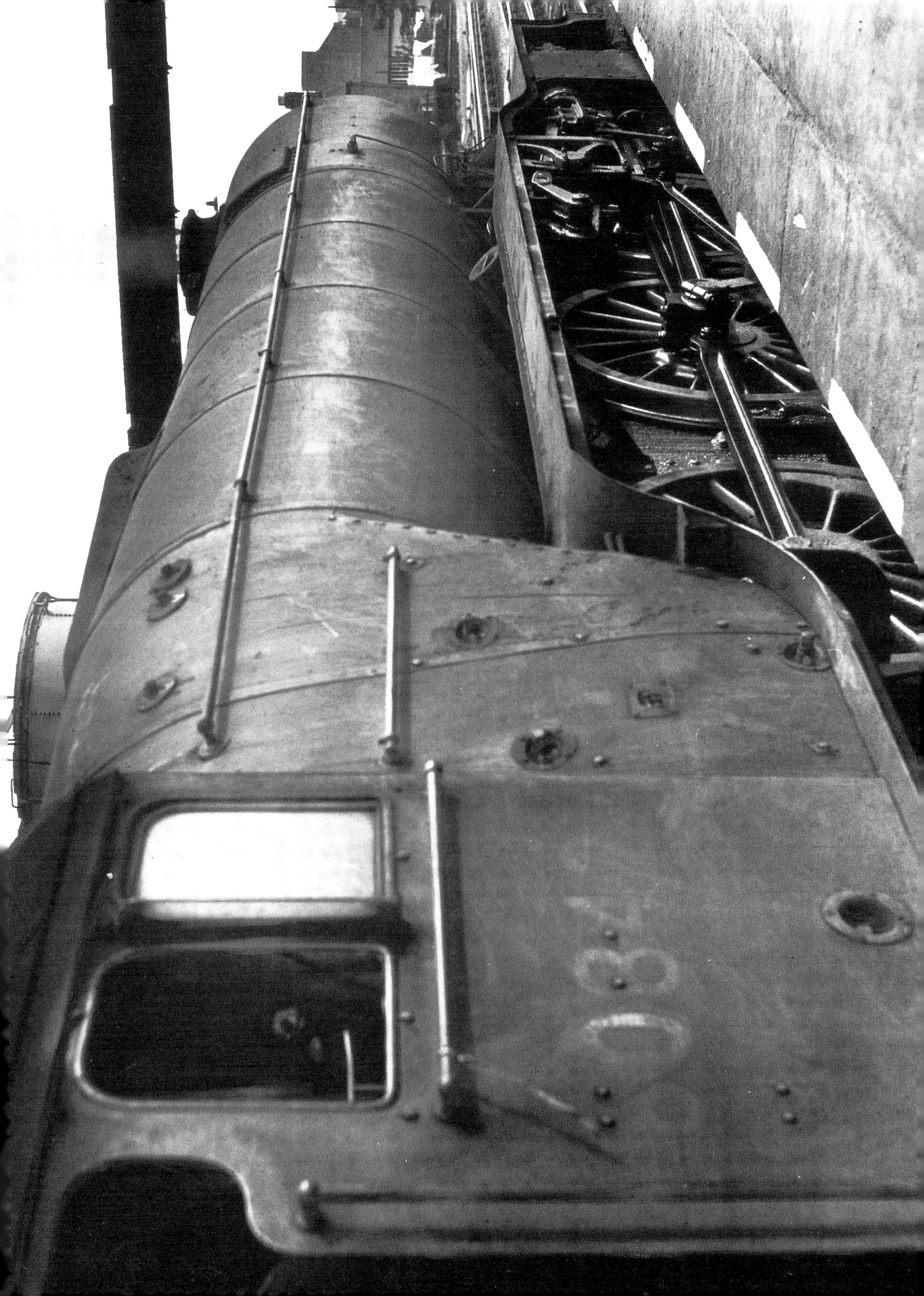

31. Both bay platforms at the south end of Leicester Central are occupied by V2s. Waiting to take over the up 'South Yorkshireman' is No 60863 while in No 4 bay is Neasden's 60876 which had earlier brought in the 10 am down express to Manchester. It will return to London with the 1.15 pm all stations from Nottingham Victoria hence the Class B lamp code below the chimney. However, as this train also included the returning

32. No 60911 moves out from Leicester Central with a relief to the up 'South Yorkshireman' on Easter Tuesday 1958.

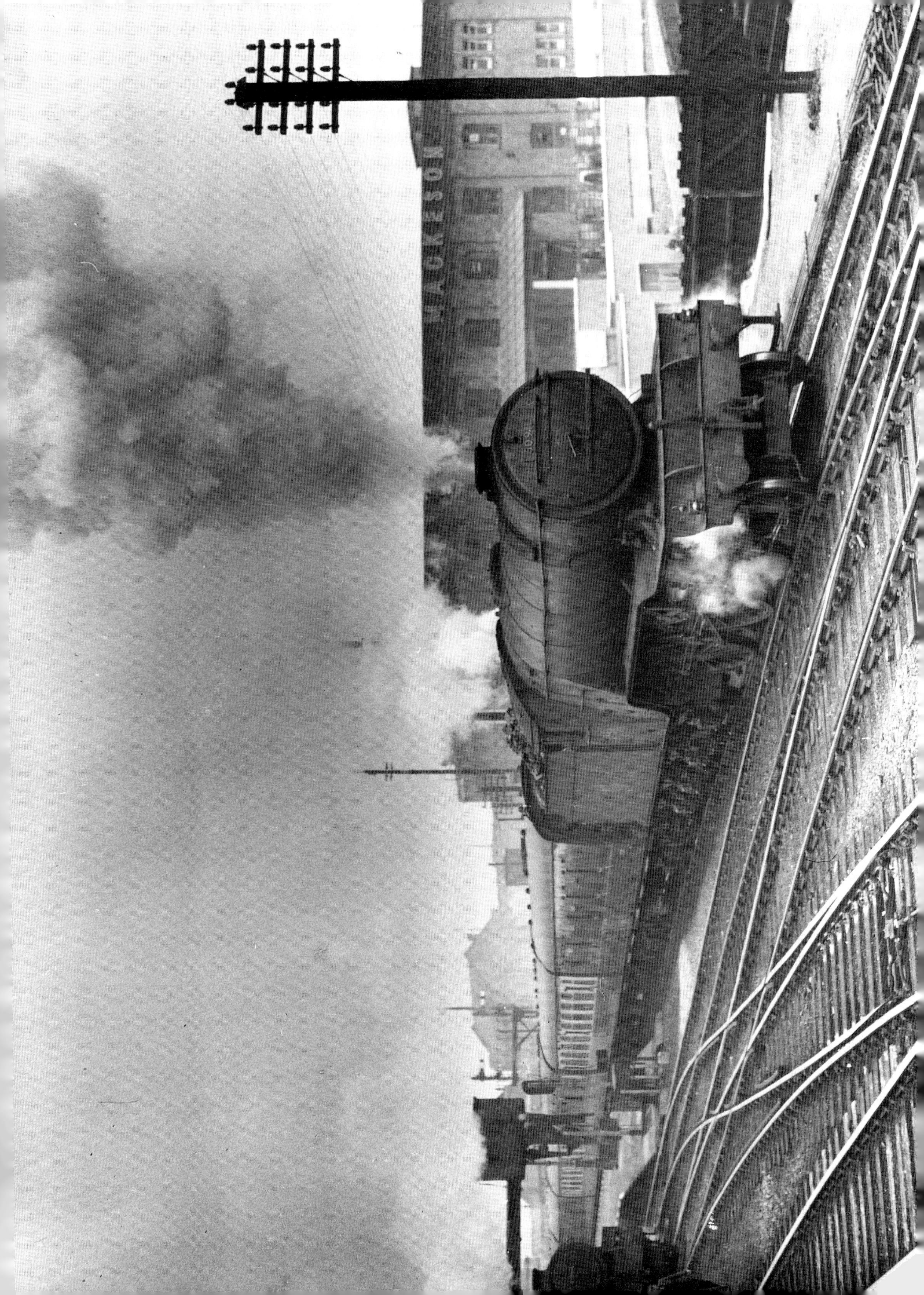

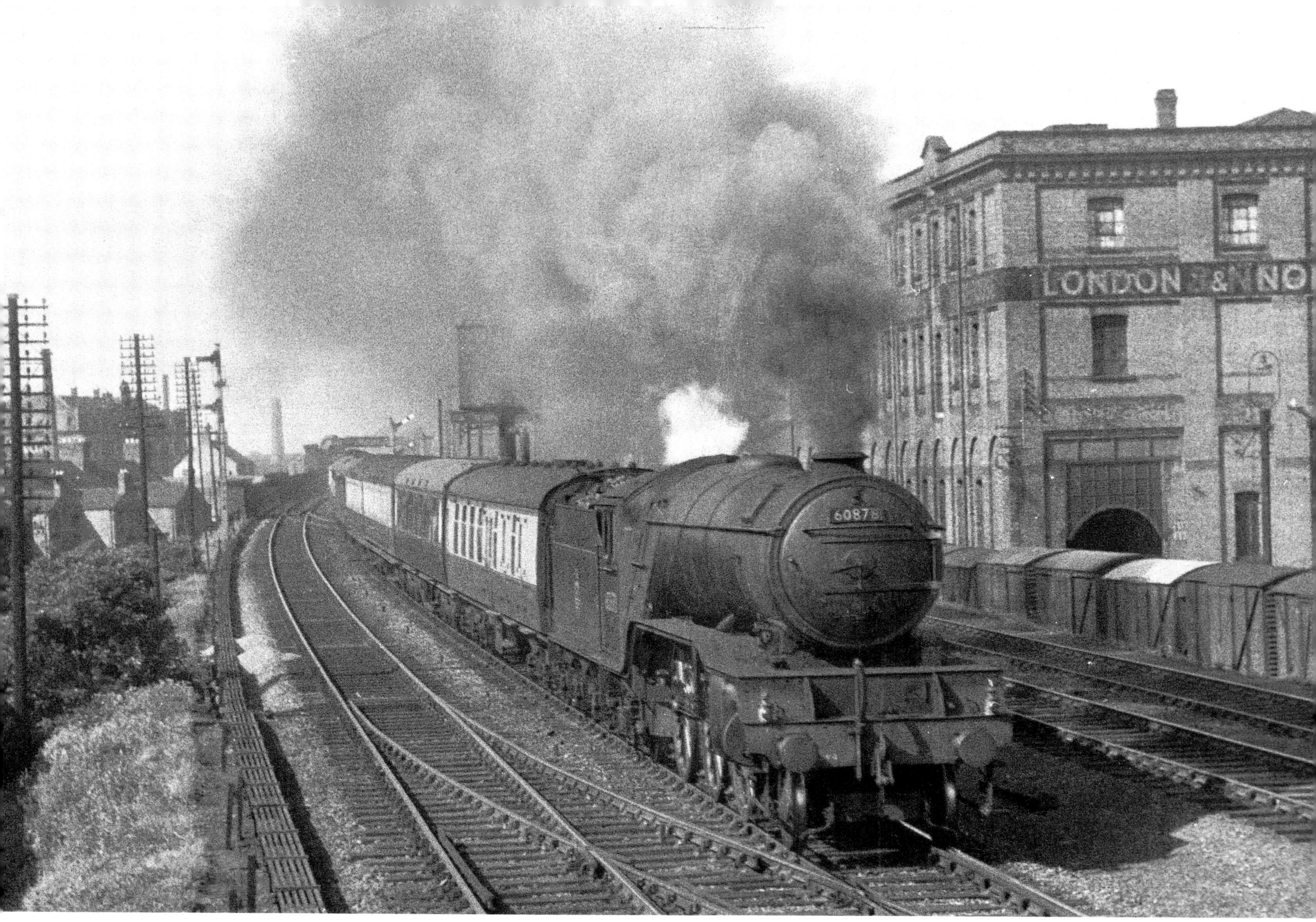

34. In the reverse direction No 60878 dashes past Ashby Magna signal box with the 3.20 pm down from Marylebone to Manchester. Driver Albert Chafer has the regulator nearly closed and the engine is accelerating down the home grade to Whetstone and Leicester. 9.8.58.

Following pages.
35. Driver Ken Davies has control of a 'borrowed' Heaton V2 from Newcastle No 60802 as he backs on to the up 'South Yorkshireman' at Leicester Central ready for the run to Marylebone. June 1958.

36. A high level shot of 60831 taken from one of the windows of the Great Central goods warehouse. The train again is the 8.30 am Manchester- Marylebone express and it is seen passing the junction with Leicester North Goods loop.

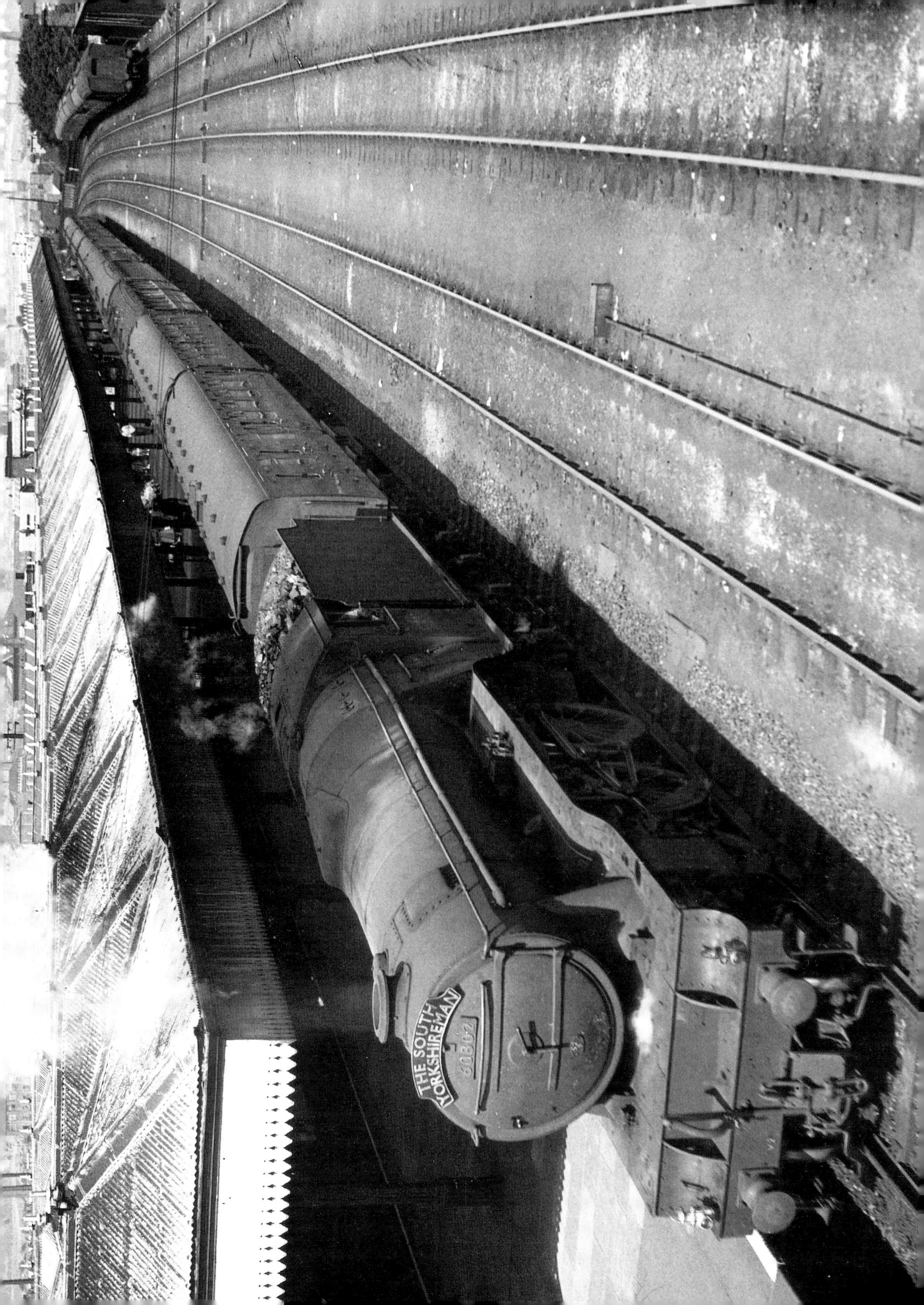
THE SOUTH YORKSHIREMAN

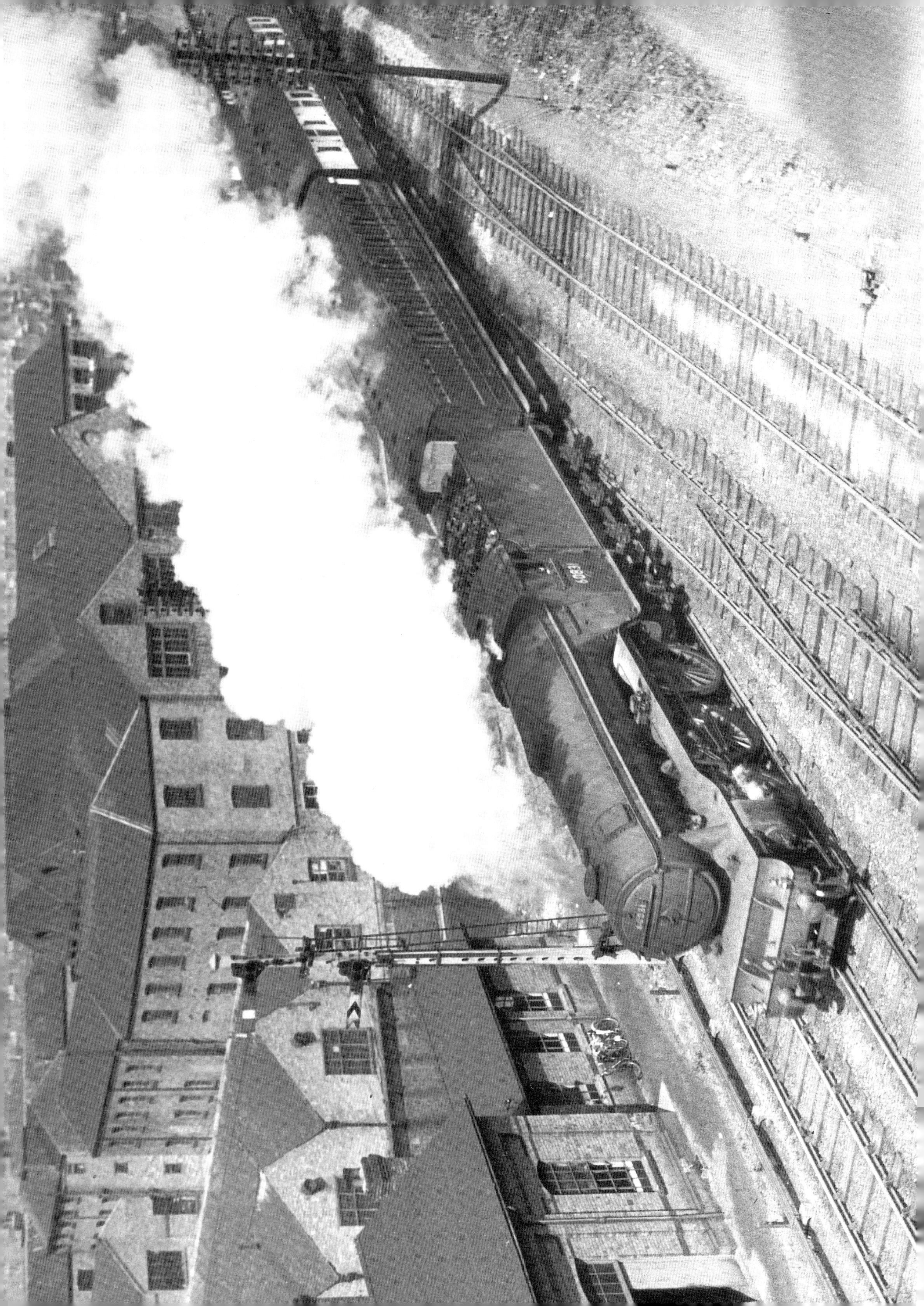

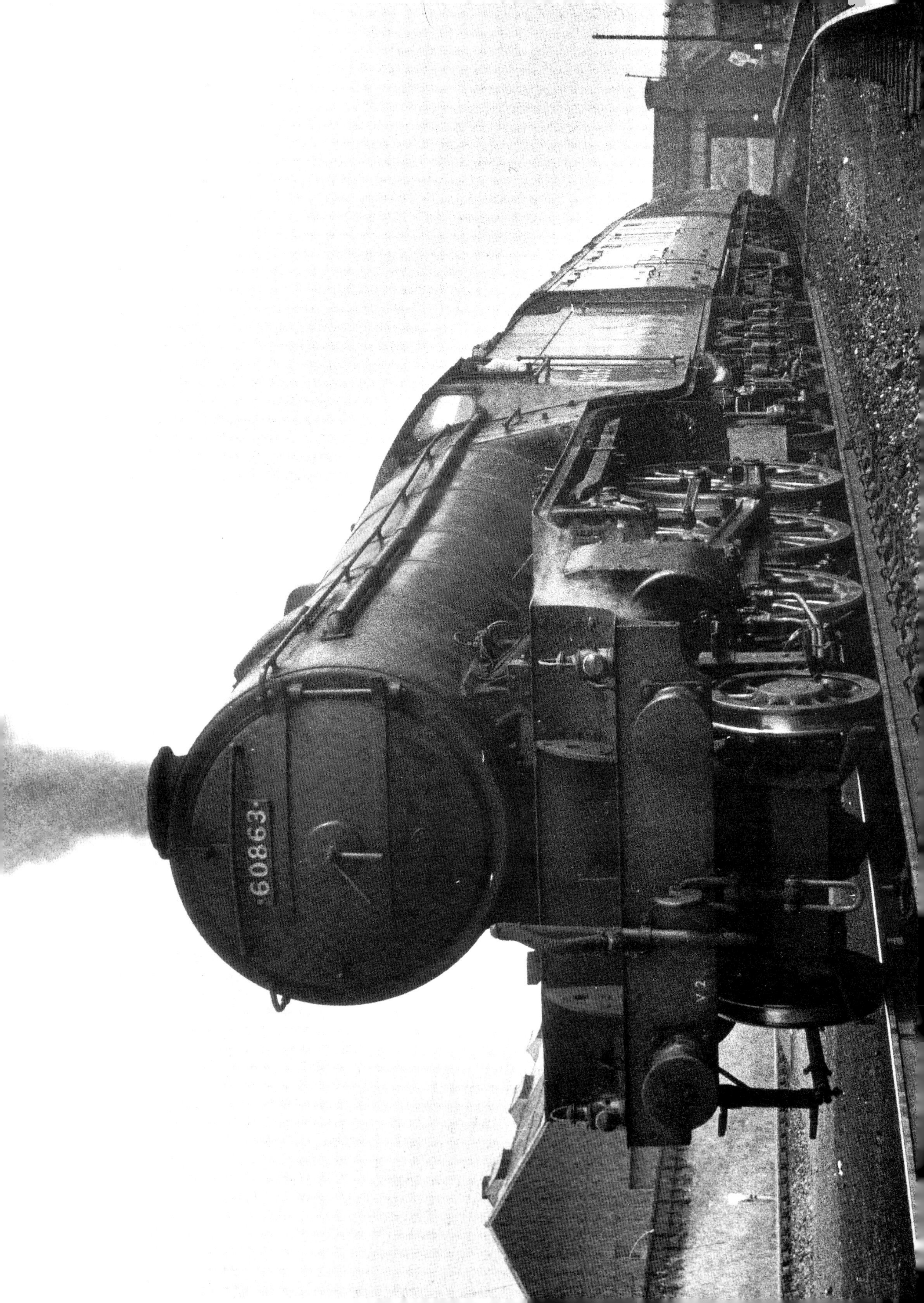
60863
V2

38. The up 'South Yorkshireman' sets off from Leicester Central headed by No 60879. Her driver is Bill Priestley and he has for company Geoffrey Dentith who has taken time off from his responsibilities at the London Midland parent depot at Wellingborough to sample a G.C. line trip before the withdrawal of the daytime Marylebone expresses in January 1960. In the bay a B1 4-6-0 waits to take over the York-Bournemouth through train.

No 60863 sets off from Loughborough Central with the 3.20 pm down from Marylebone to Manchester.

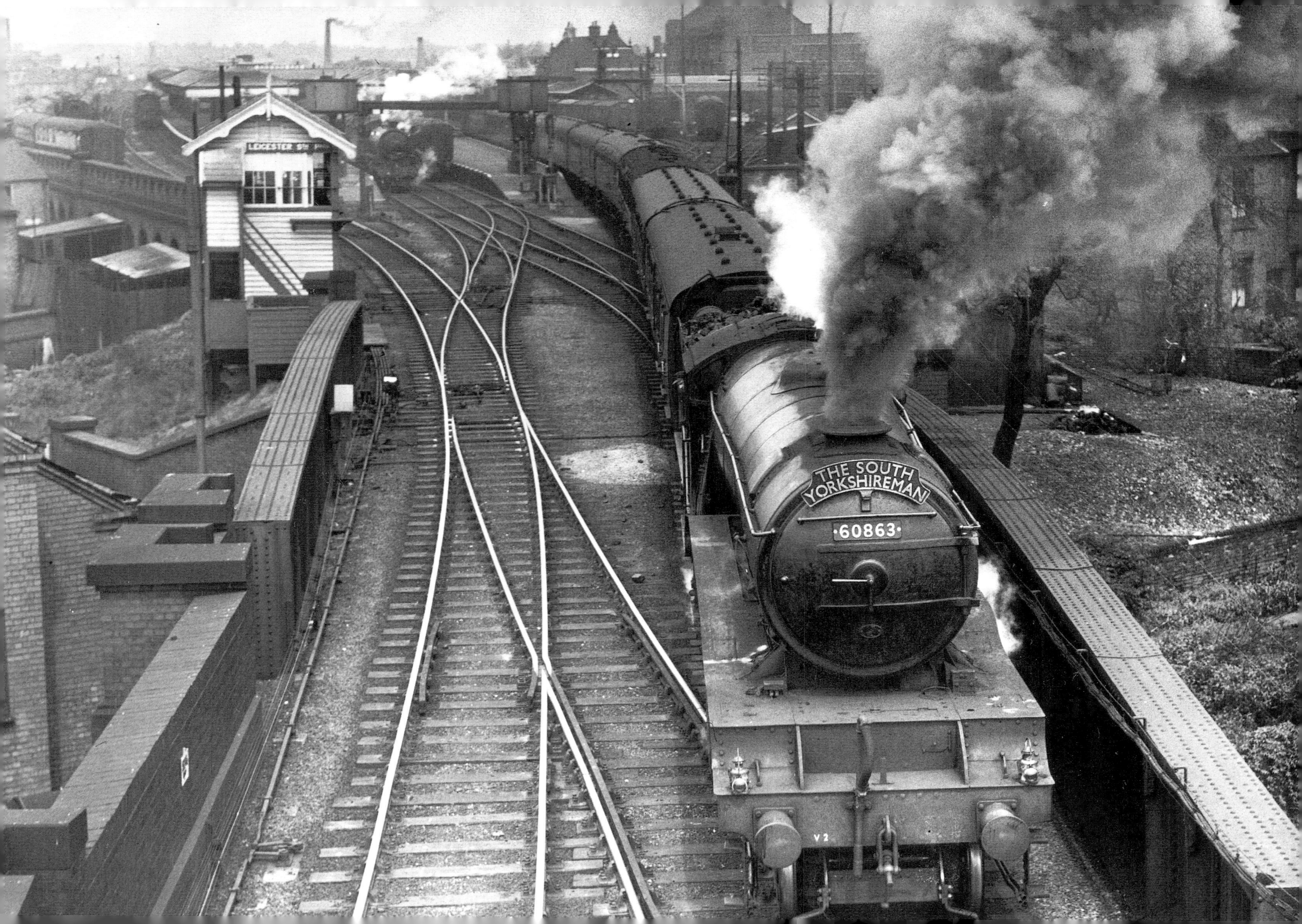
LEICESTER
THE SOUTH
YORKSHIREMAN
60863
V 2

39. Another photograph of No 60863 leaving Leicester Central with the up 'South Yorkshireman' taken from the signal gantry on Leicester's West Bridge. 20.5.58

40. A photograph taken through an archway in Leicester's Roman Jewry Wall catches V2 No 60878 pulling out of the Central station with the up 'Master Cutler'.

Following pages.
41. No 60831 gathers speed over the Leicester viaduct and approaches the North Goods loop with the 8.30 am from Manchester to Marylebone. Driver Rupe Elliot and Fireman Bill Johnson have spotted the photographer on the gantry platform.

42. No 60879 heads south past Leicester South Goods with the 8.30am from Manchester to Marylebone. Looking out for the camera are Driver George Evinson and Loco Inspector Percy Banyard. On the goods road another V2 detaches some vans from the York-Woodford fitted freight.

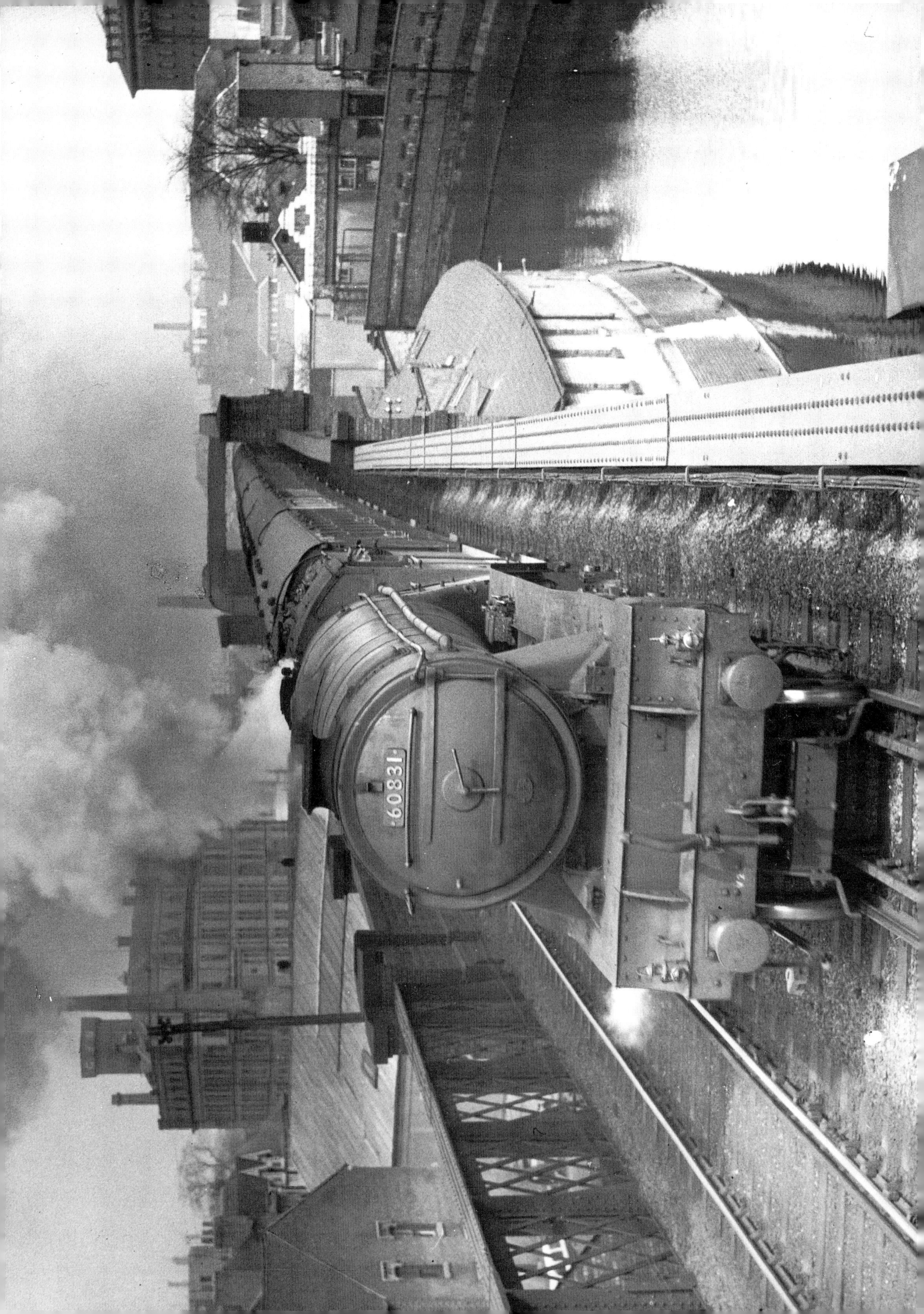
60831

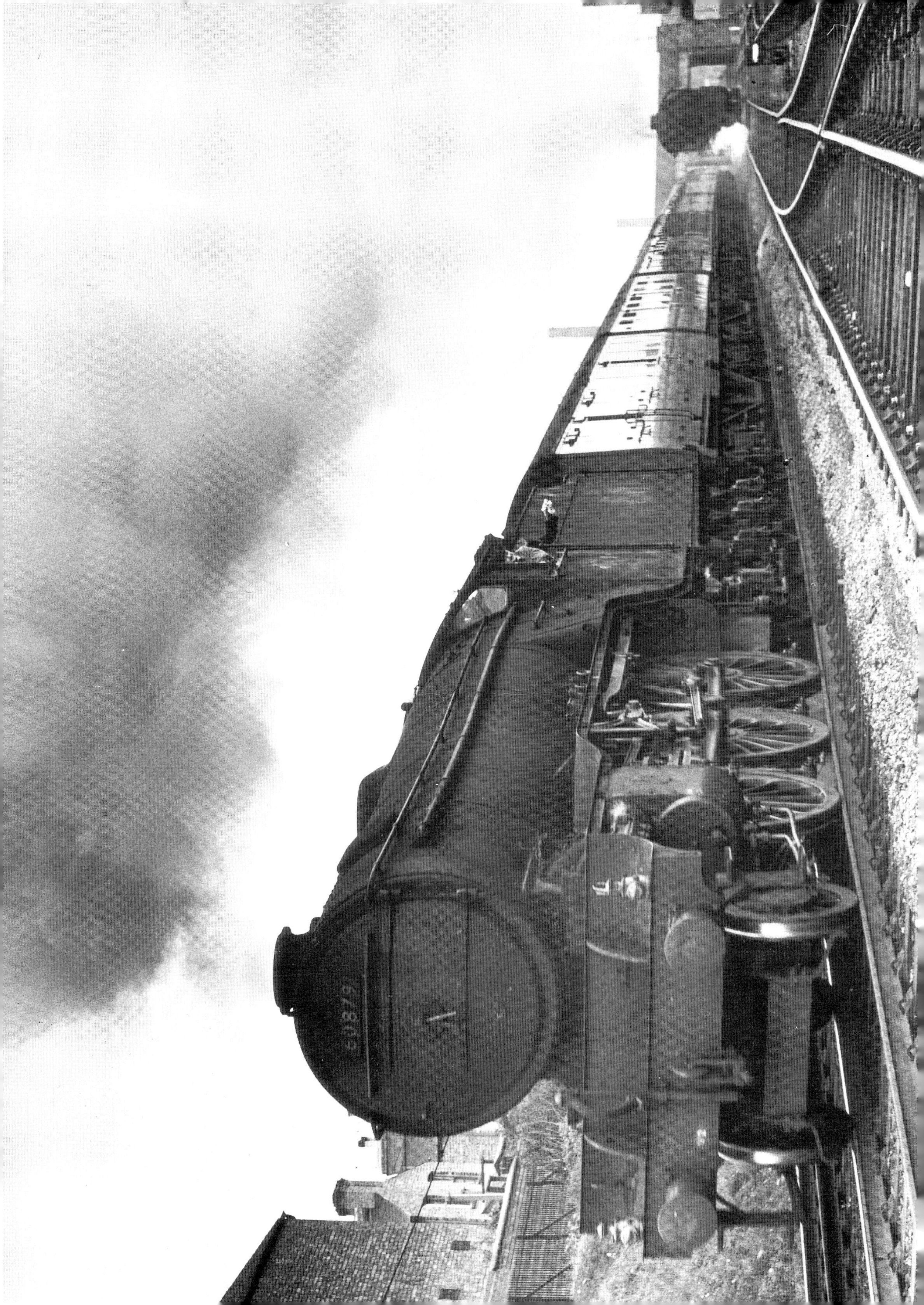
60879

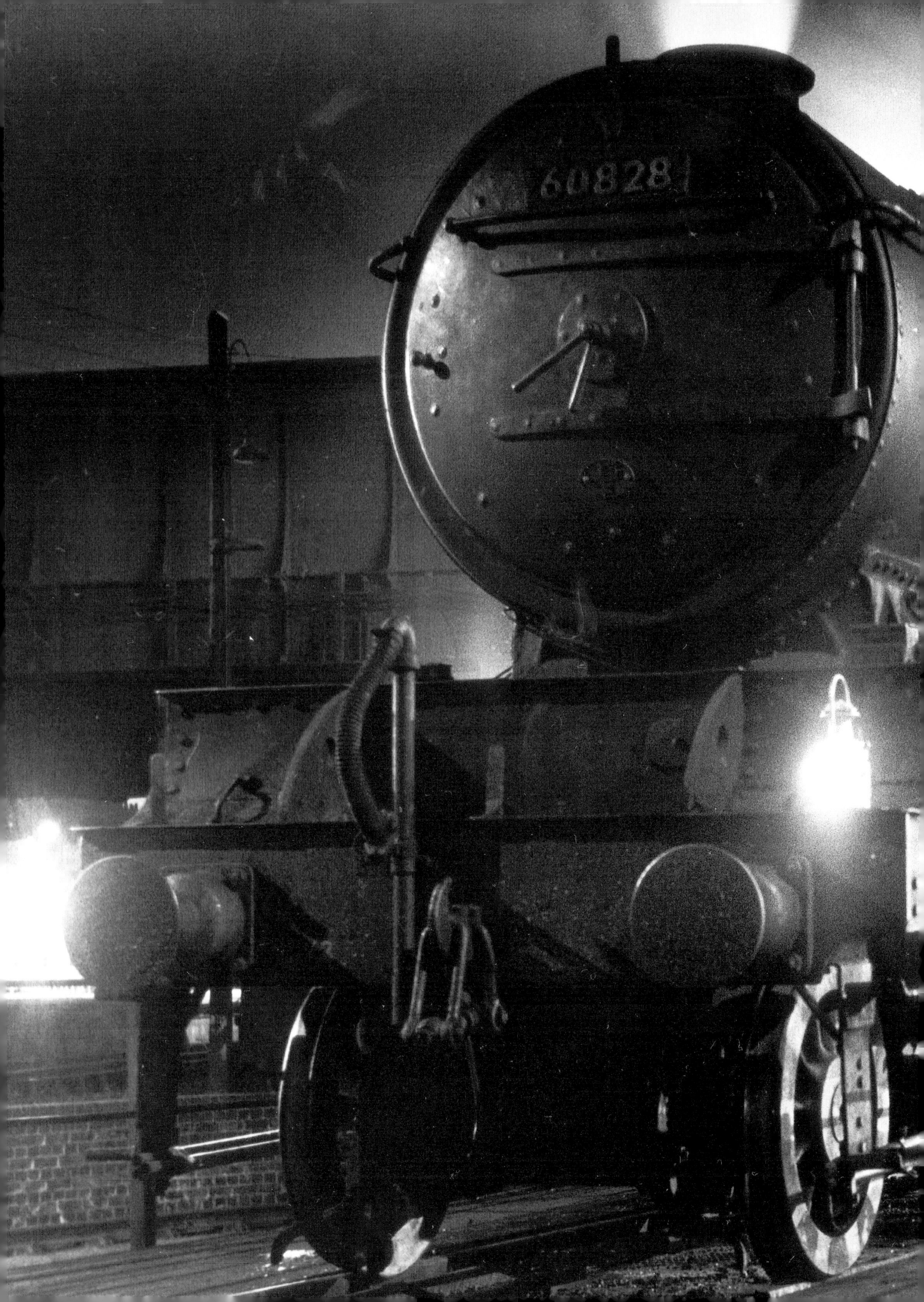
60828

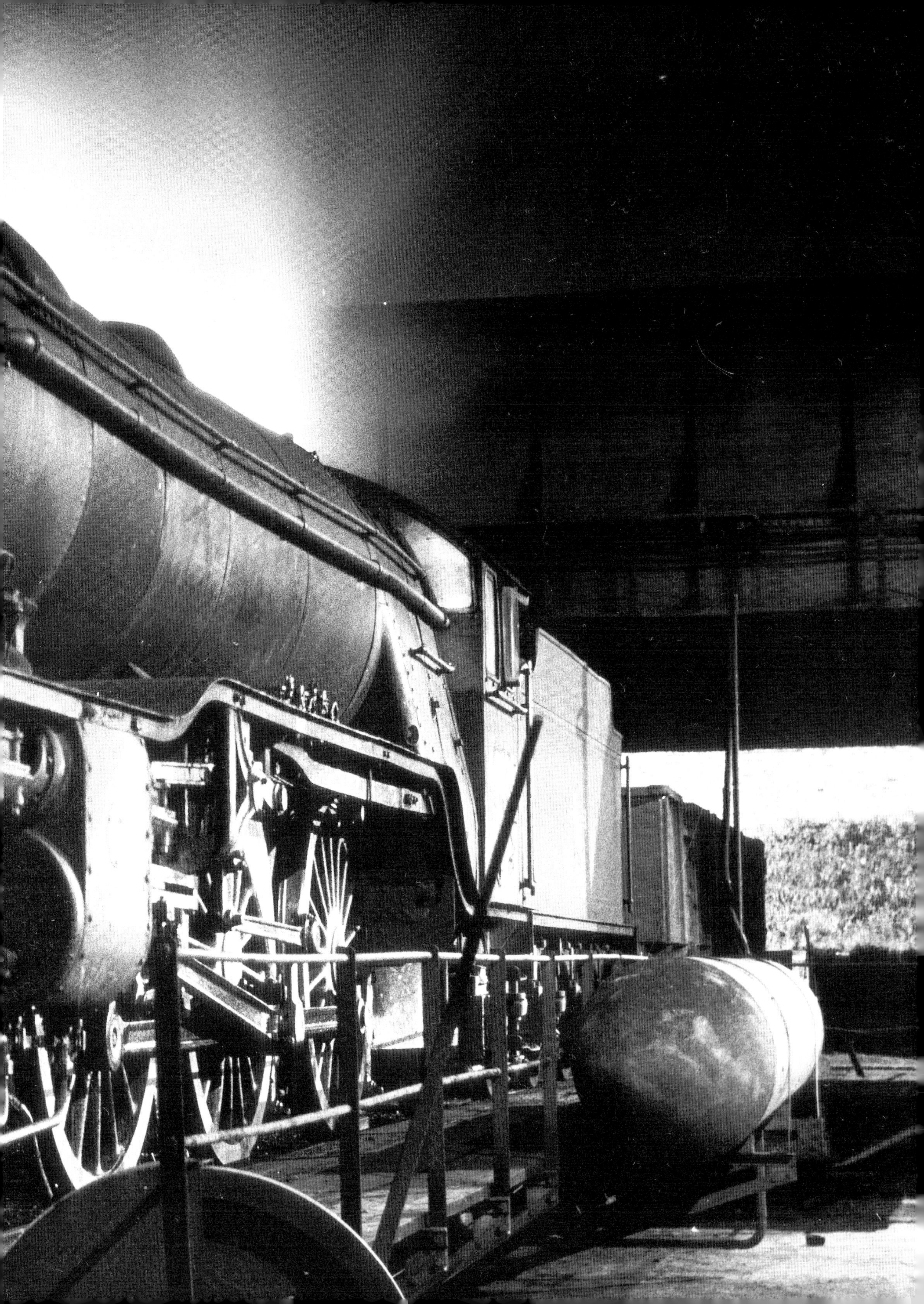

**Previous page.
43.** My trips from Leicester Central to Marylebone on the 4.5 pm express from Manchester and returning with the 1.45 am early morning 'Newspaper' express were among some of my greatest pleasures. Not least this was because it afforded the opportunity to get close to engines and photograph them without disturbance during their turn round time in the dark. So as not to attract unwelcome attentions which might put the engine crew at risk I always used the existing lamplight illumination which was discreet but which did mean long exposures sometimes under difficult conditions. In this photograph the time is thirty minutes past midnight and V2 No 60828 stands massively proud on the turntable at Marylebone before working the early morning down 'Newspaper' back home to Leicester. What a splendid looking engine the big Gresley 2-6-2s were. 29.5.58

44. Taken among the trees and shrubs near the Marylebone turntable V2 No 60828 stands in the siding after turning so as not to obstruct other engines that might wish to use the table. 29.5.58.

45. Two shots of No 60828 standing in Platform 1 at Marylebone with the down early morning 'Newspaper'. In the first picture she is seen standing near Rossmore Road overbridge raising the boiler pressure in readiness for the journey 'home'. 29.5.58

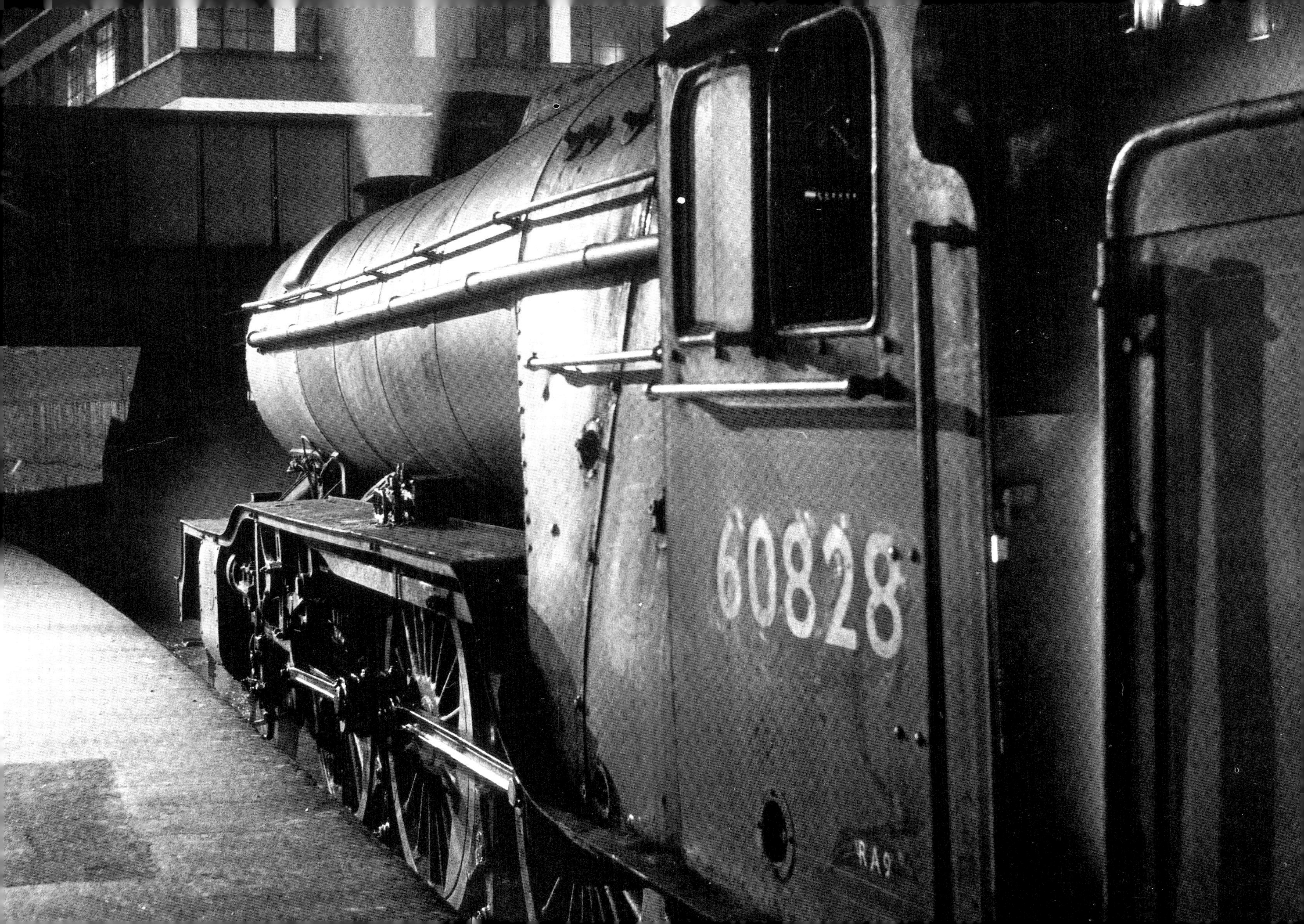
60828
RA9

46. A photograph taken looking towards the station shows No 60828 waiting for the vans to be loaded with the morning's news before its

47. A deliberate slip by request is provided by Driver Albert Chafer as he and his fireman Mick Kilby make a whole-hearted start from Leicester Central with the 8.30 am Manchester-Marylebone express with V2 No 60842.

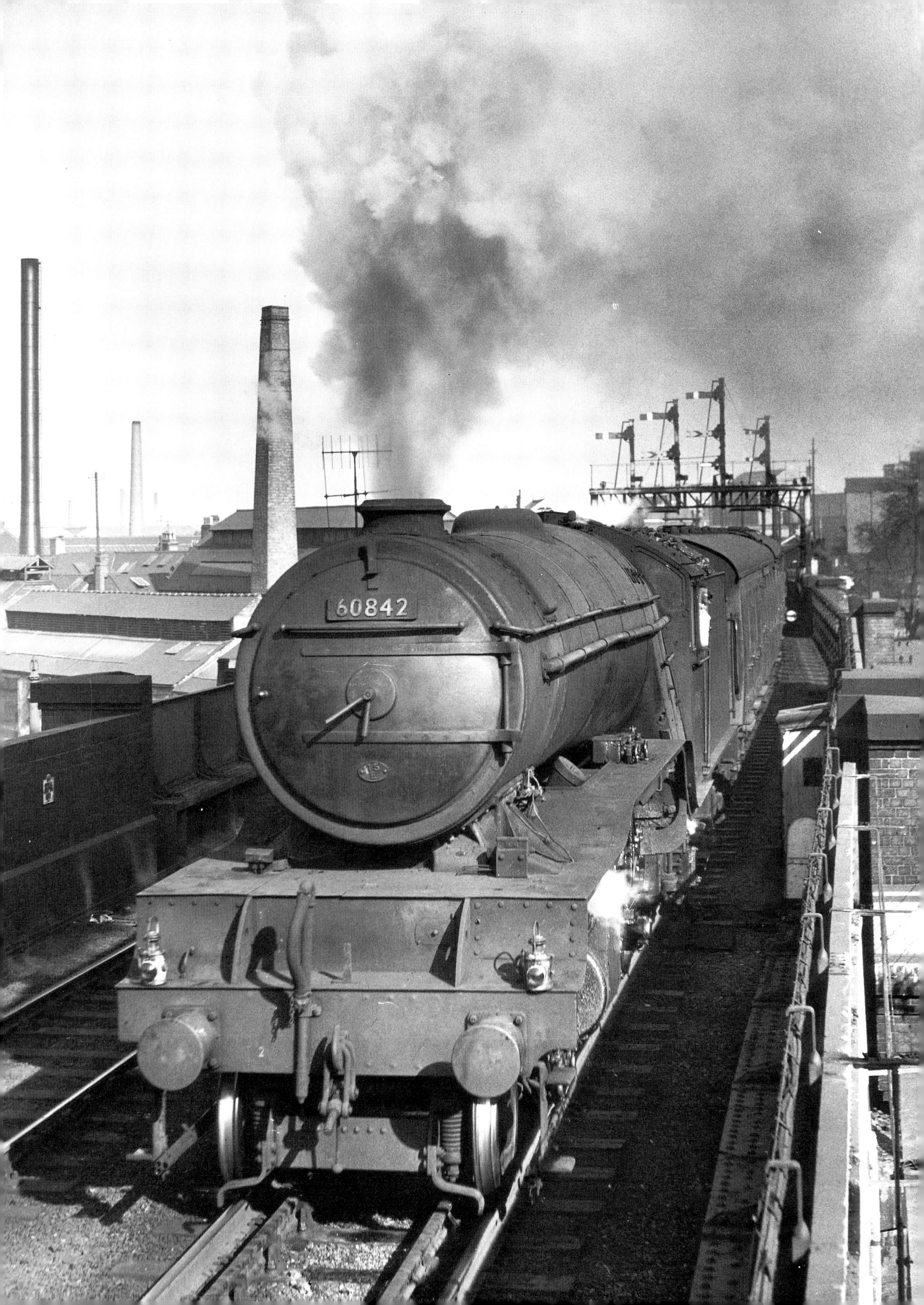
60842

48. A fine Spring morning finds Driver Sid Lees wearing a freshly laundered dust coat and looking out for the camera as he brings No 60842 out of Leicester Central and across the West Bridge viaduct with the 8.30 am from Manchester to Marylebone.

49. No 60842 stands in No 3 bay at Leicester Central with Driver Bill Priestley in charge. It is awaiting the arrival of the up 'South Yorkshireman' which has just run in to Platform 6 with 60878. A temporary shortage of headboards was only remedied by an on-the-spot transfer between the V2s.

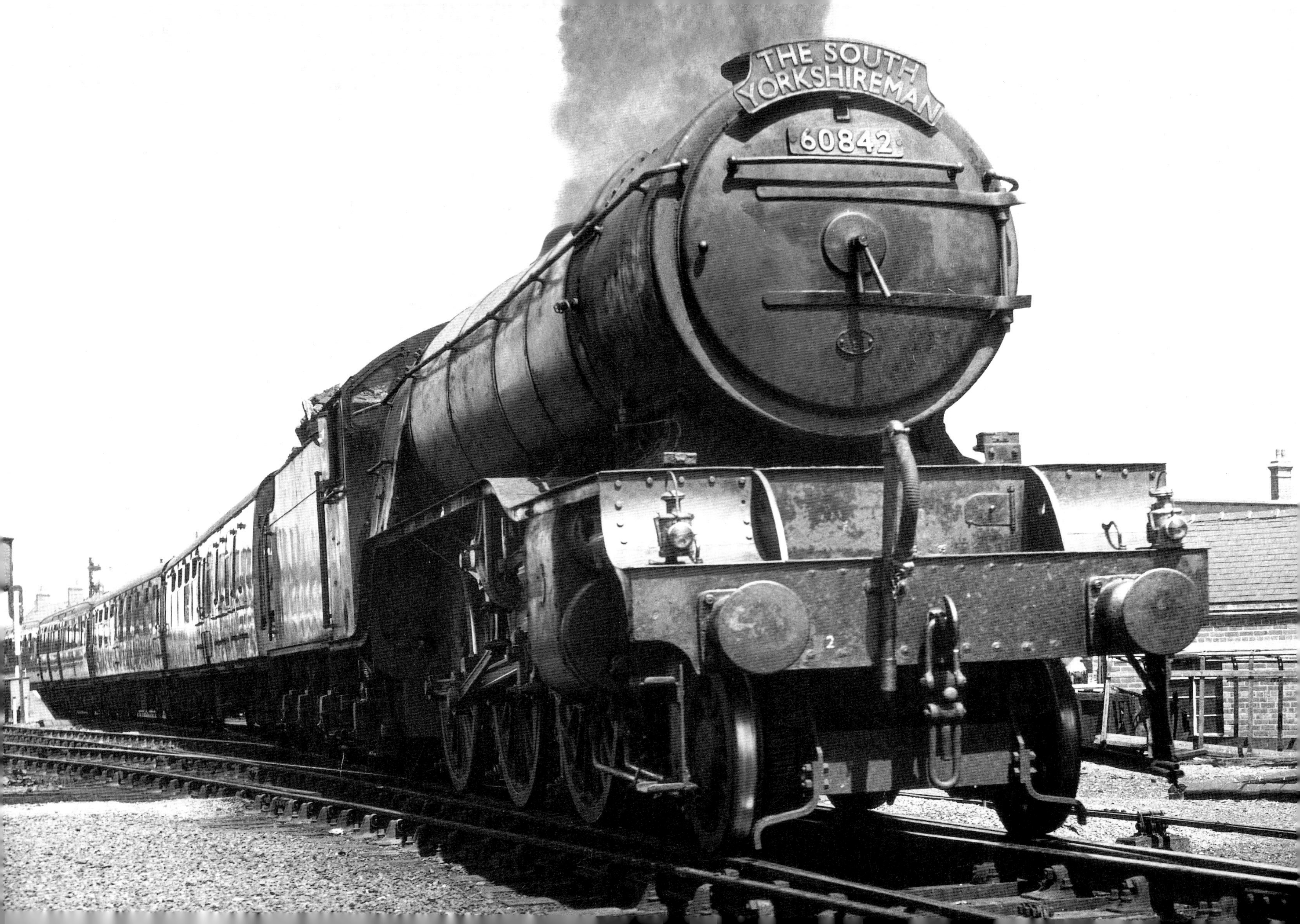
THE SOUTH YORKSHIREMAN
60842

50. No 60842 makes a stirring departure from Leicester Central with the up 'South Yorkshireman'.

51. On a Saturday in April 1959 Driver Ron Smith of Leicester's No 2 link finds himself promoted to cover for a top link driver. He is seen with No 60863 crossing the West Bridge viaduct with the up 'South Yorkshireman'.

52. V2 No 60831 stands in No 4 bay ready to take over the haulage of the 4.5 pm express from Manchester to Marylebone. Driver Sid Lees stands

53. Taken from a familiar spot No 60878 is seen gathering speed over the Leicester viaduct with the 8.30 am Manchester-Marylebone express.

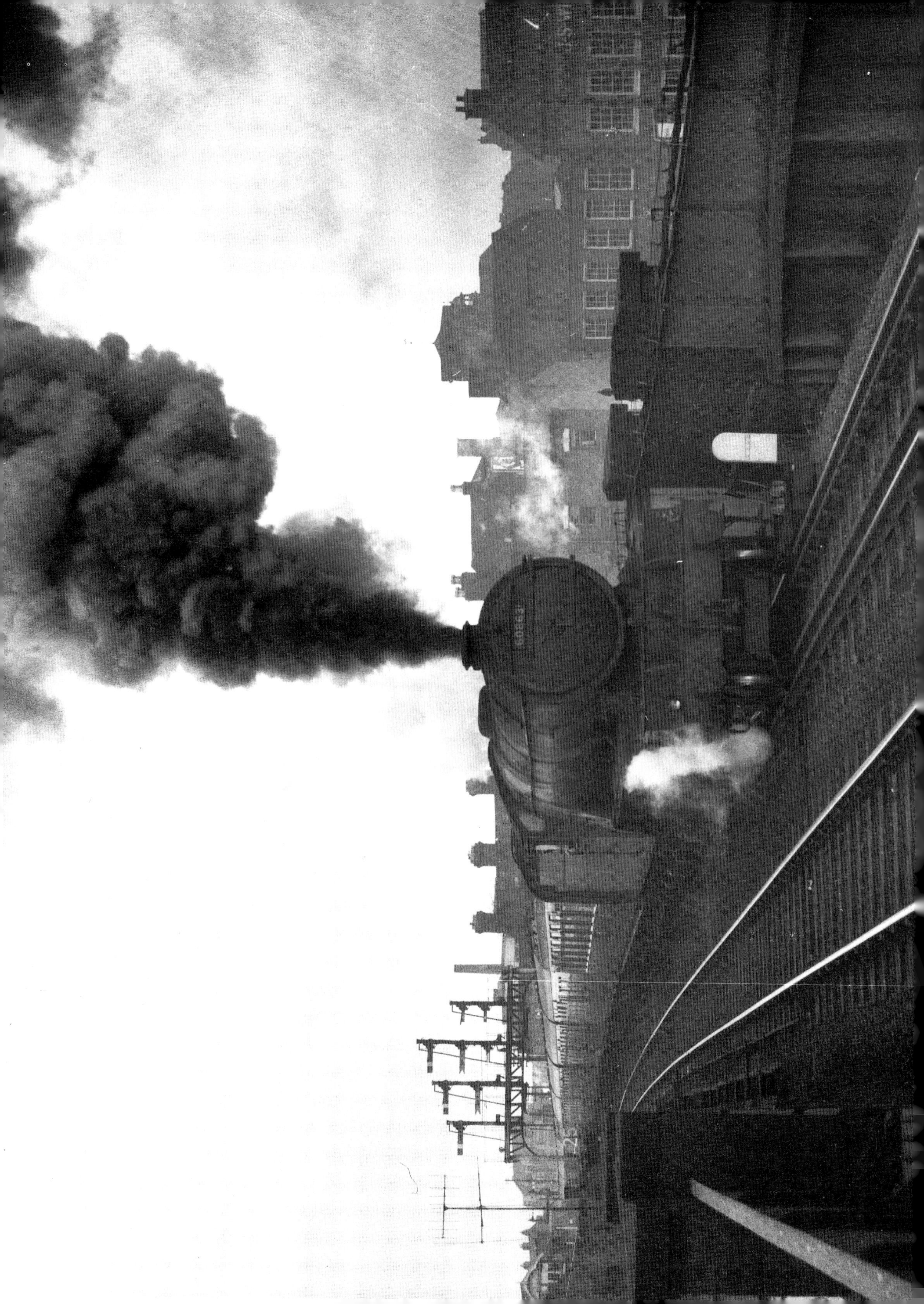

54. A plea for some smoke is perhaps answered too enthusiastically by the crew of No 60803 as she strikes off from Leicester Central and crosses the West Bridge viaduct with the 2.10 pm from Manchester to Marylebone on a sultry afternoon in 1959. The pall lingered long after the train had gone.

55. A panned shot of No 60831 taken as she was running south alongside the South Goods Loop with the 8.30 am express from Manchester to Marylebone. Already Driver Ernie Warren has her gear well pulled up and she is running on about 15% cut off with a full head of steam.

56. Due to the failure of the rostered engine at source Neasden's V2 No 60876 is commandeered to work the up 'South Yorkshireman' instead of returning to London on its usual duty which was the later and much slower 1.15 pm train from Nottingham Victoria to Marylebone. On a sunless

57. Heading for Leicester Central over the embankment north of Rugby No 60878 gathers speed on its last lap with the 12.15 pm down from Marylebone to Manchester

Following page.
58. Scruffy but unbowed, V2 No 60831 roars past Rowley Fields on the Leicester outskirts with the up 'South Yorkshireman'. As the display from the engine's chimney shows, Driver Durrington and Fireman Cassie have been 'set up' for the photograph. This was another shot taken during the school lunch break and involved a degree of self-denial in that a hastily purchased Mars Bar from a local corner shop had to be substituted for the normal life-sustaining stodge that was served up by the school kitchens.

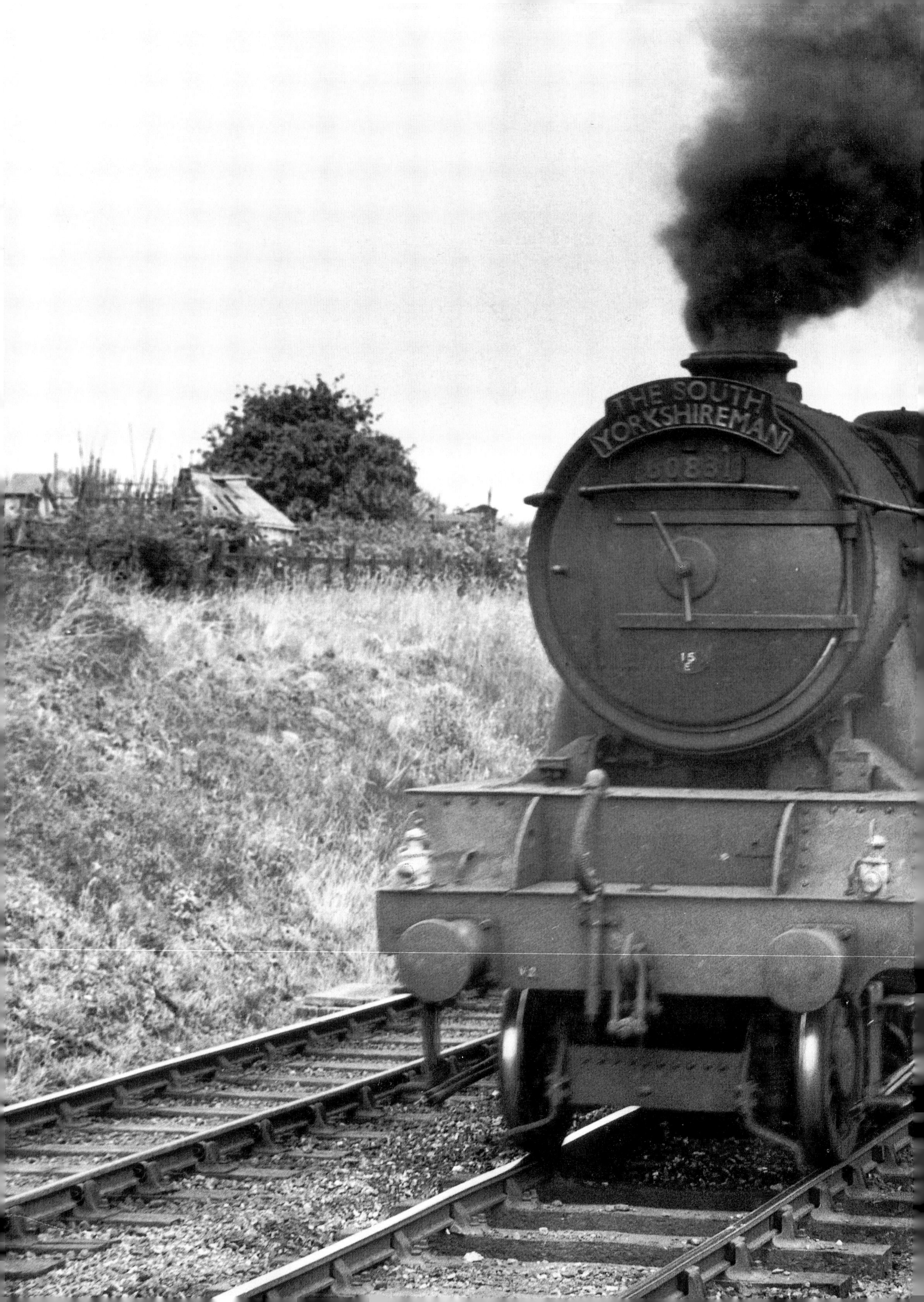
THE SOUTH
YORKSHIREMAN

¾

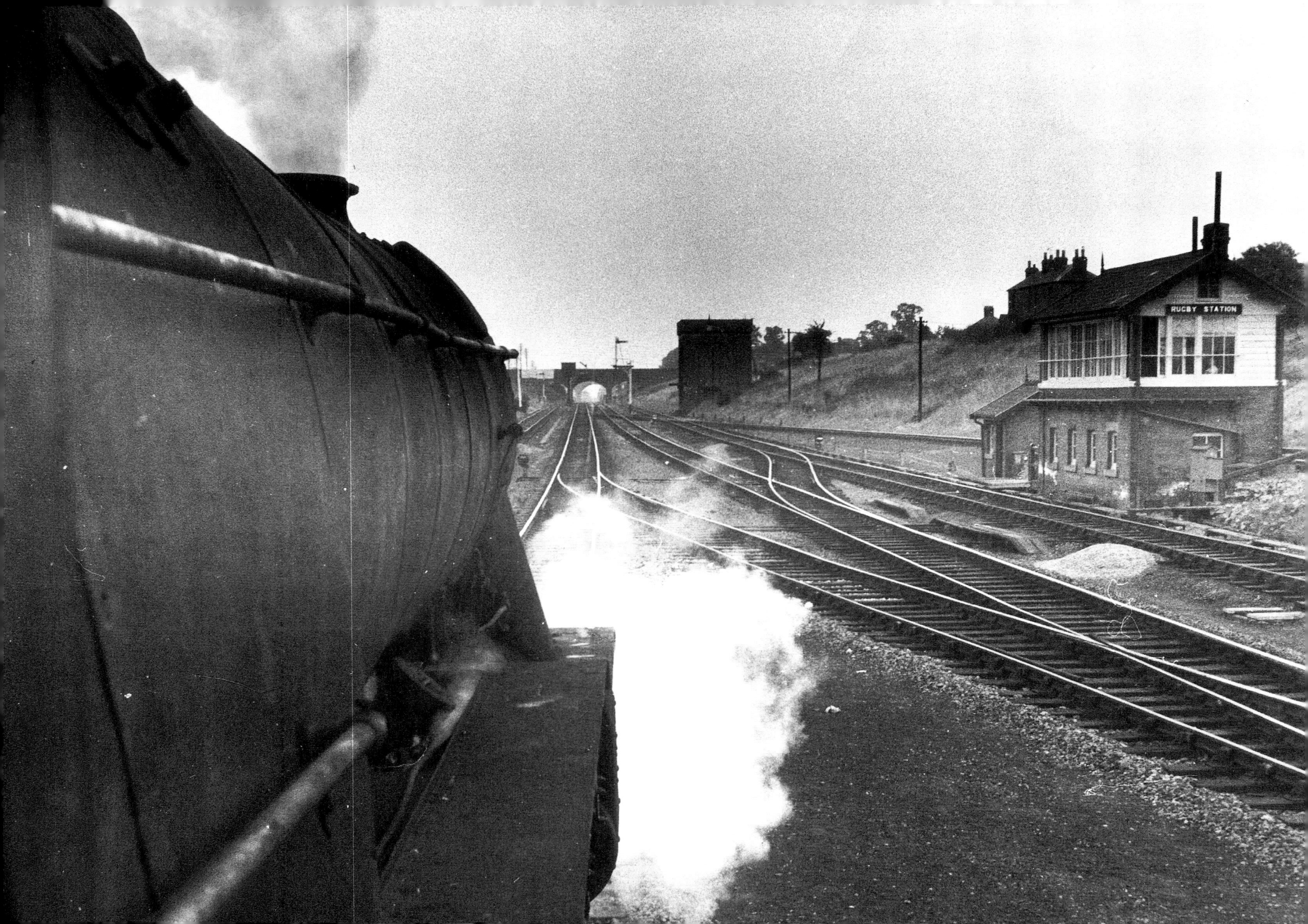
RUGBY STATION

59. A shot from the cab of No 60831 as she pulls out of Rugby Central with the 4.5 pm Manchester-Marylebone express. The start southwards from Rugby began with a slight rise as far as the first over-bridge visible in the picture following which there was 1¾ miles down the grade at 1 in 176. This gave engines a good impetus to tackle the long 6½ mile climb up to Catesby tunnel. On my numerous whirlwind evening footplate runs from Leicester to Rugby on this train I often enjoyed listening to the Gresley engines getting into their 'galloping' stride as they headed south on a quiet evening. As the sound of their effort was gradually absorbed by distance and other sounds took over one was left with a profound feeling of wistful nostalgia particularly when there was an awareness that it was all going to end and such rich moments would never be repeated.

60. Taken on a tripod perched on the vaccuum cylinder of the Marylebone turntable V2 No 6083 is seen shortly after midnight resting before its run back to Leicester with the down 'Newspaper'.

61. A frontal study of 60831 standing on the turntable at one o'clock in the morning.

62. Having hooked onto its train in Platform 1 No 60831 stands with the blower on raising steam for the journey ahead. It is a damp night with no wind and the falling droplets of vapour created a strange optical effect as they broke up and scattered the light shed by a nearby platform lamp. No 60831 had become very neglected externally and I seem to remember getting rather busy with a piece of sponge cloth before opening the shutter so as to recover her numerical identity.

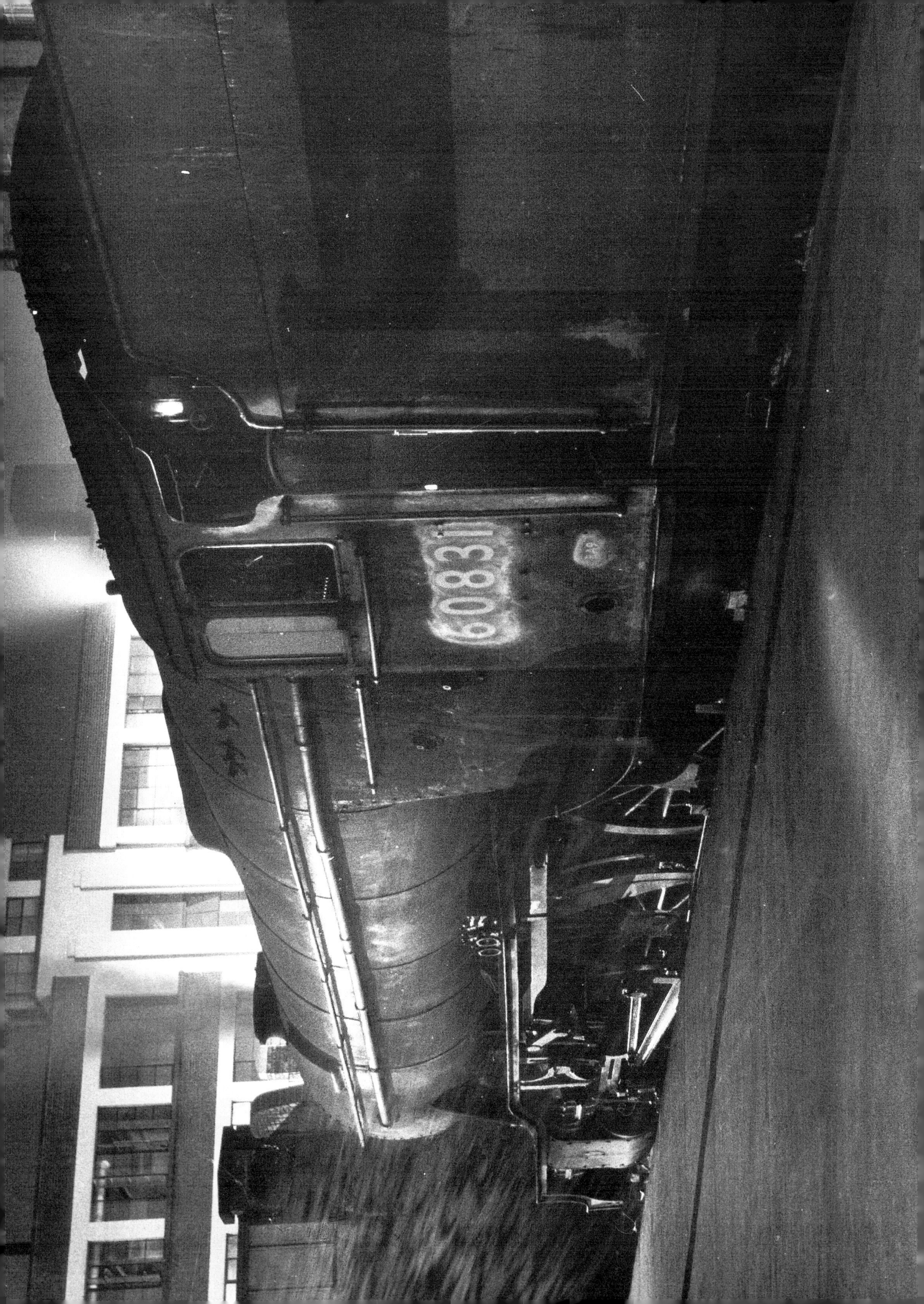
60831

63. Ron Cassie builds up the fire of a 'borrowed' Doncaster B1 No 61213 at Marylebone station before leaving with the 12.15 pm down to Manchester which took the Wycombe route back to Leicester. No 61213 was not a happy engine. On its run from Leicester to London on the 7.50am up from Sheffield its boiler had been unable to produce more than 190 lbs of steam during the whole run but thanks to a fine collaborative effort on the part of the engine crew its arrival was only 5 minutes late. An inspection at Neasden revealed that the firebars were almost solid with clinker but as there was insufficient time to remove it or provide a substitute engine the B1 had to return to Leicester in the same condition. Such situations certainly tested the skills of a driver and fireman.

64. No 61092 dashes through the Leicester outskirts near Rowley Fields with the up South Yorkshireman'. Later in the journey the B1 was to attain 92 mph near Calvert!

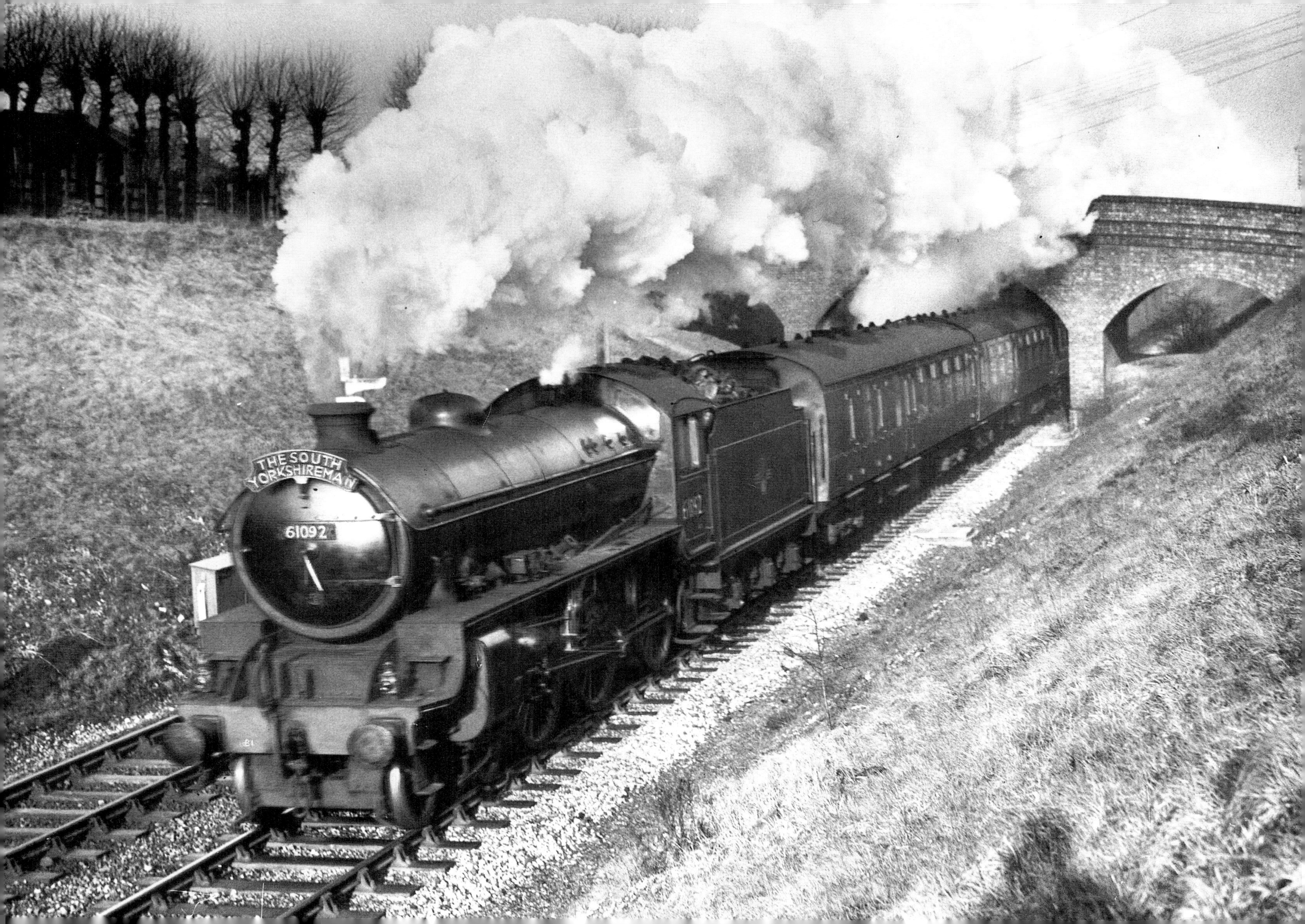
THE SOUTH YORKSHIREMAN
61092

65. No 61063 approaches the North Goods box on its way out of Leicester with the 2.10 pm from Manchester to Marylebone.

66. Dashing across Swithland Reservoir between Quorn and Rothley with the 9.20 am from Manchester to Marylebone is No 61331.

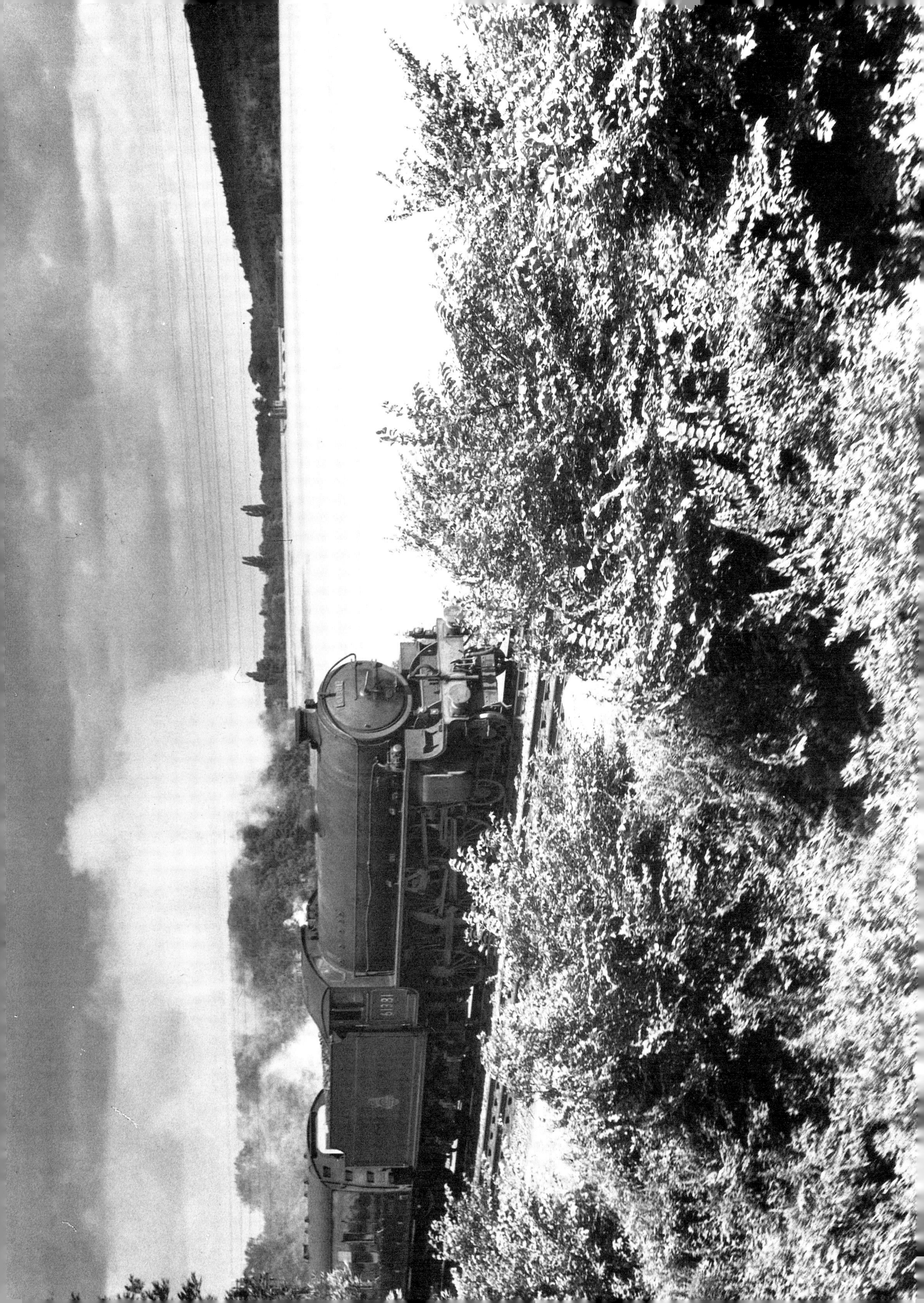

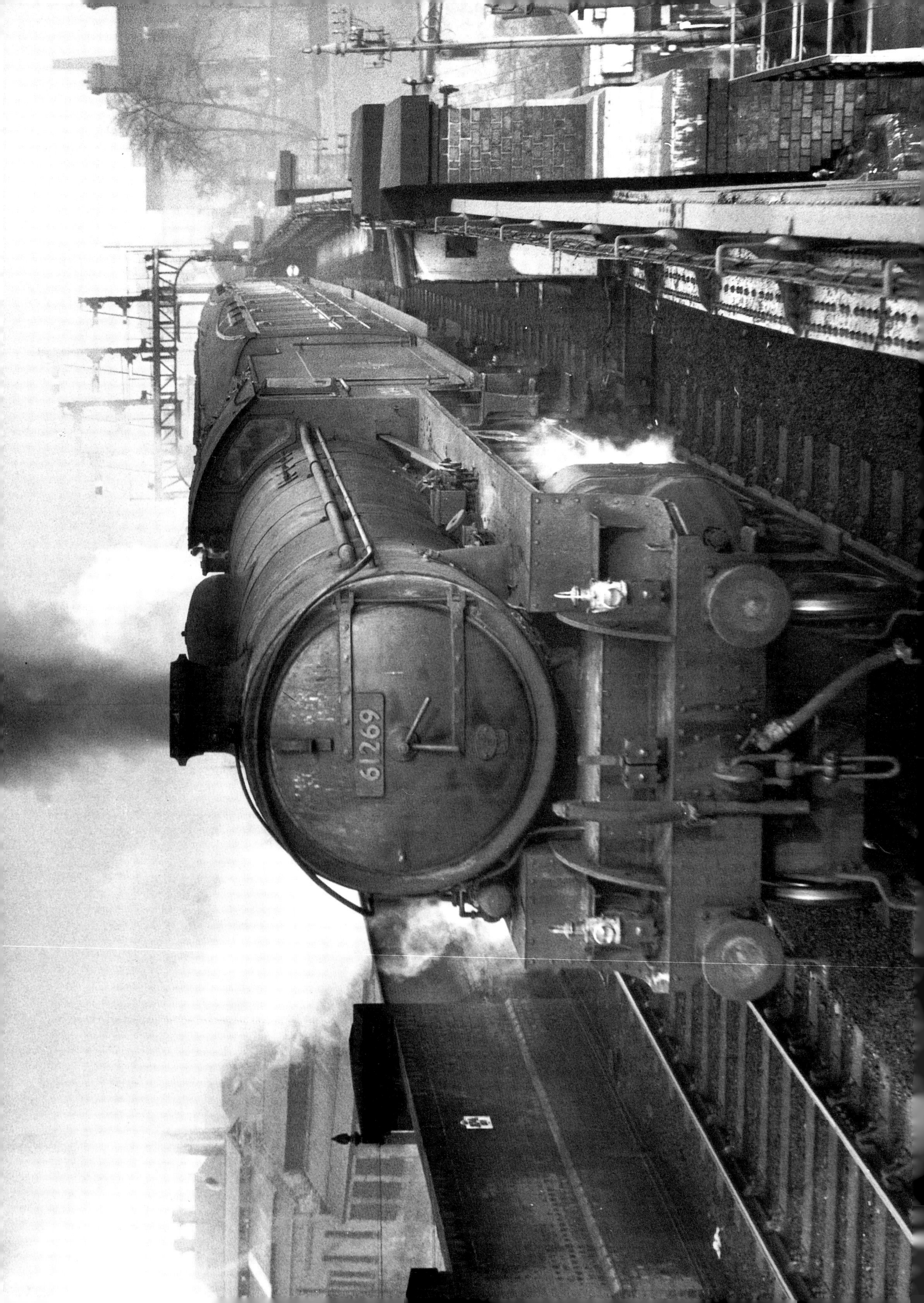
61269

West Bridge viaduct with the 8.30 am express from Manchester to Marylebone. 31.1.59.

out from Leicester Central with the final first up express of the day, the 7.40 am from Sheffield to Marylebone. Her driver was Len Woodhead and his fireman Mick Kilby.

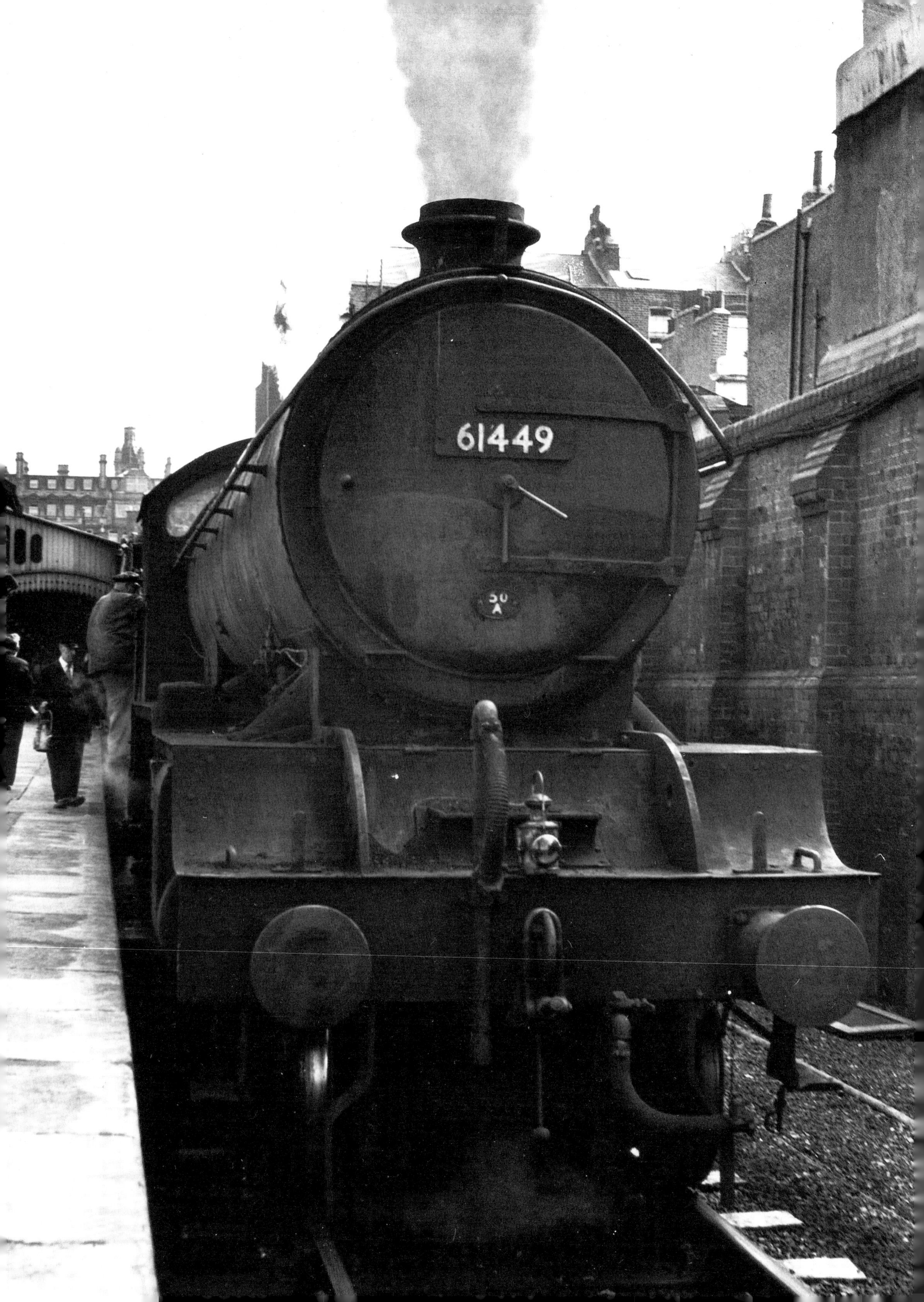
61449

69. Driver Albert Chafer climbs into the cab of B16 No 61449 which has just backed down onto the 3.20 pm down to Manchester in No 4 platform at Marylebone while the guard holding the tender lamp checks the coupling up process. This photograph illustrates the entertaining 'bloodspitter' episode described in the book's introduction. 6.10.58.

70. Signs of the London Midland Region take-over. A Stanier Class 5 4-6-0 No 45006 passes the South Goods loop as it leaves Leicester with the up 'South Yorkshireman'.

71. Approaching the top of the climb between Ashby Magna and Lutterworth another Black 5 No 44821 heads for Marylebone with the 4.5 pm express from Manchester to Marylebone. 9.8.58.

72. The Summer of 1958 was memorable for the use of vaccuum fitted 9F 2-10-0s on some of the G.C. expresses and Saturday cross country holiday trains. What was probably quite a reasonable decision by the London Midland Region where their own trains were concerned completely misjudged the audacious spirit that pervaded engine crews on the Great Central section. The result was that the 9Fs acquired almost an entertainment value and were pushed along at speeds into the 80s until anxious reports flooded in to the top echelons of the Motive Power Department which instantly clapped a 60 mph restriction on the big 2-10-0s.

In this photograph No 92125 from Wellingborough shed is seen at Leicester Central waiting to take over the 3.20 pm down Manchester

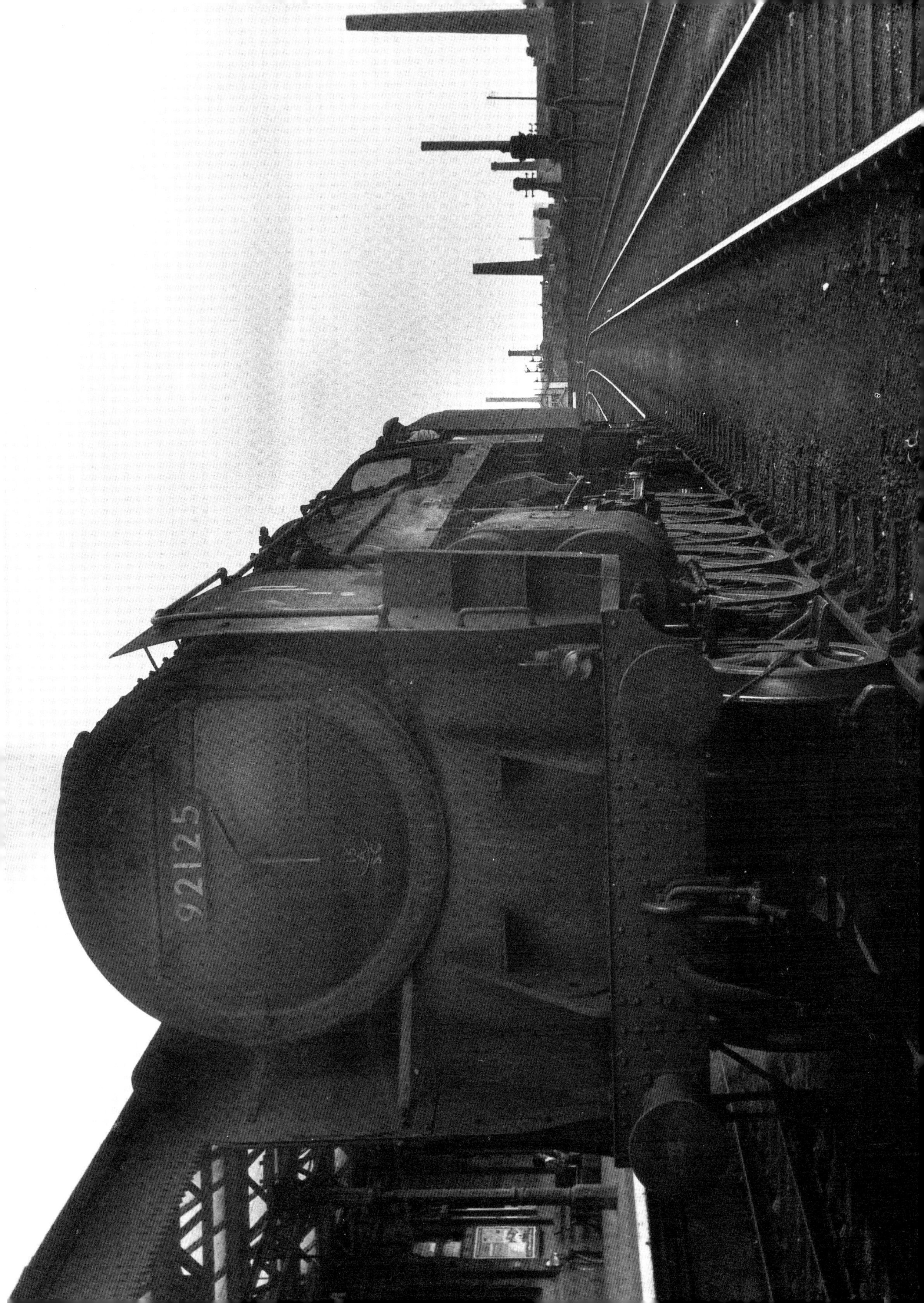
92125

73. A shot from the cab of No 92125 as it crosses the River Soar on its way out of Leicester with the 3.20 pm express from Marylebone to Manchester.

74. Driver George Evinson looks out as he sets off from Loughborough Central with No 92125 bound for Nottingham Victoria and Sheffield where the 9F will come off the train. The 3.20 pm down will complete its journey to Manchester London Rd with electric haulage.

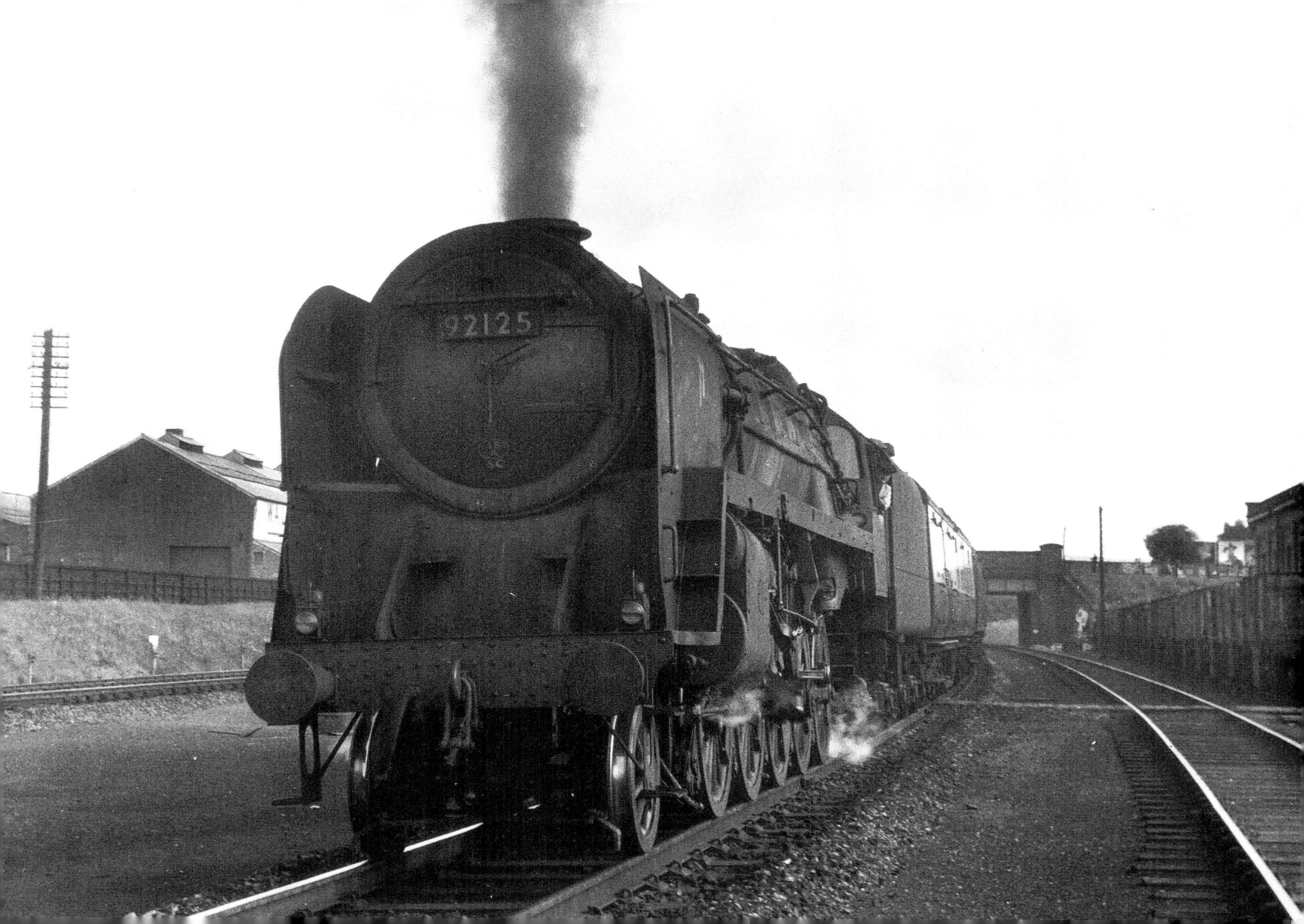
92125

75. At Leicester Central a Standard Class 5 No 73045 relinquishes its train, the 7.40 am from Sheffield Victoria to Marylebone, and makes for the shed. In No 4 bay B1 No

76. During its final week of running the up 'South Yorkshireman' climbs to Ashby Magna on the last day of 1959 under threatening skies. The engine is Standard 5 No

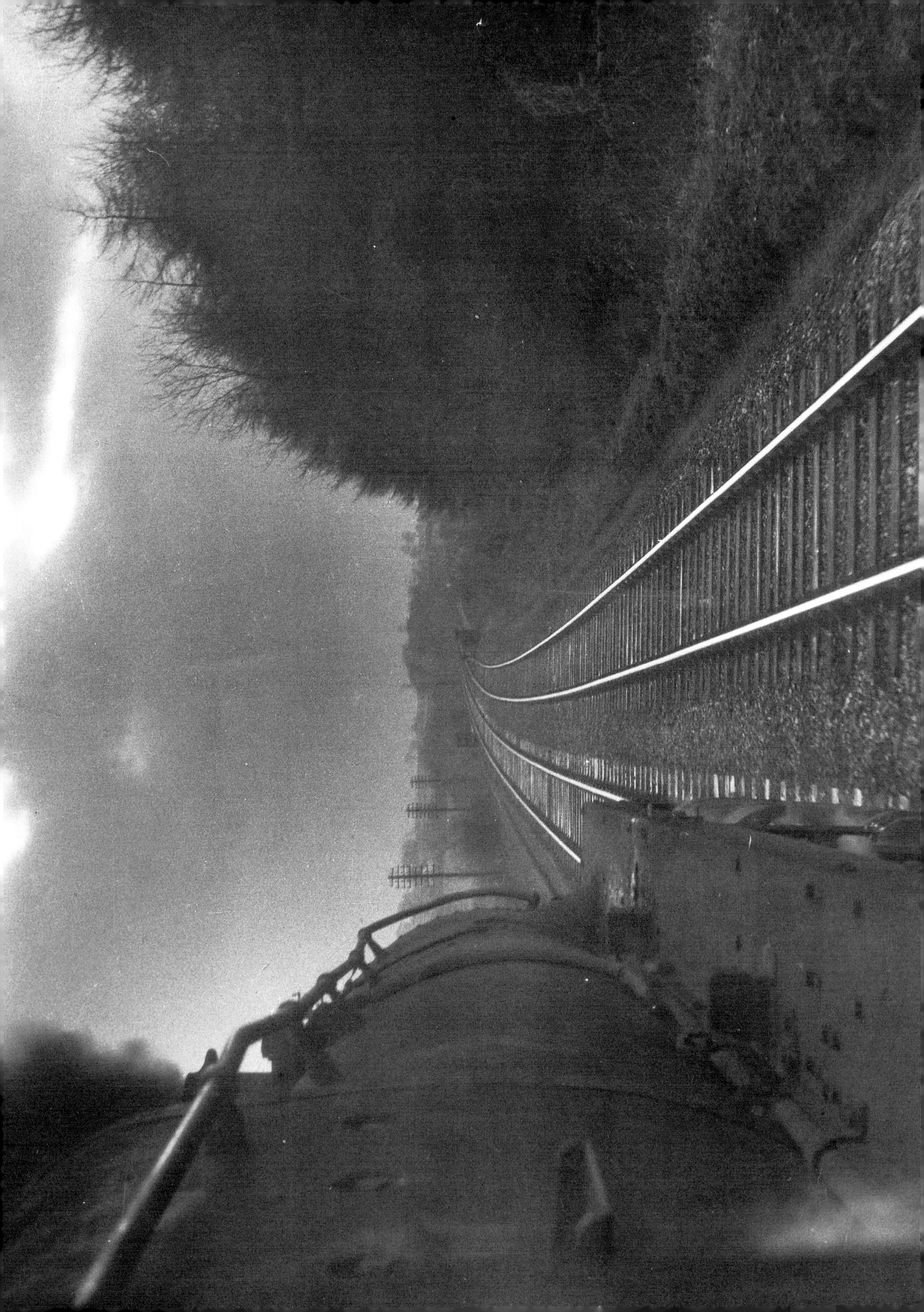

Marylebone Express Finale.
77. Driver Ken Davies and Fireman Jack Freer are in charge of Standard 5 No 73053 for the run to Marylebone with the last 8.30am from Manchester on January 2nd 1960.

78. In the down direction as the gloom settles another Standard 5 No 73069 makes a vigorous start from Leicester Central with the final 12.15 pm from Marylebone to Manchester. Driver Jack Jacques and Fireman Barry Frost from Leicester's No 2 link make a punctual departure.

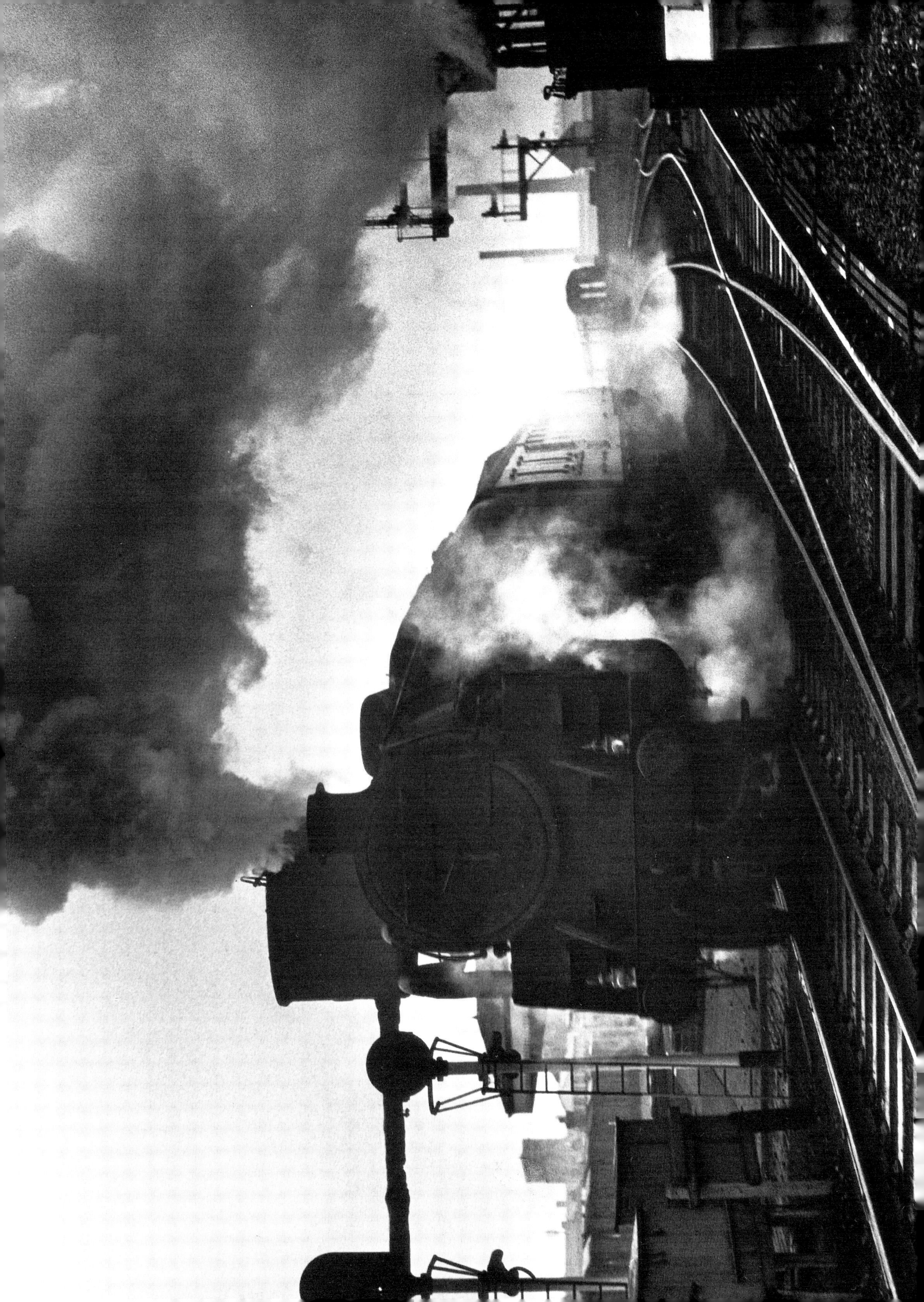

The York-Bournemouth and Cross Country expresses.

79. V2 No 60881 from Doncaster shed stands in No 3 bay at Leicester Central having been 'borrowed' for a run to Banbury with the Newcastle-Bournemouth through train.

80. No 60881 sets out over the West Bridge viaduct at Leicester with the up 'Bournemouth' and crosses the Soar Navigation. Above and beyond the engine can be seen the wagons and tracks of the Midland's West Bridge yard.

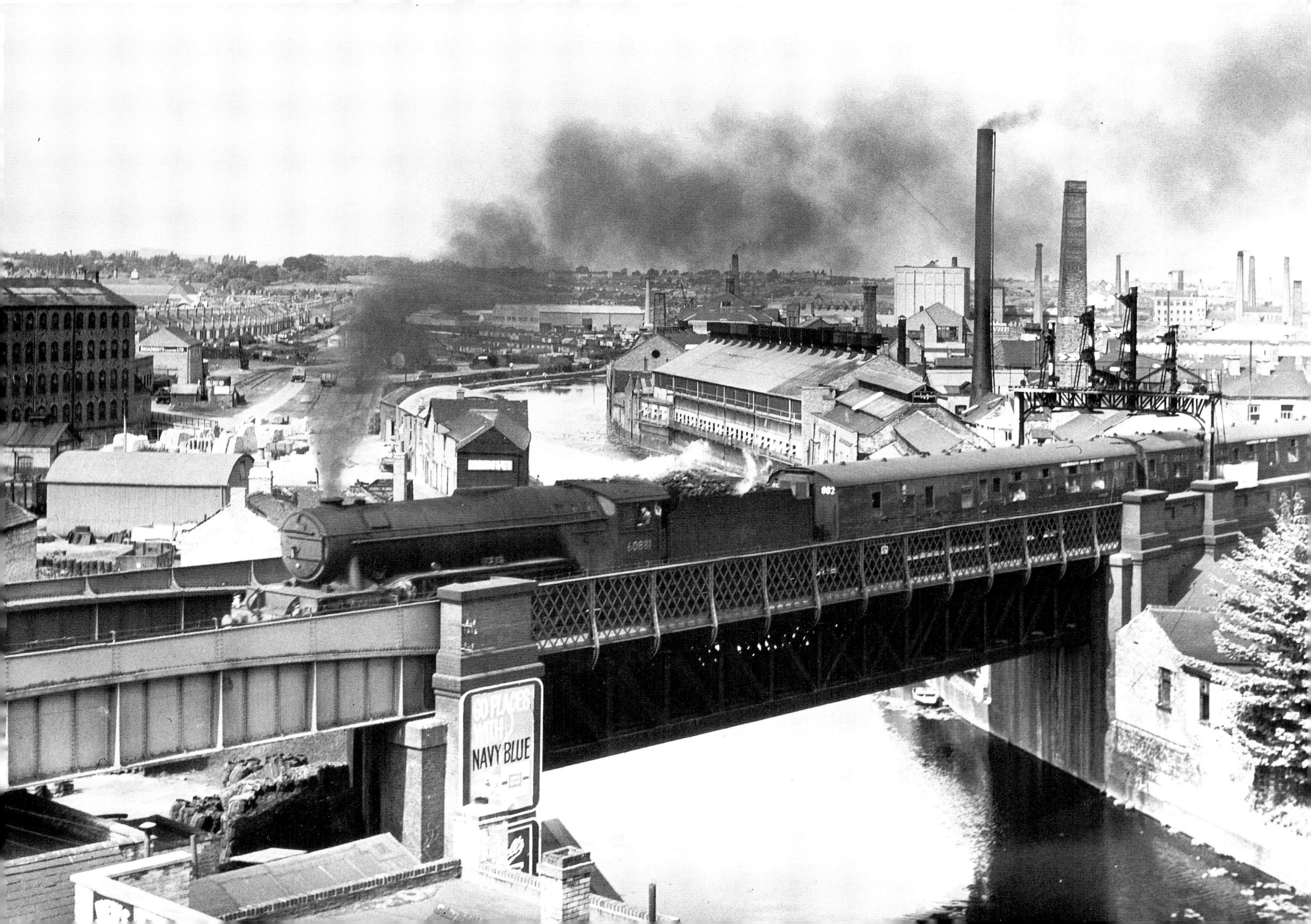
GO PLACES WITH
NAVY BLUE
60881
982

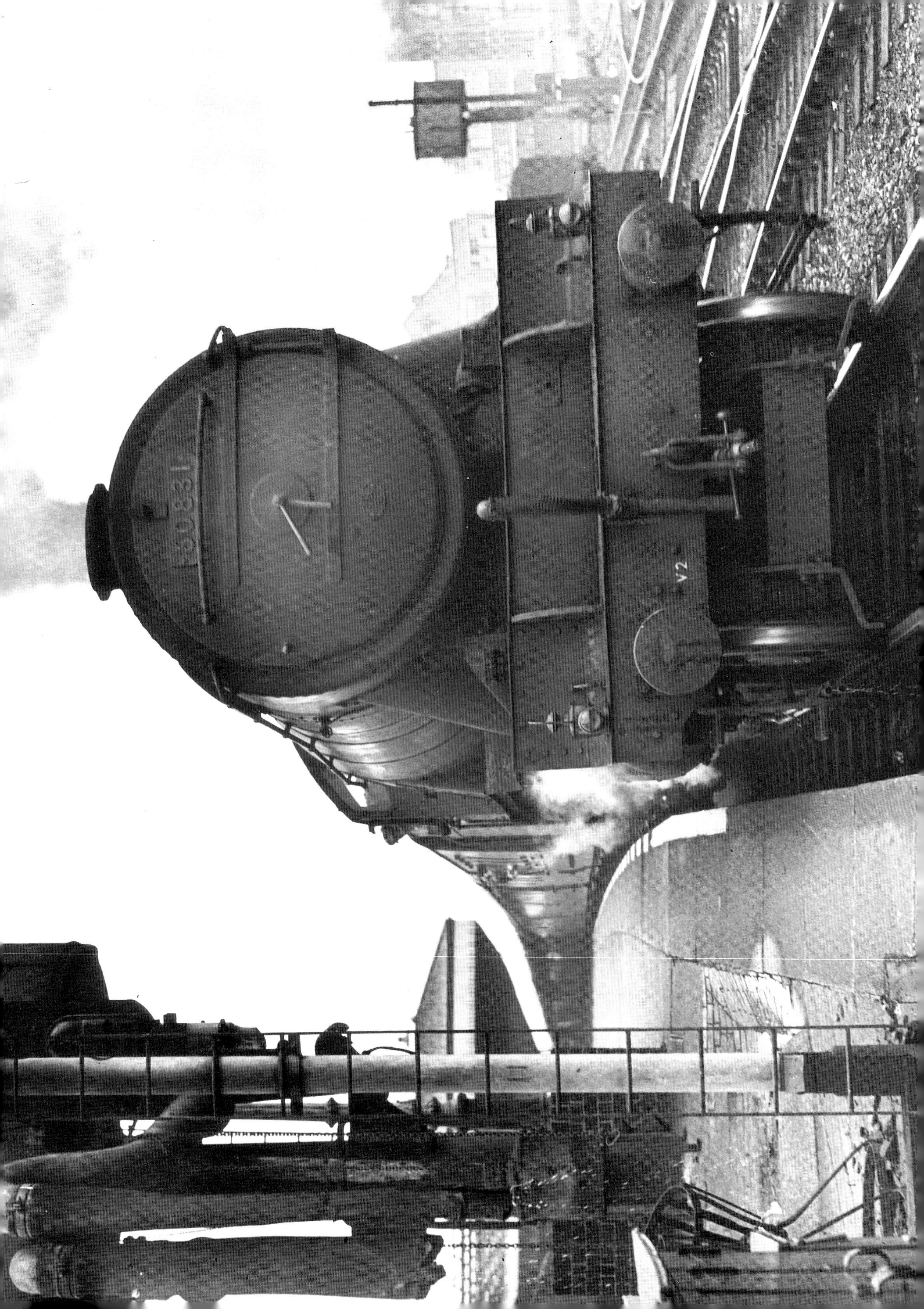
60831
V2

No. 61078 takes a (Sat) holiday train bound for Bournemouth out of Leicester Central on a Summer Saturday in 1959.

off from Leicester Central with the Newcastle–Bournemouth in August 1958.

83. The sun is high overhead on a hot and humid Summer Saturday as a York B16 4-6-0 coasts into Leicester Central over the Soar Navigation with a relief to the Bournemouth-Newcastle

84. An Annesley 9F 2-10-0 No 92043 takes a rest from 'windcutting' and with Leicester driver Bill Priestley at the regulator makes an effortless start from Leicester Central with a through

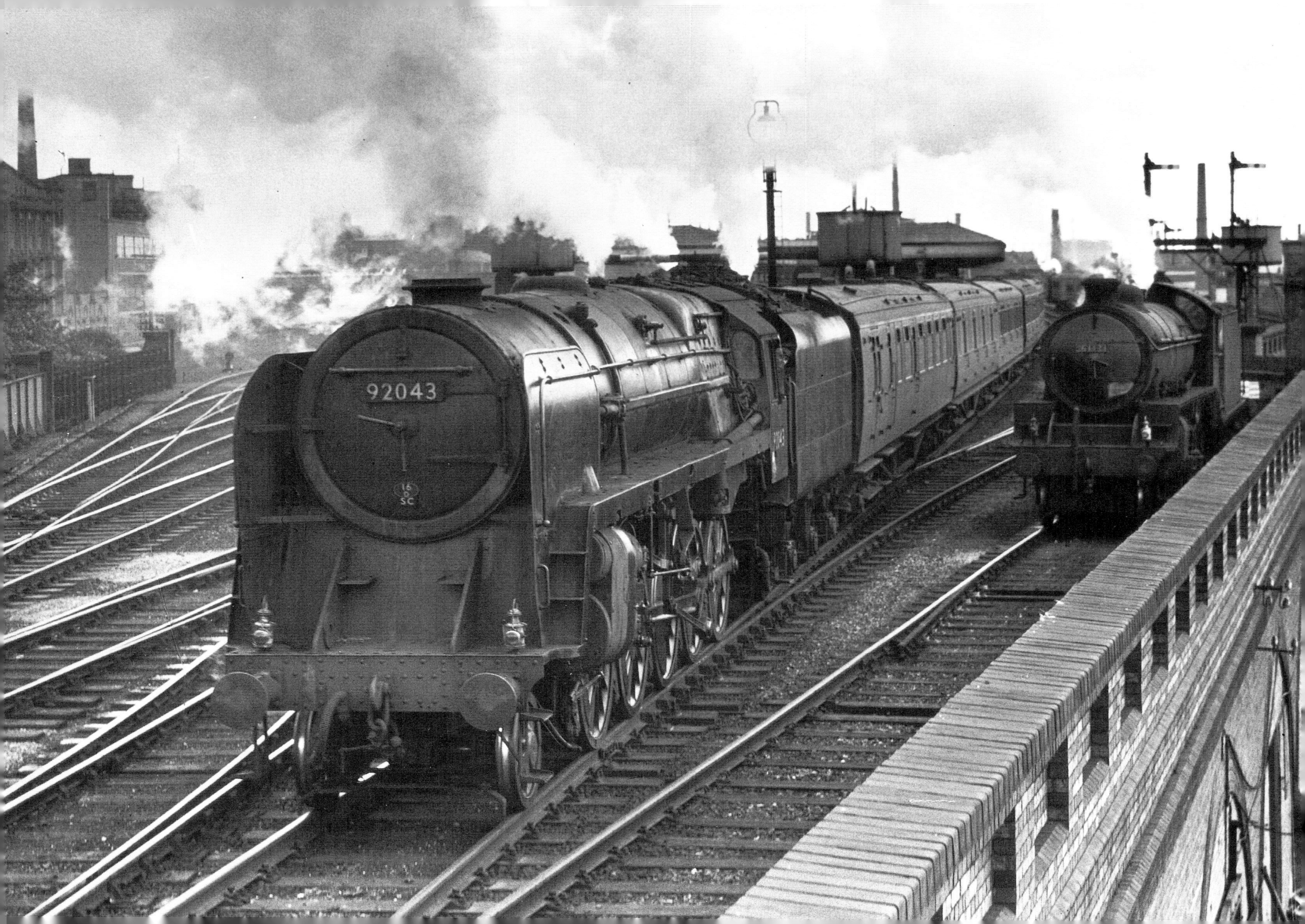
92043

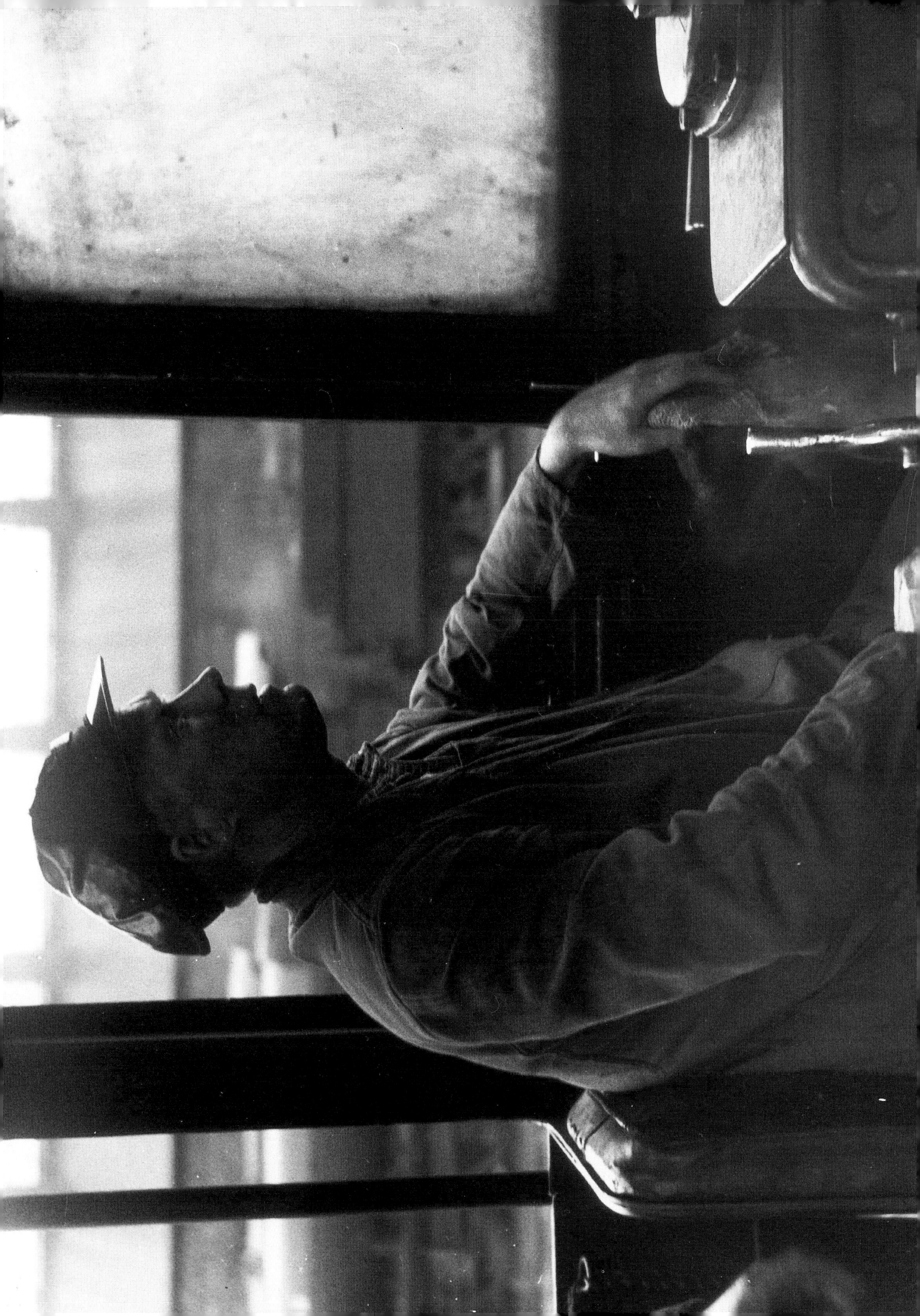

85. Driver Ron Smith with Standard 5 No 73135 has a look of growing irritation on his face as his engine is held on the down main line outside Banbury shed in the pouring rain. He is travelling back from Oxford to Leicester light engine after working a Saturday relief to the Newcastle-Bournemouth.

86. On the other side of the engine his fireman for the day, Harry Elford, takes life easily and scans the gauges. I still have the most cordial memories of this trip. I had spent much of the day photographing the busy activities at Oxford where continuous heavy rain had set in during the morning. However, mindful of the fact that such scenes would shortly disappear and would never be repeated I decided to continue with my mission and received a thorough soaking as a reward for the dedication. At the end of the afternoon after things had quietened down I was faced with the grim prospect of making my way to the outskirts of Oxford over 2 miles away from where I would endeavour to hitch lifts back to Leicester. In my saturated condition I had little optimism.

I was on the point of leaving the station when I noticed a somewhat unkempt Standard 5 waiting to enter the station from the north and as it drew its train into the platform and came to a stop my spirits soared as I recognised the face of Driver Ron Smith. Not only did he rescue me by giving me a ride back to Leicester but he also stopped and dropped me off near a bus stop. How dramatically the fortunes could change!

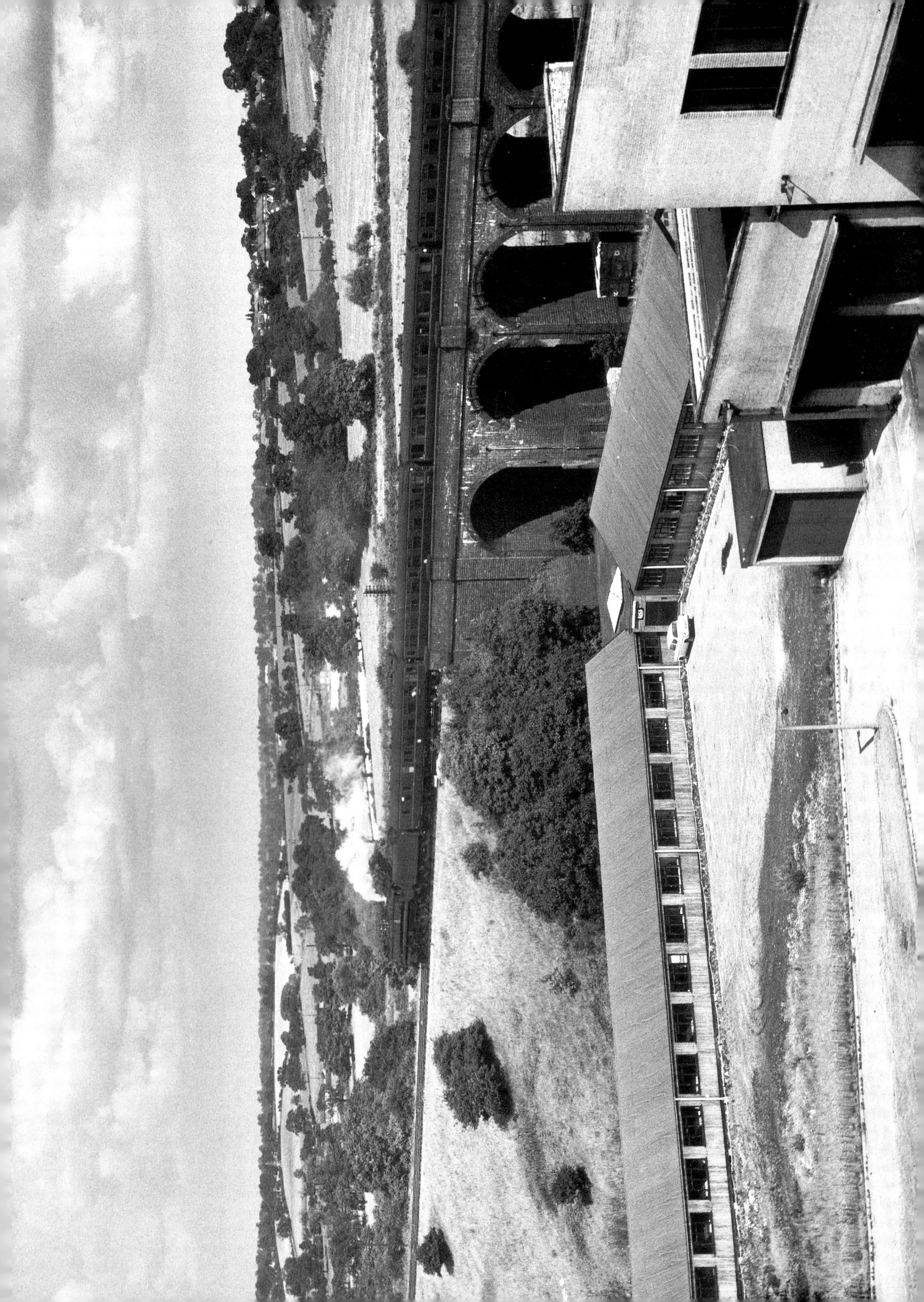

88. The Saturday 10.5 am from Bournemouth West to Bradford train has run into Leicester Central headed by a Western Region 'Hall' class 4-6-0 No 7923 'Speke Hall'. Its task accomplished it prepares to hand over to London Midland 'Jubilee' class No 45646 'Napier' which will complete the run to Bradford. 22.6.63.

89. After taking over the train No 45646 'Napier' sets off from Leicester Central 22.6.63.

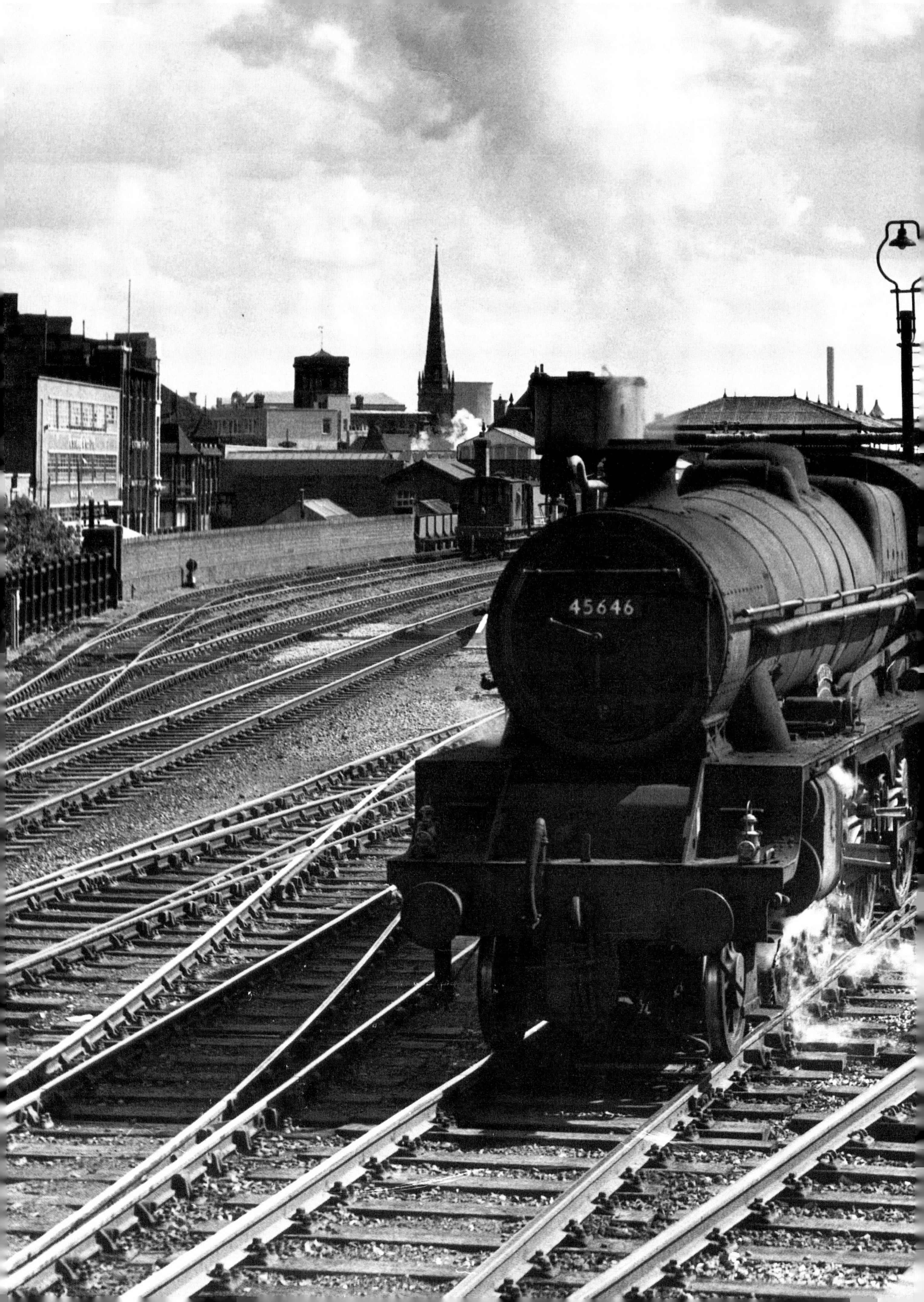
45646

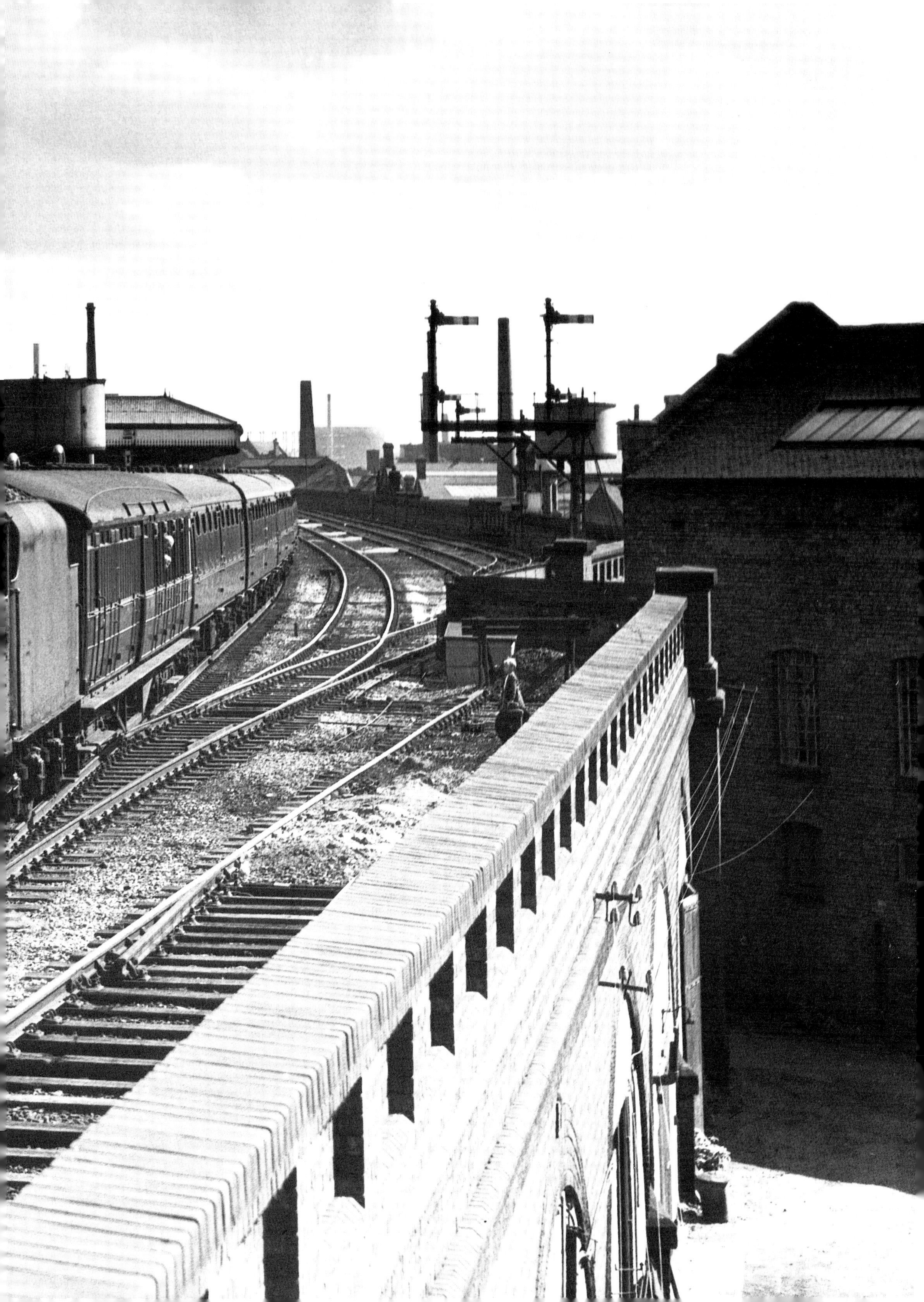

CATCH POINTS

91. A sister engine No 44691 approaches the same spot with the 12.25pm from Ramsgate to Derby Friargate. 22.6.63

92. Another 'Black 5' No 45234 crosses the Soar viaduct North of Loughborough with a train from Bournemouth

93. A Stanier Class 5 climbs the long bank to Barnston tunnel out of Loughborough with a Summer Saturday train from Hastings to

94. A 'Britannia' Pacific No 70040 'Clive of India' hurries into Leicester between Birstall and Abbey Lane with the 1.28 pm from Cleethorpes to

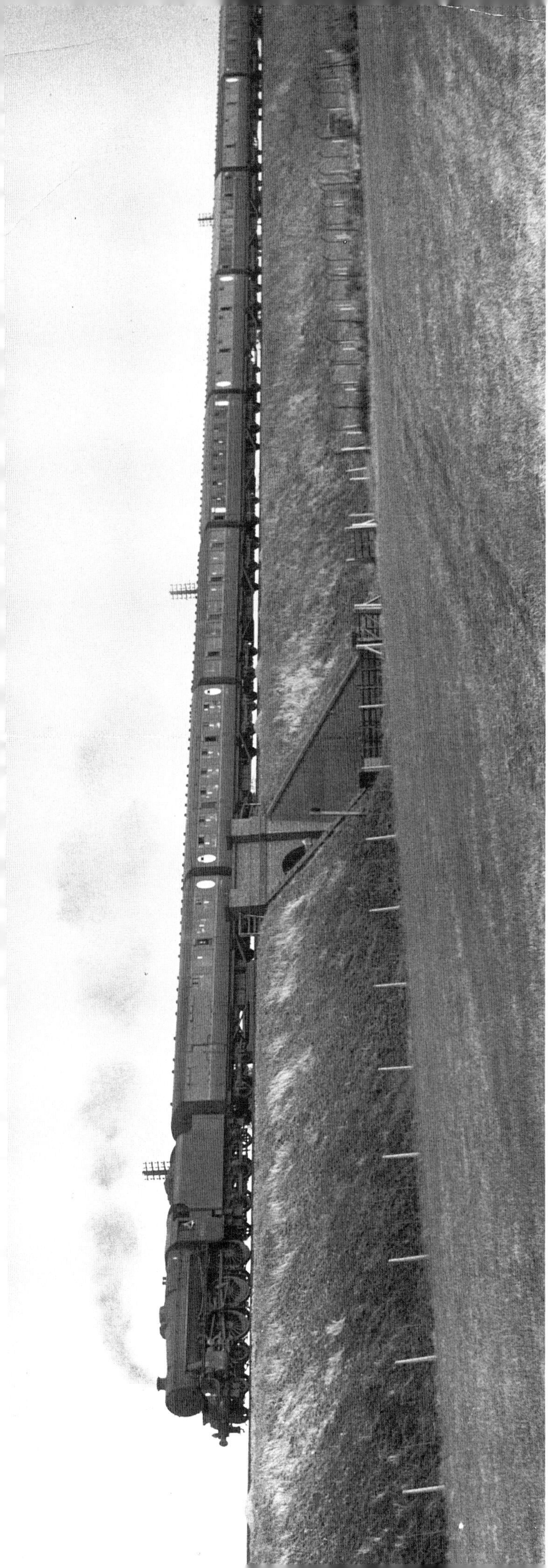

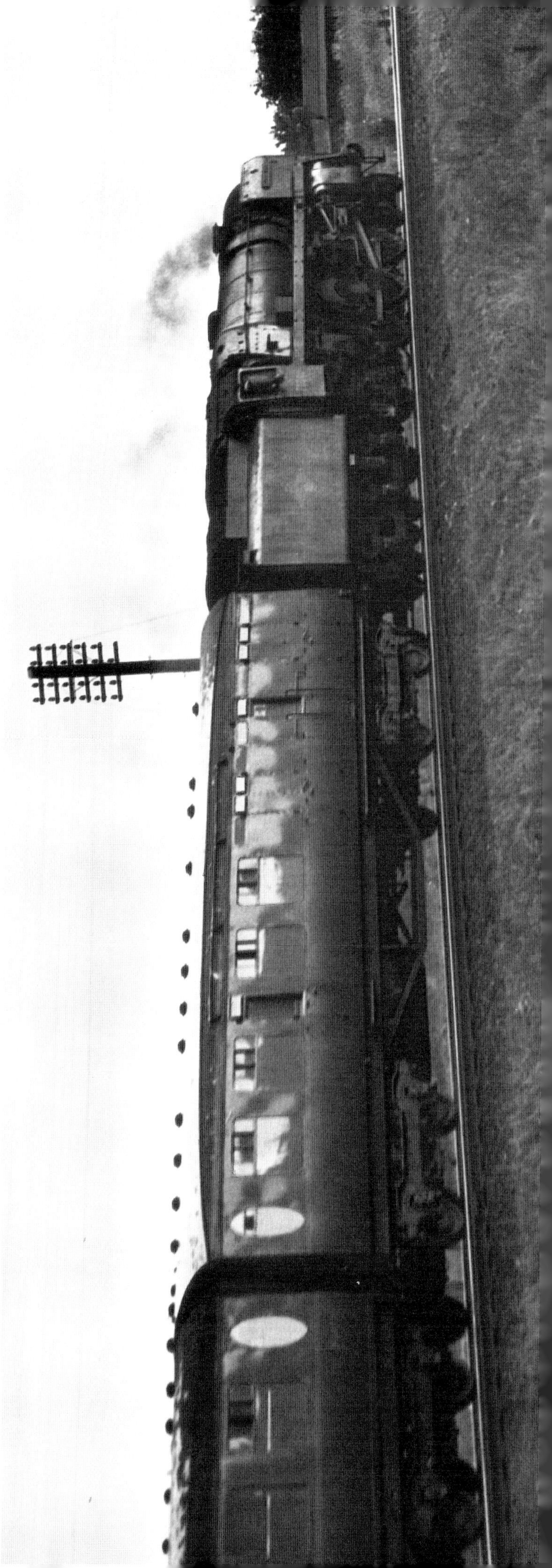

95. I took a number of shots of London Midland 'Jubilee' No 45708 'Resolution' on the afternoon of Saturday, June 29th 1963 before and during a footplate trip when she was working from Leicester Central on the 10.34 am train from Bournemouth West to

96. A photograph from the driver's side taken just before departure from Plat-

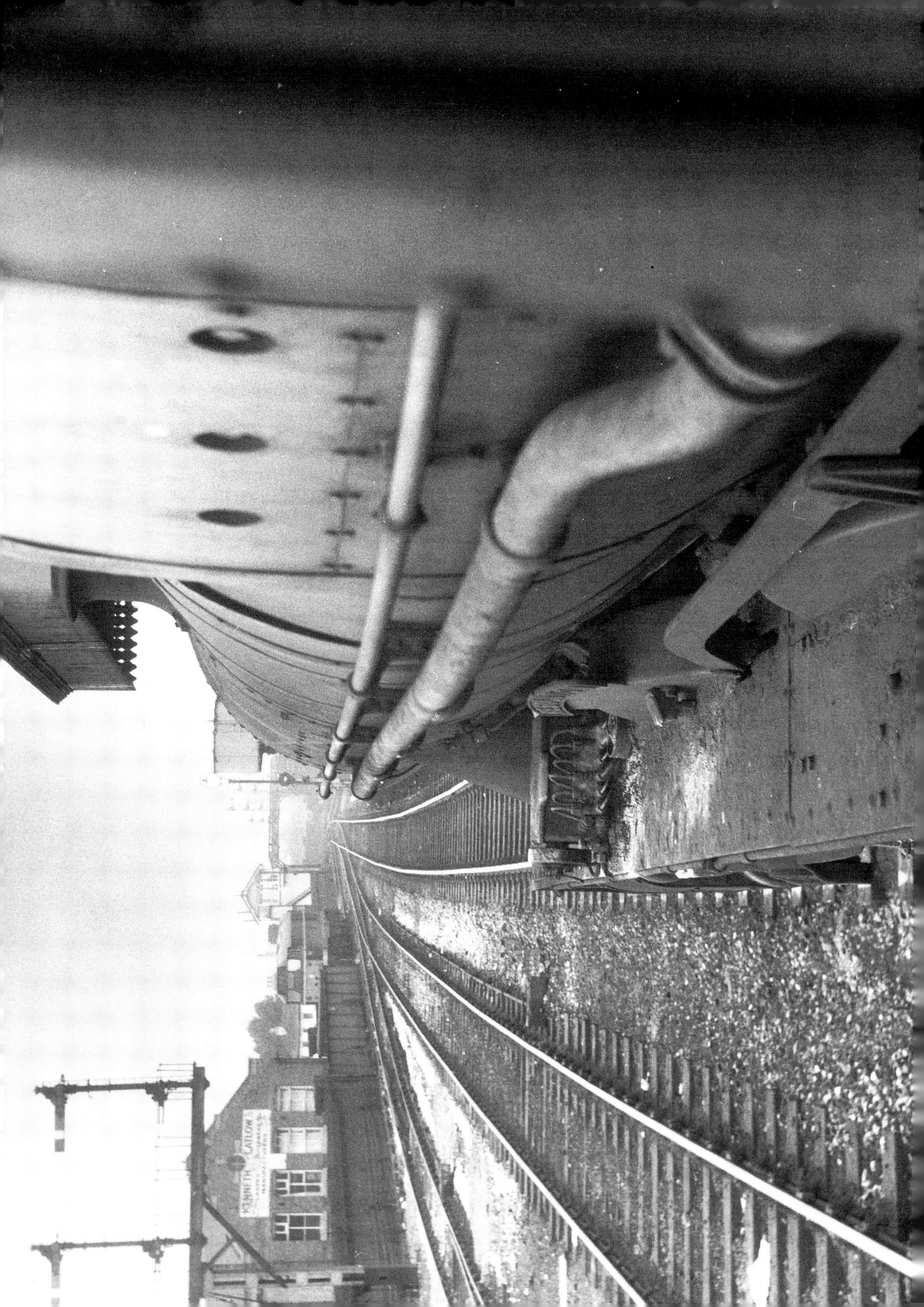
KENNETH CATLOW

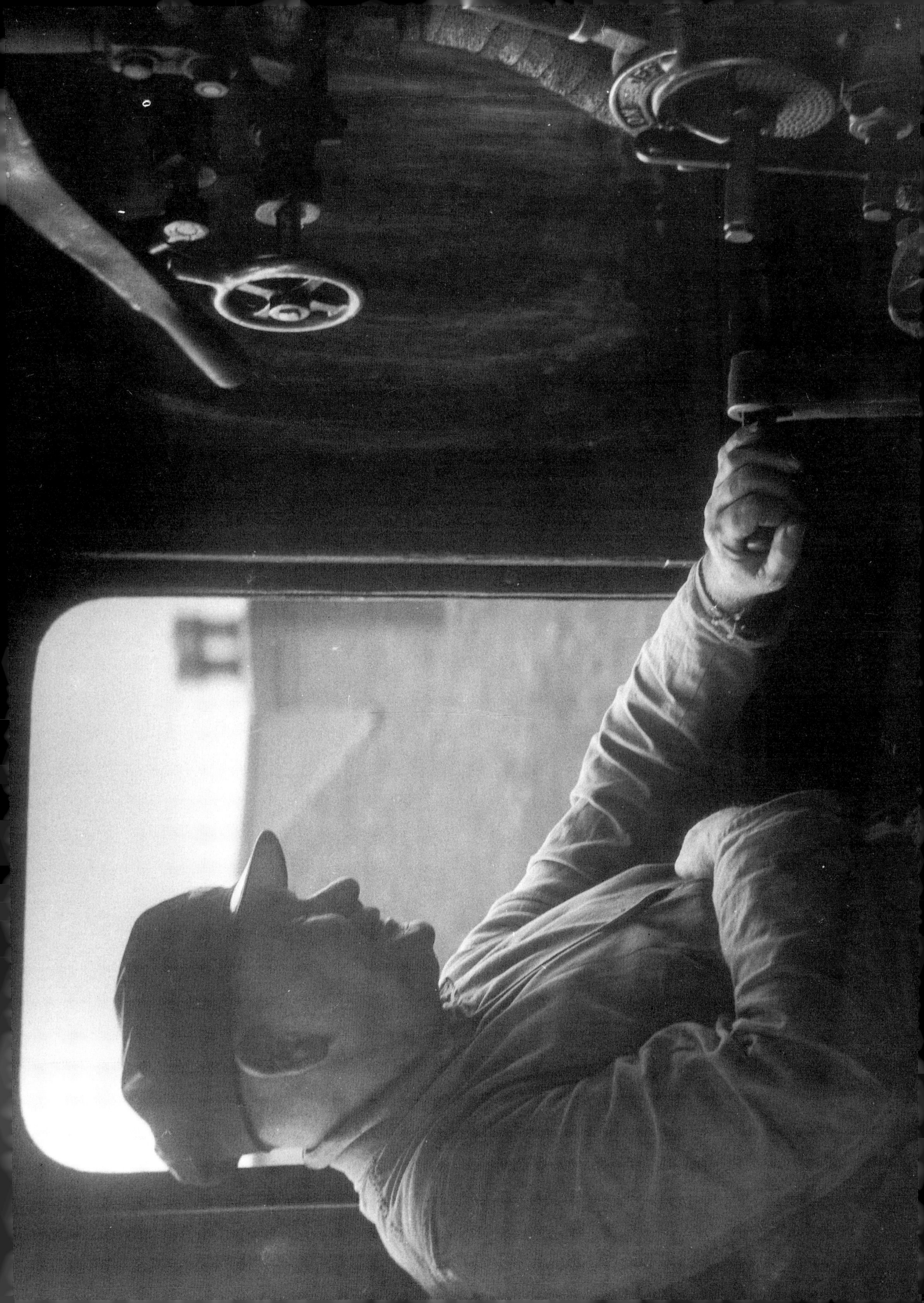

97. Sheffield Driver Ernie Wilson gives the wide-open-regulator treatment to No 45708 as it pulls away from Leicester over the Northgate viaduct.

98. After crossing the River Trent No 45708 approaches Queens Walk and Nottingham where a Stanier 'Black 5' heading a southbound Summer Saturday train exchanges greetings.

99. In 1962 the York-Bournemouth train was provided with diesel haulage throughout between Sheffield and Banbury, the engine returning with the northbound train. Leicester Central's steam contribution was thus ended. Photographed between Rothley and Birstall English Electric

Local Passenger.

100. Colwick driver Walter Dawson with a Robinson A5 4-6-2 tank No 69825 marshals some empty stock at Nottingham Victoria before working a local passenger train to Leicester.

Following pages.

By 1958 apart from the odd A5 tank and J11 0-6-0 there were very few original Great Central engines to be seen at work over the London Extension. An interesting regular exception however was provided by the 5.49 pm local passenger train that ran from Sheffield Victoria to Leicester Central each weekday evening which produced a former Great Central 'Director' 4-4-0.

Its return from Leicester only 23 minutes after its arrival meant that very smart work was put in by the station pilot in removing the empty stock and taking it onto the West Bridge viaduct where it was held while the D11's engine crew put in some urgent endeavour to turn the engine on the station turntable before backing on to the waiting coaches and taking them into platform 3. This snappy piece of operating gave rise to a nickname being attached to this train of 'The Spitfire'.

The 'Director' used came from the mainly freight engine depot at Staveley and it was supplied from the Sheffield parent depot at Darnall specifically for this working combined with local passenger duties between Sheffield and Chesterfield.

During the summer of 1958 the regular engine was No 62663 'Prince Albert' and thanks to Mr. Frank Haywood, the Staveley shedmaster, its smokebox was given a coat of black paint to improve its looks for the camera. At a depot where engine cleaning had almost become a lost art it was a generous gesture and the gratitude lingers still.

The 'Directors' were a finely proportioned engine combining good looks with good performance. In their heyday they had been a formidable competitor to the 4-4-0s on the the rival Midland Railway and like them had once worked the fastest expresses throughout between London and Manchester.

I made a number of trips to photograph 'Prince Albert' and also enjoyed two footplate rides to and from Leicester Central. A selection of memories follow.

101. Before the application of some black paint No 62663 stands beneath the road bridge at Belgrave and Birstall with the return 8.55 pm local from Leicester Central to Chesterfield.

102. At Chesterfield Central No 62663 'Prince Albert' waits to leave with the 12.03 pm train to Sheffield Victoria. The guard and driver wonder what all the fuss is about. 21.6.58.

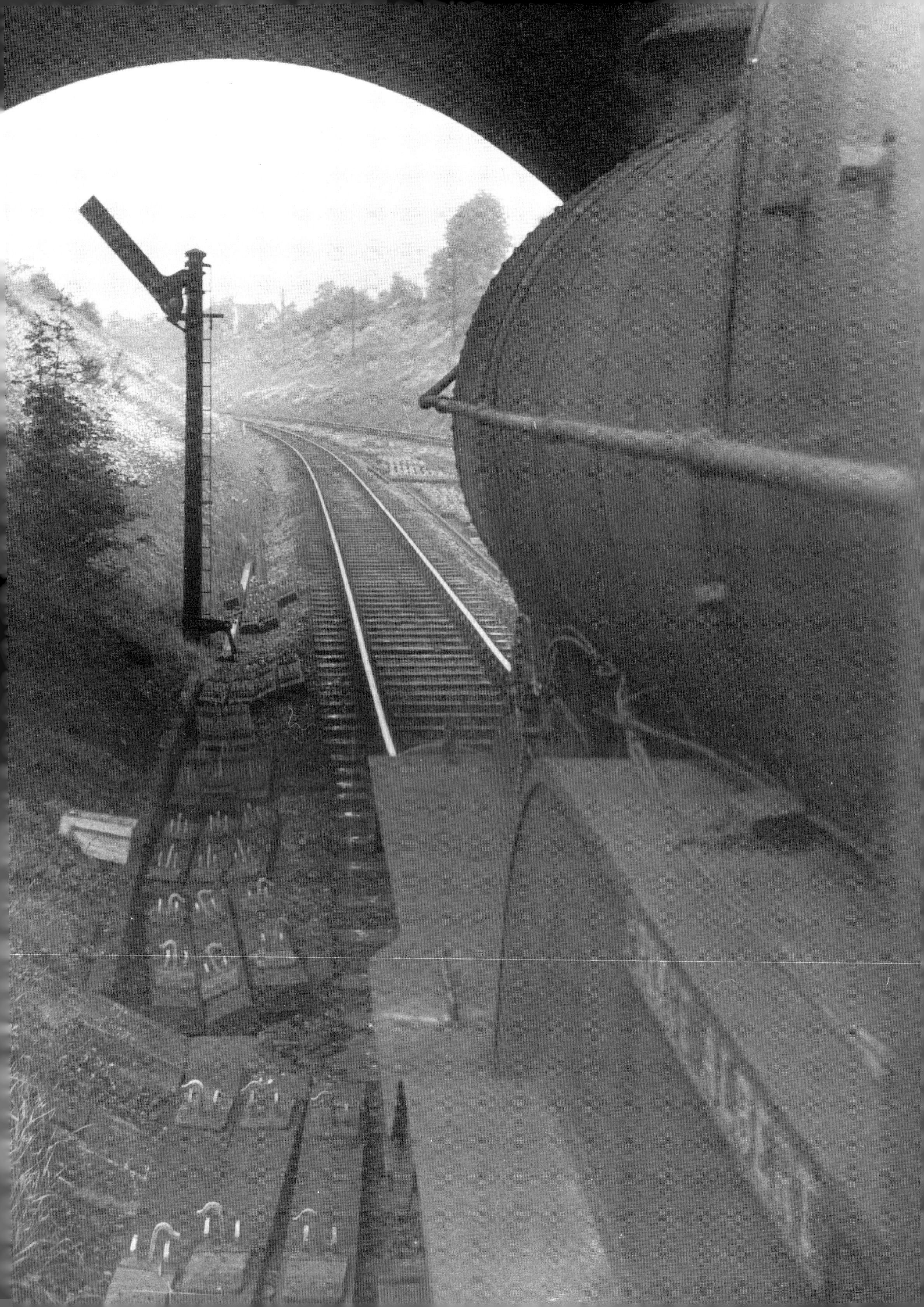

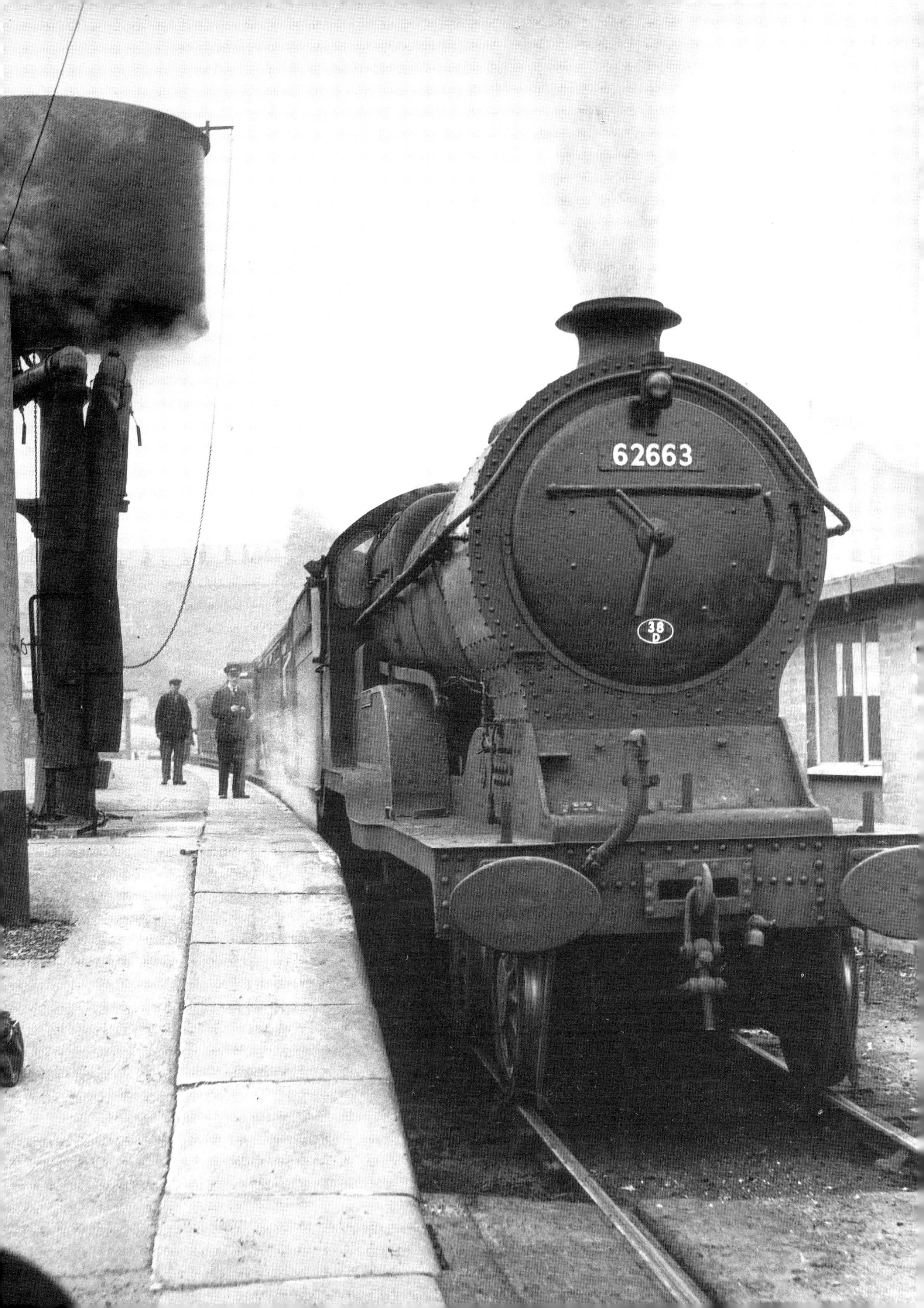
62663
38 D

103. No 62663 has just arrived in Platform 7 at Nottingham Victoria with the 5.49 pm from

104. Having paused beneath the station roof at Nottingham Victoria No 62663 moves up the platform to the water column before continuing its journey to Leicester. 23.6.58.

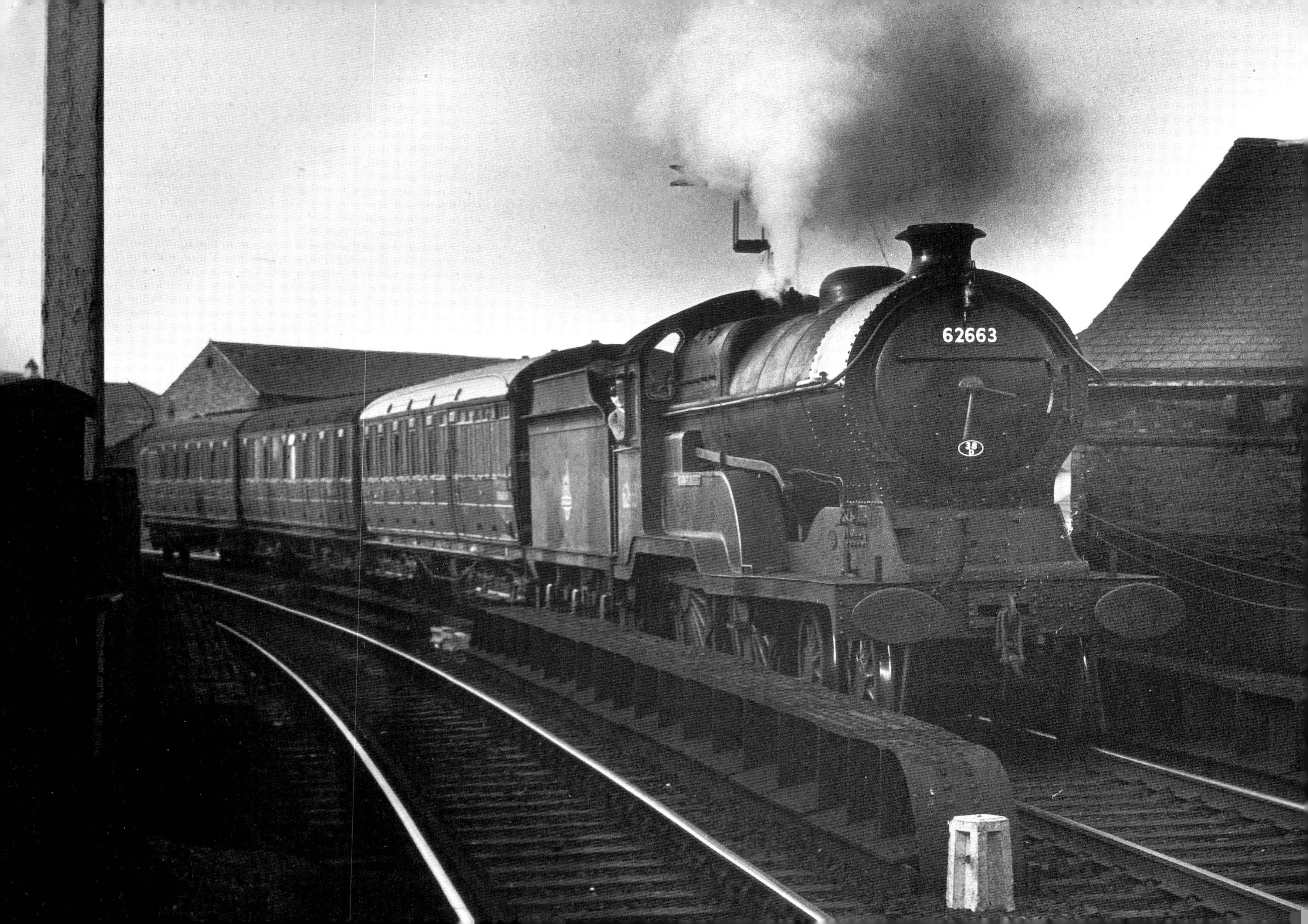
62663

105. 'Prince Albert' takes the curving approach to Nottingham Arkwright Street with the up 'Spitfire'. Staveley Driver Harry Turner obliges with a smoke and a full head of steam. 24.6.58.

106. No 62663 calls at East Leake with the 5.49pm from Sheffield to Leicester Central.

107. Driver Harry Turner from Staveley opens up the regulator of No 62663 'Prince Albert' as the engine leaves Leicester Central and crosses the Northgate viaduct with the return 'Spitfire'. 28.6.58.

108. Neasden's V2 No 60877 wearing a Class B lamp code attempts a little self-concealment as it stands in No 3 bay at Leicester Central after arriving from Marylebone with the 10 am down Manchester express. Its return to London will be on the 1.15 pm all stations from Nottingham Victoria which will include the empty newsaper vans. In the background a sizeable crowd on platform 6 awaits the arrival of the up 'South Yorkshireman'.

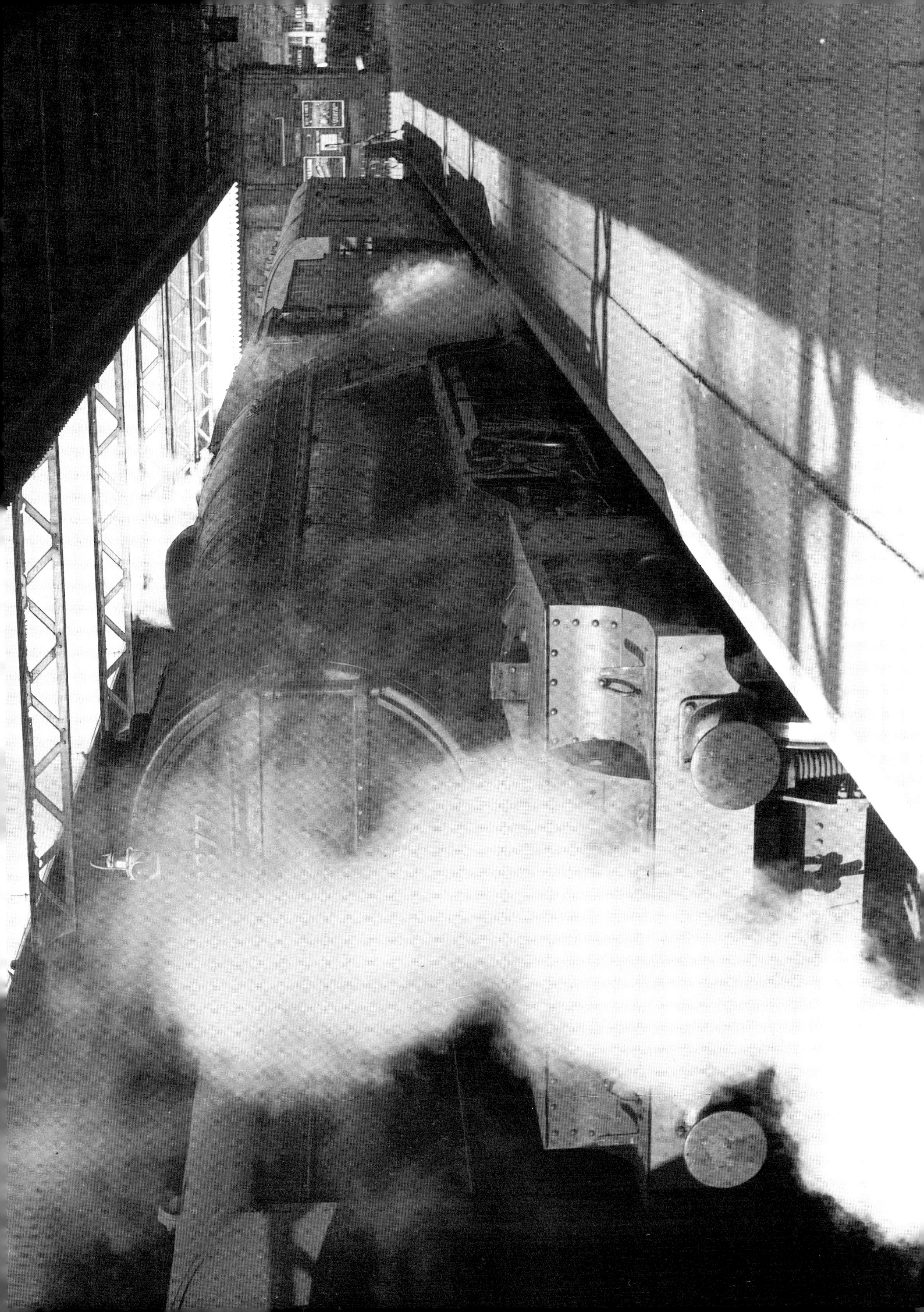

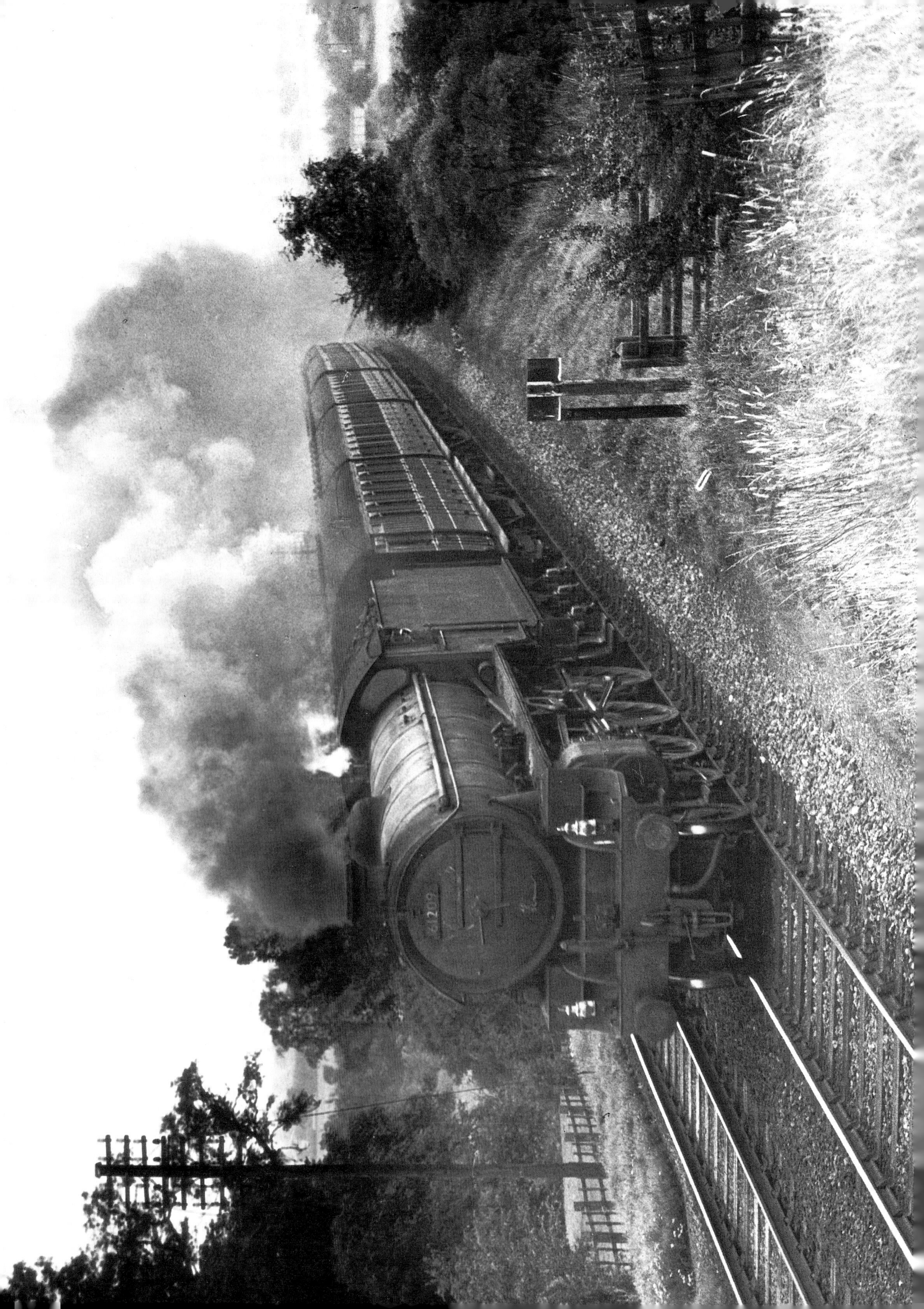

110. The same working taken near the same spot finds B1 No 61265 this time wearing the correct headlamp code.

hustled up the climb from Loughborough to Barnston near Stanford on Soar by B1 No 61209 which insists on wearing Class A headlamps.

111. Though not strictly a Great Central line working this train from Grantham to Derby Friargate with L1 2-6-4 tank No 67790 on the front is nevertheless joining the formerly shared tracks of the G.N. and G.C at Nottingham's Weekday Cross Junction.

112. Another 'Director' No 52667 'Somme' sets out from Sheffield Vic-

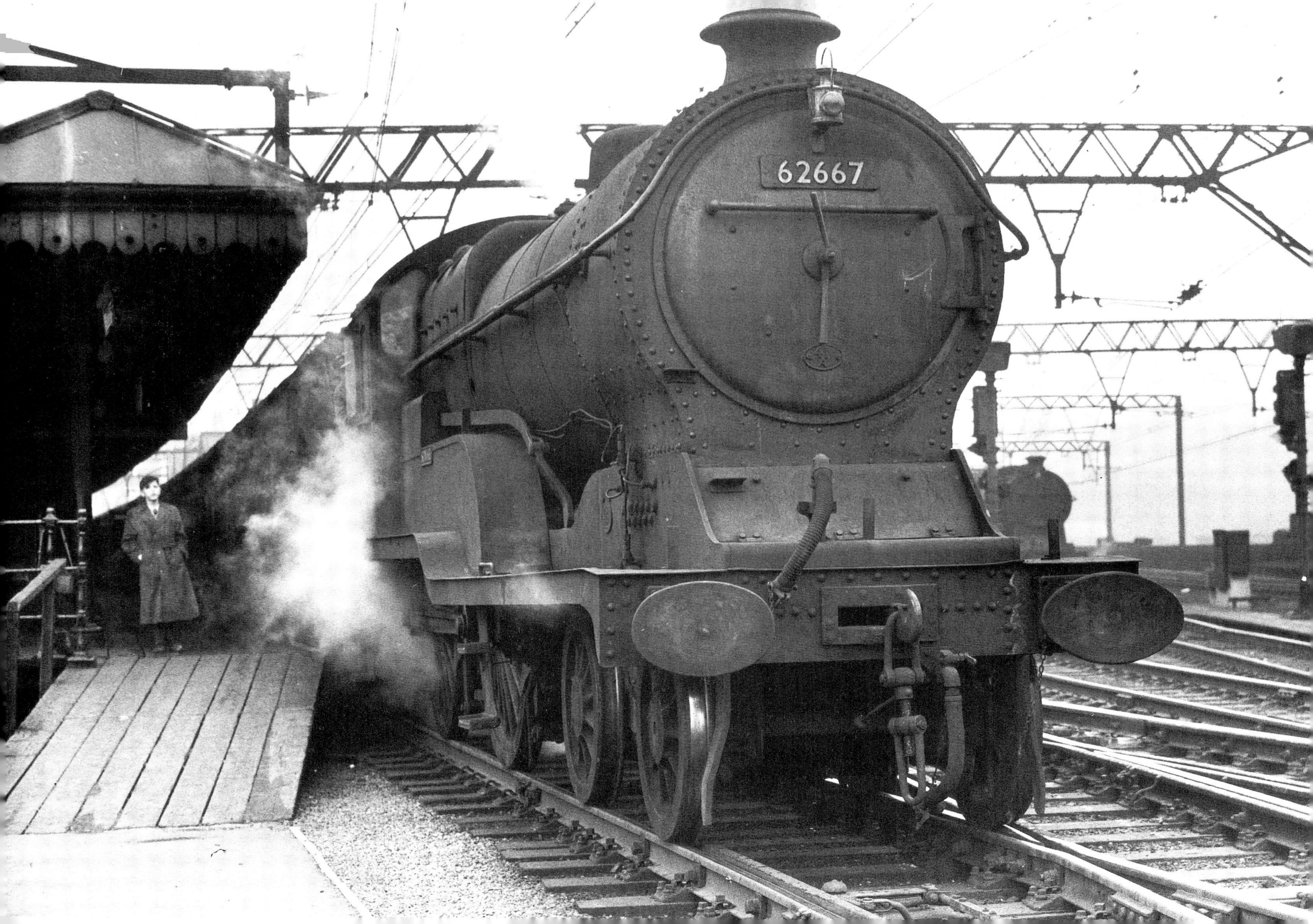
62667

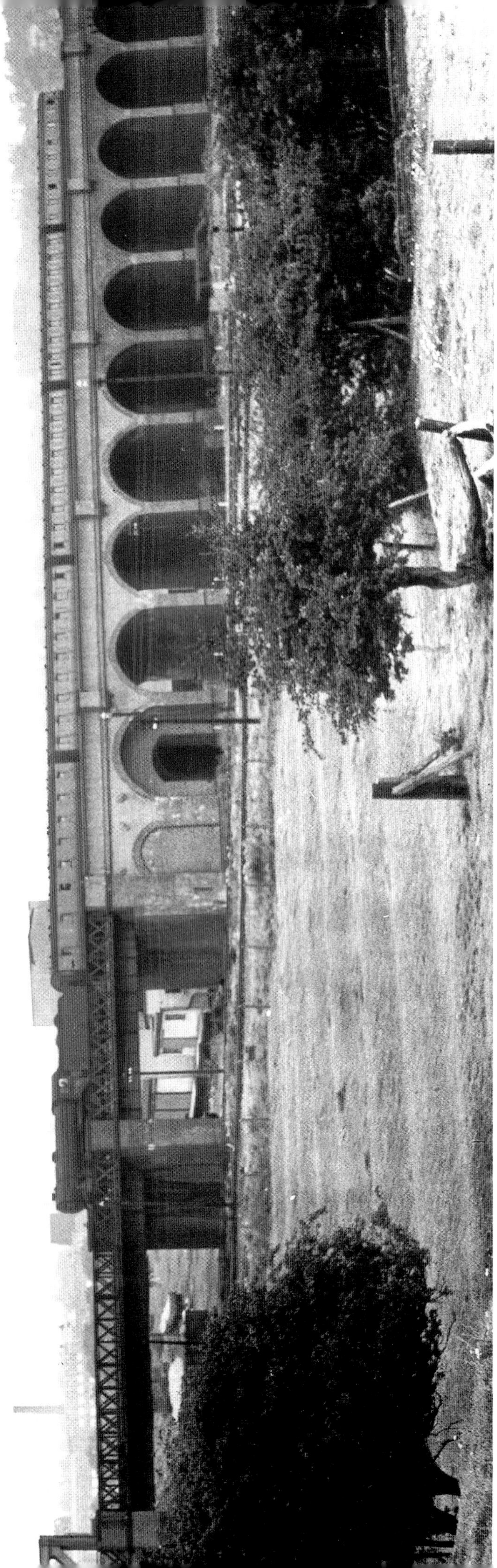

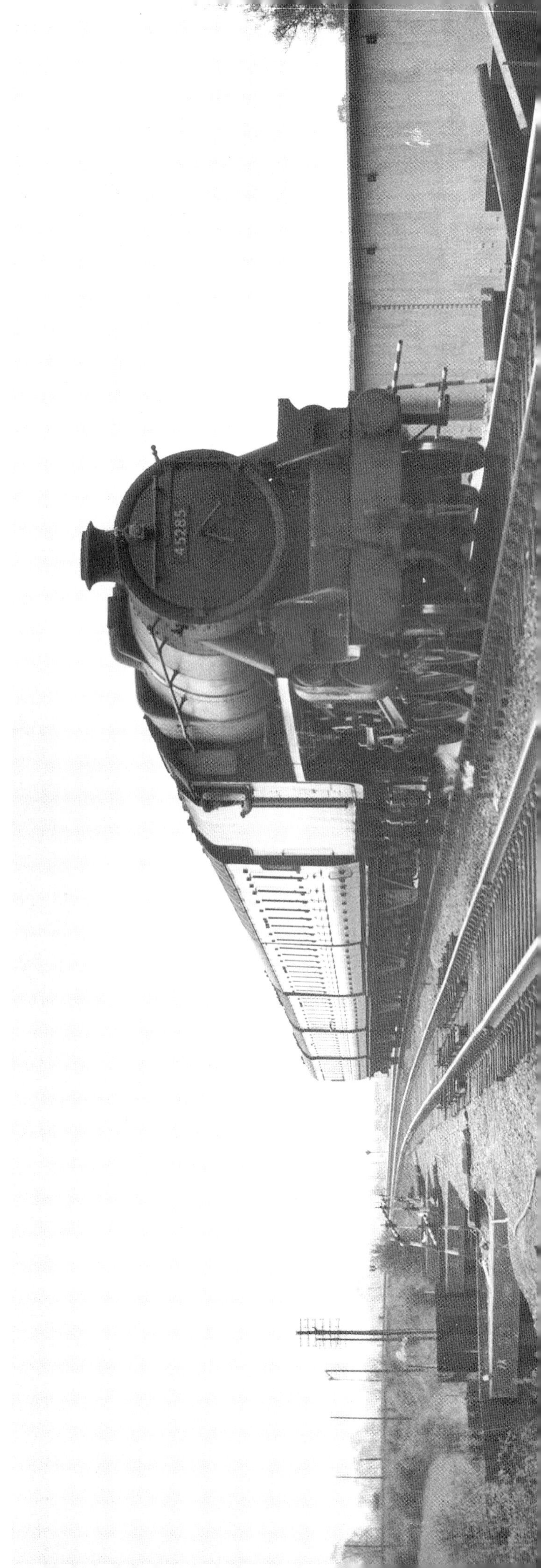
45285

Woodford with a K3 2-6-0 providing the power hurries into Rugby over the Avon viaduct and crosses the London Midland's Western Division line to Market Harborough.

local from Rugby to Nottingham drifts round 'Cosby Corner' and slows to a crawl over the bridge being constructed over the new M1 motorway. The Great Central main line was actually closed for the afternoon on 18th May 1963 while the bridge was lifted into position.

11th 1963 a Stanier 'Black Five' No 45342 coasts over Swithland reservoir with the 5.20 pm local from Rugby to Nottingham

116. In the fading light of the afternoon of March 26th 1959 a former G.C. A5 4-6-2 tank working bunker first hurries a local train for Pinxton through the remains of Carrington station in Nottingham between the Mansfield Road and Sherwood Rise tunnels.

117. A York B16 4-6-0 in unrebuilt condition heads the 5.20 pm local from Leicester Central to Woodford out of Ashby Magna. 9.8.58.

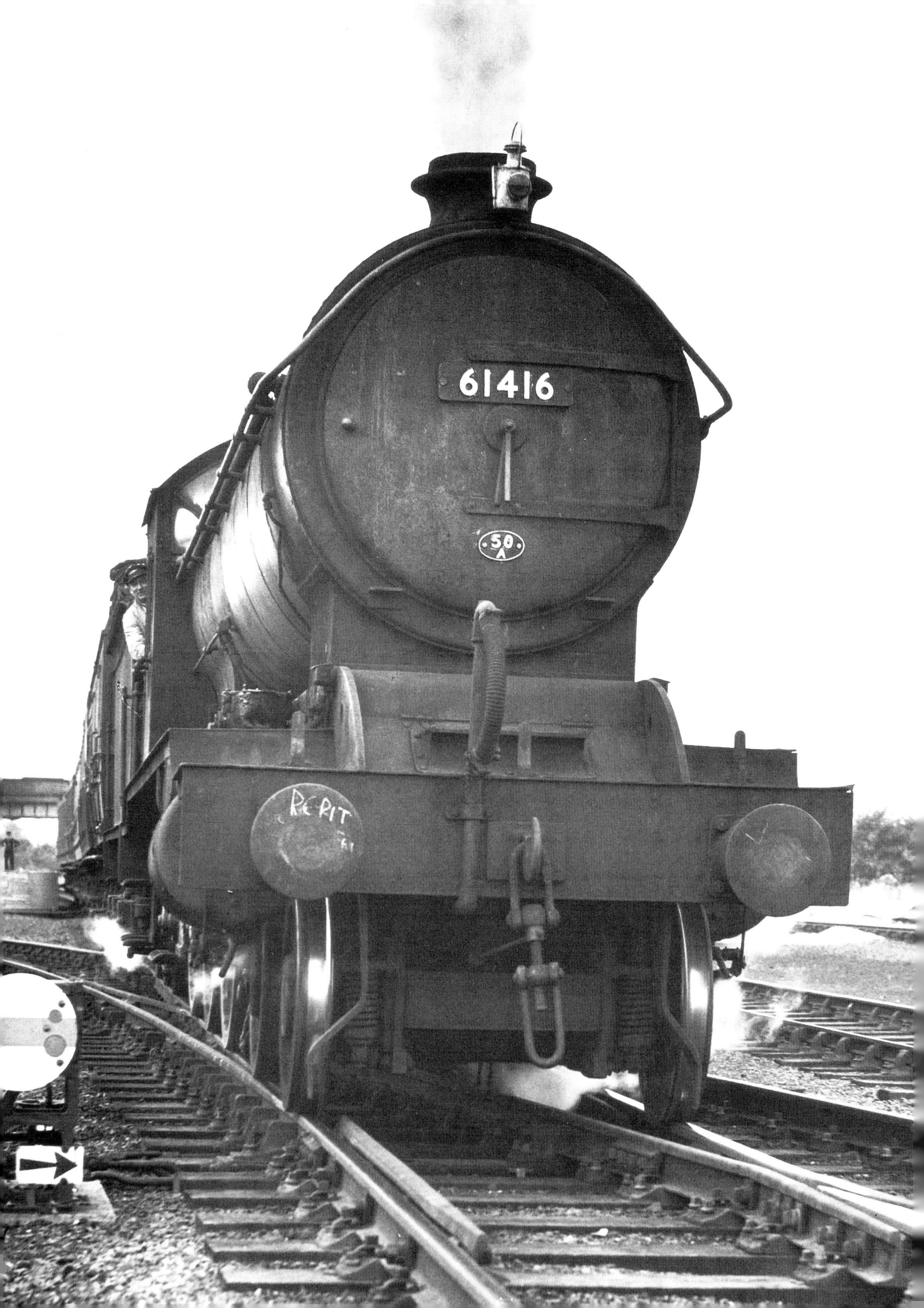
61416
50A

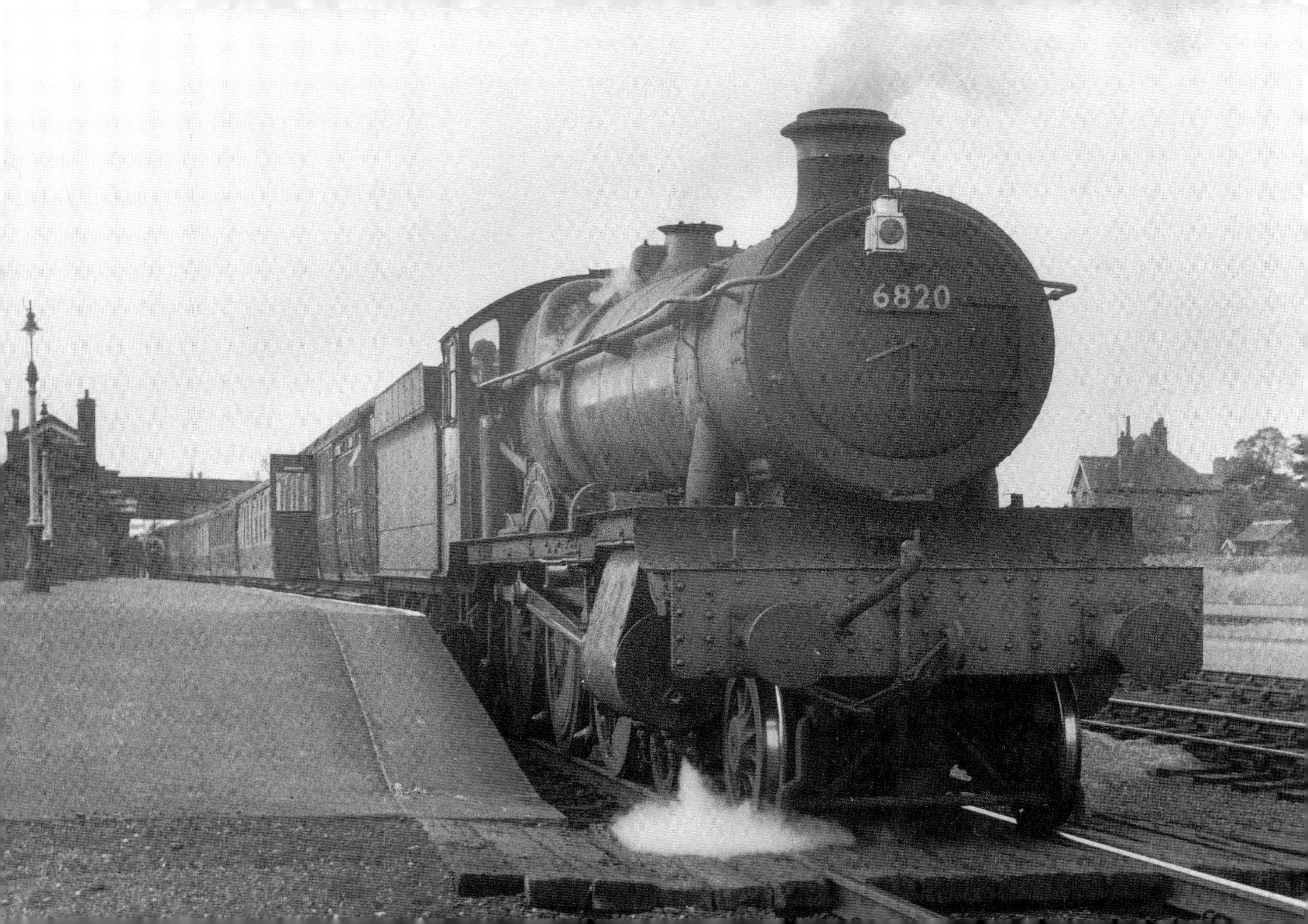
6820

118. A Western Region 4-6-0 No 6820 'Kingstone Grange' is commandeered to work the 1.20 pm local from Leicester Central to Nottingham and its return working at 5.45pm. The 'Grange' was sent from Old Oak Common after a local B1 on a special to Marlow became derailed at Old Oak and was unable to make the return journey. No 6820 is seen stopping at Quorn on its run back from Nottingham to Leicester. 16.6.58

119. No 6820 arrives in Leicester Central with the 5.45 pm local from Nottingham Victoria. 16.6.58.

120. On another occasion a 'Hall' No 5986 'Arbury Hall' is assigned to the same duty with top link Driver Tommy Chamberlain and his mate Fireman Charlie Vaughan as crew. The 'Hall is seen during its stop at Rothley.

121. No 5986 'Arbury Hall' makes its last stop before Leicester at Belgrave and Birstall.

Following page.
122. An Ivatt Mogul No 43032 hurries down the grade near Aylestone Fields between Whetstone and Leicester on a morning of Winter sunshine with the

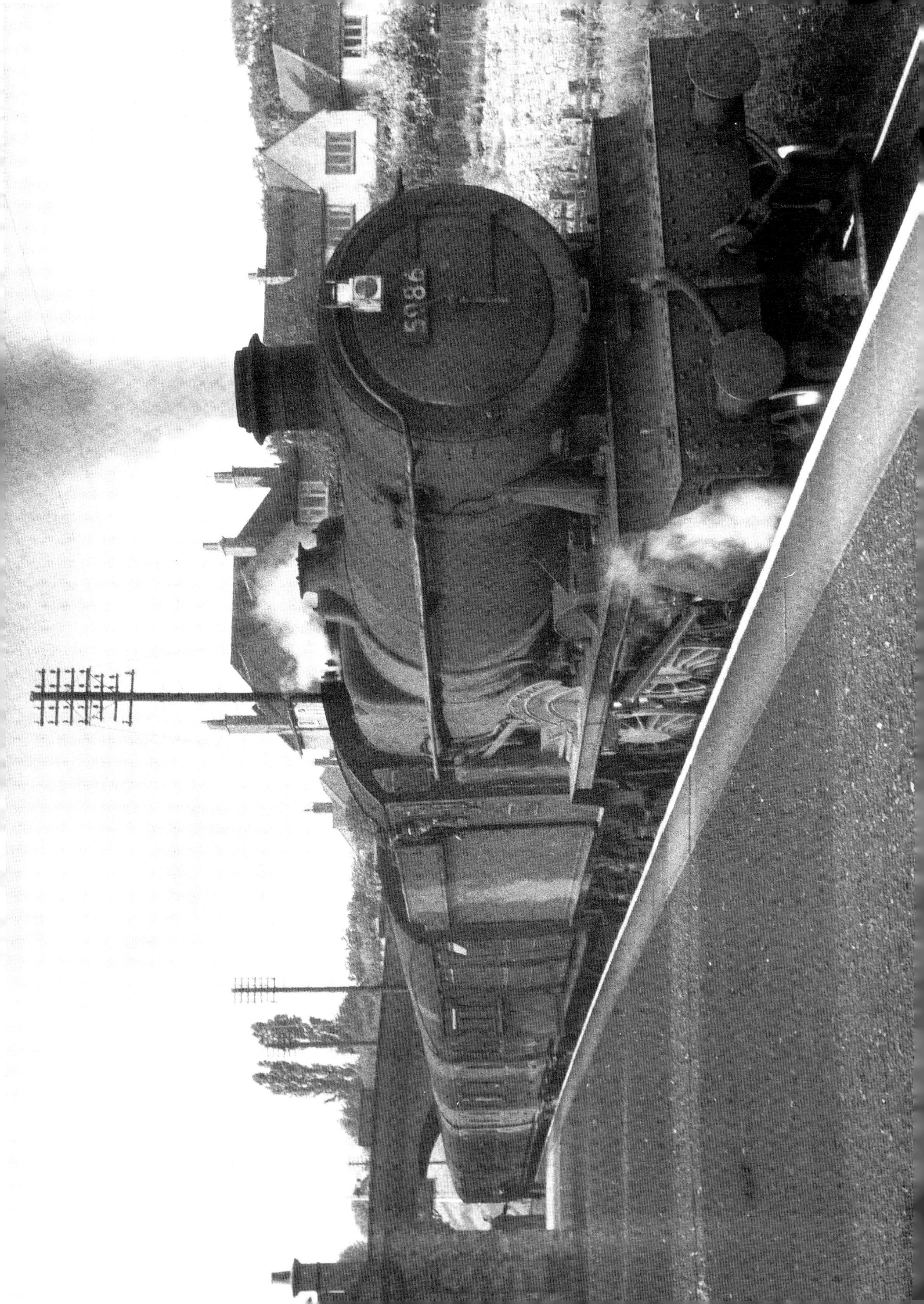
5986

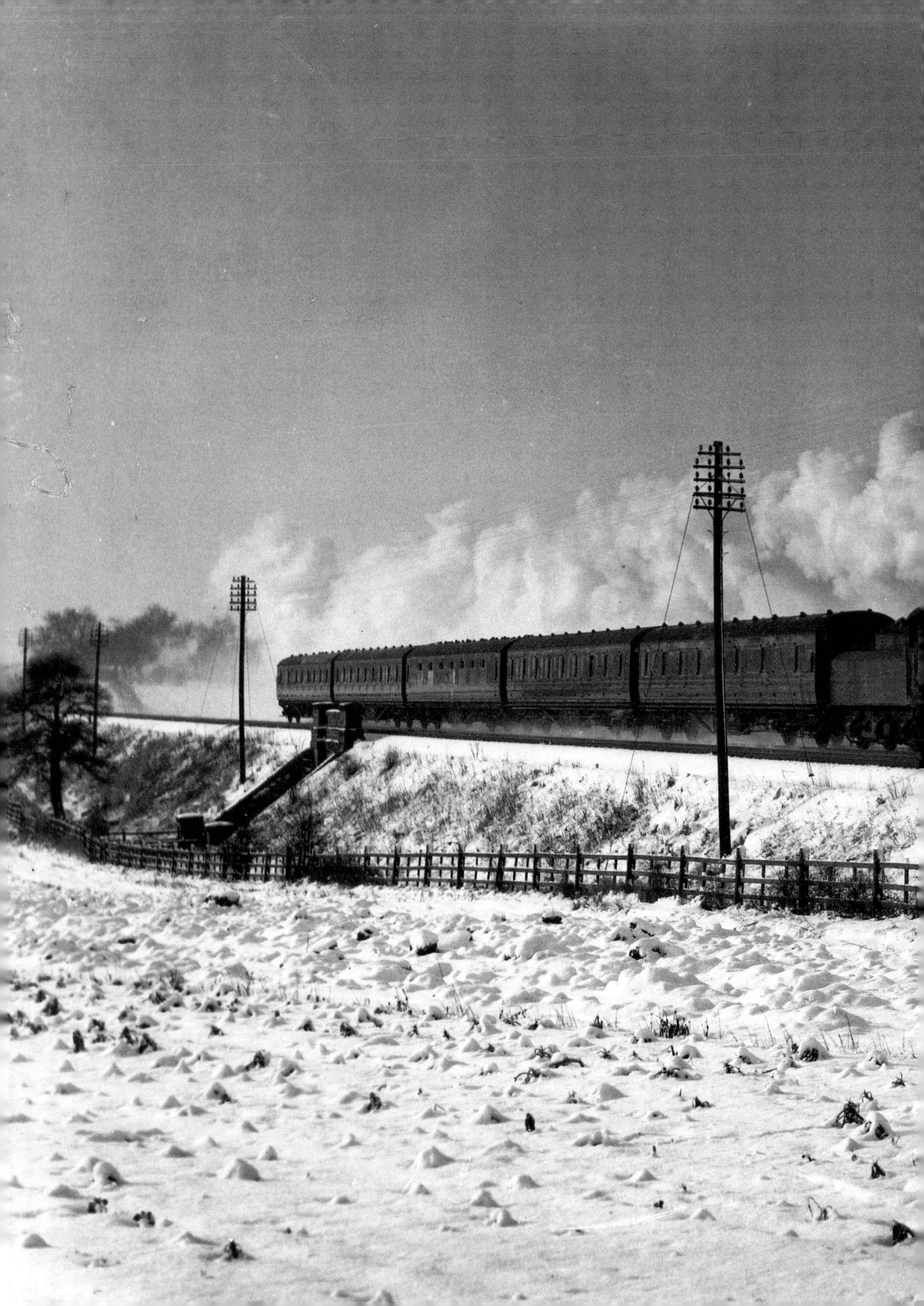

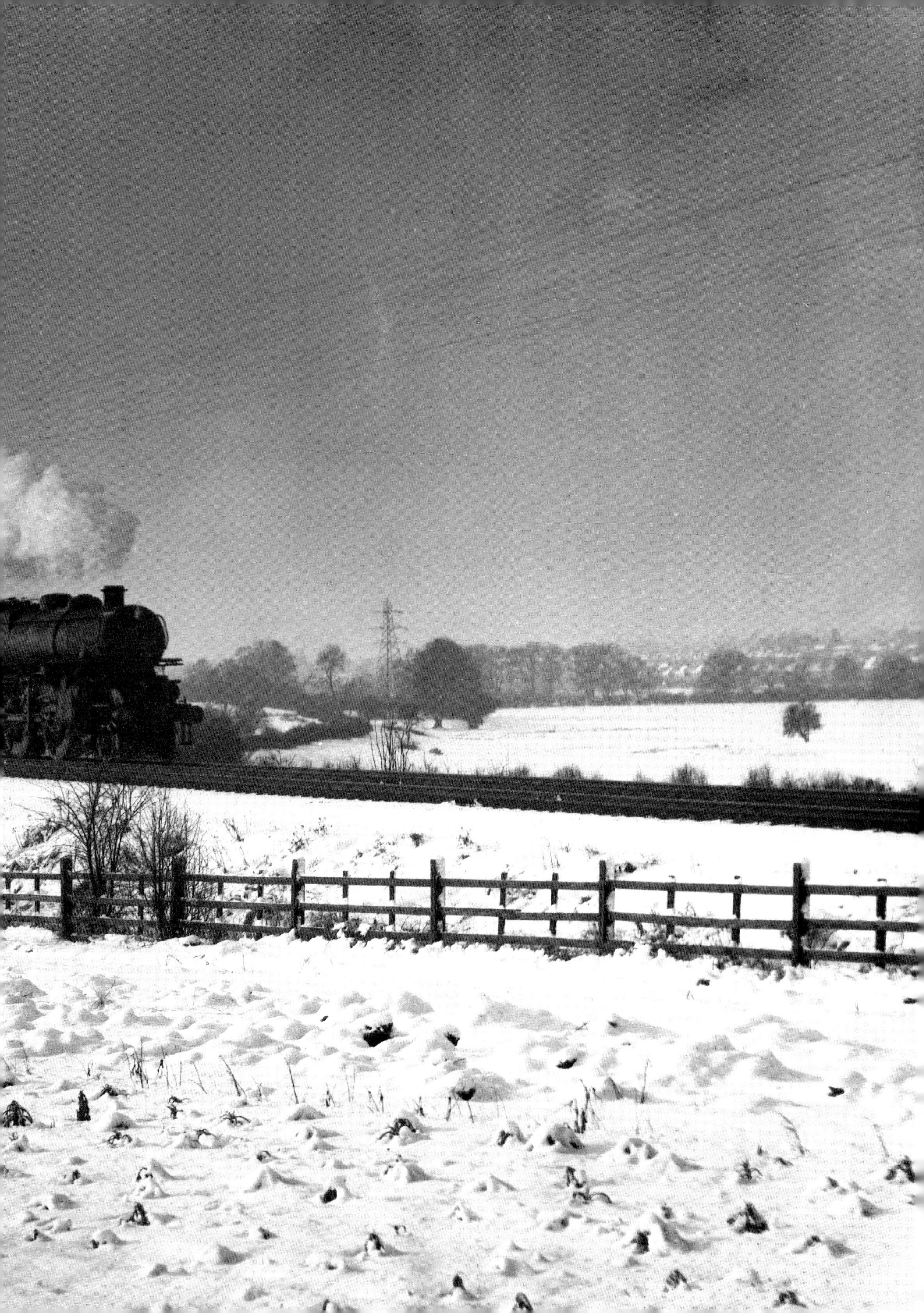

Superpowered stoppers.

123. For a very brief period in the summer of 1962 two London Midland 'Royal Scot' 4-6-0s were allocated to Leicester Central shed for working the heavy Newcastle-Bournemouth train as far as Banbury. However their stay came to a swift end when it was decided to run an English Electric type 3 diesel from Sheffield right through to Banbury from where it would return with the balancing

124. On cup final day 1961 when Leicester City appeared at Wembley rebuilt 'Patriot' No 45540 'Sir Robert Turnbull' acted as standby engine at Leicester Central to cover any cup special failures. Its services were not required and later it was used on the York-Bournemouth to Banbury. It returned to Leicester with the 7.20 pm local from Woodford to Nottingham and is seen here being held at Ashby Magna for a return cup final special to Sheffield to pass it on the down loop line. 6.5.61.

125. At Nottingham Victoria a K3 Mogul No 61873 marshalls empty stock before working out with an up G.C. line local.

126. A G.C./Met line local stands in the bay platform at Aylesbury while the fireman of Standard Class 4 2-6-4 tank No 80141 looks down the four coaches of Metropolitan suburban stock to watch the antics of a young man who is not certain whether to become a passenger or not.

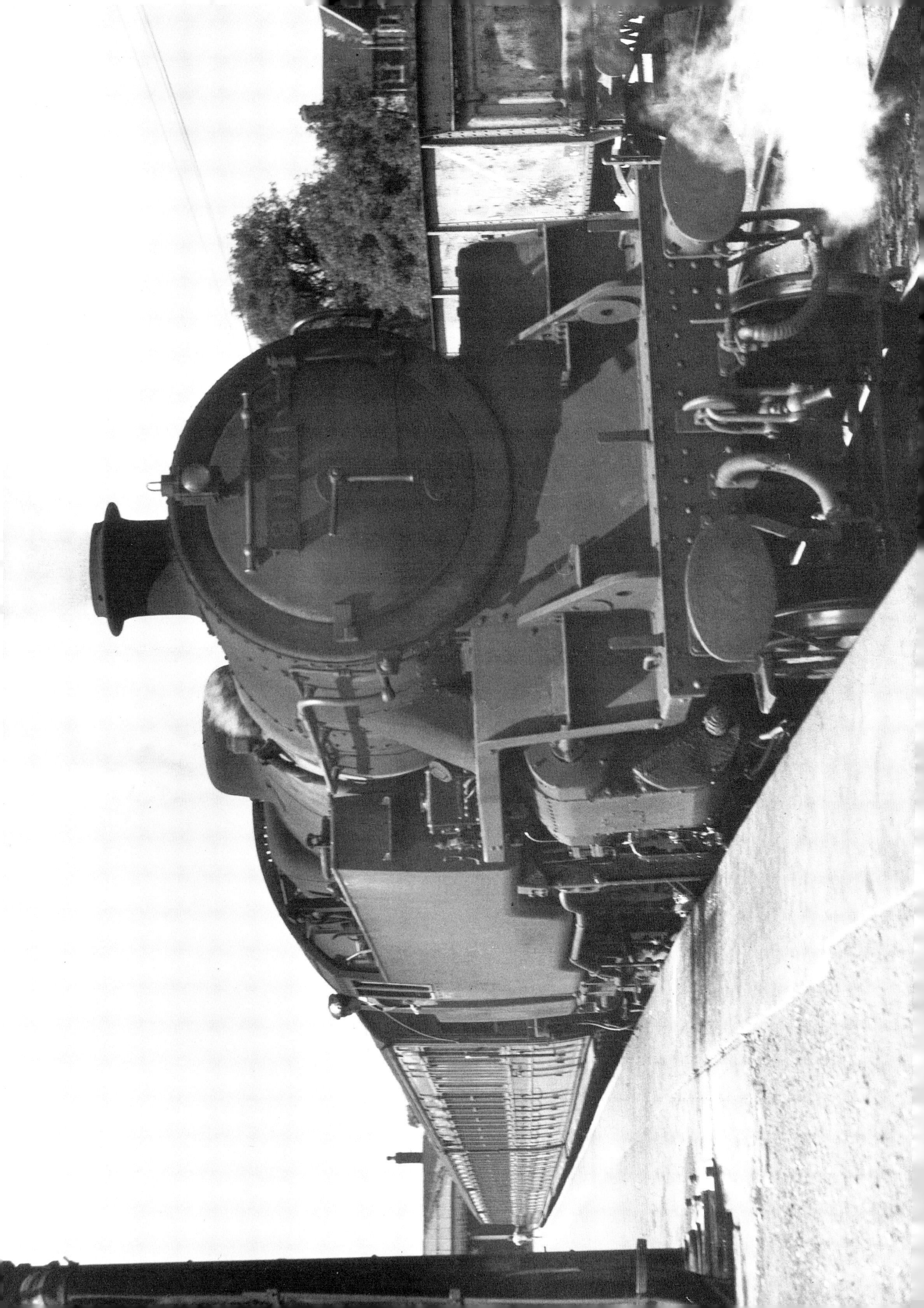

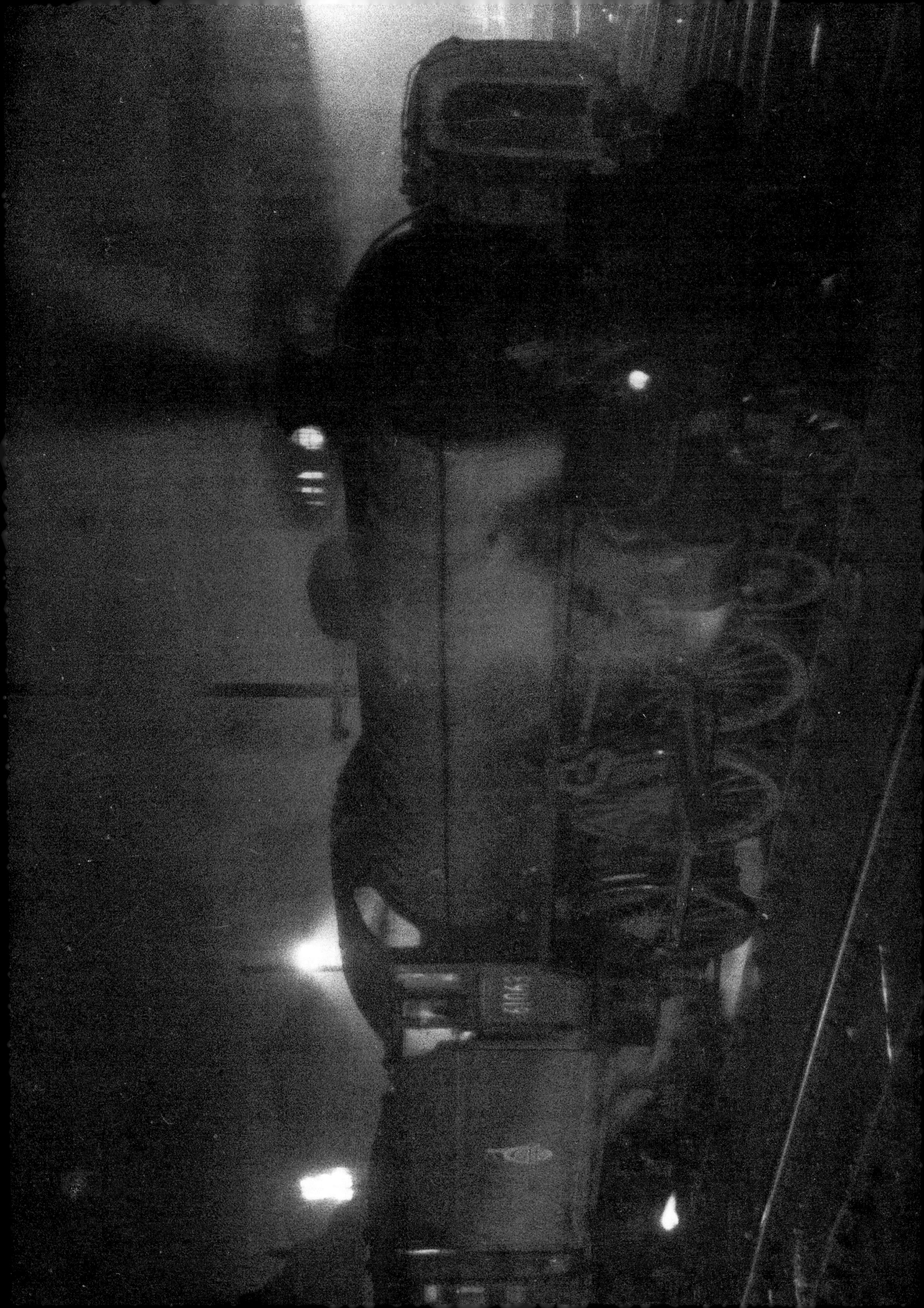

Pilots, shunters and shed.

127. Some experiments on a damp, murky night at Leicester Central station using 2 second exposures with fast, grainy film and no flash. Discernable in the subdued lamp light is B1 No 61063 which is on station pilot duty and pausing between shunting operations.

128. Driver George Evinson watches the author's antics with the tripod and camera while No 61063 stands on the turntable road beside the water column at Leicester Central.

129. Empty stock disposal. A Robinson A5 Tank No 69800 propels a rake of coaches into the carriage sheds at Leicester North Goods on a Summer afternoon in 1958.

130. Yard shunter. Until 5th April 1958 when it was withdrawn for scrapping a J.52 0-6-0 tank No 68839 shunted the goods yard at Leicester. As a sign of the new management it was replaced by No 47203, a London Midland 'Jinty' complete with condensing pipes which had seen long years of service at Cricklewood and the London underground widened lines. This, in turn, was replaced by a sister engine of later vintage No 47442 which is seen here taking a 'breather' near

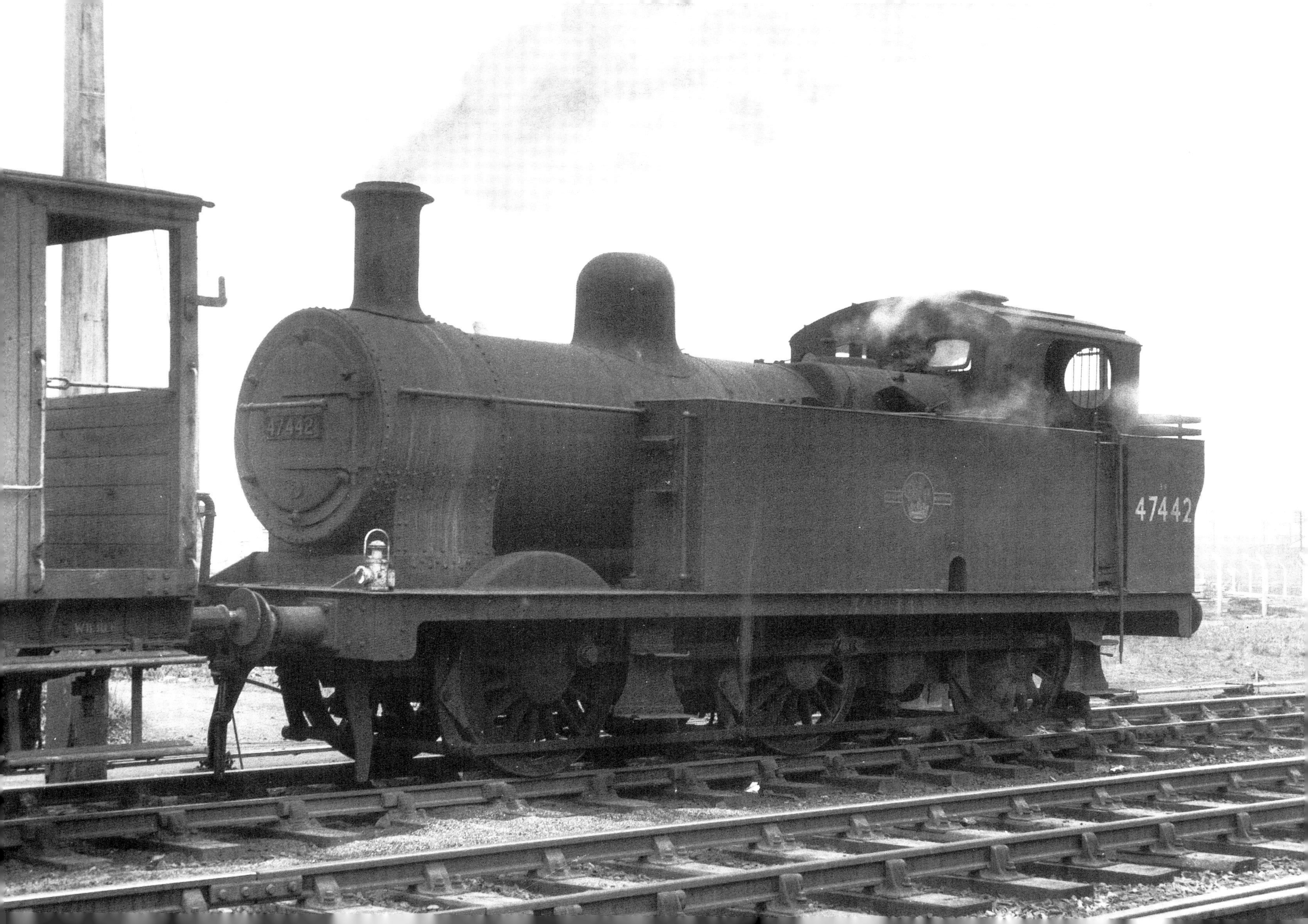
47442
47442

131. A shot from the cab of No 47442 taken during shunting operations at Leicester South Goods.

Leicester Central Shed.
132. Leicester Central was a four road shed built to house between 15 and 20 engines. By the time this photograph was obtained it was occupied by a motley collection including three local 31s Nos 61008 'Kudu', 61063 and 61376, a 9F 2-10-0, 'Jinty' No 47203 and a Colwick J6 No 64183.

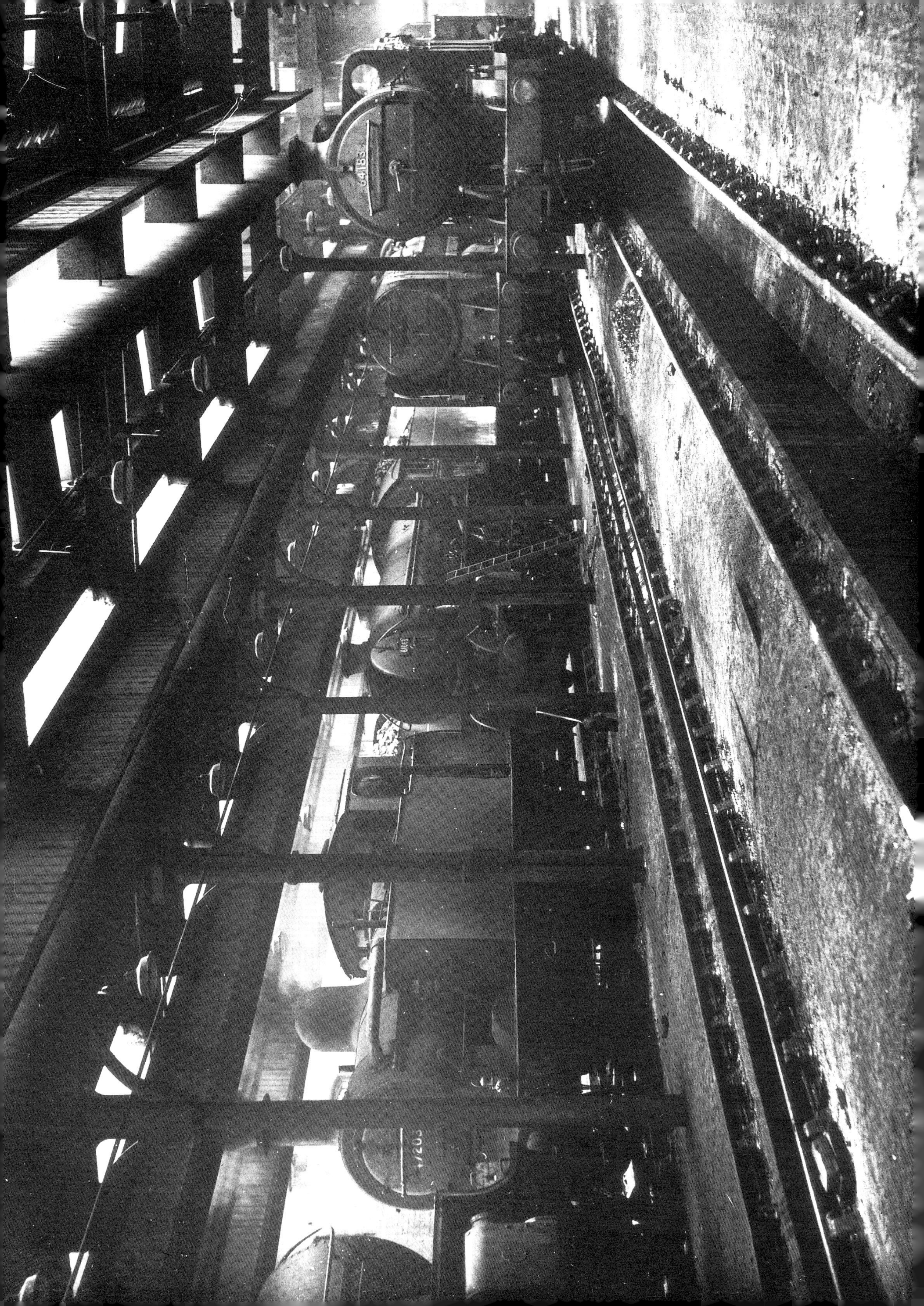
64183

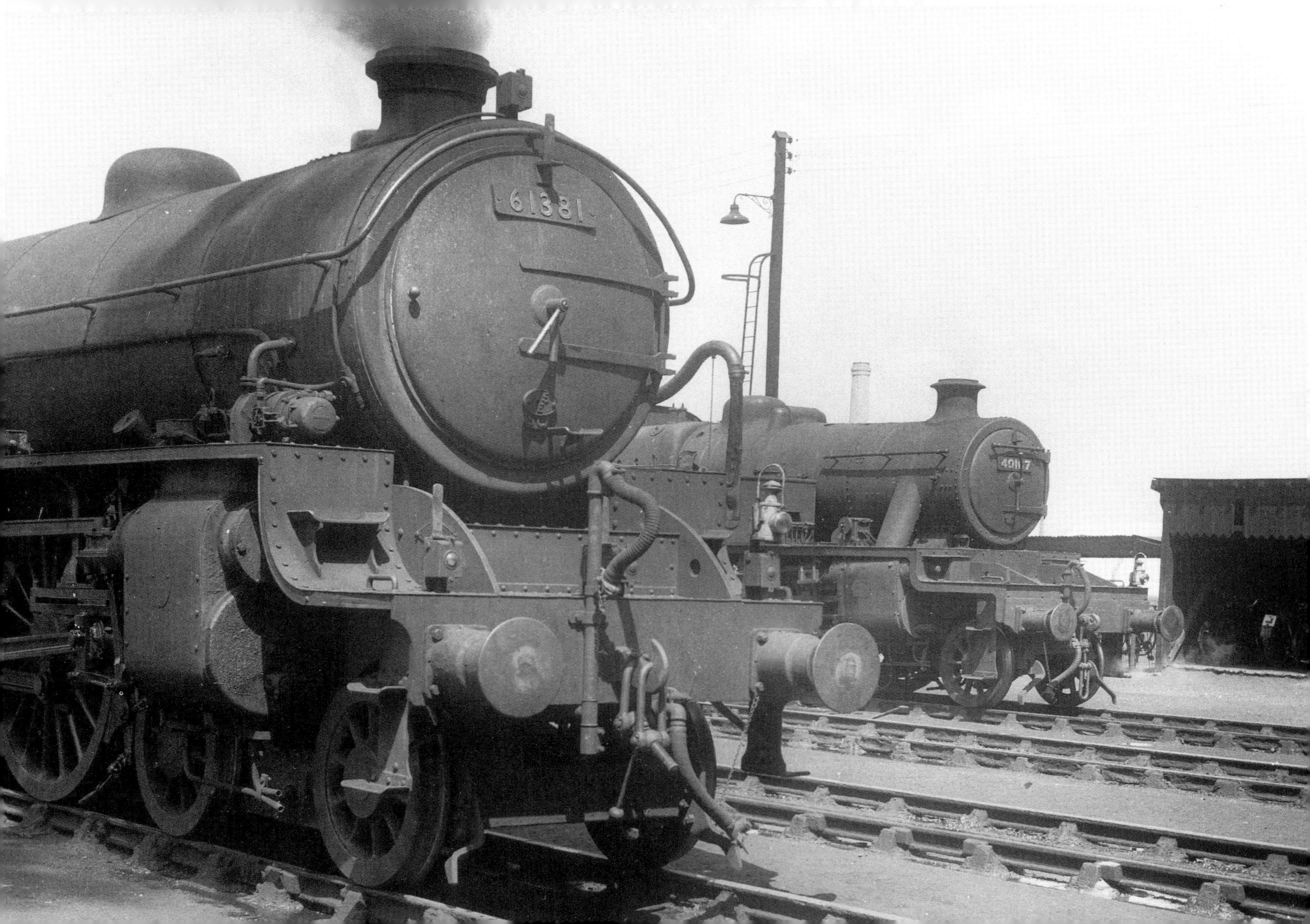
61381
49117

133. Signs of Change. A B1 No 61381 stands outside the shed in the company of Stanier 3P Tank No 40167 which was attached to the depot in 1959 for 16 months to undertake local passenger and pick-up freight duties. 14.5.59.

134. A distinguished, long serving resident was V2 No 60863 which belonged to Leicester for nine years. Here she waits at the front of the shed ready for express passenger duty.

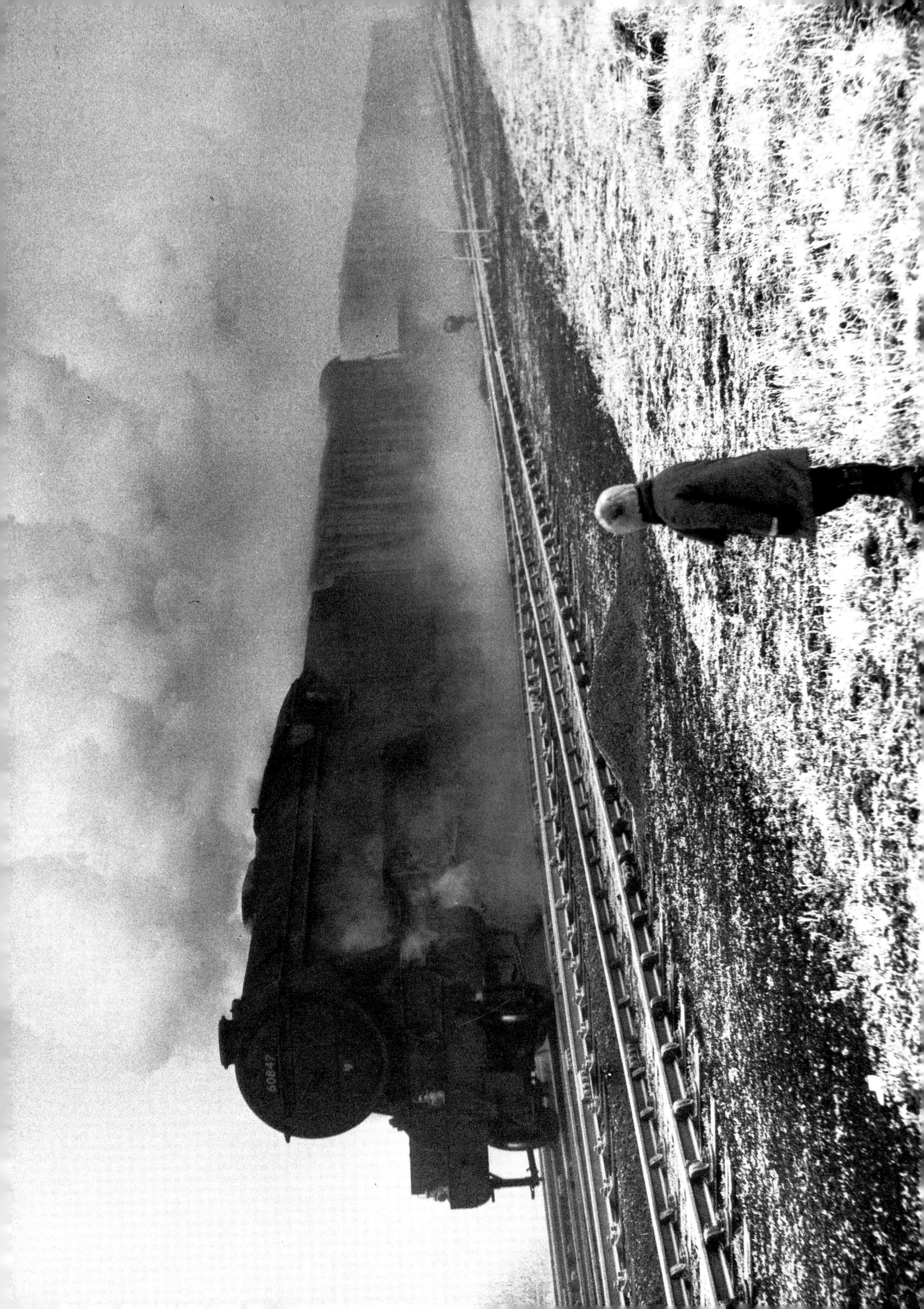

135. The Great Central's London Extension was a remarkably free flowing route along which both freight and passenger traffic could run unimpeded by thrombotic junctions and bottlenecks.

A number of fitted freight trains travelled its tracks each weekday carrying merchandise, parcels and fish. During the morning there was a trio of trains all running from the Dringhouses yard at York. Their destinations were Bristol, Cardiff and Woodford respectively. The Bristol and Woodford freights usually brought V2s and B16s through from York and this gave them an air of distinction. Together with the York-Bournemouth express these fast freights also maintained the line's historic link with the north-east of England even after its transfer into the London Midland Region.

In this photograph of the York-Bristol a V2 No 60847 'St. Peter's School, York' is seen climbing through Whetstone on a morning of freezing fog in February 1963. A young Walker, suitably wrapped up to withstand the cold observes the action. 25.2.63.

4.50 pm fast freight from Woodford. Crossing Swithland Reservoir on a summer evening No 60805 coasts down the grade to Loughborough under easy steam.

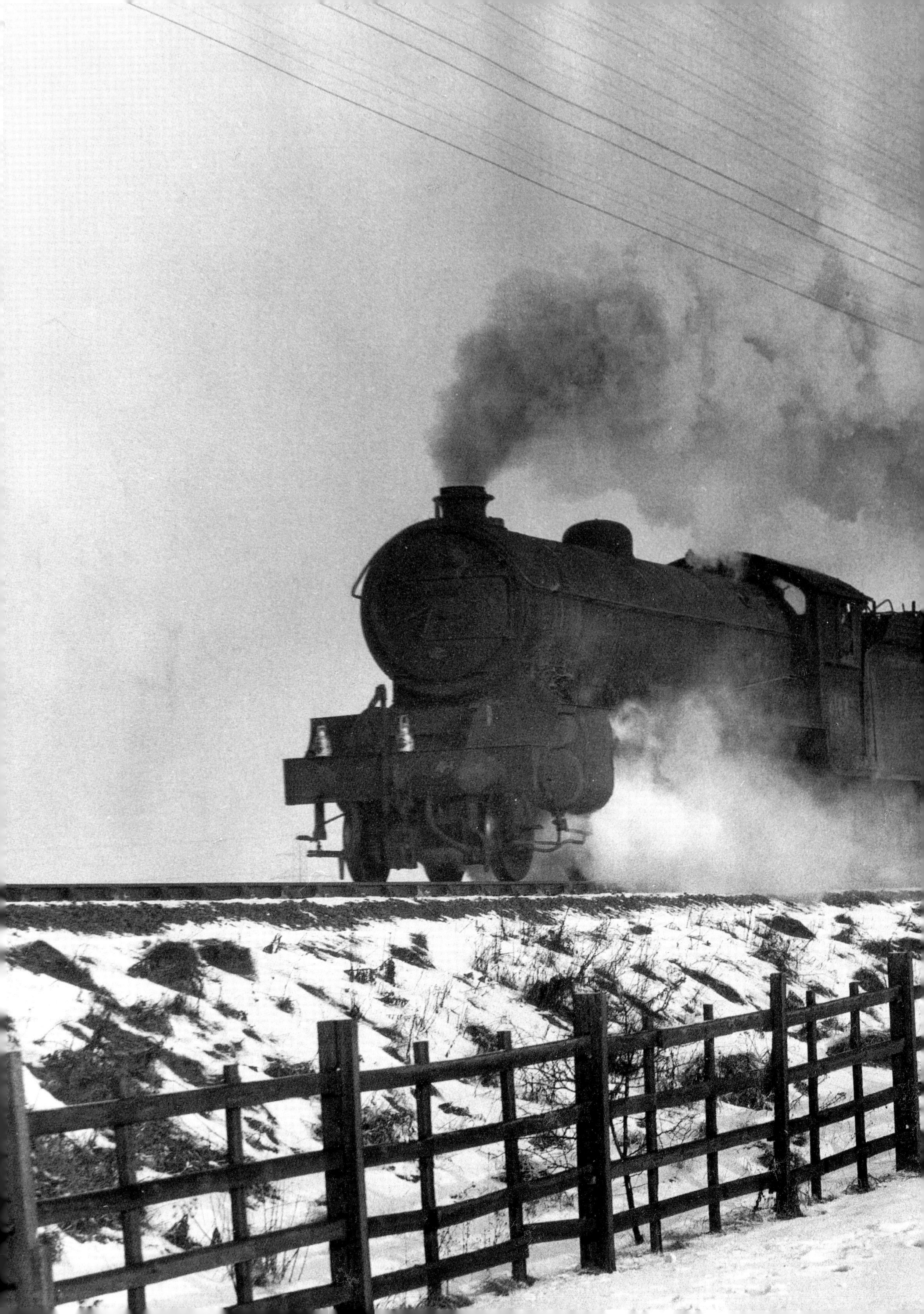

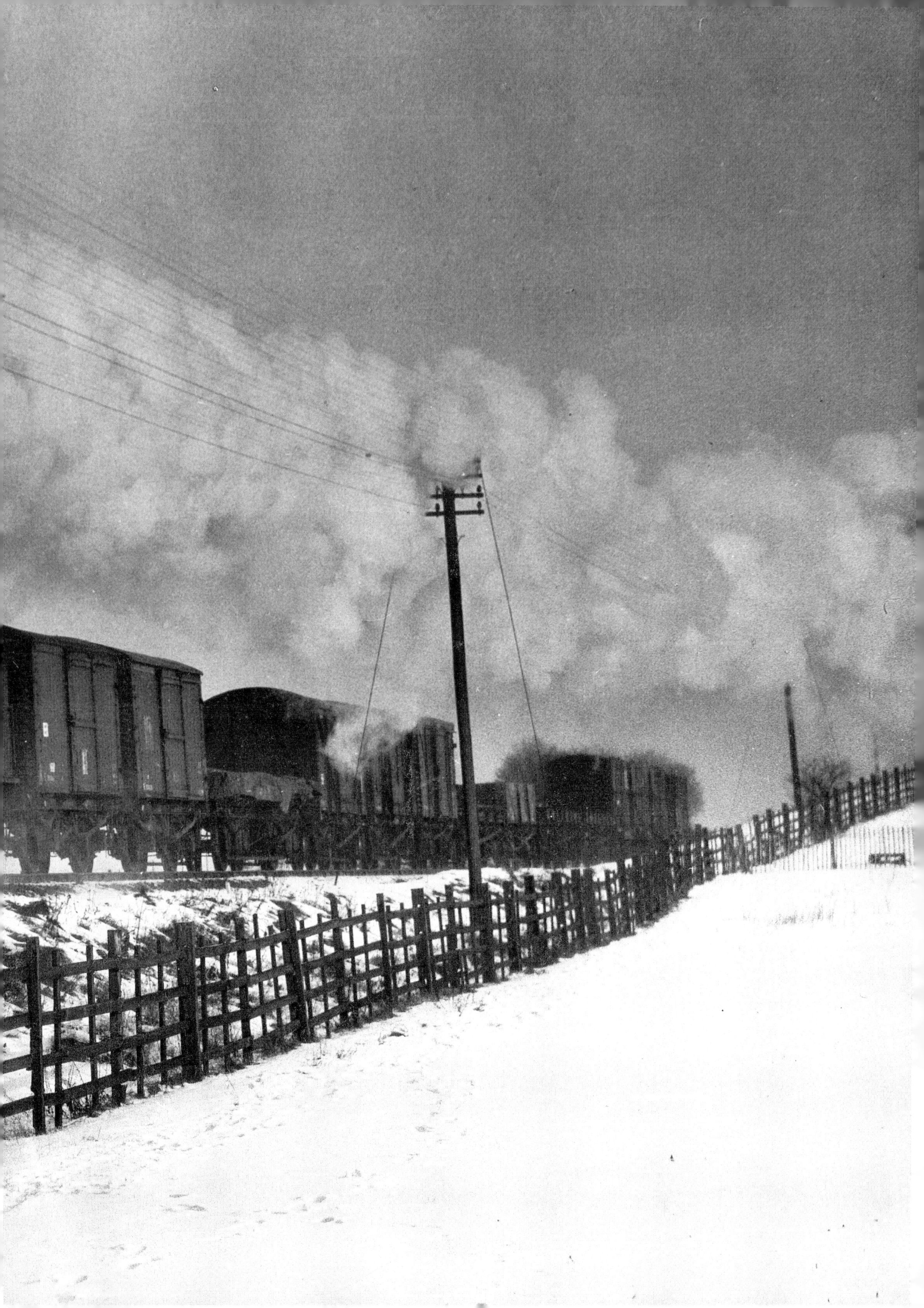

Previous page.
137. A B16 4-6-0 makes a lusty acceleration away from Leicester with the York–Woodford on a day of snow and freezing temperatures in January 1963.

138. York V2 No 60961 having run through Leicester Central under easy steam with the 4.50 pm fast freight from Woodford opens up again ready for the climb to Birstall. No 60961 was a York engine for the whole of its working life of over 21 years.

139. The 3.10 am from York to Woodford was the last of the three up morning express freights and provided an excellent daily service from the North East to intermediate centres between York and Woodford like Nottingham and Leicester. A York B16 No 61449, one of the Thompson rebuilds and hero of the Albert Chafer 'episode' detaches vans at Leicester South Goods on 7.9.61.

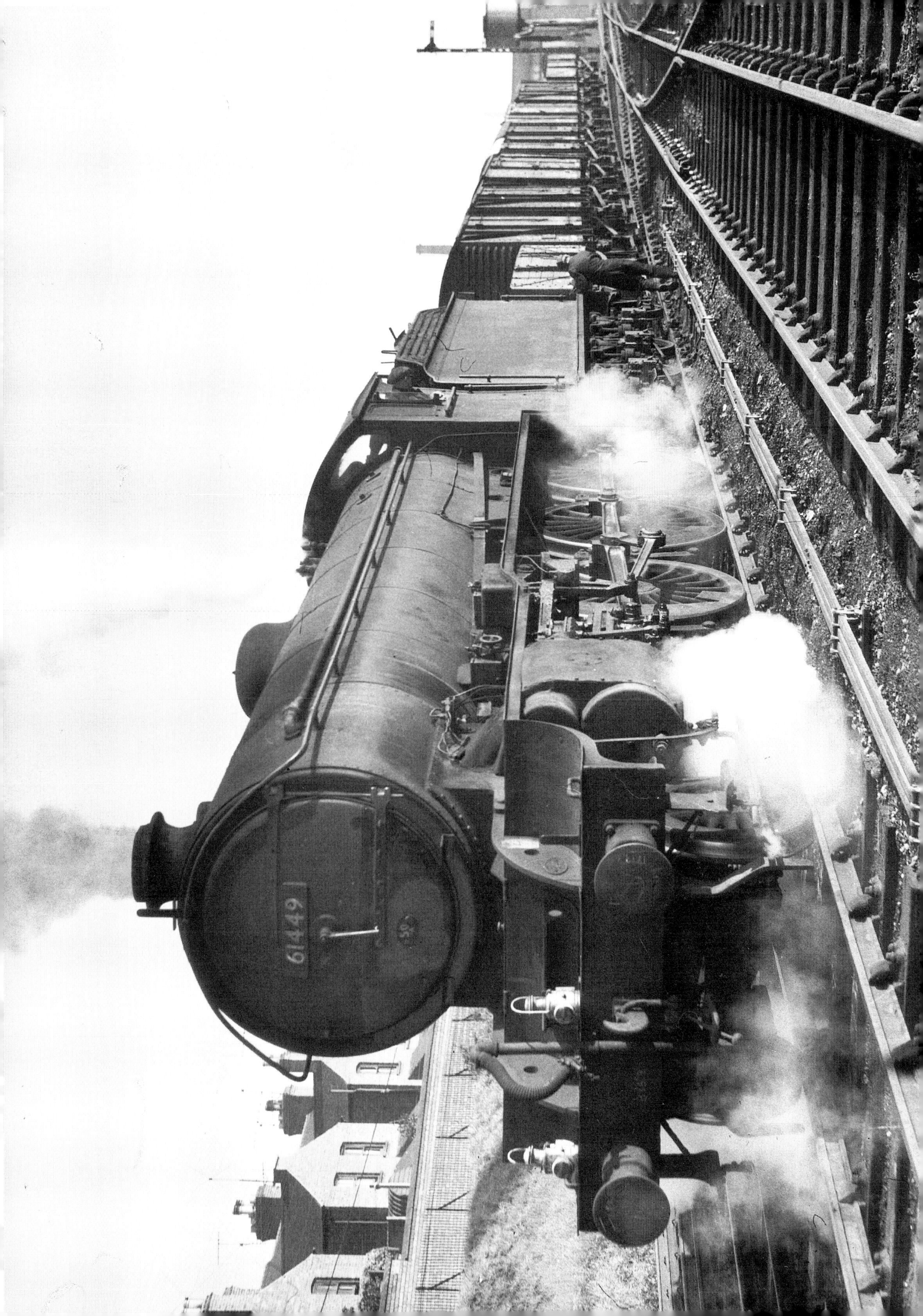
61449

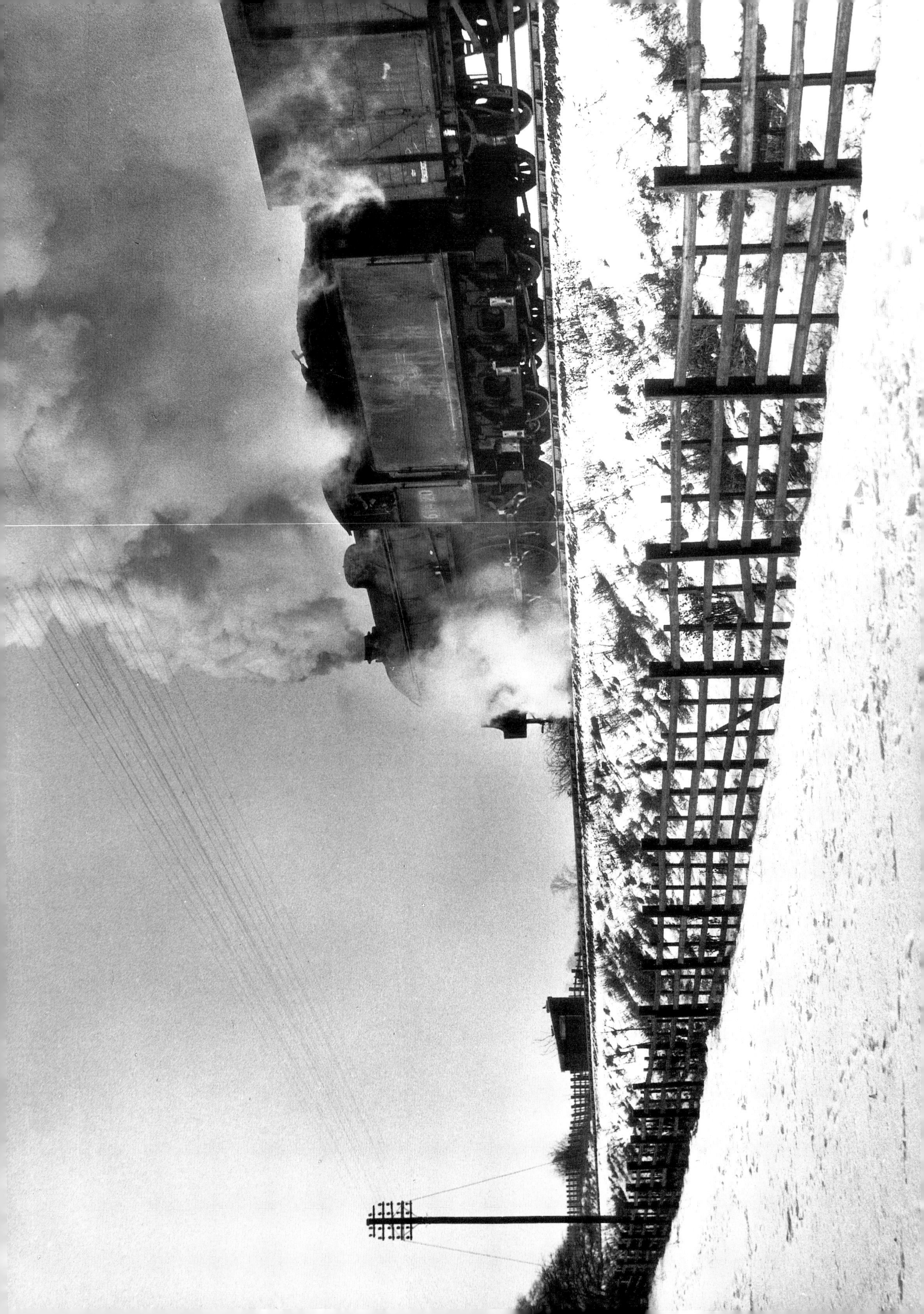

140. In the snow of January 26th 1963 another 'bloodspitter' No 61420 makes a steamy climb past Aylestone Fields between Leicester and Whetstone with the York-Woodford.

141. Woodford driver Caesar Webb at the controls of York B16 4-6-0 No 61416. This was one of the unrebuilt engines with steam reversing gear. They were not too popular with G.C. line crews.

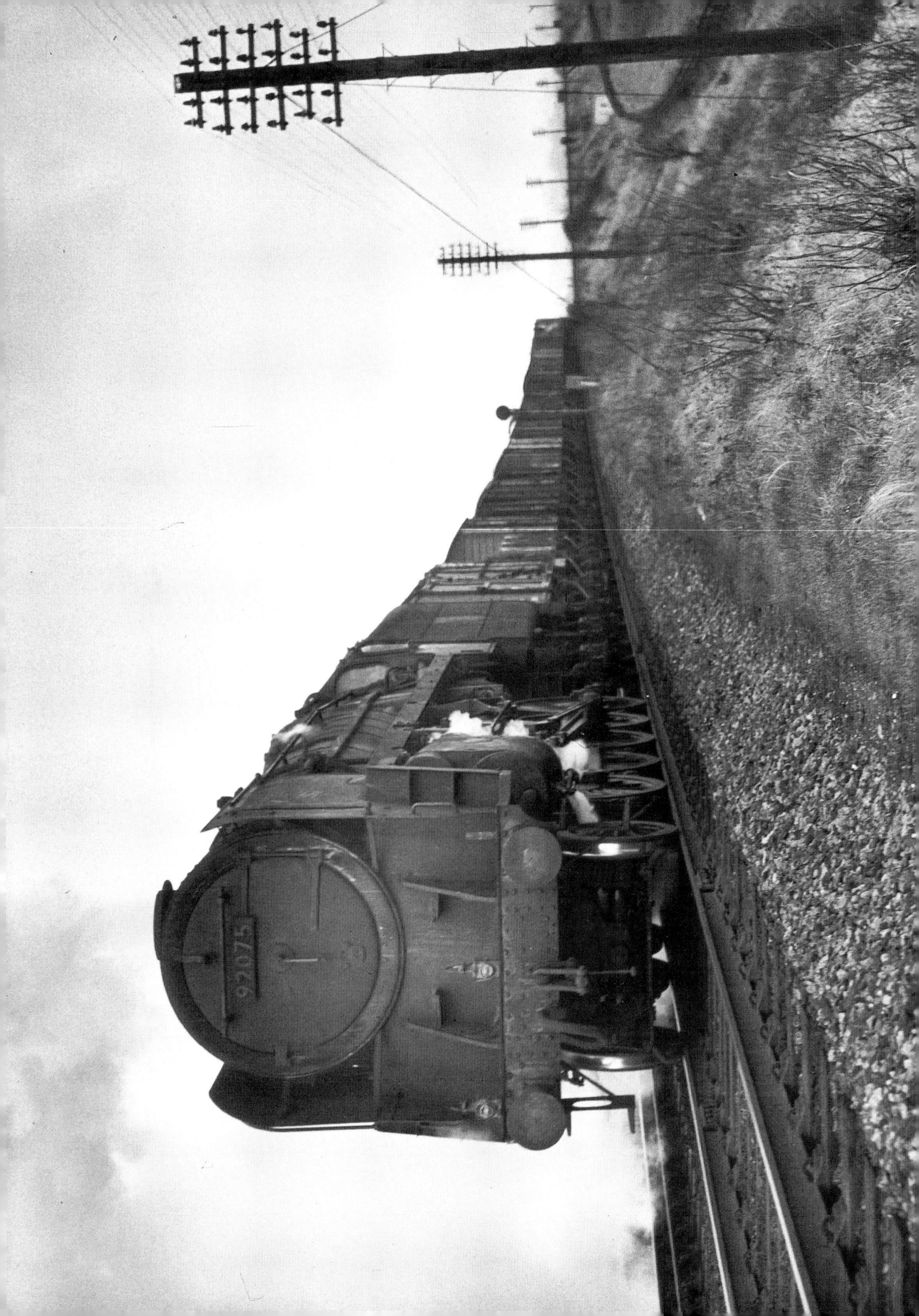
92075

provided. No 92075 rounds 'Cosby Corner' on the climb to Ashby Magna.
fitted freight.

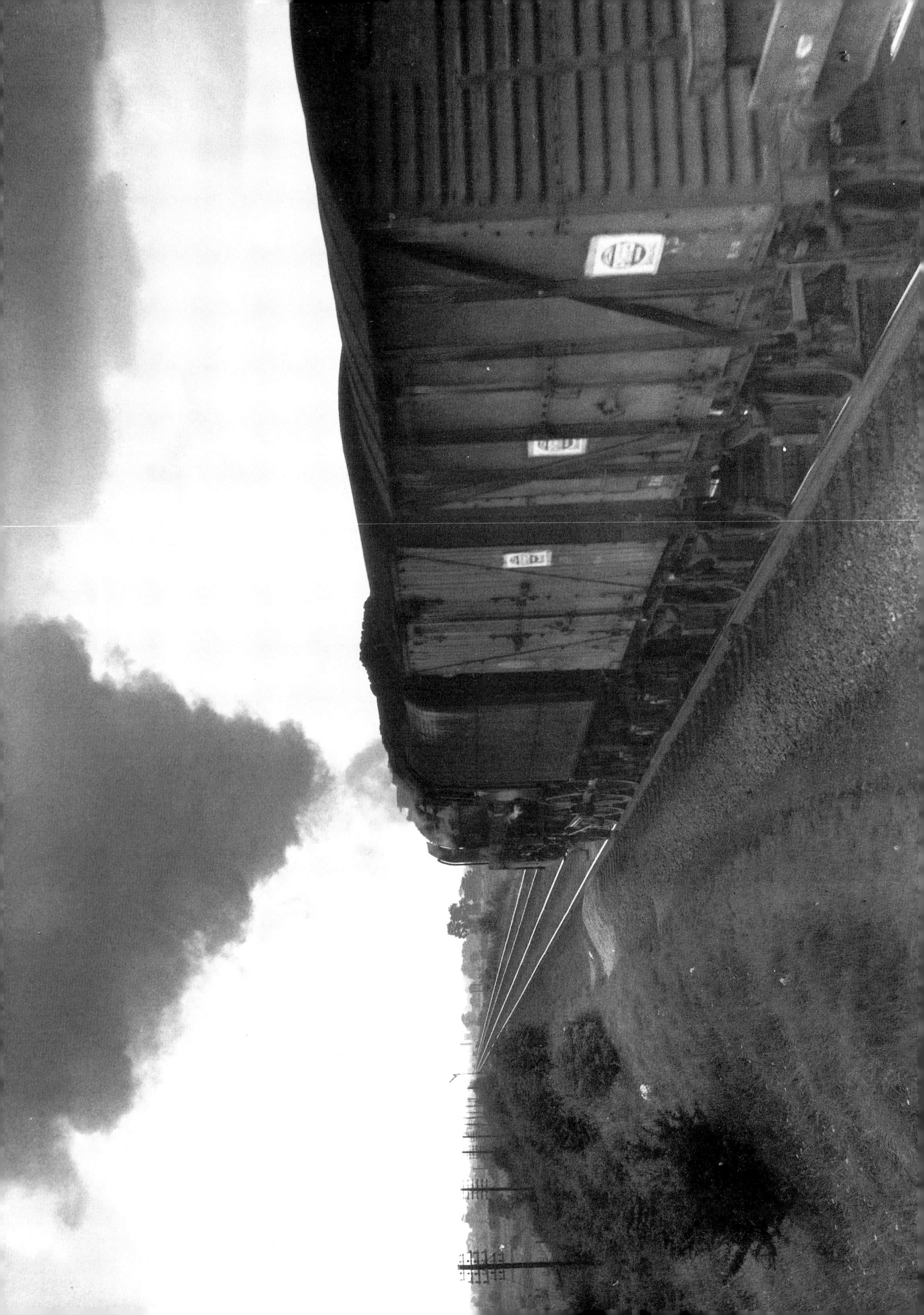

York- Bristol on 28.8.63. Leicester and Birstall with the 4.50 pm from Woodford to York.

146. A photograph taken near Stanford on Soar catches 9F No 92067 with the same

Fish trains.

147. For many years the Western engine bringing in the Bournemouth-York express to Leicester Central made its return to Banbury with the 12.50 pm fish from Hull. The Braunstone Gate warehouse clock reads five past six as 'Hall' class No 6979 'Helperly Hall' passes Leicester North Goods box with a well loaded train.

148. Bound for Grimsby on a murky late afternoon on 26th March 1959 an Immingham K3 No 61912 hustles a train of empty fish vans through the disused

149. The fish train from New Clee to Banbury hurries off the Leicester viaduct and passes the North Goods loop junction headed by a Woodford Standard 5 No 73159. 9.8.63.

Following pages.

150. The 4.30 pm fish from Grimsby to Whitland in South Wales was a high priority train and together with the other Great Central line fish trains was accorded a column in the London Midland Region's passenger working timetables. From 1961 it was assigned to an Immingham 'Britannia' Pacific between Grimsby and Banbury. A stop was made at Leicester Central for water and a crew change. These two photographs taken on 7th June 1963 show, first, No 70036 'Boadicea' setting off from Leicester Central on the next stage of the journey to Banbury with a full head of steam and a Woodford crew. 7.6.63.

151. No 70036 'Boadicea' crosses the West Bridge viaduct on its way south.

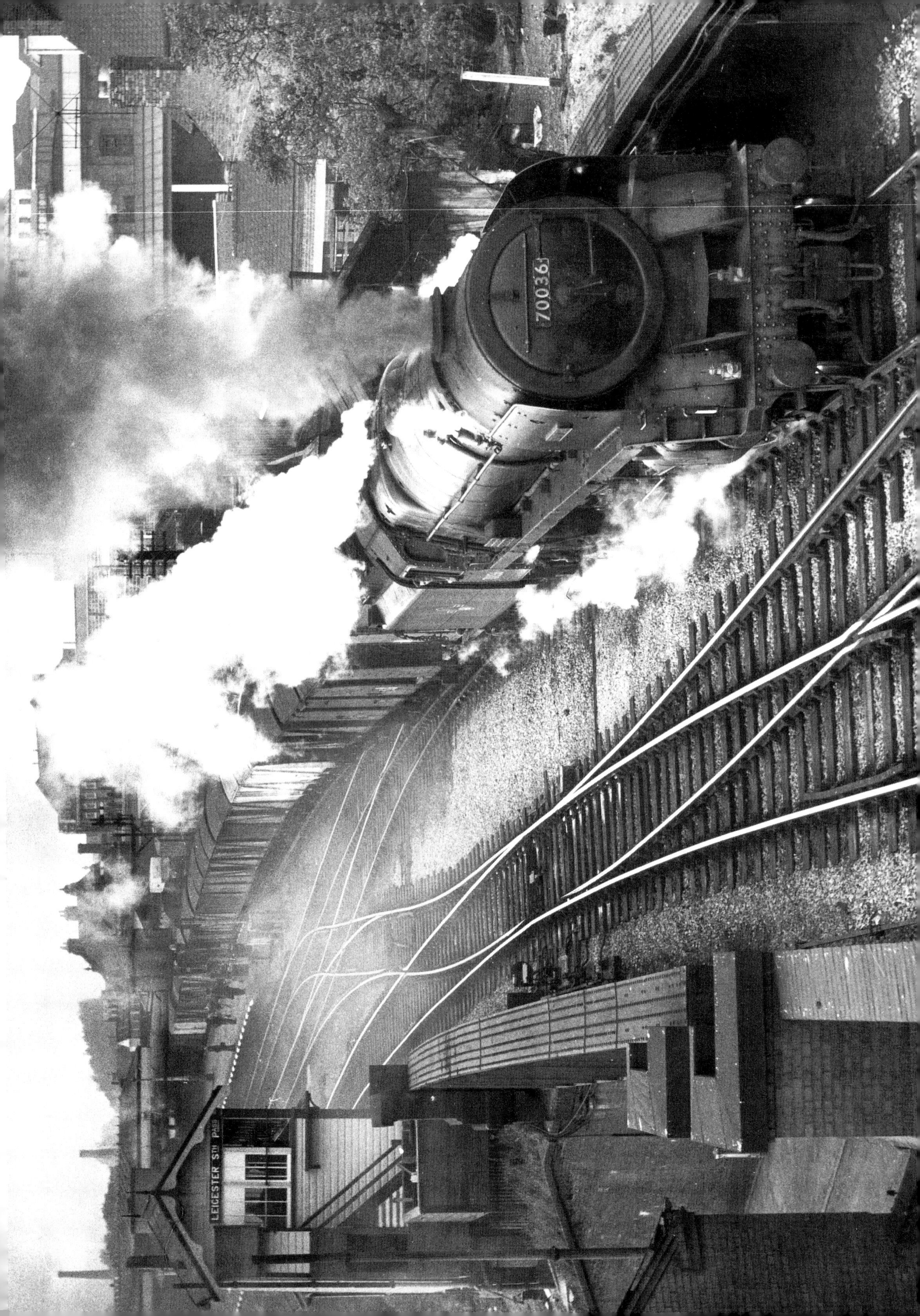
70036
LEICESTER

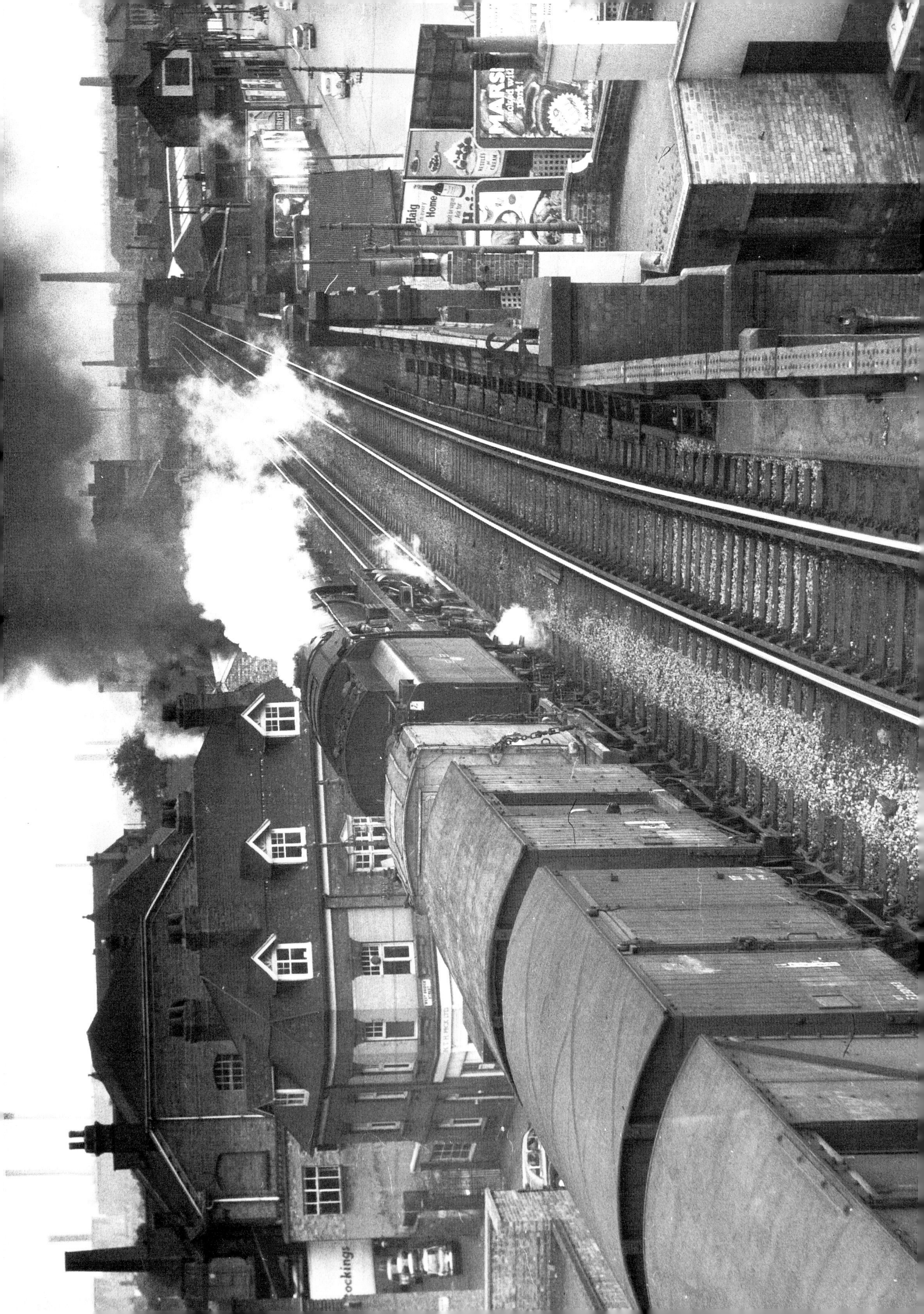
MARS

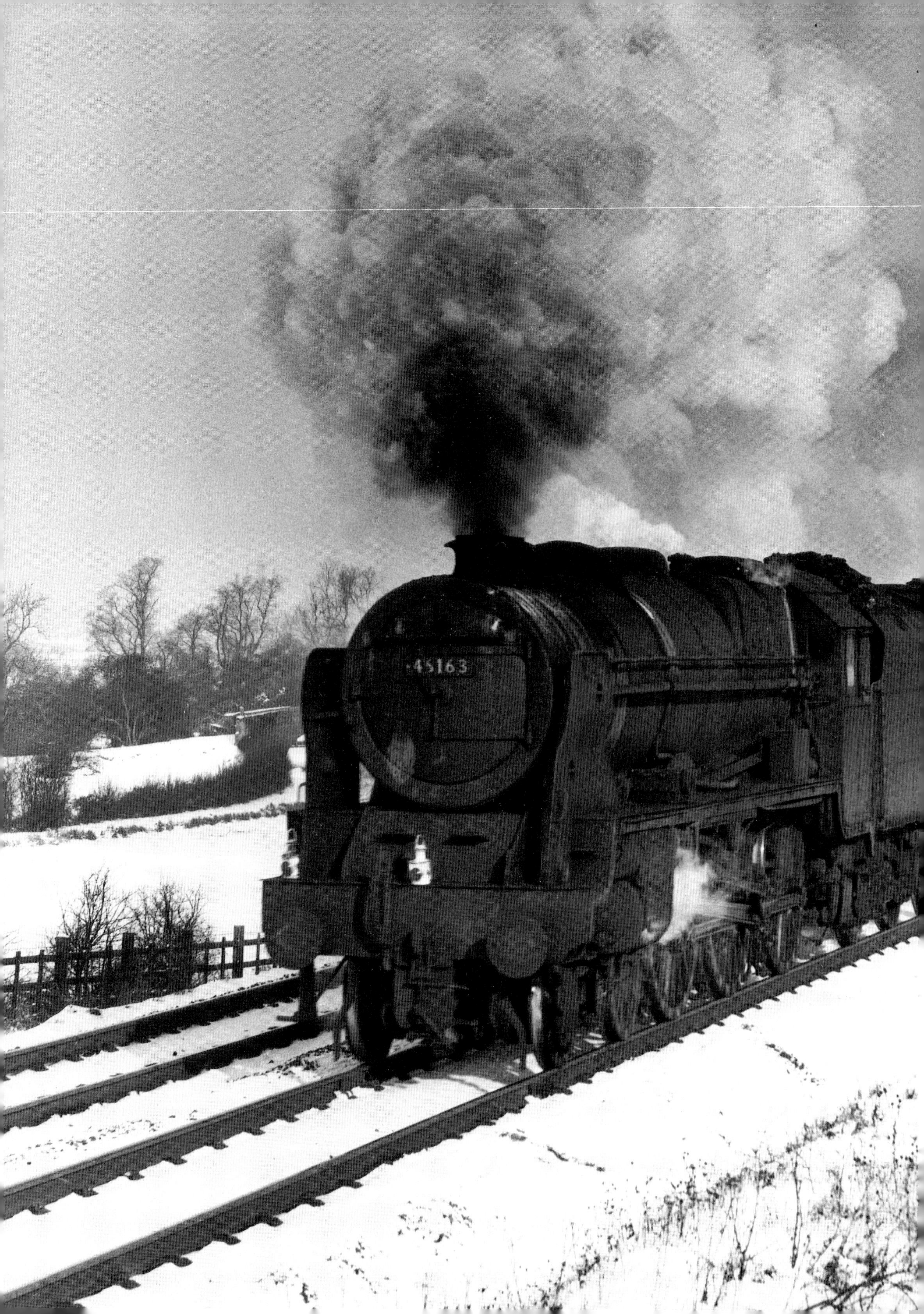
45163

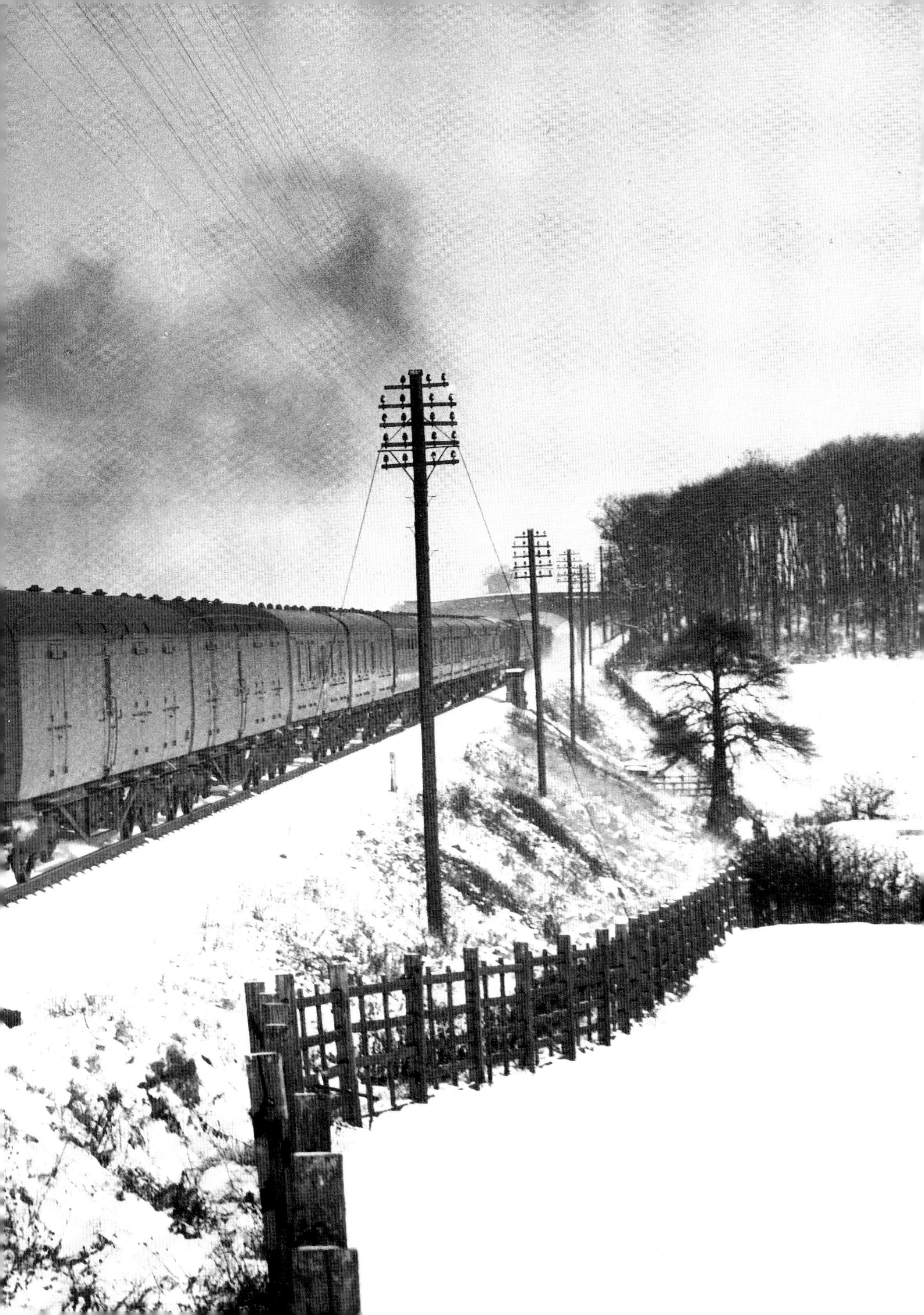

Previous page.
152. The Nottingham-Marylebone Parcels. After passing into the control of the London Midland Region and the subsequent withdrawal of the Great Central line's local passenger services south of Rugby a new morning parcels train was introduced between Nottingham and Marylebone which included in its composition the empty newspaper vans which had worked down from London in the early hours. The train became a regular duty for Annesley 'Royal Scots' working out their last days and in this photograph No 46163 'Civil Service Rifleman' provides a spectacle to warm the blood on a glorious Winter morning on 2nd February 1963 as she climbs through the snow to Whetstone with the Nottingham-Marylebone parcels.

153. A shot from the cab of 'Britannia' No 70041 'Sir John Moore' working the Grimsby-Whitland fish train seen approaching Ruddington in the fading evening light of 26th August 1963. On the down main line a London Midland 8F heads north light engine. 26.8.63.

154. No 70041 'Sir John Moore' with the Grimsby-Whitland fish stands in Leicester Central with 'the bag in' filling its tender tank as dusk sets in at 8.20 on the evening of August 26th 1963.

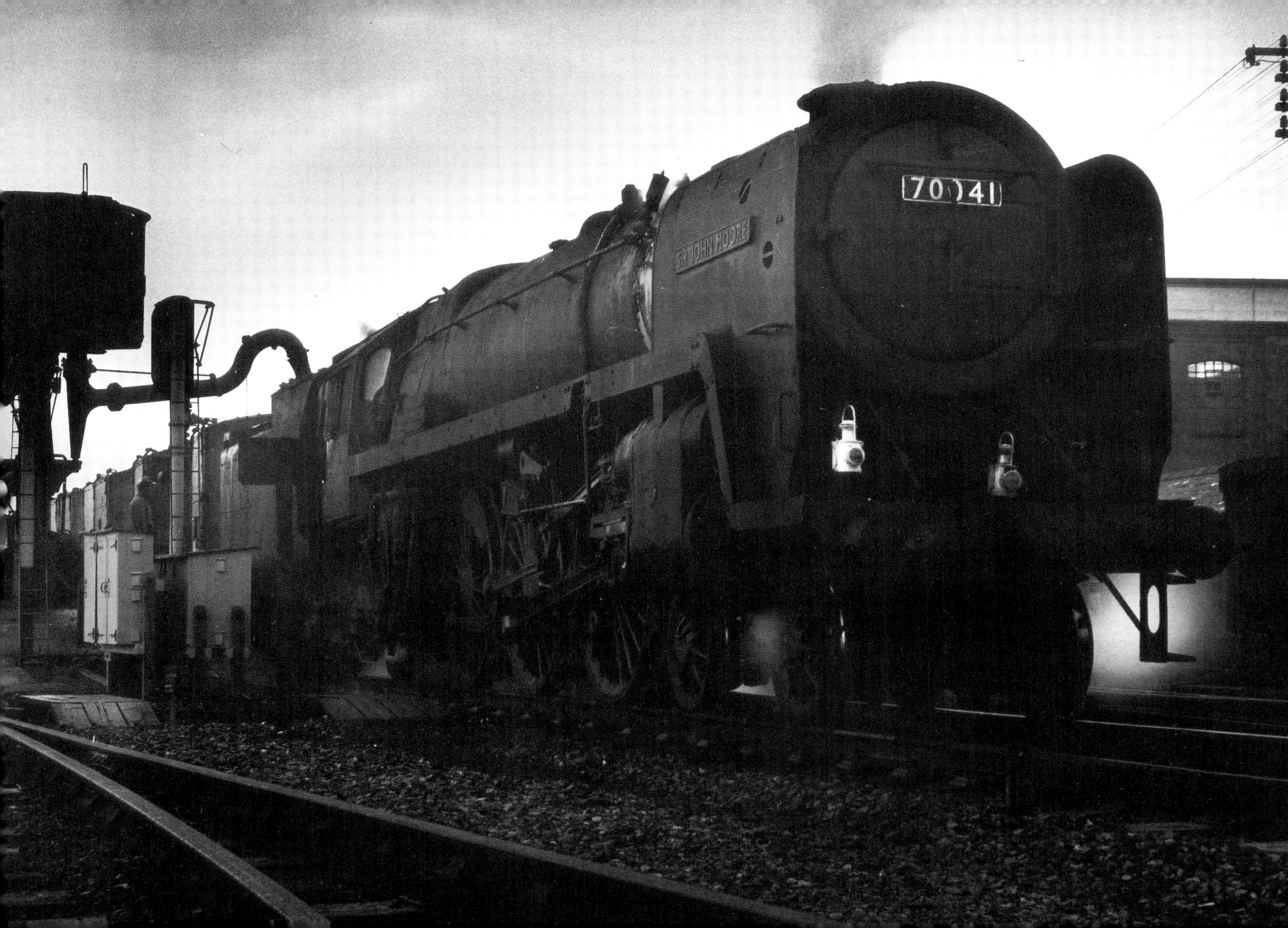
SIR JOHN MOORE

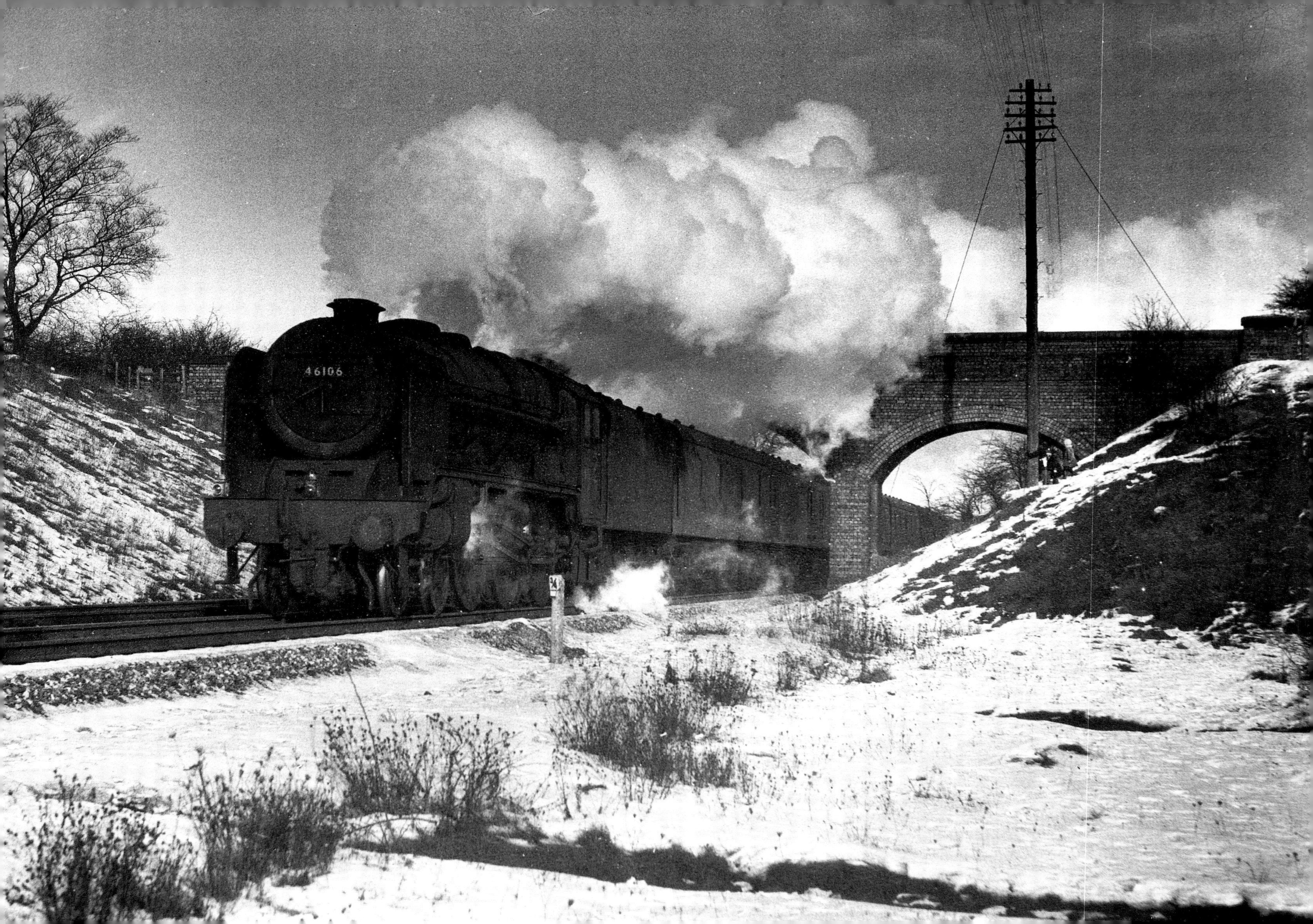
46106

155. No 46106 'Gordon Highlander' which was always recognizable by its straight smoke deflectors is seen in wintry conditions heading south between Aylestone Fields and Whetstone on 26th January 1963.

156. No 46122 'Royal Ulster Rifleman' climbs away through Whetstone with the Nottingham-Marylebone parcels on 28th August 1963.

157. No 46125 '3rd Carabinier' makes a massive departure from Leicester Central on 7th April 1964.

158. A photograph from the cab of 'Royal Scot', No 46163 with the Marylebone parcels taken at a rather unsteady moment as it negotiated the crossovers leading to the mouth of Parliament Street tunnel at Nottingham Victoria.

159. No 46143 'The South Staffordshire Regiment' with not a square inch of green paint to be seen on her, opens up after some cautious 'treading' over the new bridgeworks being constructed over the M1

Freight. The Annesley-Woodford 'romp'.

The time interval service of freight and steel traffic between the yards at Annesley and Woodford was a typical piece of lively Eastern Region enterprise. It exploited admirably the uncomplicated directness of the Great Central's London Extension and its freedom from obstacles. A high frequency of freight trains was timetabled around the regular express and local passenger services and by running them into sidings and loops drivers were given the incentive of a clear road which they siezed upon with enthusiasm. The introduction of the Standard 9F 2-10-0s in 1957 with their free running characteristics and massive capacity for work injected some tremendous sparkle into the service and their performance over the Great Central section became a legend. They also symbolised the last ray of hope and demonstrated the line's true value before negative policies took over and destroyed it.

The 9Fs.
160. 9F No 92096 dashes out of Catesby tunnel with a down 'runner'.

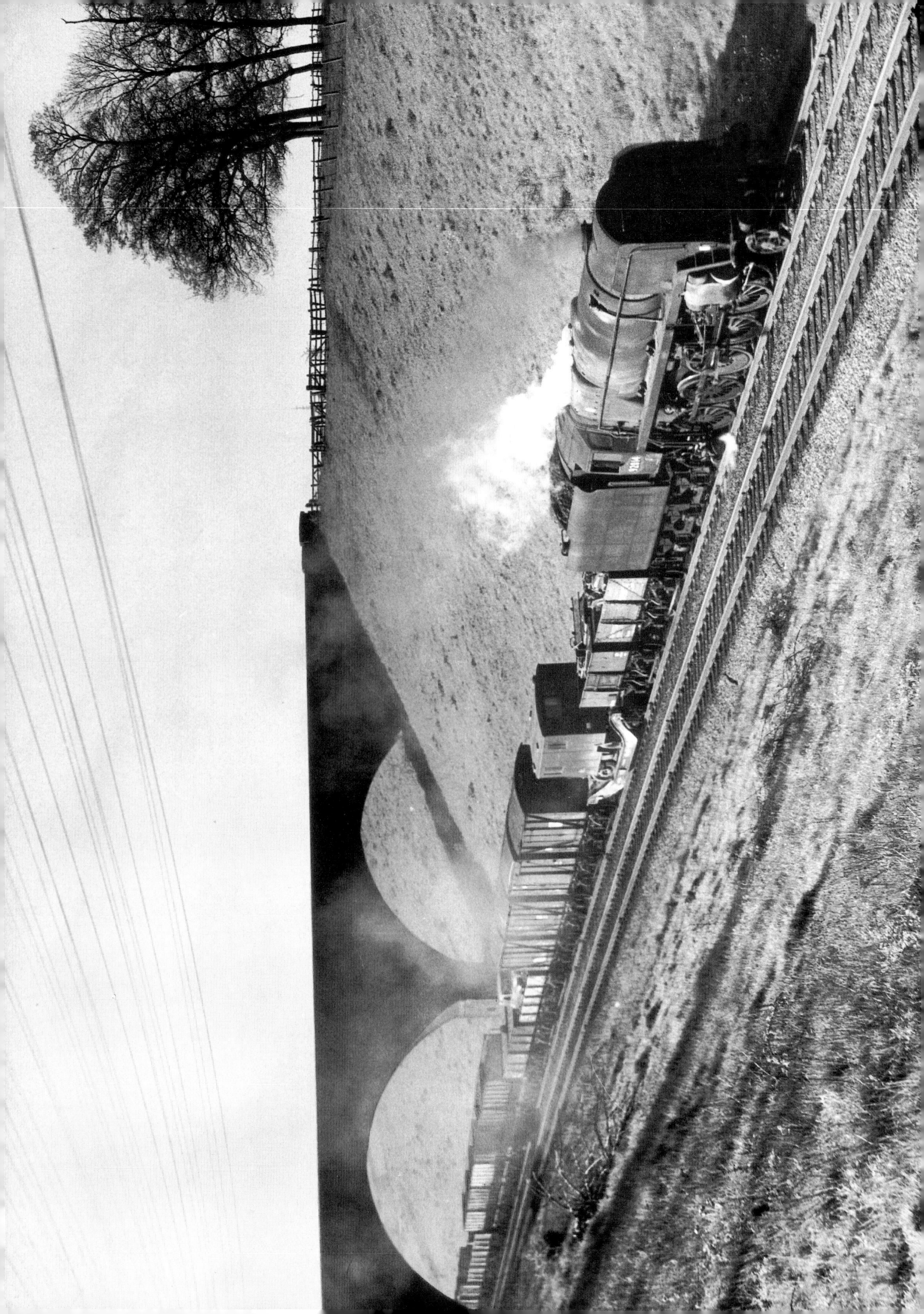

Catesby tunnel and approaches Staverton Road with a long northbound train which includes some vehicles bound for the Ministry of Defence depot at Ruddington. 9.5.64.

begins the curve of 'Cosby Corner'. The track here was on a well cambered bend which had no effect on the visibility of down trains but effectively masked off the lower part of the wheels of up trains. 29.6.64.

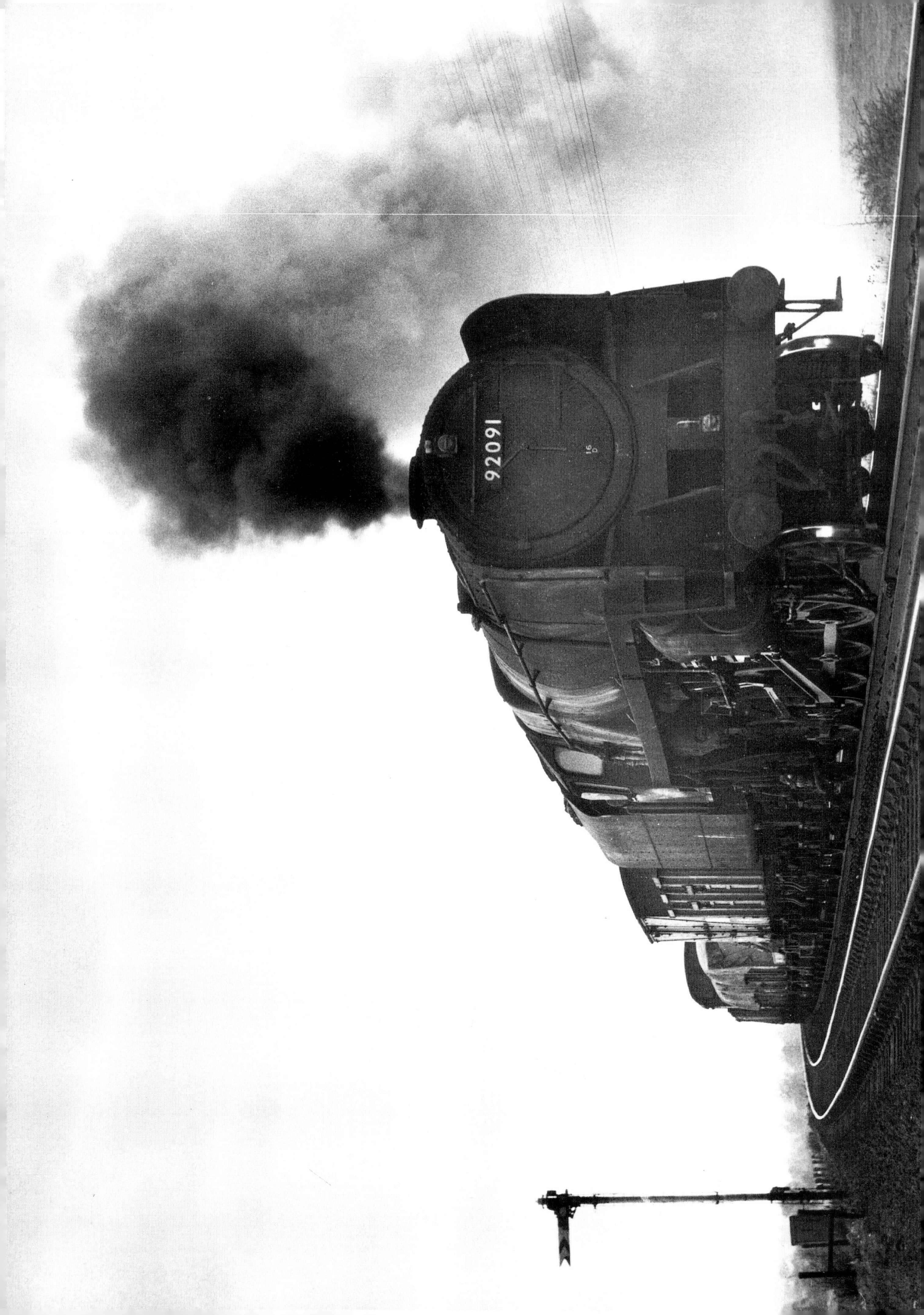
92091

163. No 92091 thunders round the curve of 'Cosby Corner' on its way up the climb to Ashby Magna with a southbound 'windcutter'.

164. The shadows are lengthening as late on a summer evening No 92093 lifts an up 'windcutter' away from Whetstone and round the curve of 'Cosby Corner' on its way up Ashby Magna bank.

165/166. Coming and Going. 9F No 92167 hauling an up mixed train of coal and steel pounds round 'Cosby Corner' and puts up an impressive smoke screen

Following page.
167. No 92087 enjoys a clear road over the Nottingham viaduct as she coasts past Weekday Cross junction with

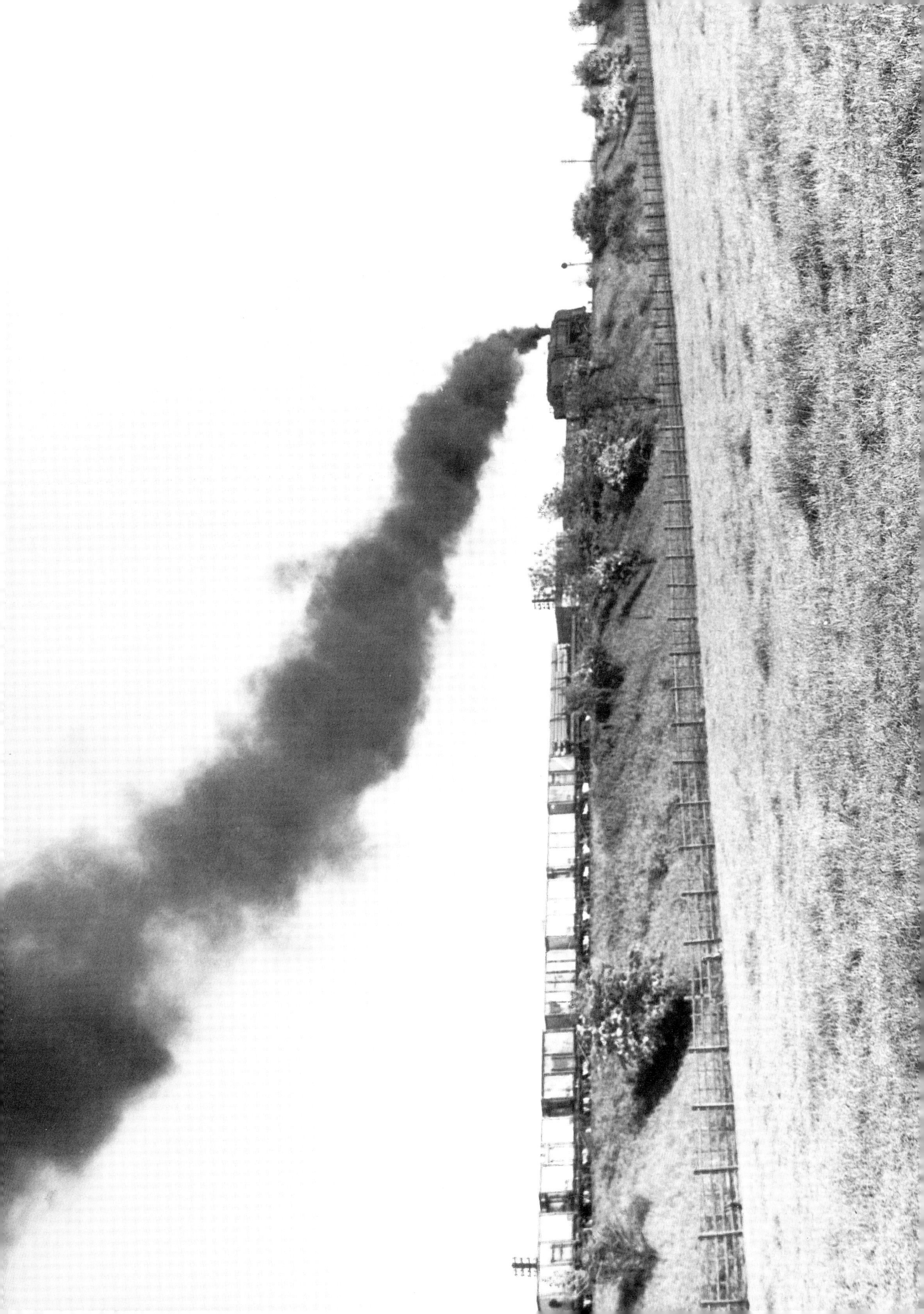

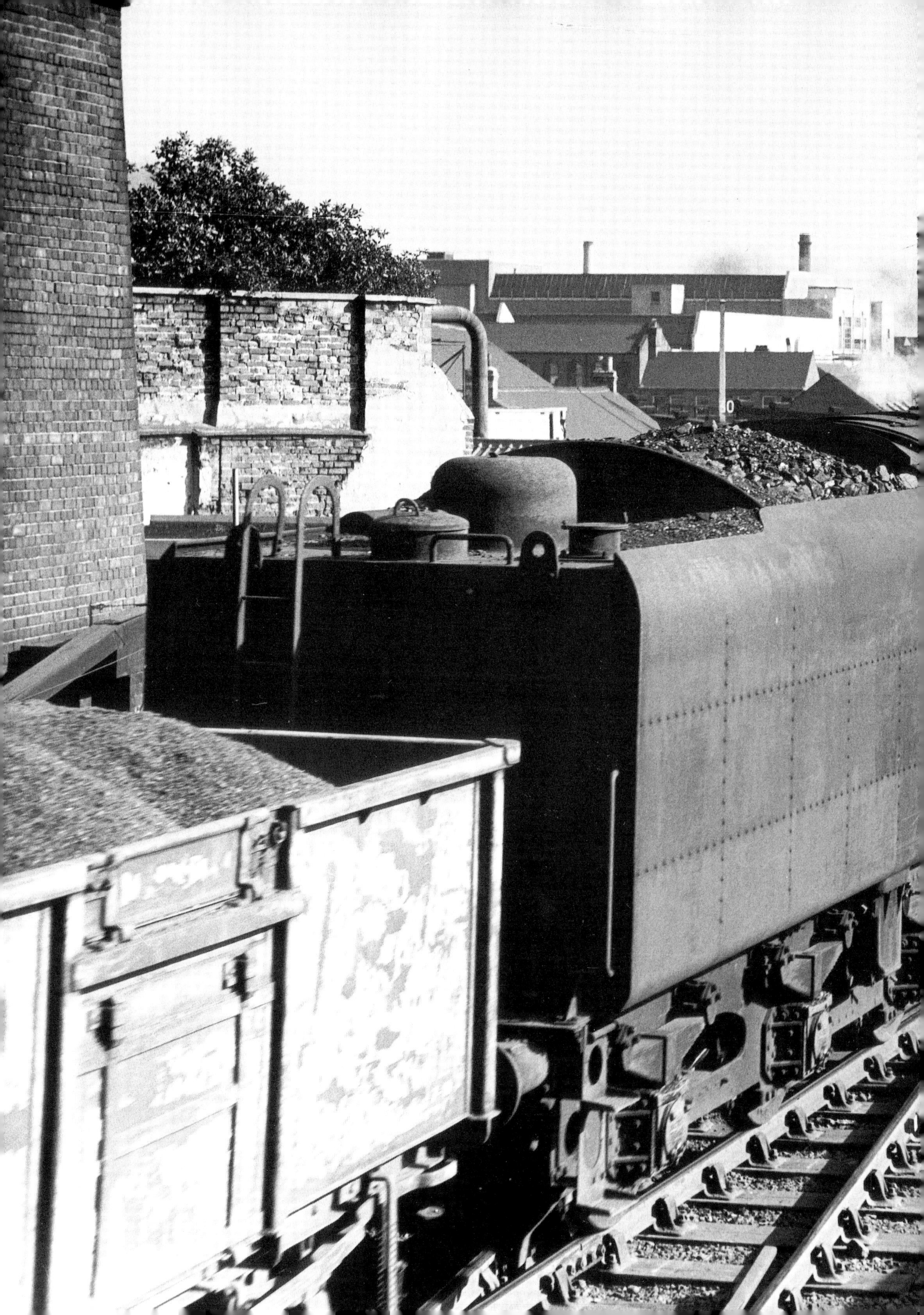

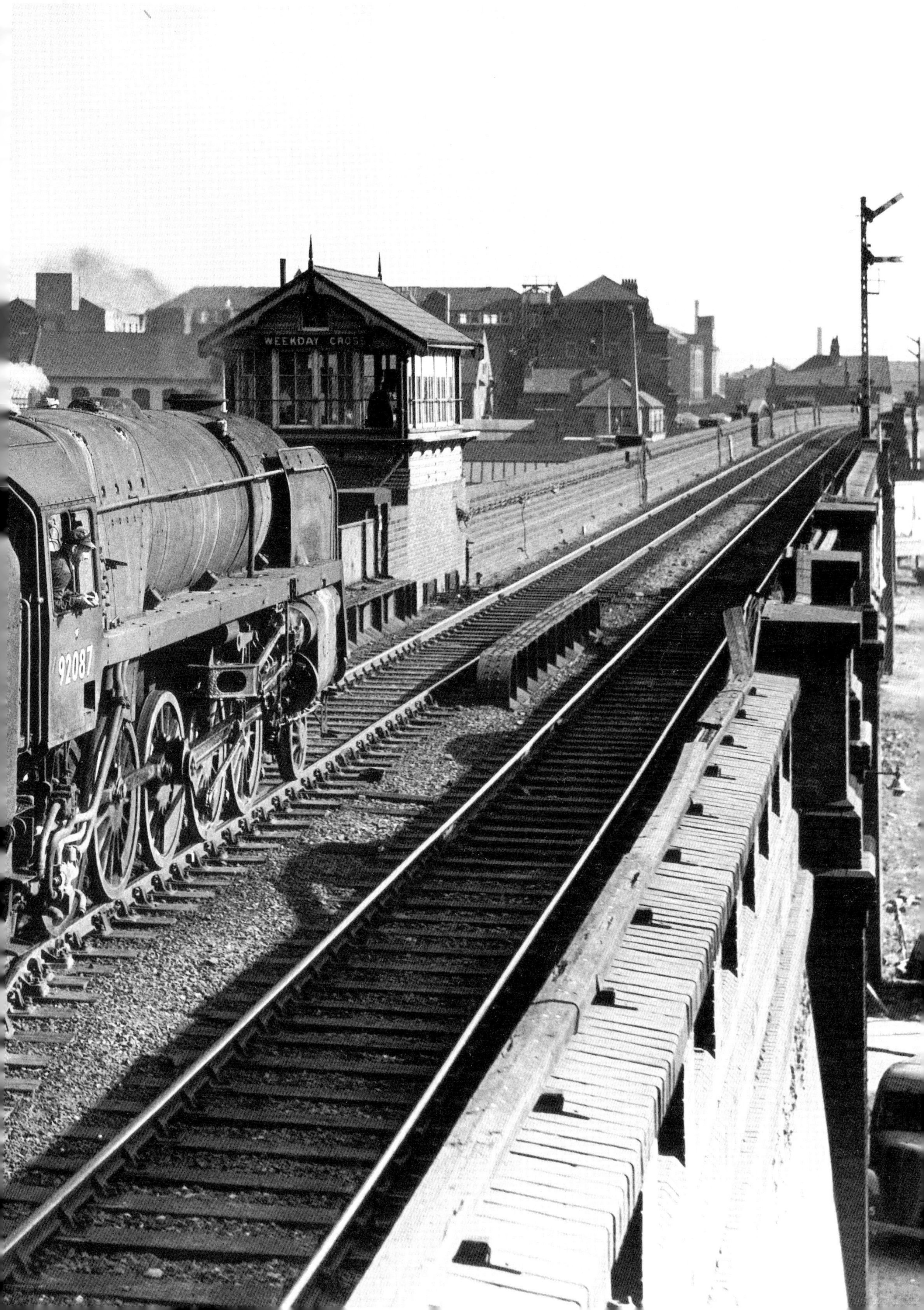
WEEKDAY CROSS
92087

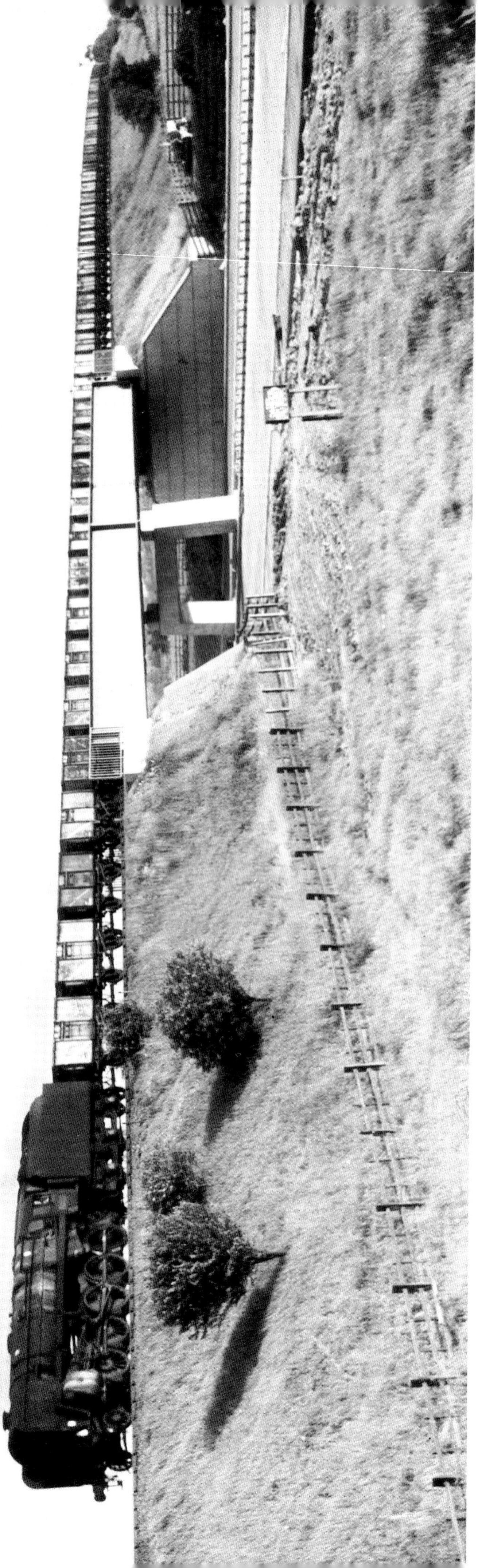

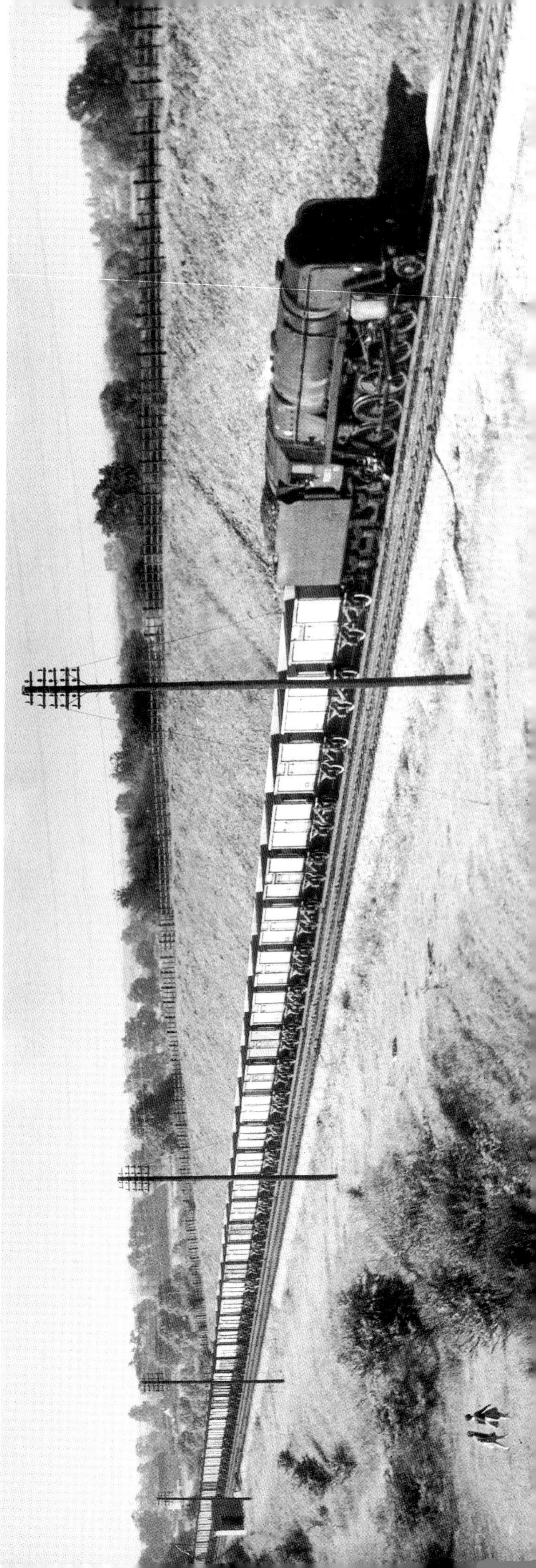

92089 rattles a long train of coal empties down Ashby bank towards Whetstone and Leicester on a summer evening.

81 train of 50 empties is whisked towards Leicester by 9F No 92012.

170. No 92091 climbs through Whetstone with a mixed up 'runner' on a peaceful Summer evening in June 1964. 29.6.64.

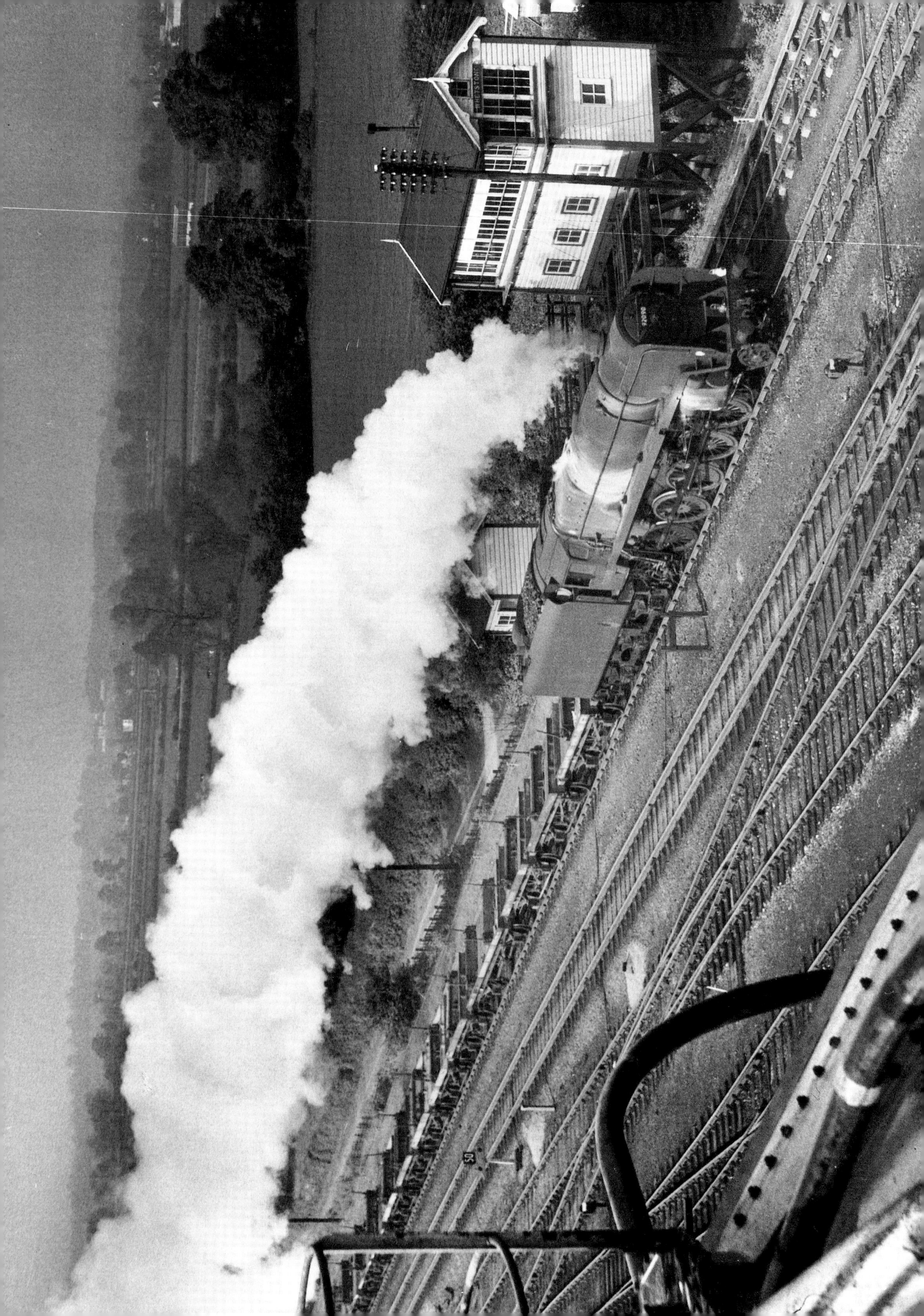

cry as she sweeps past Whetstone signal box at nearly a mile a minute with a train of steel empties destined for Scunthorpe. 25.5.63.

is seen again nearing Whetstone on the up with a southbound 'runner'. 28.8.63.

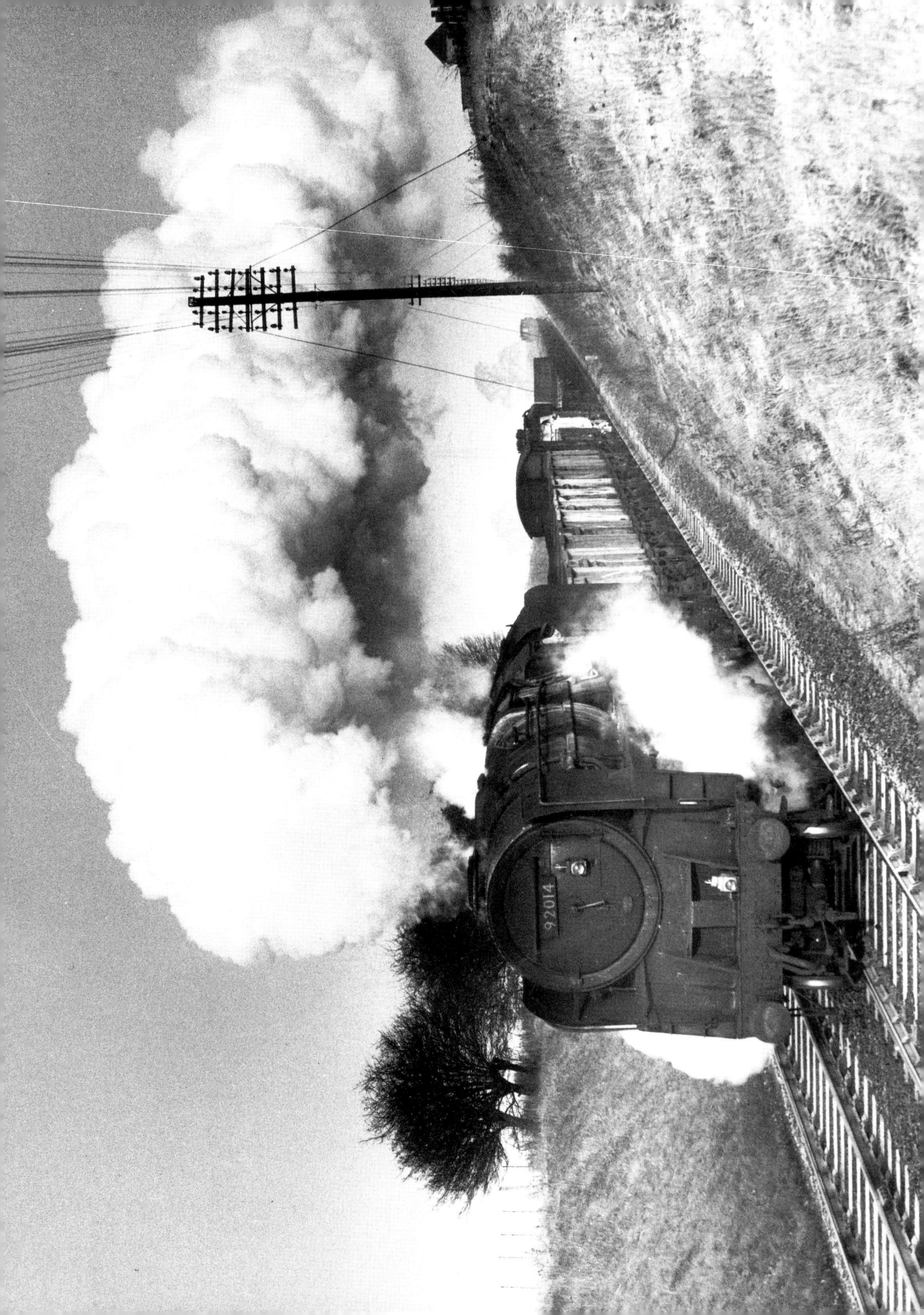
92014

174. Through the snow 9F No.92011 revels in the freedom of a clear road as it races towards Whetstone with another train load of coal. 26.1.63.

snatches a glance at the camera as his engine blazes away up the main line towards Whetstone with an Annesley-Woodford 'non-stop'.

175. It was always a matter of some amusement to me that many drivers of 'windcutters' seemed reluctant to close the regulator and coast down the gradients when they were in their favour and here is a perfect example of what I mean.

On a freezing January morning in 1964 No 92092 is entering the outskirts of Leicester at Aylestone fields and has been descending for 3 miles. However, the regulator is still well open and she is blazing

176. Heading south on the same morning is No 92075 with loaded steel for South Wales.

177. The fireman of No 92069 with an up train of coal has caught sight of a distant 'on'

178. 'Windcutter' superpower. An unbalanced engine working finds a brace of 9Fs Nos 92072 and 92013 passing Leicester North Goods with an up working.

Following pages.
179. No 92091 gathers speed again after crossing the Leicester viaduct with an up coal train on an April morning in 1963.

180. Another 9F No 92032 with an Annesley-Woodford coal train makes a vigorous acceleration past Leicester North Goods.

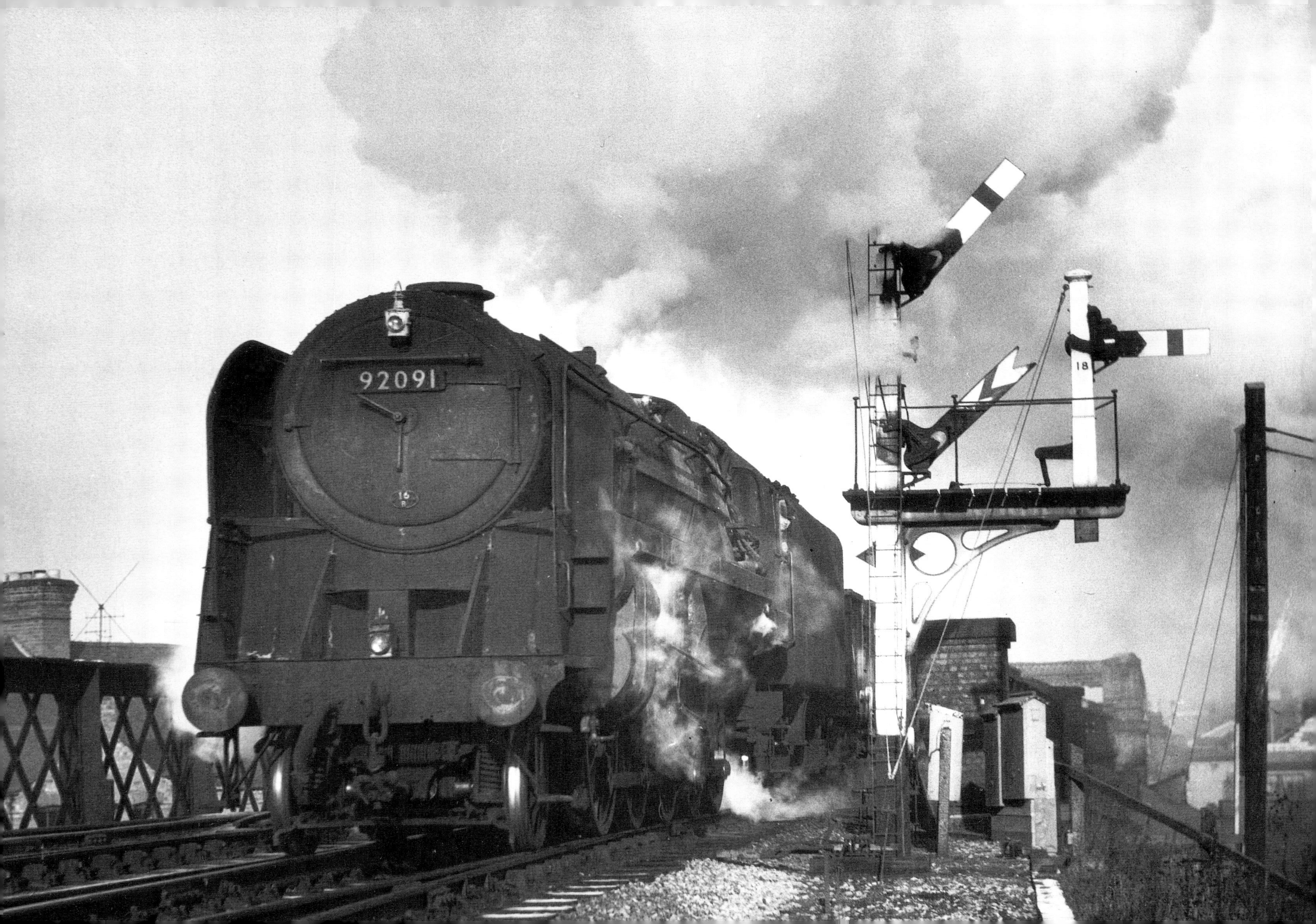
92091
18

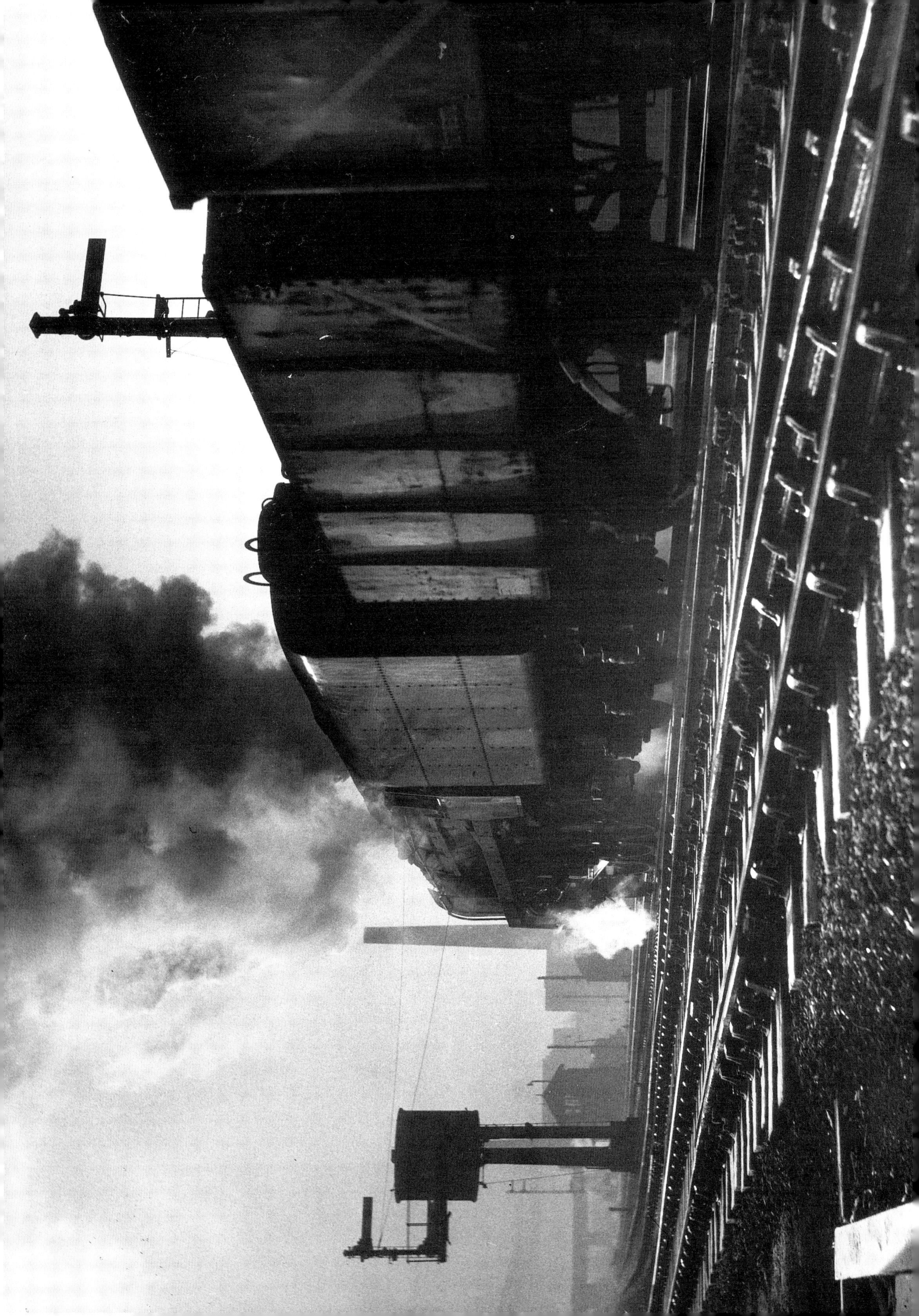

181. No 92075 makes an energetic climb away from Leicester and approaches Whetstone with an up mixed 'runner'.

9Fs in the freezing fog.
182. At the other end of Leicester near Birstall on a day when road traffic was paralysed and the Midland lines were in chaos, the boards are all 'off' for No 92071 as she confidently swings down the 1 in 176 into Leicester with an up coal train. 2.1.62.

Following page.
183. Another photograph taken on the morning of 2nd January 1962 finds 9F No 92095 looming through the fog as it climbs lustily towards Birstall with a down 'runner'.

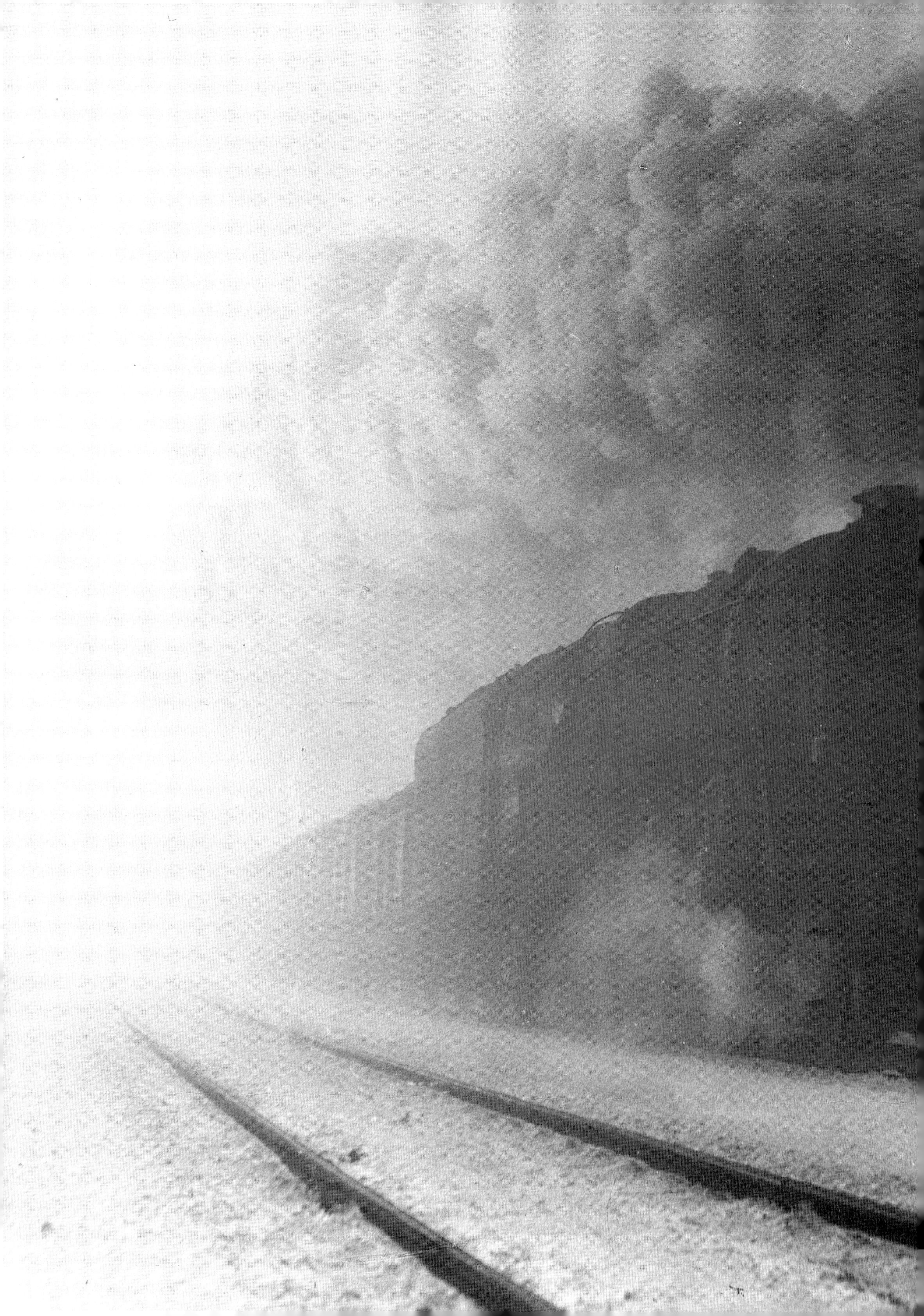

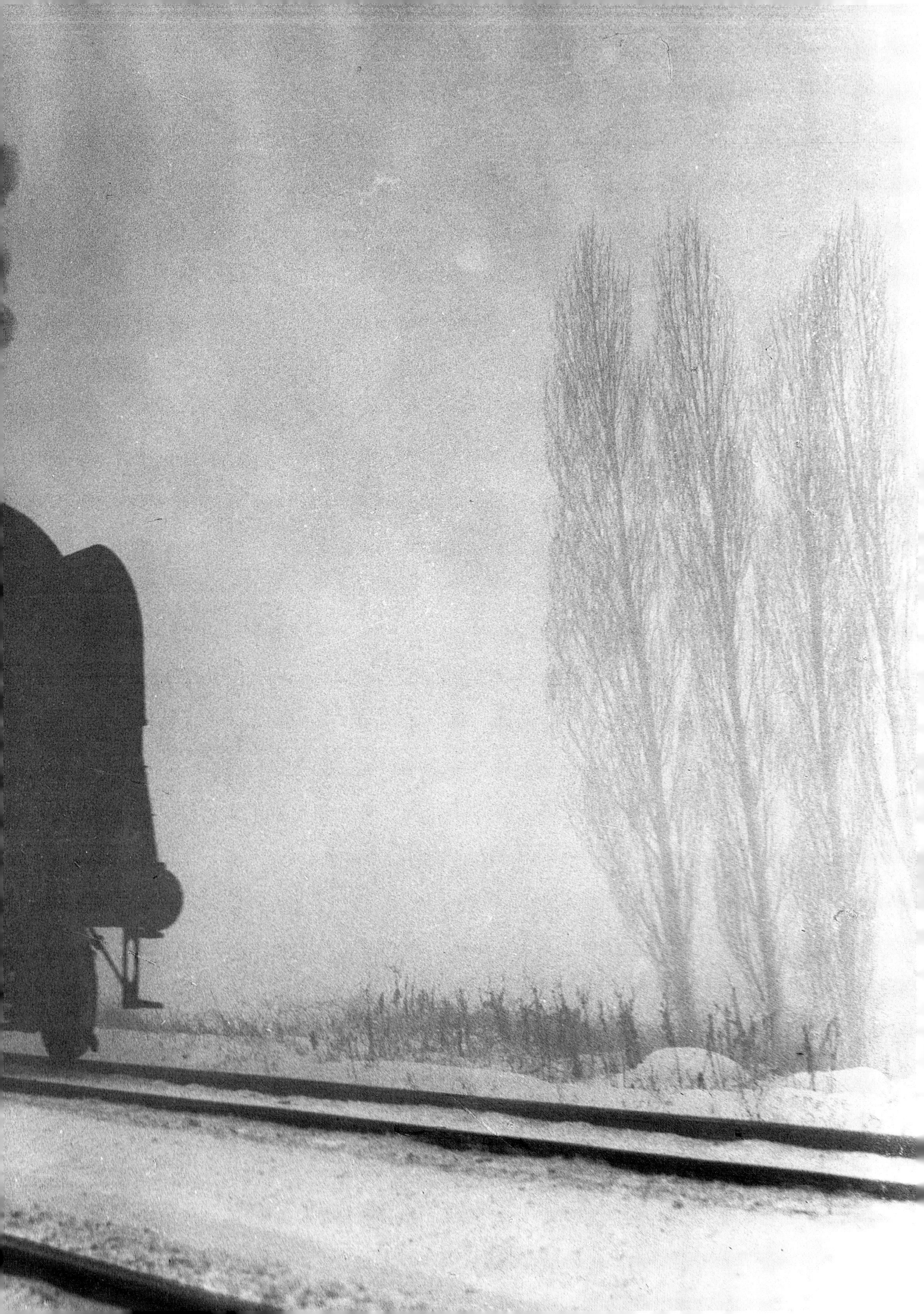

184. A photograph, taken from the windows of the goods warehouse in Braunstone Gate in the winter of 1963 catches No 92031 scurrying past Leicester North Goods box with a 50 wagon train of coal empties. Collecting coaches from the carriage sheds is a

185. Another winter shot in 1958 catches 9F No 92088 clattering past Abbey Lane

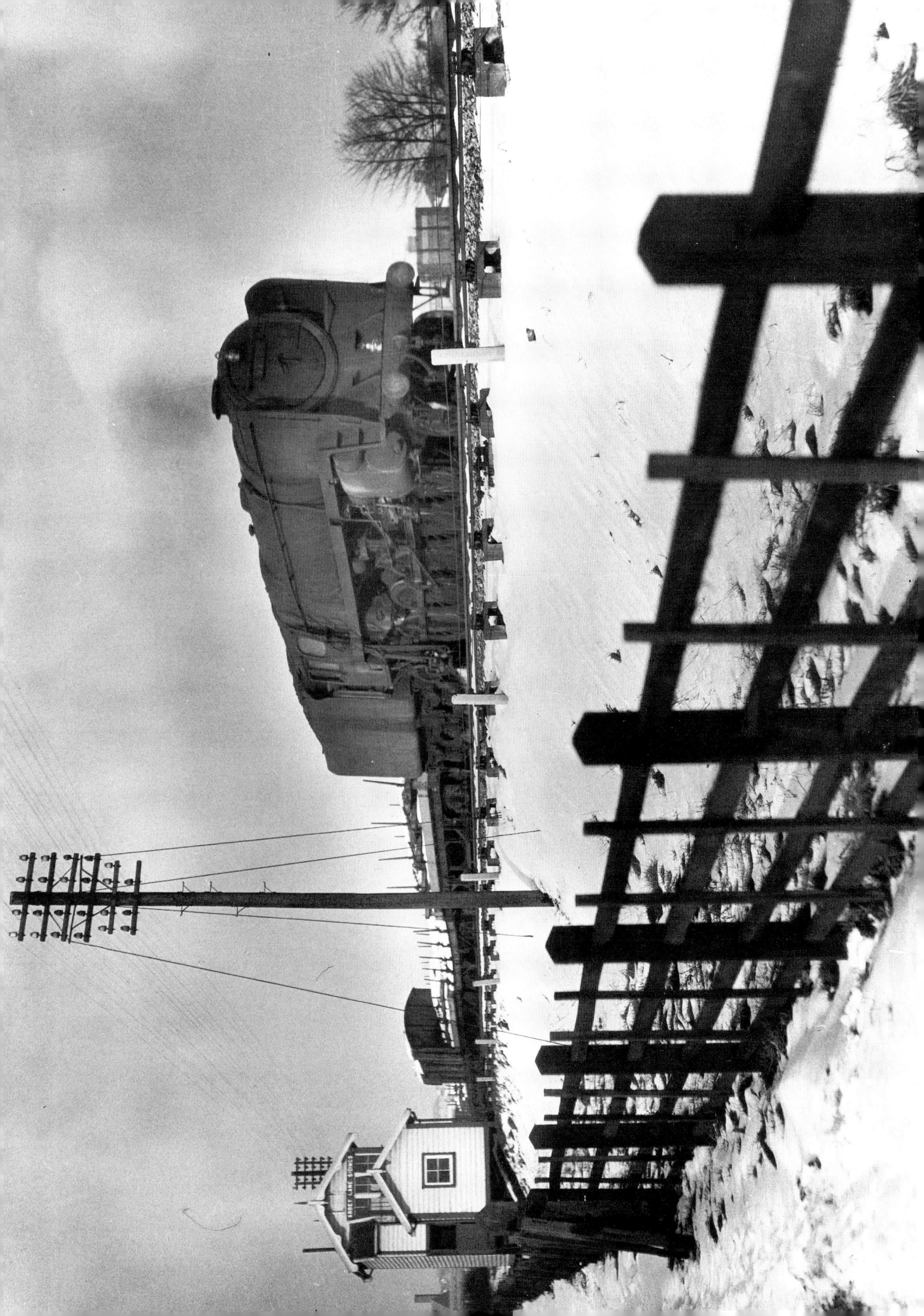

186. Two platelayers going off duty pause to watch No 92068 as it dashes past Abbey Lane sidings with a northbound mixed train of empties.

187. Surrounded by a jungle of abandoned and overgrown neighbouring plots a dedicated gardener is too deeply absorbed in his digging to spare a glance at 9F No 92030 as it storms past his allotment at Beaumont Leys between Leicester and Birstall with a northbound

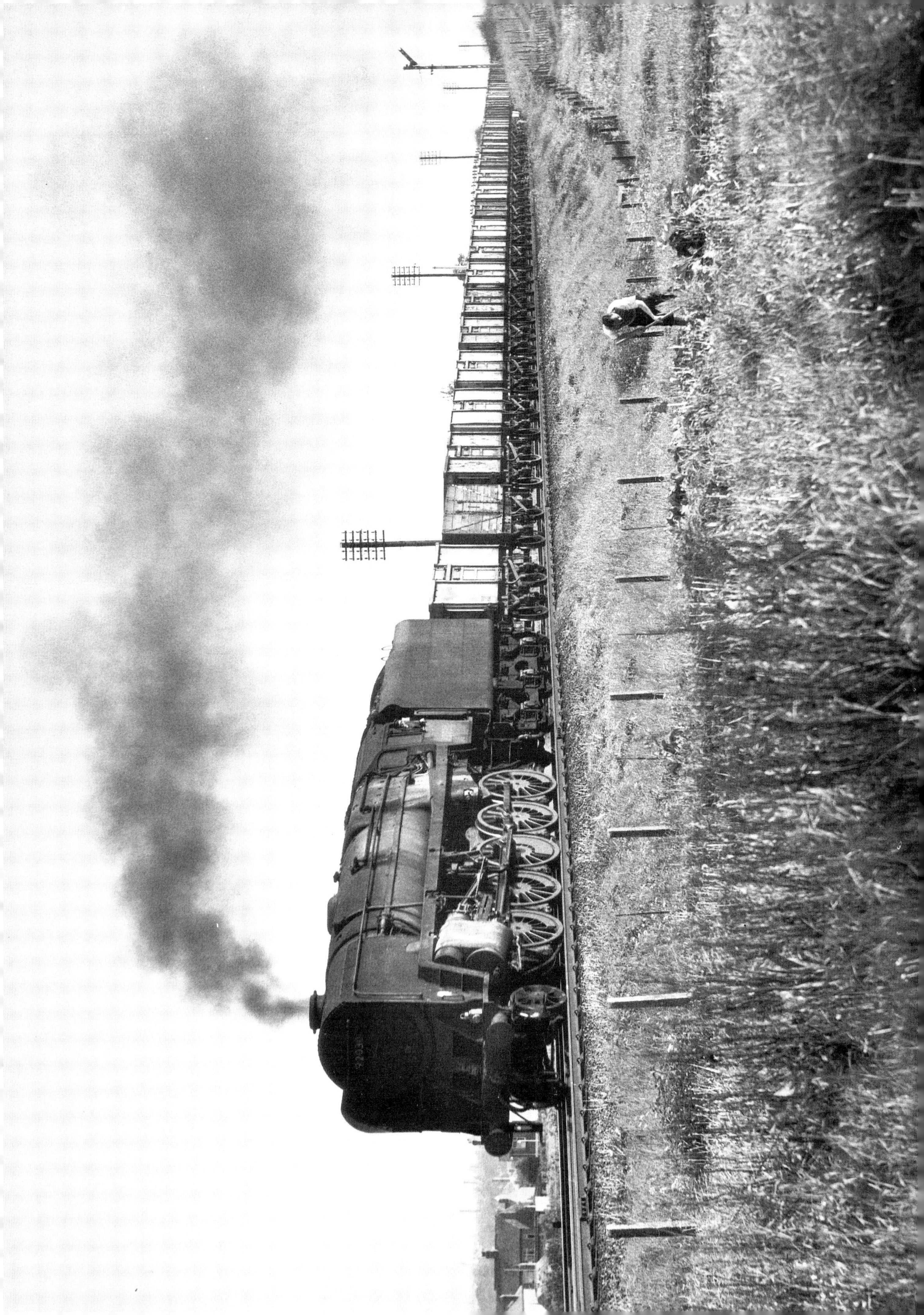

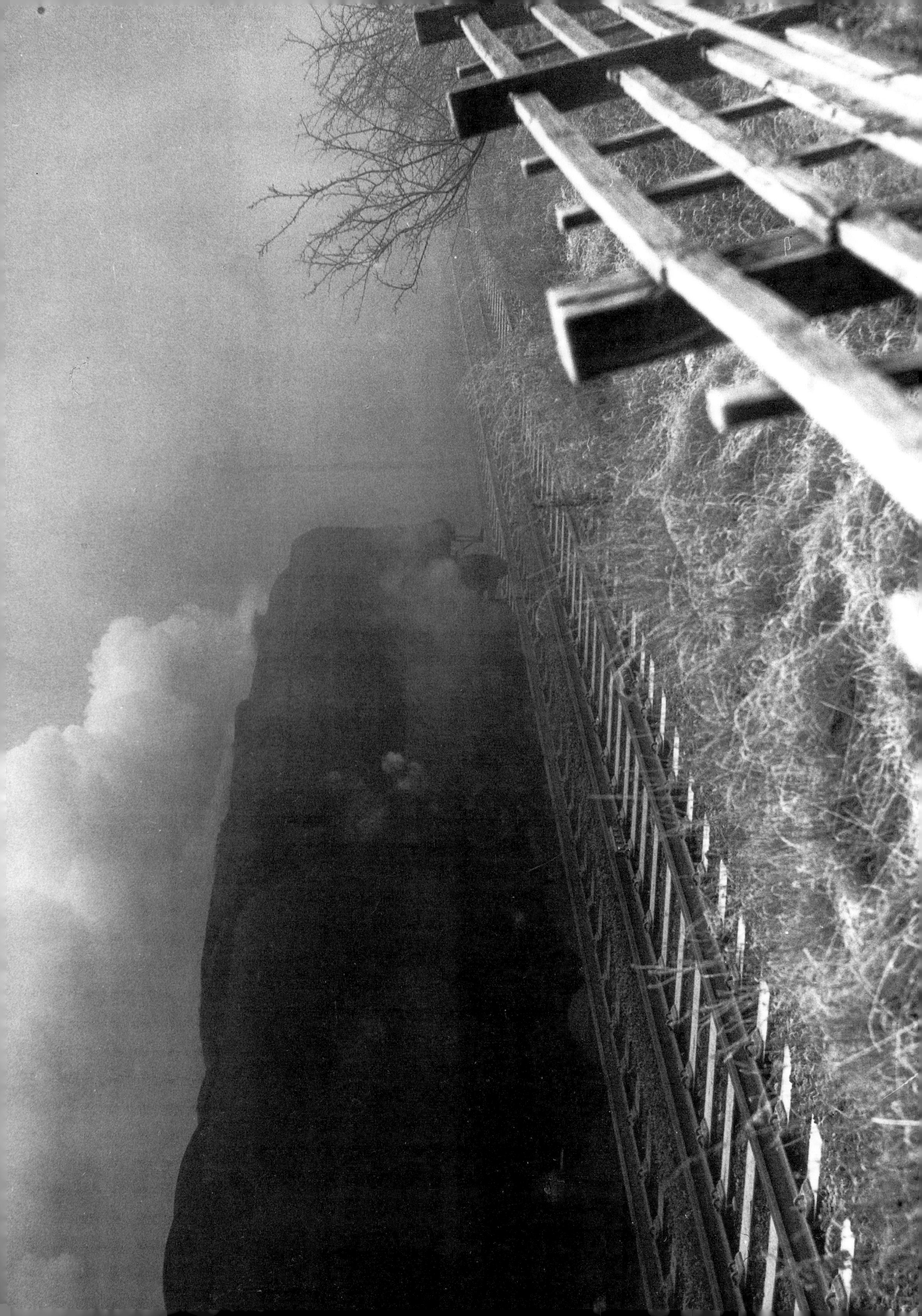

188. No 92092 passes near to the village of Thurcaston between Rothley and Birstall with an up coal train and rushes the 1 in 176 rise before descending to the Soar valley at Leicester. January 1964.

189. In the other direction No 92124 hurries north with balancing coal empties. January 1964.

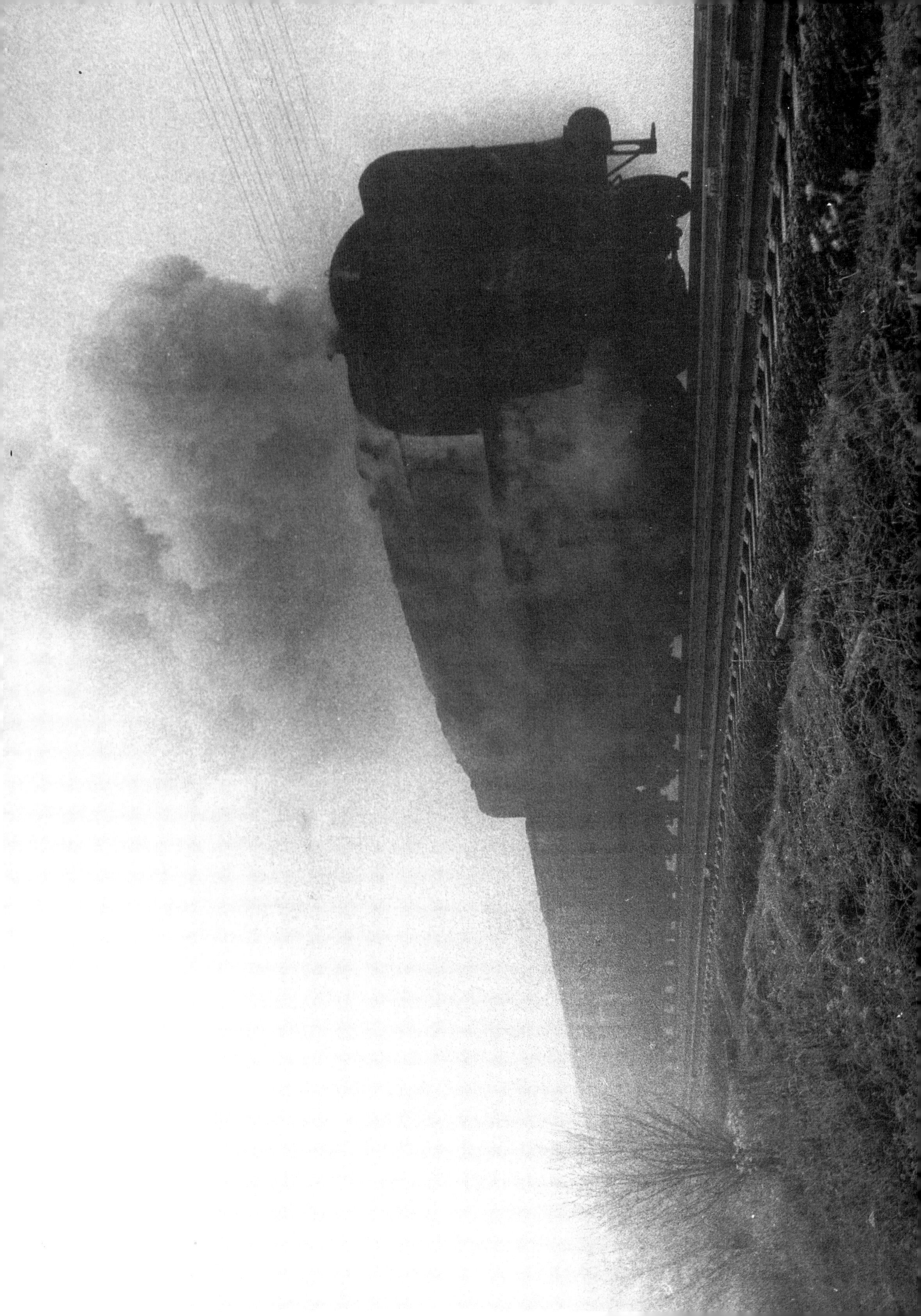

a frosty morning in January 1964 ... through the fog near Rothley with winter coal, January 1964.

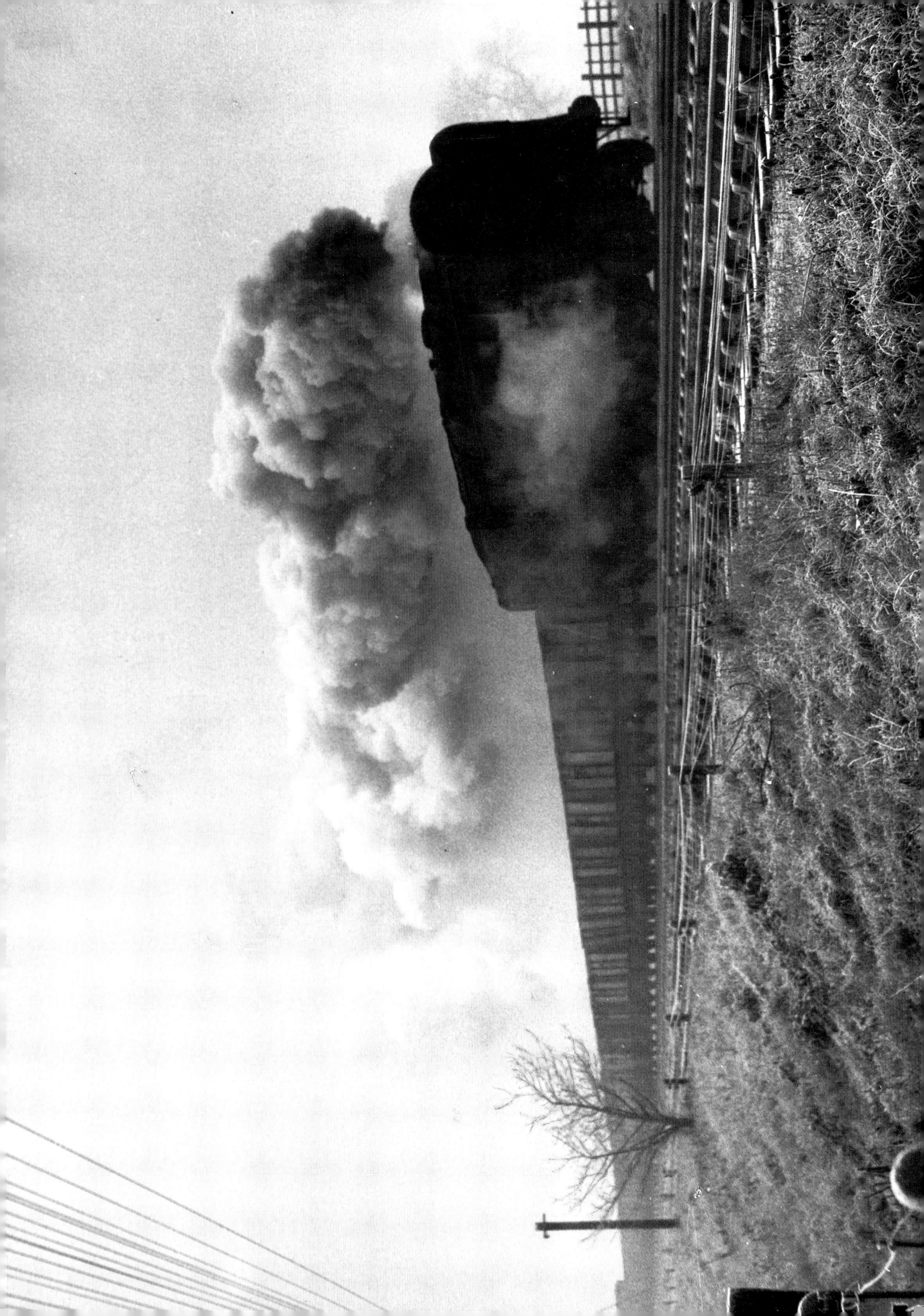

She is seen running hard near Thurcaston hollow between Rothley and Birstall with a southbound train of coal and steel. 24.12.62.

past Swithland sidings with an up all-coal 'windcutter'. January 1964.

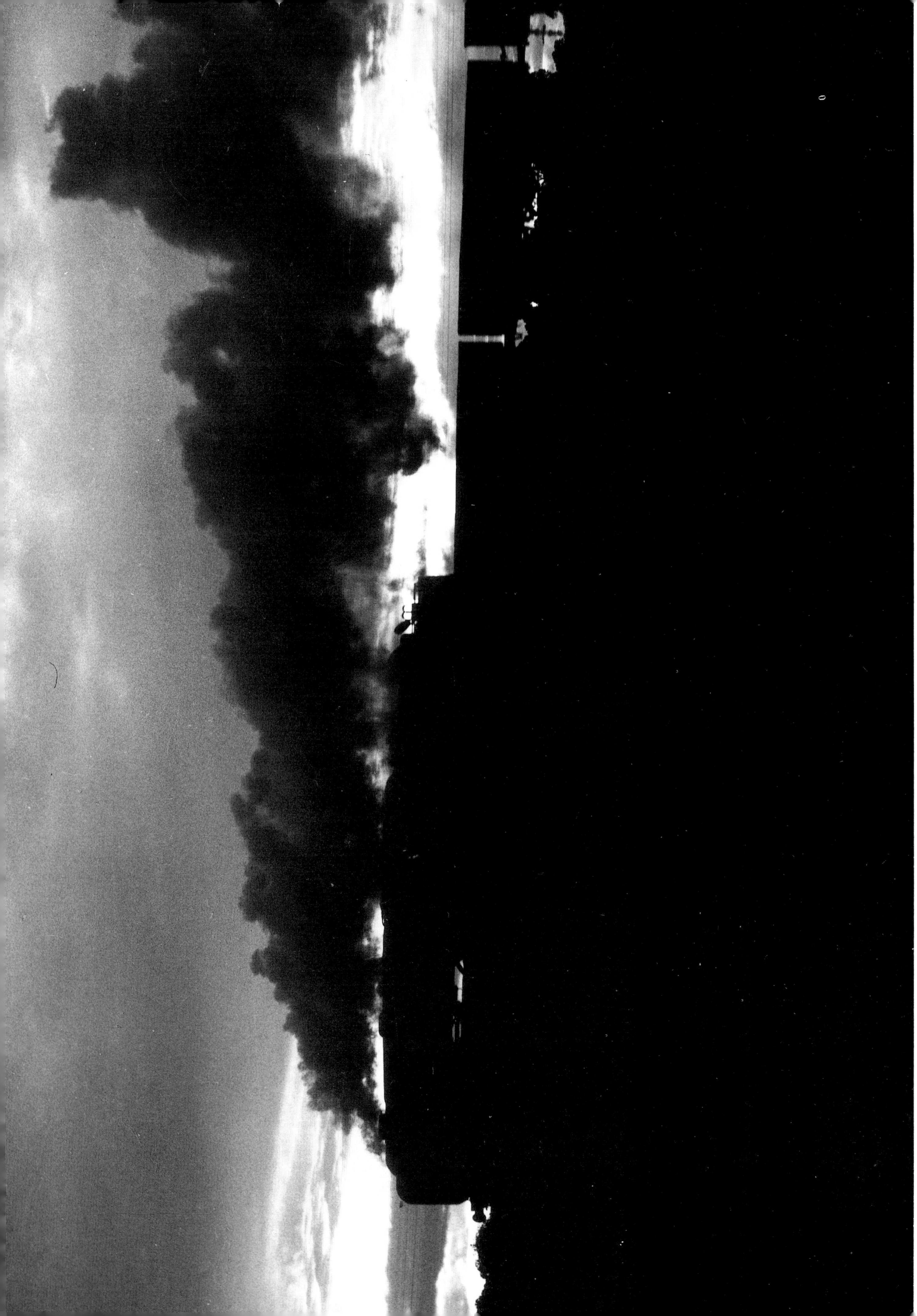

Black 5s
195. It is a Summer Saturday and No 44777 drifts cautiously into Leicester from Birstall with an Annesley-Woodford coal train in the wake of a holiday passenger train. 30.5.63.

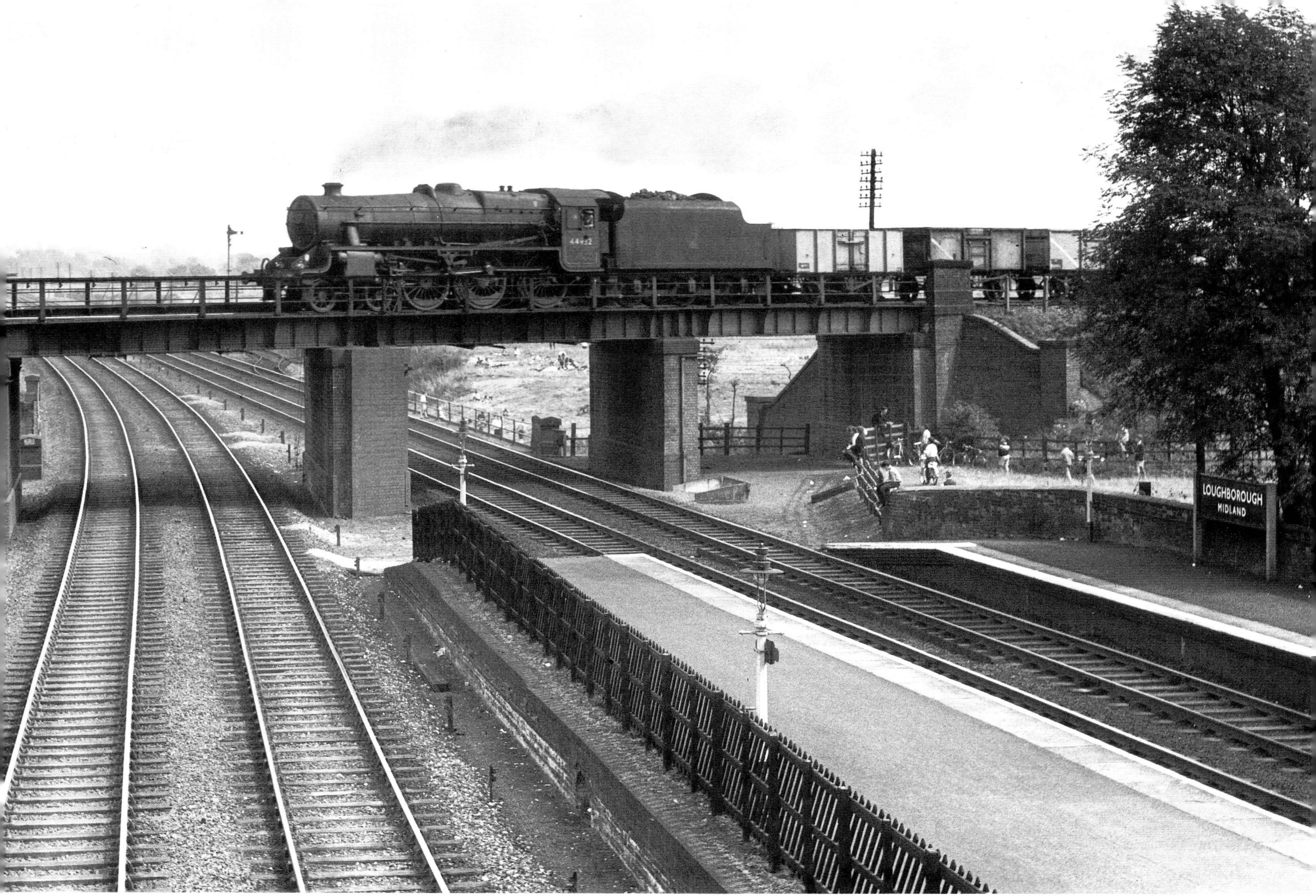
44952
LOUGHBOROUGH
MIDLAND

197. A B1 4-6-0 No 61327 races through Whetstone towards Leicester also with up coal empties. 20.5.64.

Following page.
198. Another V2 on 'windcutter' duty. On a crisp December day in 1962 an old and familiar friend, No 60831, by now a York engine, revives the spirits as she heads an up coal train out of Leicester and crosses over the Soar Navigation at Aylestone.

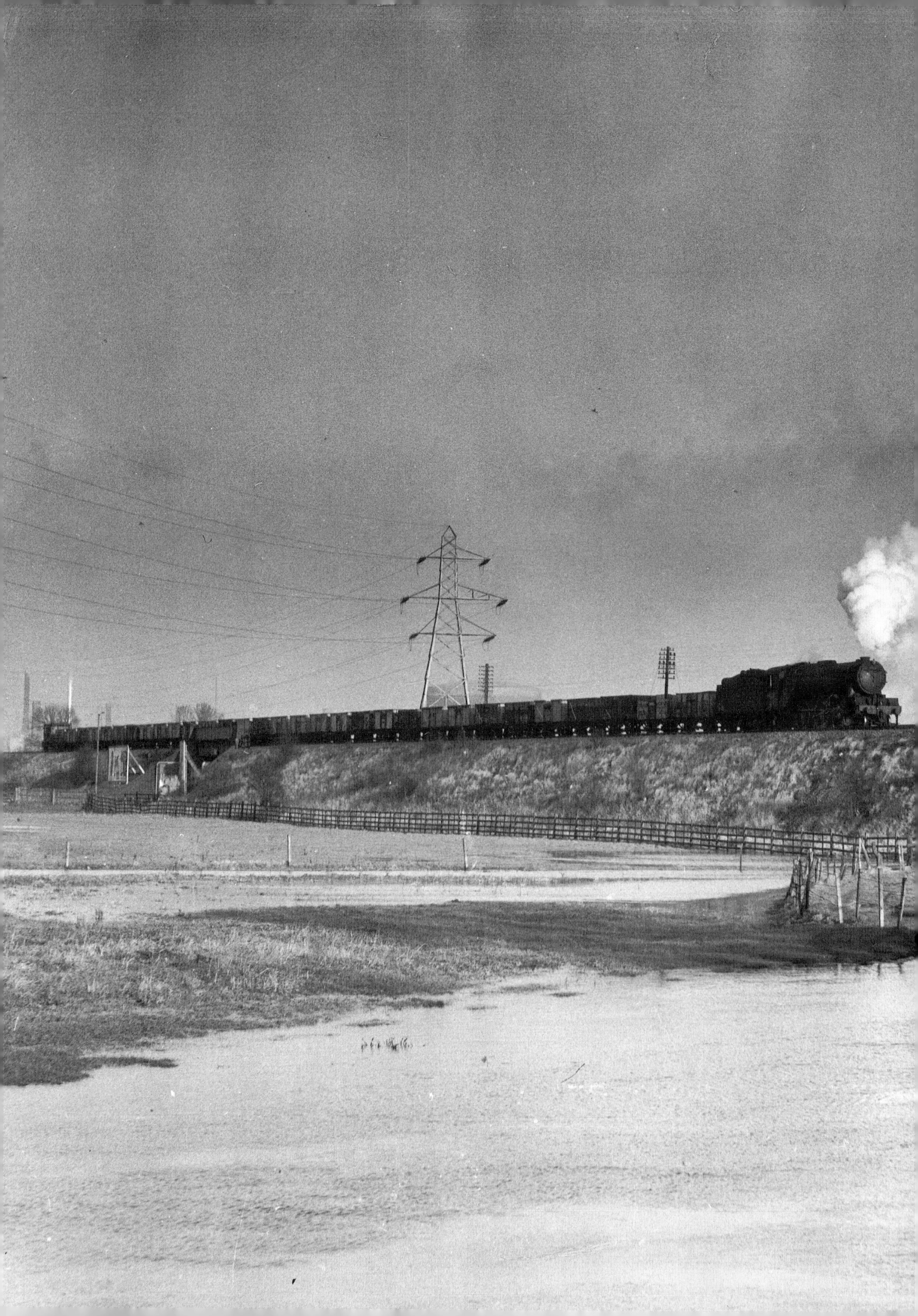

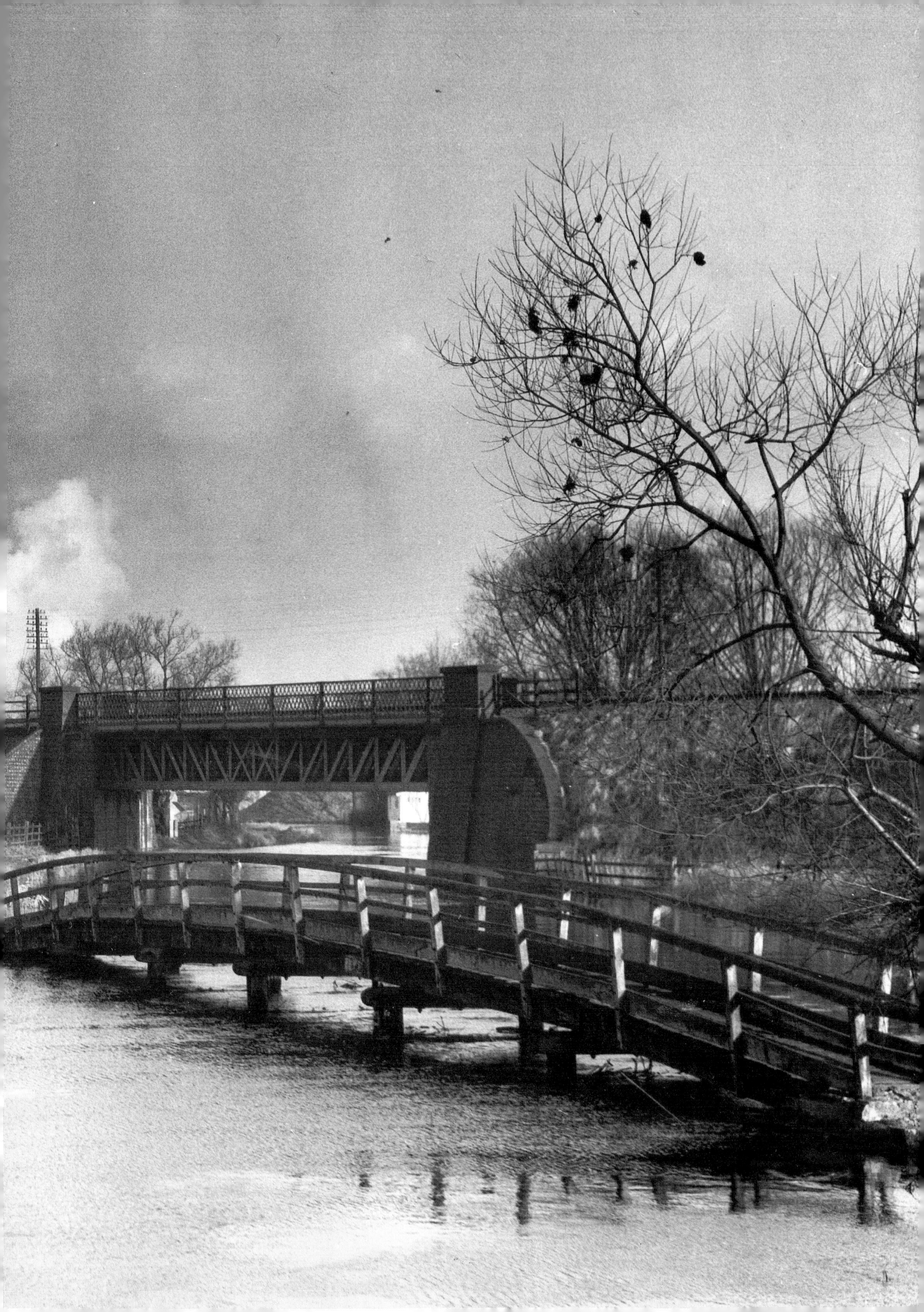

199. After being delayed by an enthusiasts' special on Saturday, April 7th 1964 a V2 No 60895 puts on steam again and quickens the pace as it heads south from Leicester over the River Soar navigation with an up

200. The onward movement of freight from Woodford yard tended to travel at a somewhat reduced pace compared with that to and from the north. However, in this photograph a Western Mogul No 6368 has got off to a very snappy start and is heading for Culworth Junction and

201. Local and Pick-up Freight. A former Great Central A5 4-6-2 tank No 69807 brings a rake of empty wagons and a hopper of ashes from Abbey Lane sidings along the goods loop at Leicester North Goods.

202. Stanier Class 5 No 45416 takes the up loop line at Leicester Central with the local freight from Ruddington on a January day in 1964.

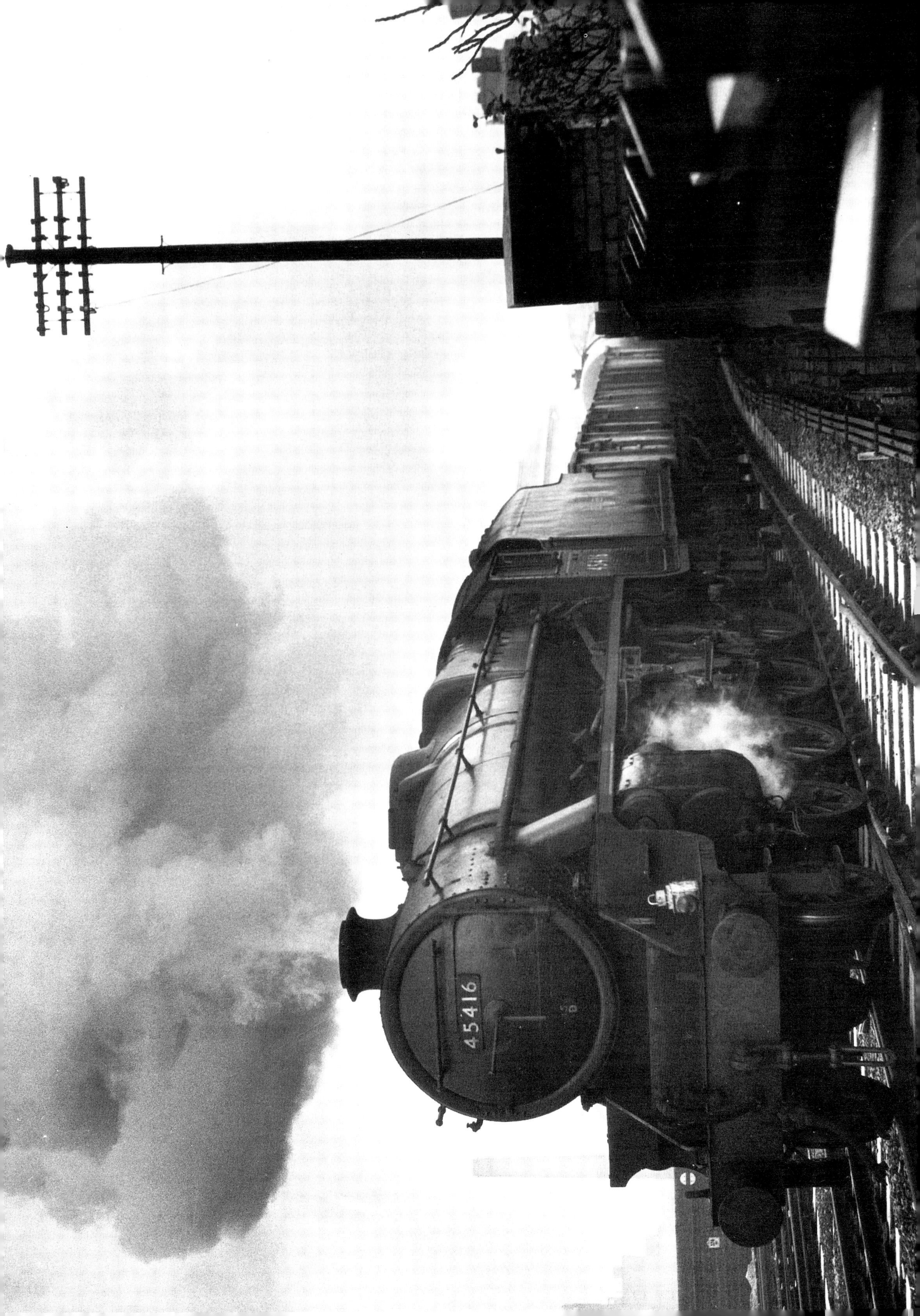
45416

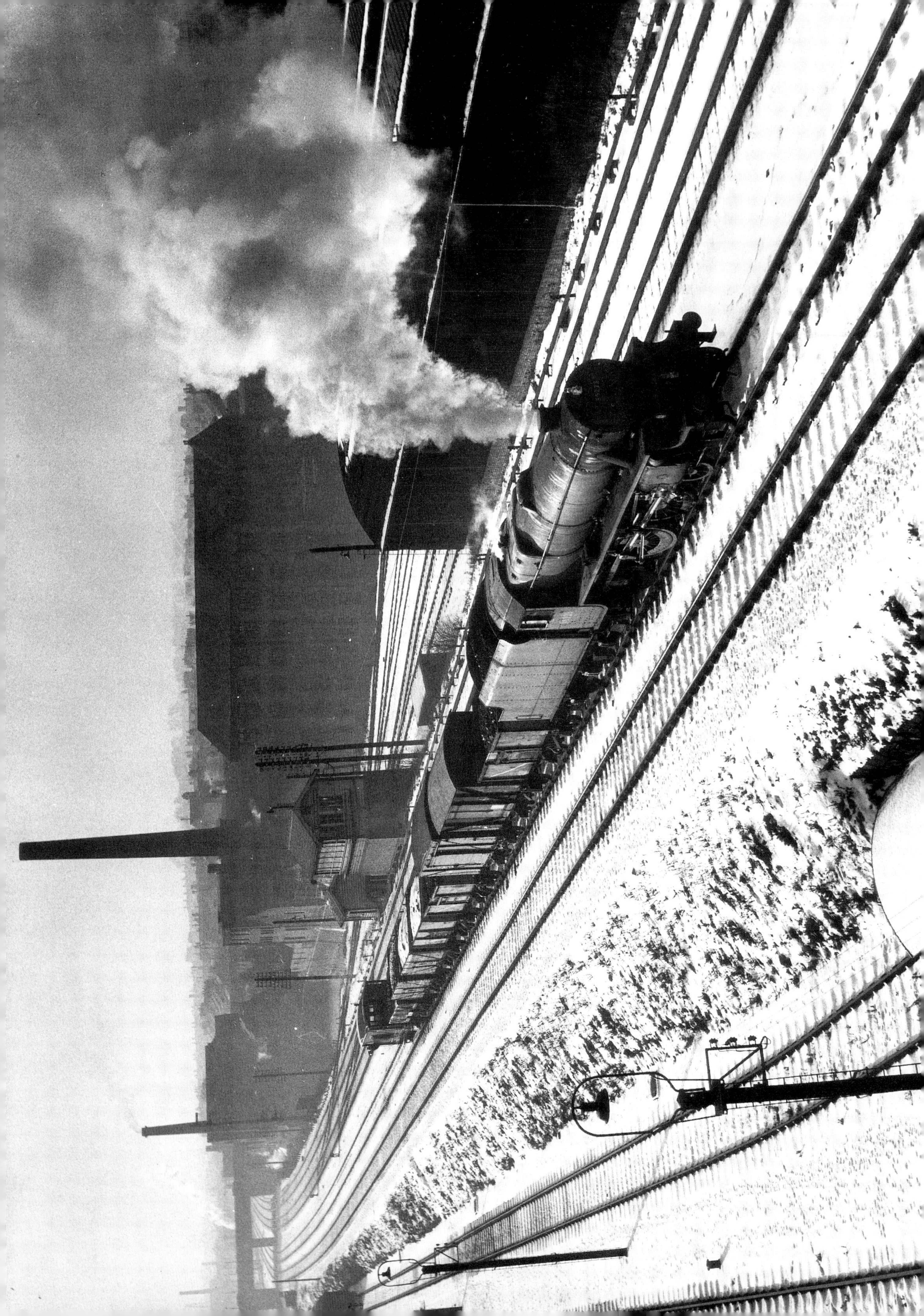

at Leicester North Goods with a short transfer freight on a day in January 1964 when the county was in the grip of a hoar frost.

205. In similar weather conditions but with the addition of quite dense, clinging fog a Stanier 8F No 48700 shunts wagons in the sidings at Whetstone. 25.2.63.

206. The same working provides employment for an 'Austerity' 2-8-0 which is seen shunting at Whetstone during a cold spell in February 1963. After the arrival of the 9Fs at Annesley it was not all that common to see

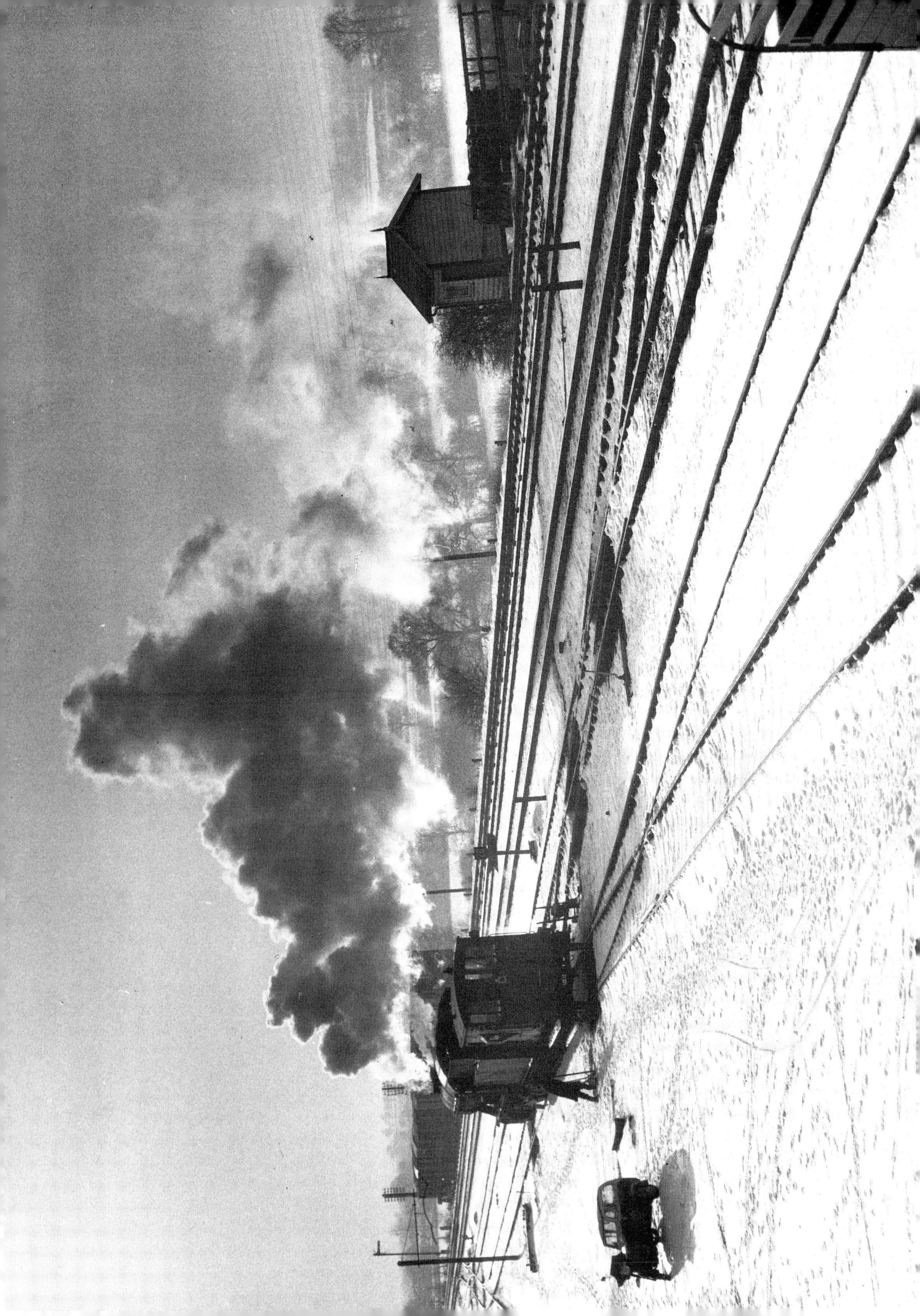

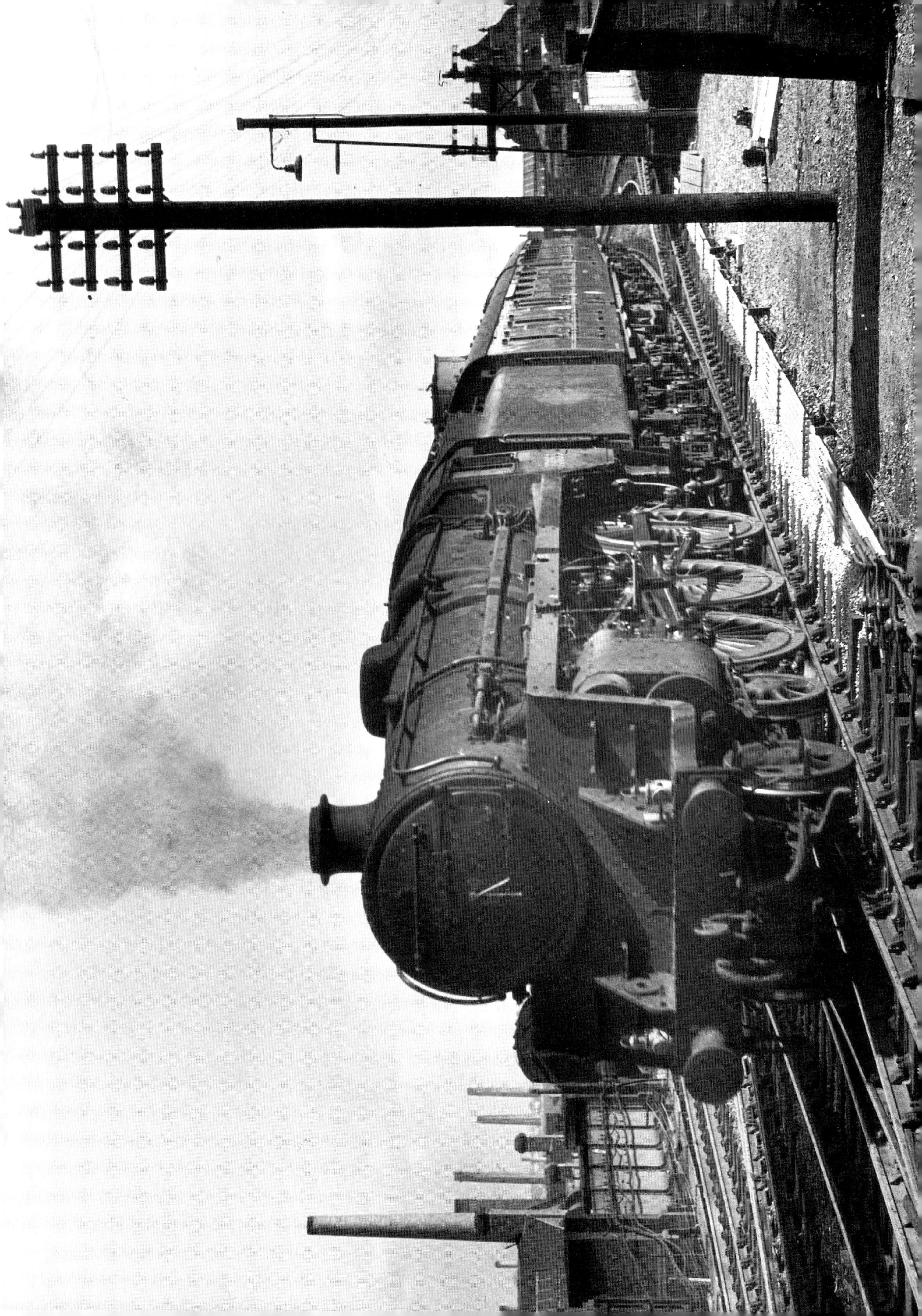

207. Following the withdrawal of the Marylebone expresses in January 1960 a deliberately unenterprising semi-fast service was introduced running between Marylebone and Nottingham. There were three trains in each direction each day calling at eight stations and initially an optimistic rake of seven coaches was provided with Stanier and Standard Class 5 haulage. In 1963 despite the much proclaimed dearth of servicing facilities the first down train from Marylebone and 12.25 pm return from Nottiingham was turned over to a four coach diesel set.
In this photograph Standard 5 No 73053 strikes off from Leicester Central with the 8.40 am up semi-fast from Nottingham Victoria to Marylebone June 1960

208. Stanier Class 5 No 44832 heads north from Rugby and approaches Shawell with the 12.25pm from Marylebone. 5.8.61.

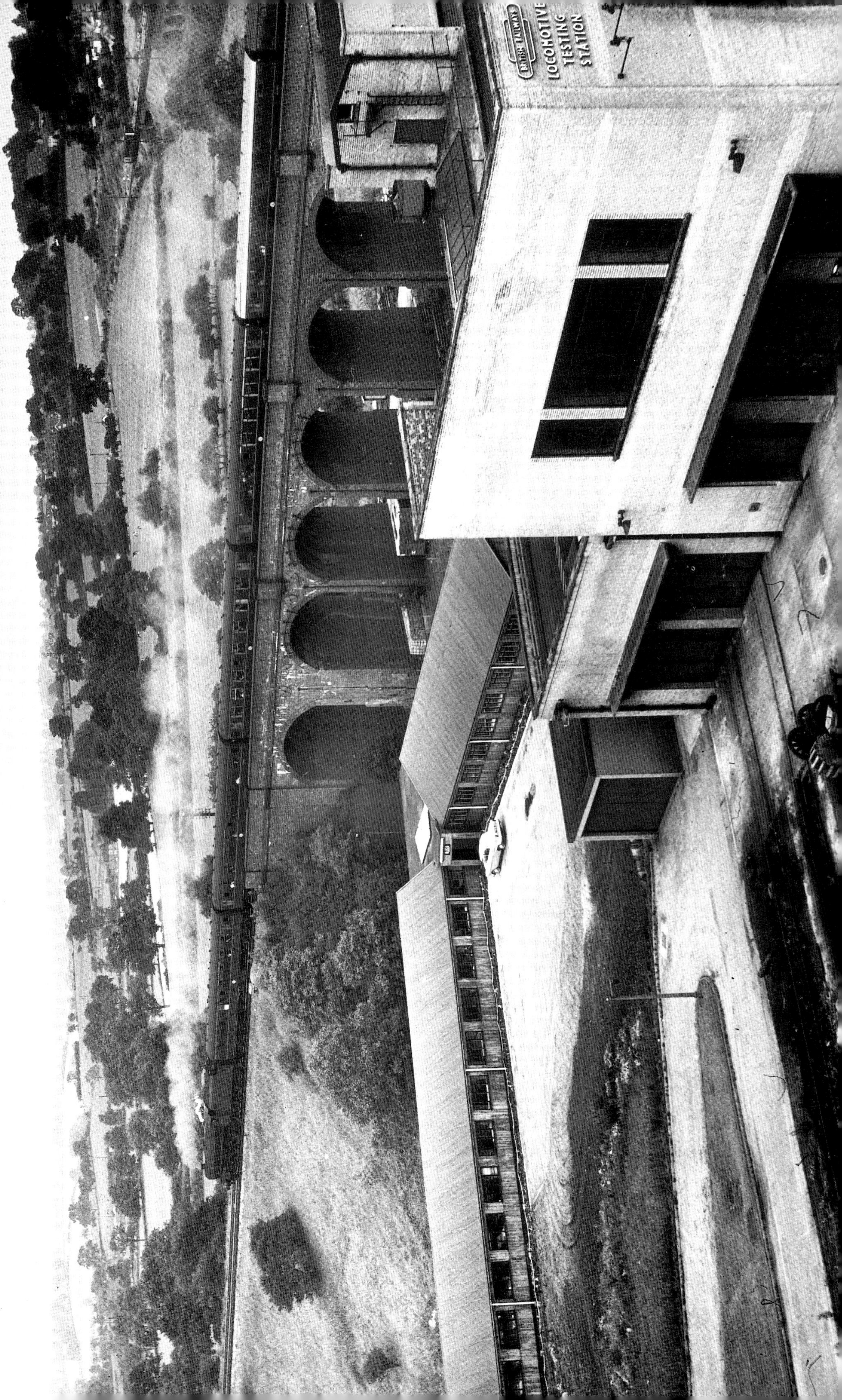
BRITISH RAILWAYS
LOCOMOTIVE
TESTING
STATION

short-lived locomotive testing station and beyond to the Great Central main line where a Stanier 'Black five' is seen crossing the Avon viaduct with the 2.38 pm from Marylebone to Nottingham. 17.8.63.

reservoir with the 2.38pm semi-fast from Marylebone to Nottingham. 11.6.63.

211. A panned shot of Stanier 'Black 5' No 45342 seen hurrying towards Birstall with

212. Standard 5 No 73011 passes Leicester South Goods with the 5.15 pm up semi-fast from Nottingham to Marylebone.

Following page.
Royal Scots.
213. A 'Royal Scot' No 46125, by now stripped of its nameplates, arrives in Woodford and is failed with injector trouble. Alongside stands the replacement engine Standard 5 No 73011 and behind it waiting for the road to Banbury is Western 2-8-0 No 3820 with an up freight. 16.5.64.

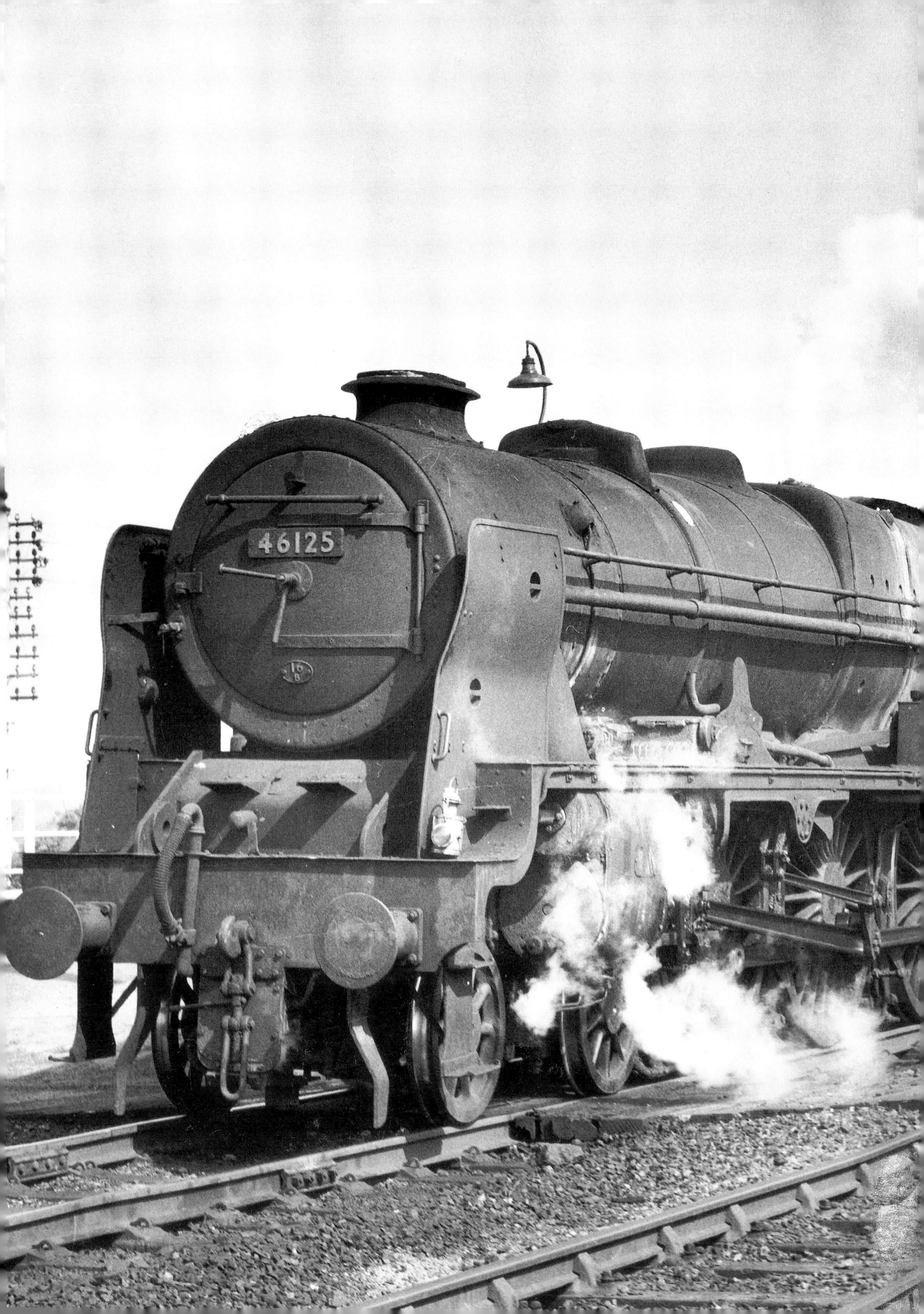
46125

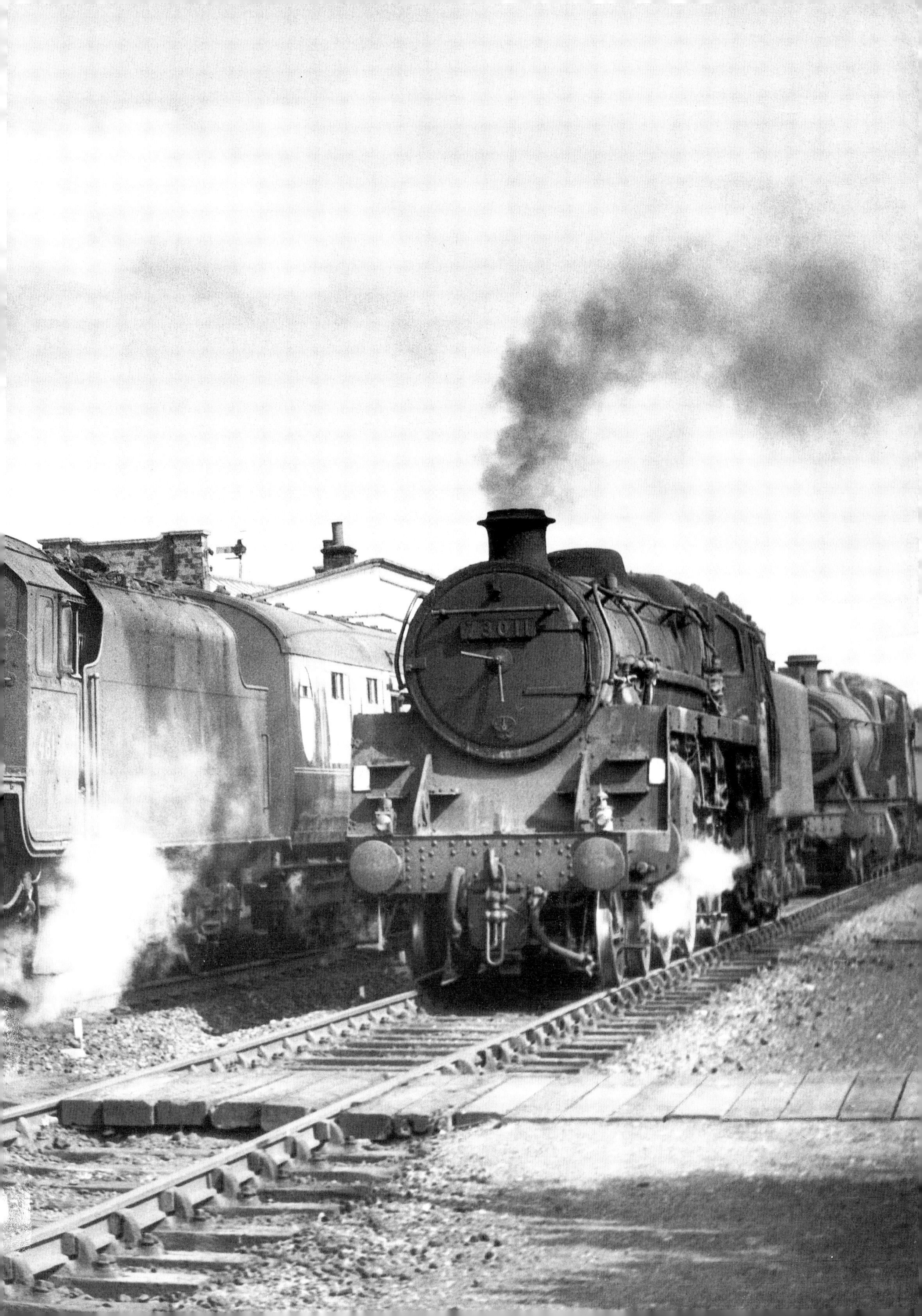

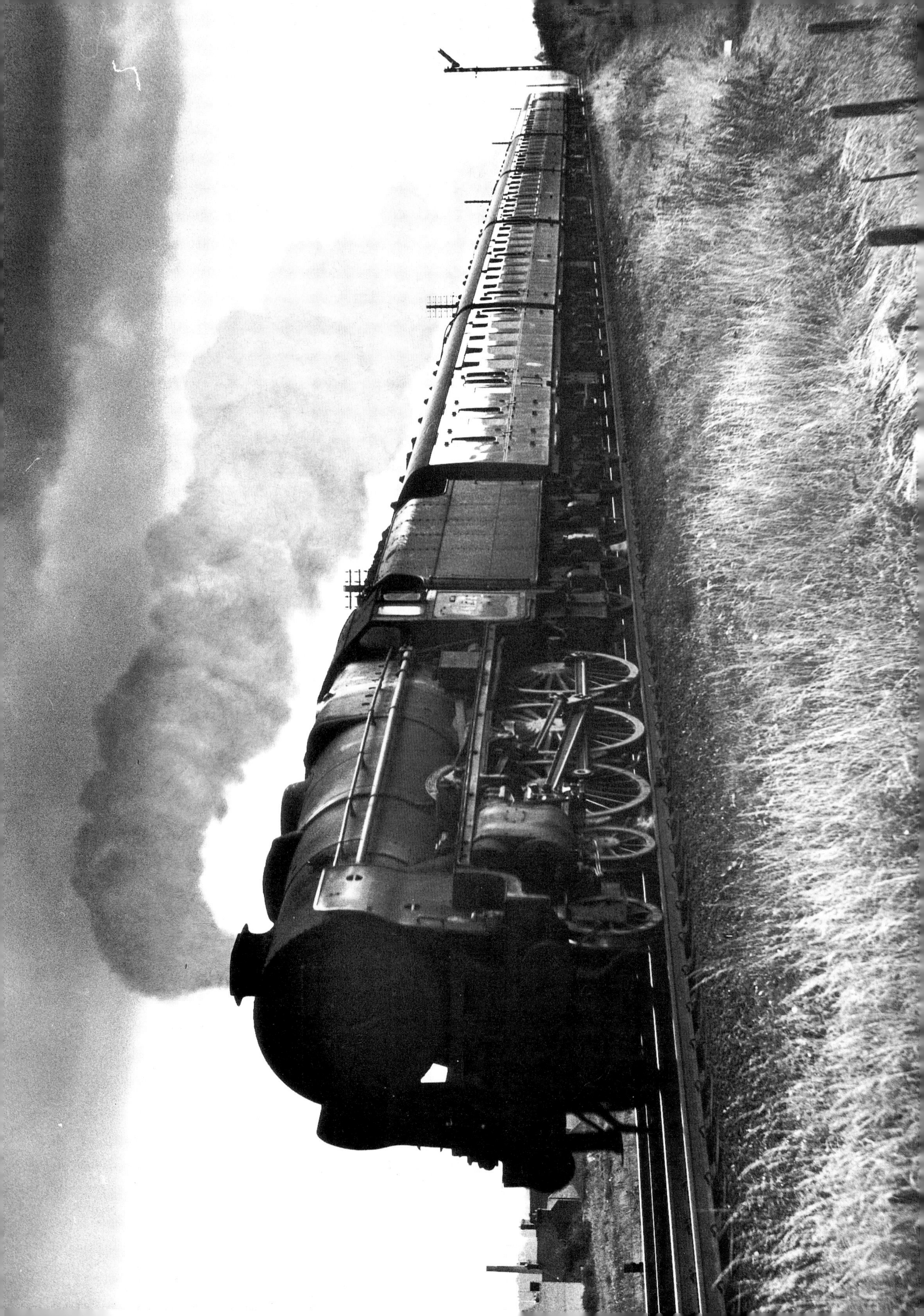

Leicester with the 5.15 pm semi-fast from Nottingham to Marylebone. This was the last up semi-fast of the day and was made up to 7 coaches to cope with the large number of commuters who used the train between Nottingham and Rugby. June 1963.

from Leicester and passes Beaumont Leys with the 4.38 pm down semi-fast from Marylebone to Nottingham.

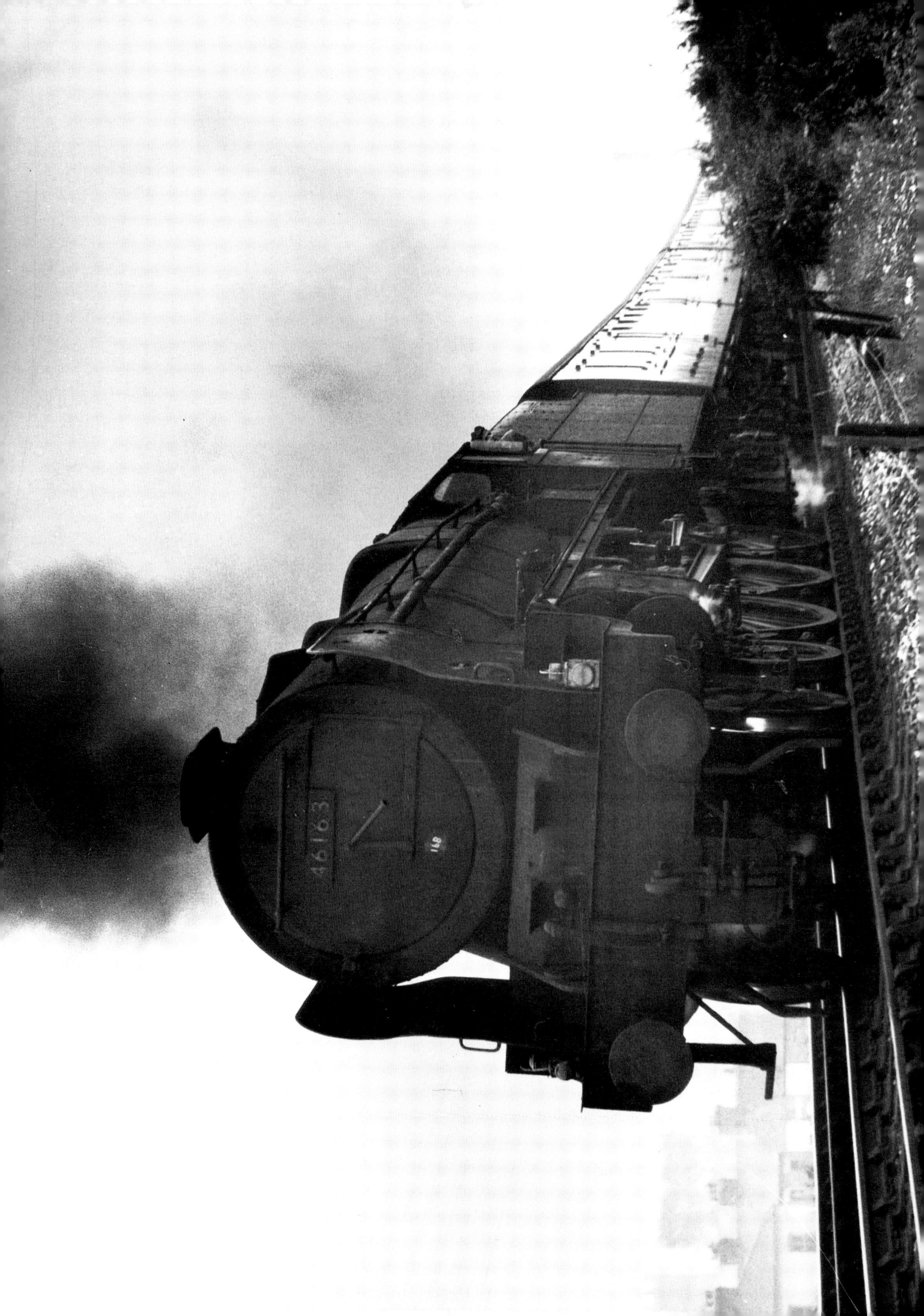
46163

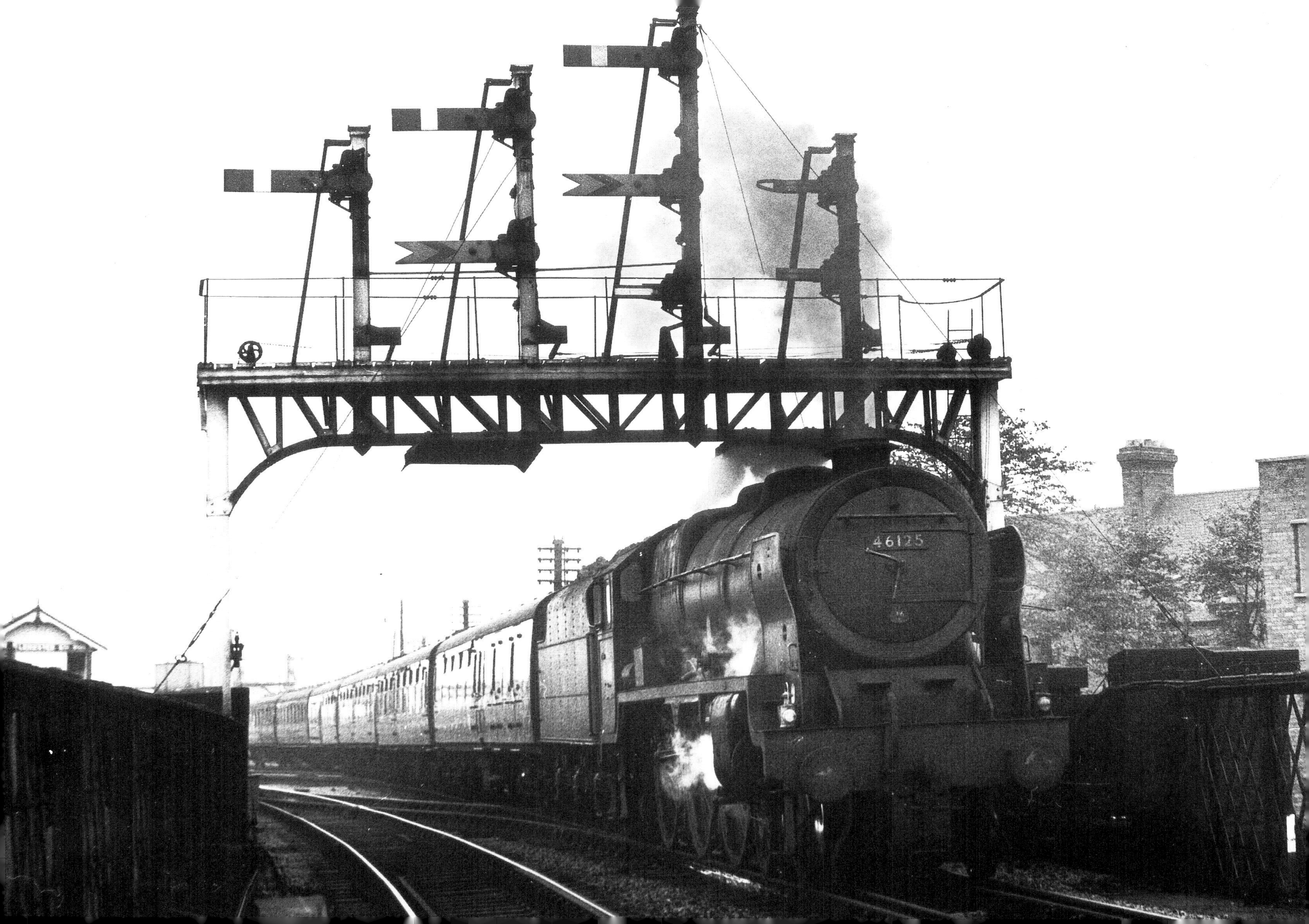
46125

Previous pages.
216. Passed Fireman Ron Cassie is in charge of 'Royal Scot' No 46163 'Civil Service Rifleman' on the 2.38 pm semi-fast from Marylebone to Nottingham. The train is seen approaching Abbey Lane on its way north from Leicester. The emission from the engine's chimney suggests that the old conspiracies continued to operate even after Ron had relinquished the shovel!

217. No 46125 '3rd Carabinier' crosses the West Bridge viaduct at Leicester with the 5.15 pm semi-fast from Nottingham to Marylebone.

218. No 46111 receives the wide-open regulator treatment from Annesley driver Lauriston Yates working the 5.15 pm up semi-fast from Nottingham Victoria to Marylebone. Though primarily reared in a freight train tradition, Annesley crews were not averse to running hard when the occasion demanded it and their sparkling experience with the 'windcutters' proved to be of enormous value when it came to 'changing hats' and working passenger trains.

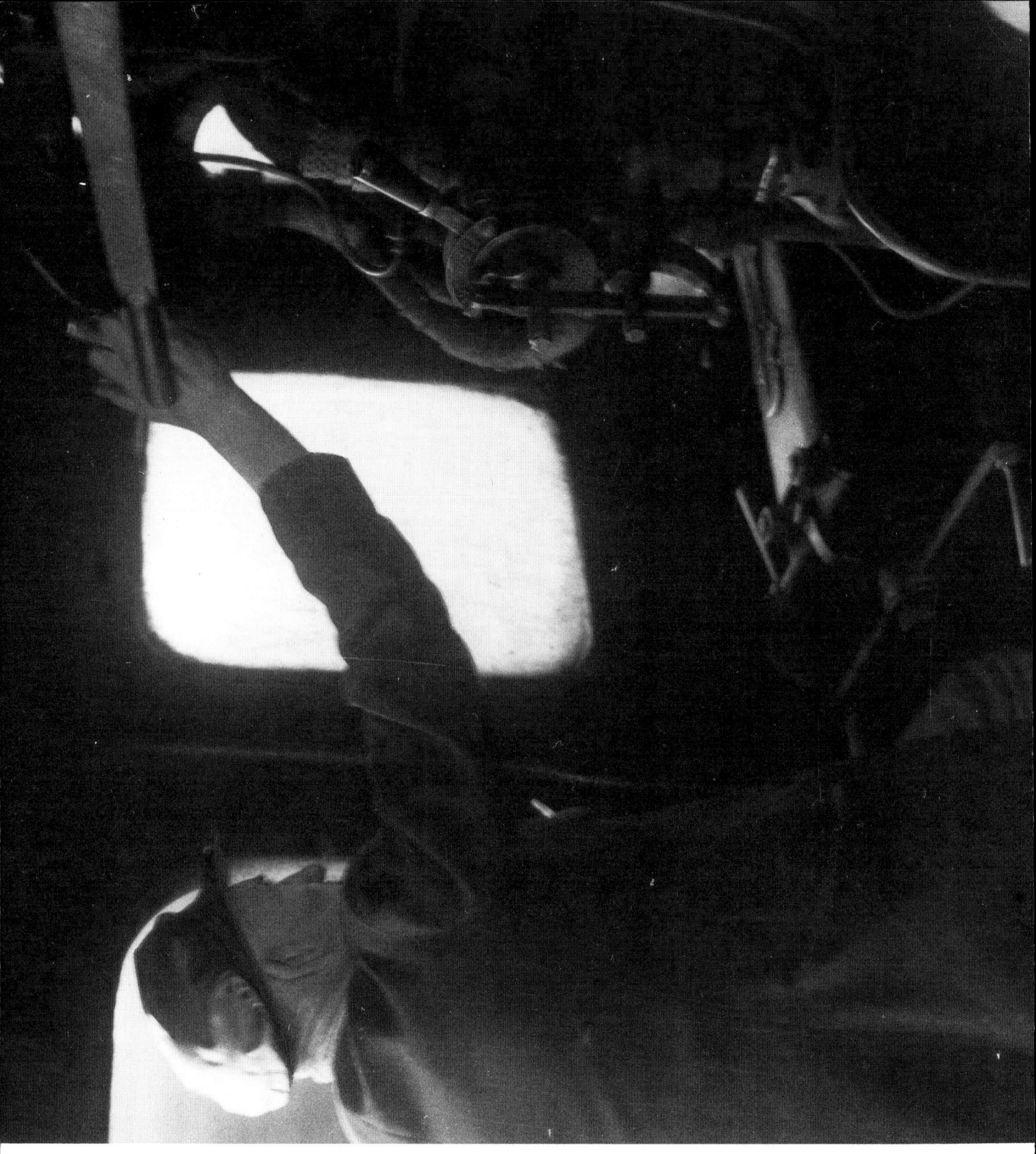

219. Driver Yates's fireman takes a brief rest from his labours with the shovel after No 46111 has called at East Leake.

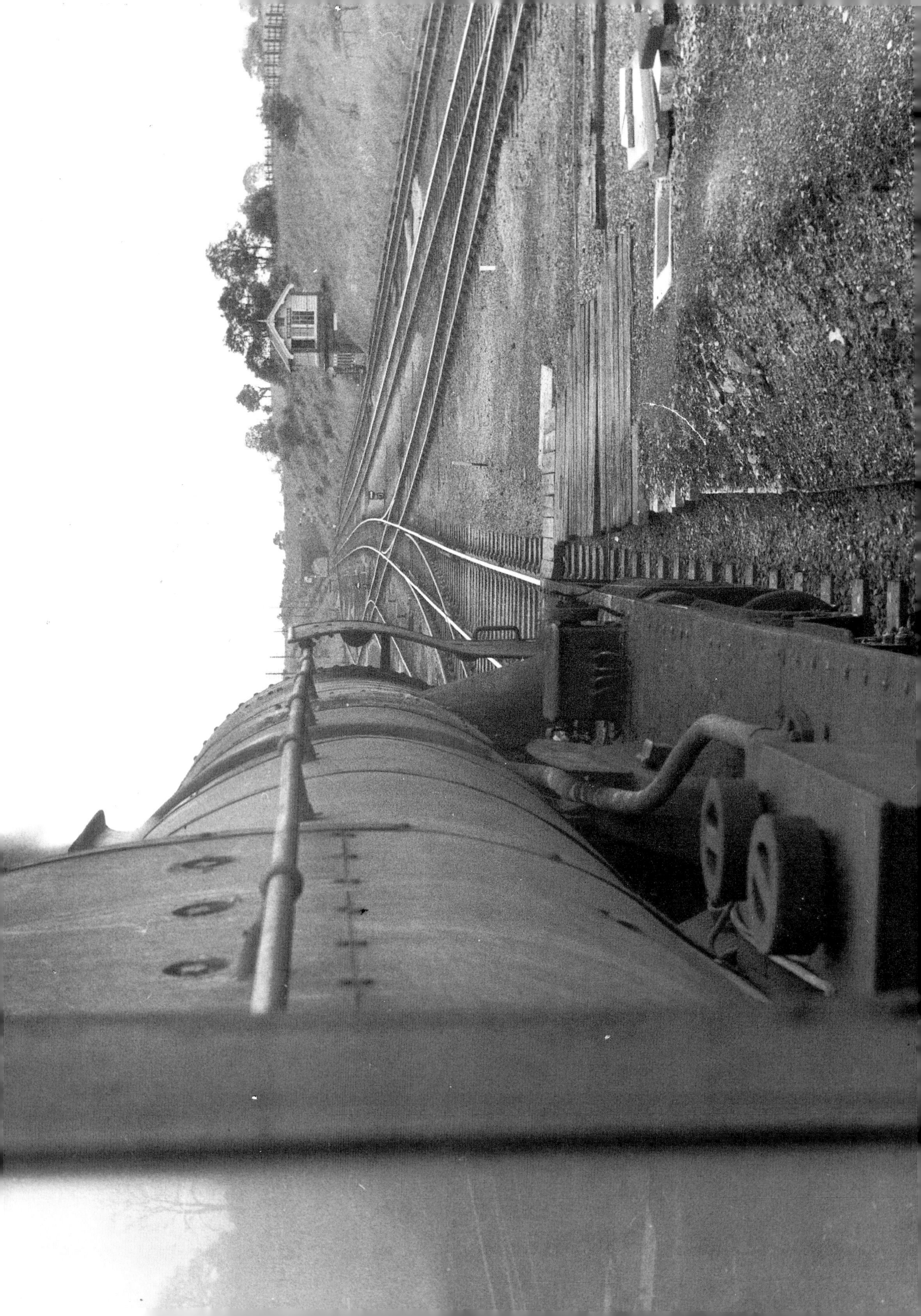

named 'The Ranger(12th London Regiment)' but now also stripped of its nameplates, moves out of Ashby Magna with the 5.15 pm semi-fast from Nottingham to Marylebone.

Central section enginemen as a symptom of the line's planned decline. Whenever the opportunity arose any V2 working in from York and the North Eastern Region would be 'hi-jacked' and have a trip stolen out of it on a semi-fast round trip. Approving memories lingered and were revived by such practices.

In this photograph No 60954 on its way back home hurries away from Leicester up the climb to Birstall with the 4.38 pm semi-fast from Marylebone to Nottingham. 15.6.63.

222. B1 4-6-0 No 61169 dashes into Leicester and approaches Abbey Lane with the

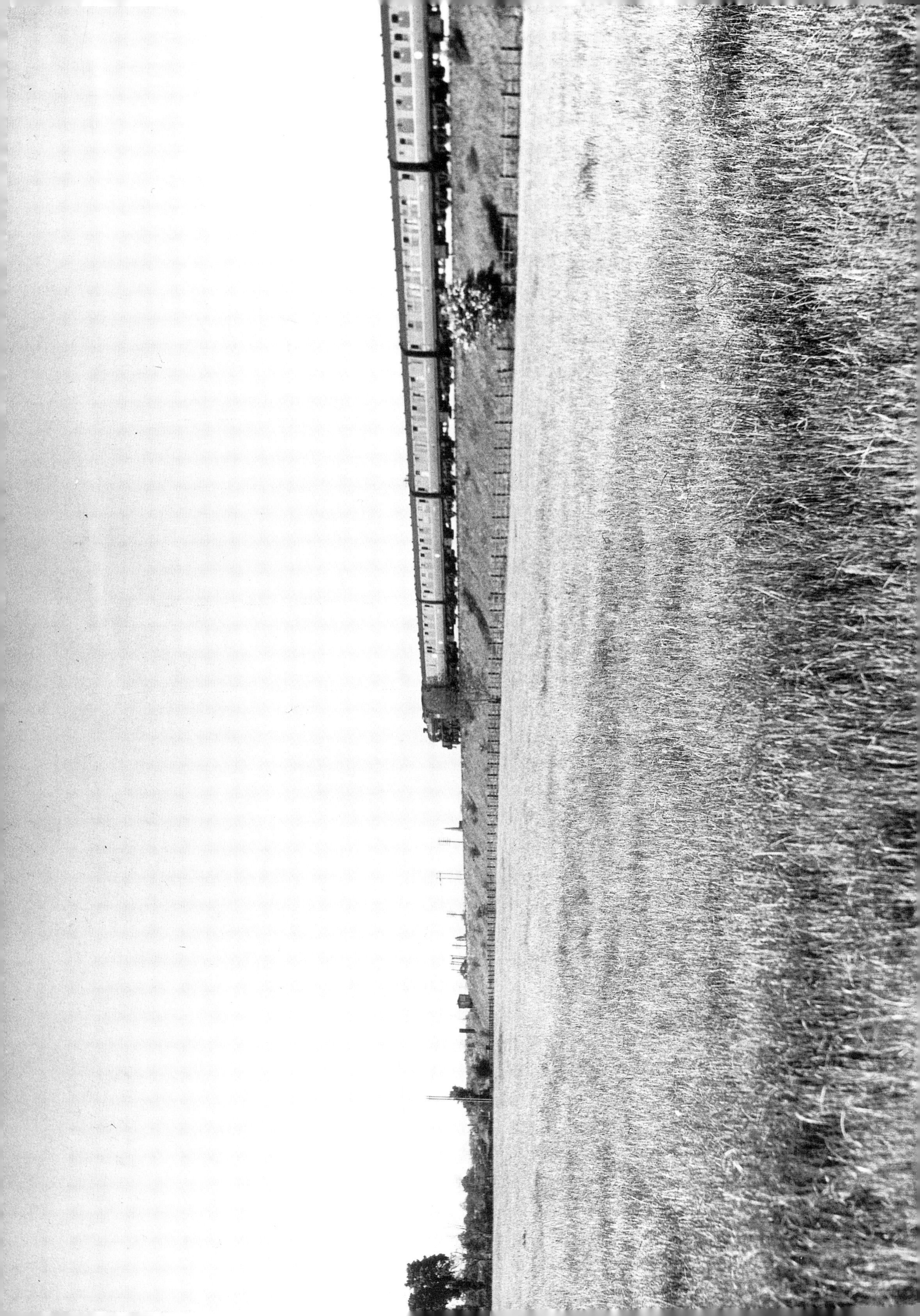

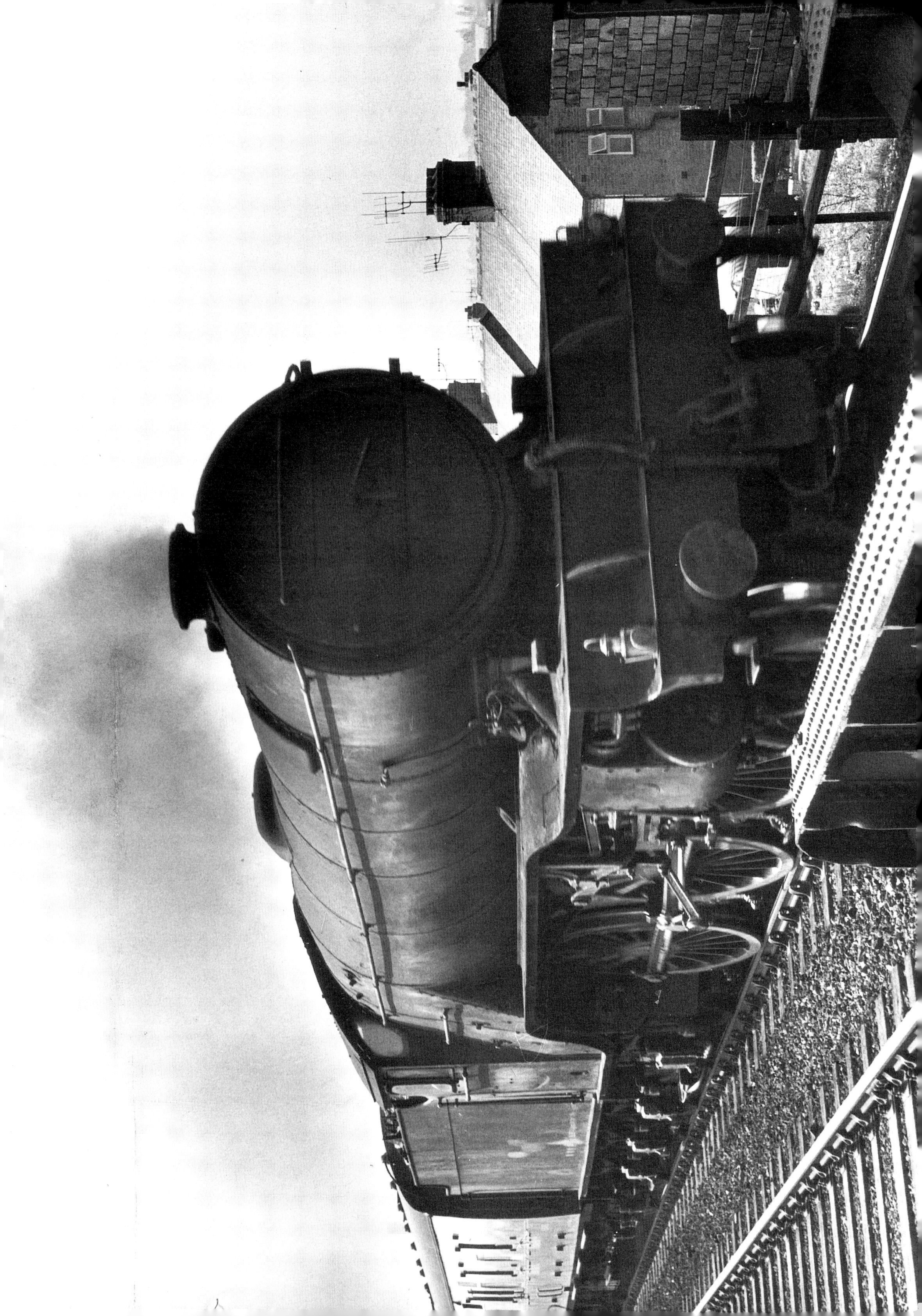

224. Another York V2 No 60864 is caught in close-up as it accelerates away from Leicester and nears Abbey Lane with the 4.38 pm down semi-fast from Marylebone to Nottingham. September 1963.

[illegible] down to Stanier Class 5 haulage in its final years. By now reduced to an absurd four coach formation the 8.15 am semi-fast from Nottingham to Marylebone is whisked up the 1 in 176 climb to Catesby tunnel by 'Black 5' No 44932. 9.5.64.

226. During the last year of the Great Central as a through route I was resident in Oxfordshire and was only able to make snap visits to the line usually at Brackley. Here a Stanier Class 5 with cylinder cocks open restarts the 5.15 pm semi-fast from Nottingham to Marylebone away from Brackley Central on a late Spring evening in 1965 before the removal of the station's loops and sidings.

227. No 44970 drifts into Brackley on a glorious summer evening in 1965 with the 4.38 pm from Marylebone to Nottingham.

Following page.
228. It is nearly midnight on Saturday, September 3rd 1966 and the air weighs heavy with memories as a Stanier Class 5 No 44858 stands quietly in the turntable siding at Nottingham Victoria. It is waiting to take over the night mail from York to Swindon which was the last up steam working over the Great Central before its closure north of Nottingham.

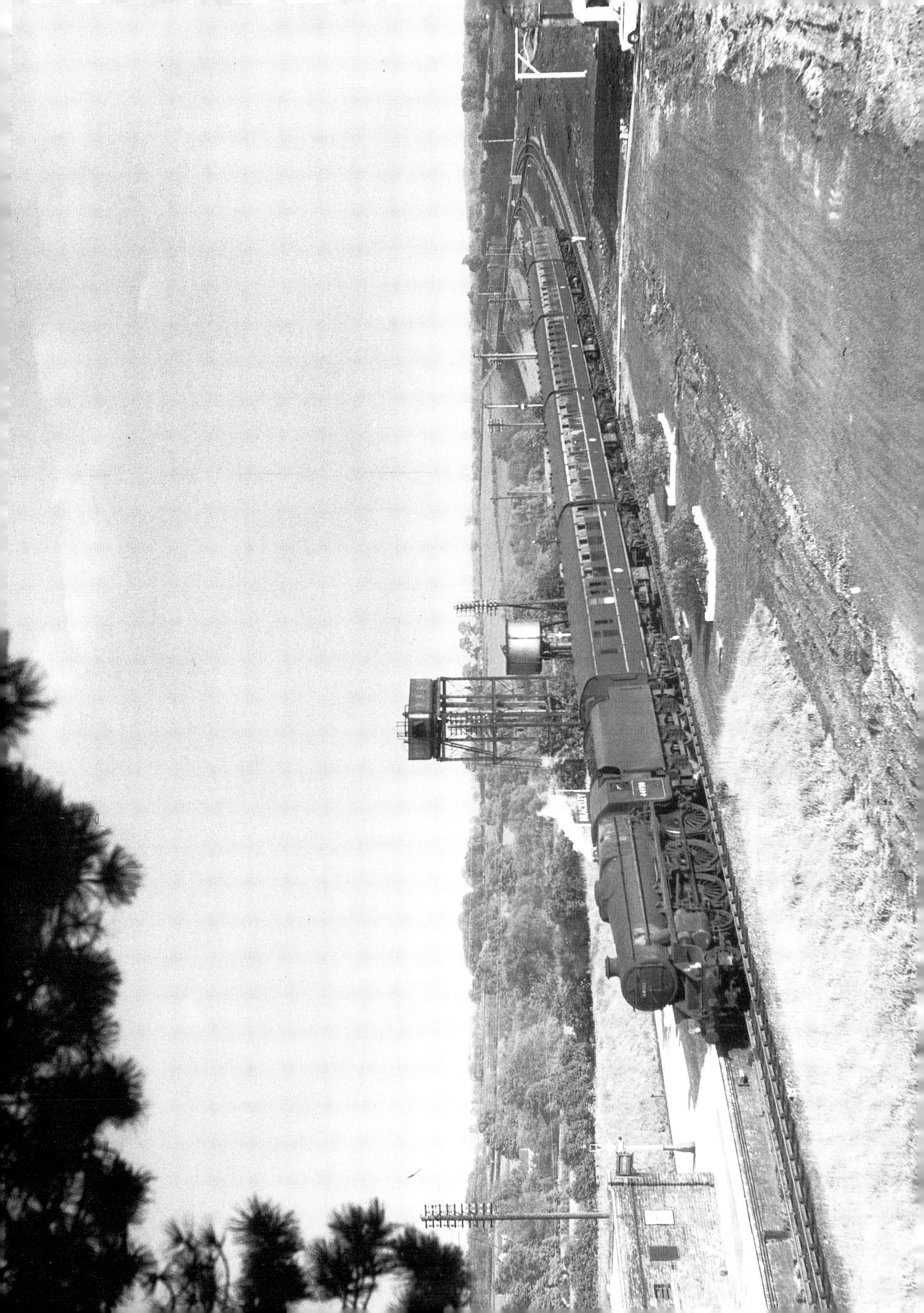

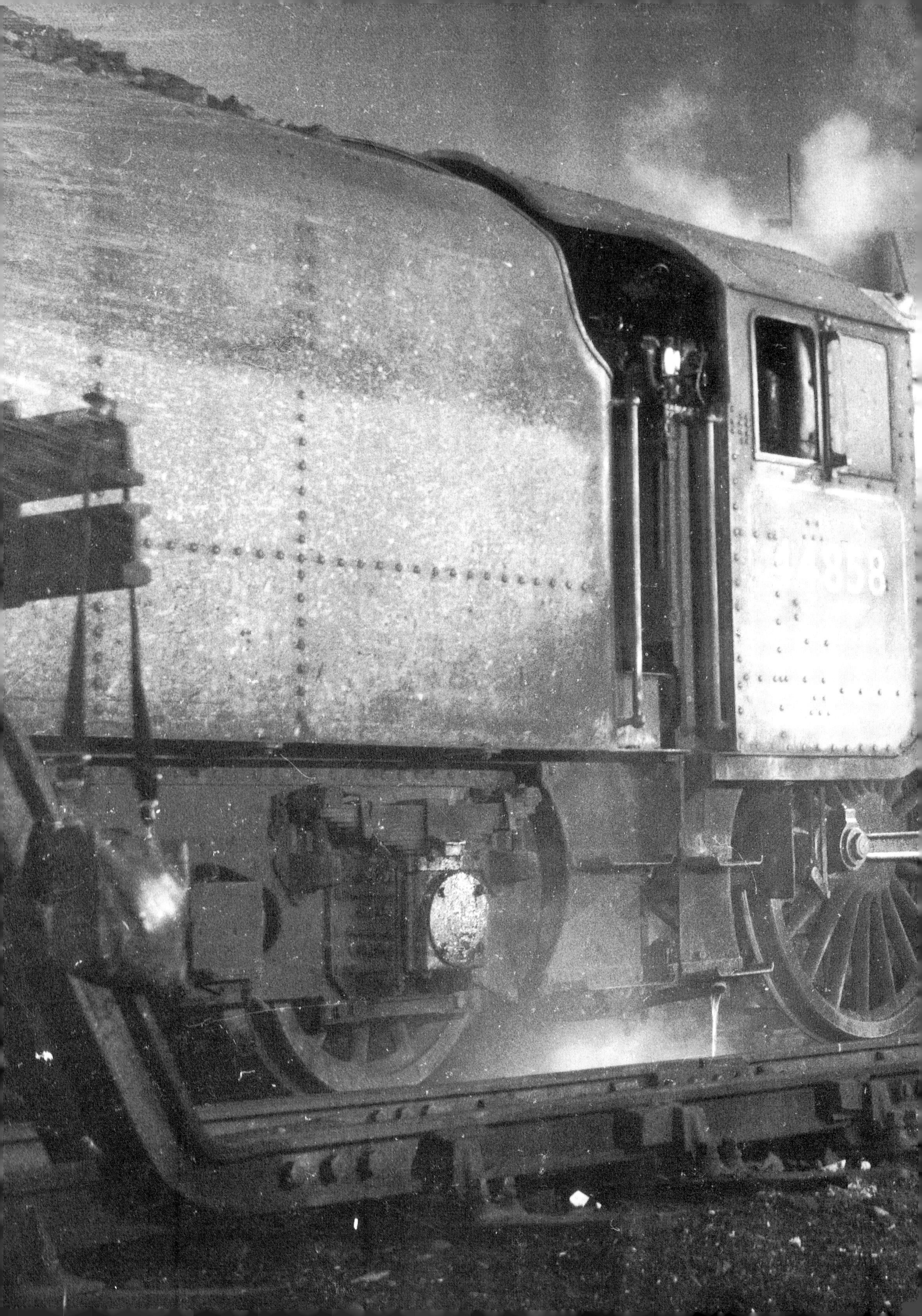

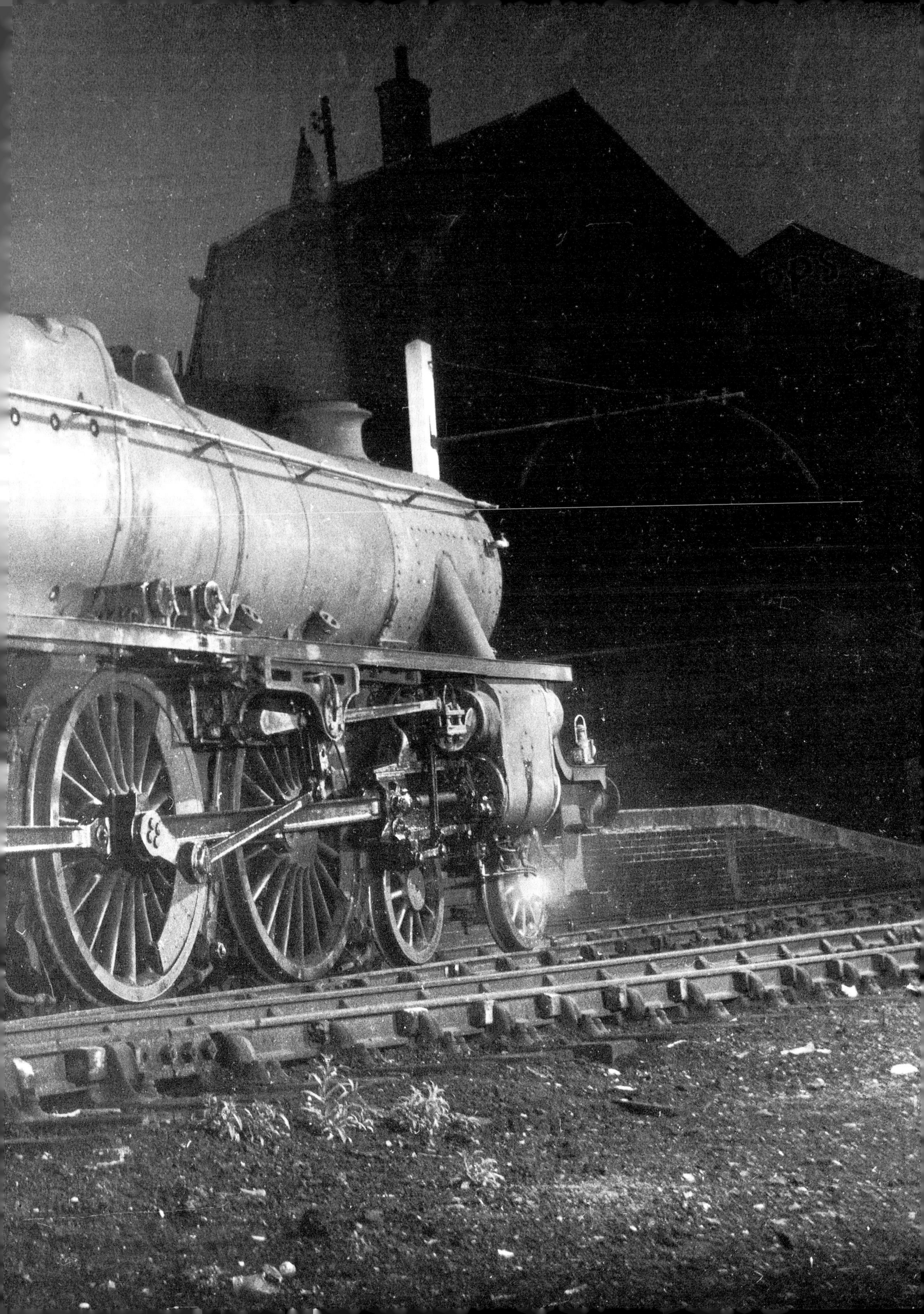

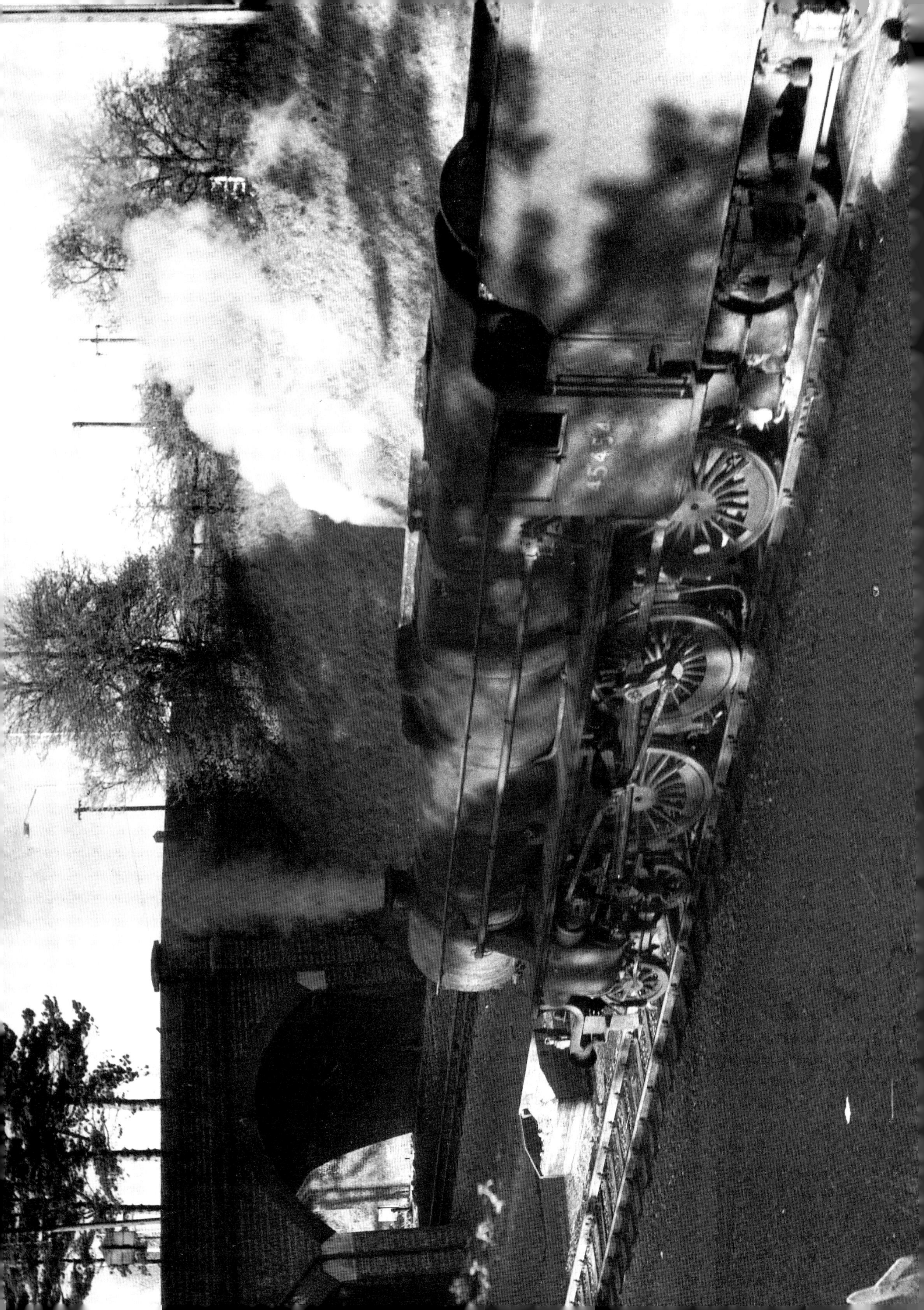
45454

230. No 44825 slips off steam as it passes Culworth Junction and prepares to stop at Brackley with the 4.38 pm down semi-fast from Marylebone to Nottingham.

231. No ———— during its stop at Woodford with the 2.38 pm semi-fast from Marylebone to Nottingham.

231. The semi-fast service is in its last month as another Stanier Class 5 hustles into Leicester over the West Bridge viaduct with the 2.38 pm from Marylebone to

232. All the sidings and loops at Brackley have been removed and the loading gauge left stranded in this

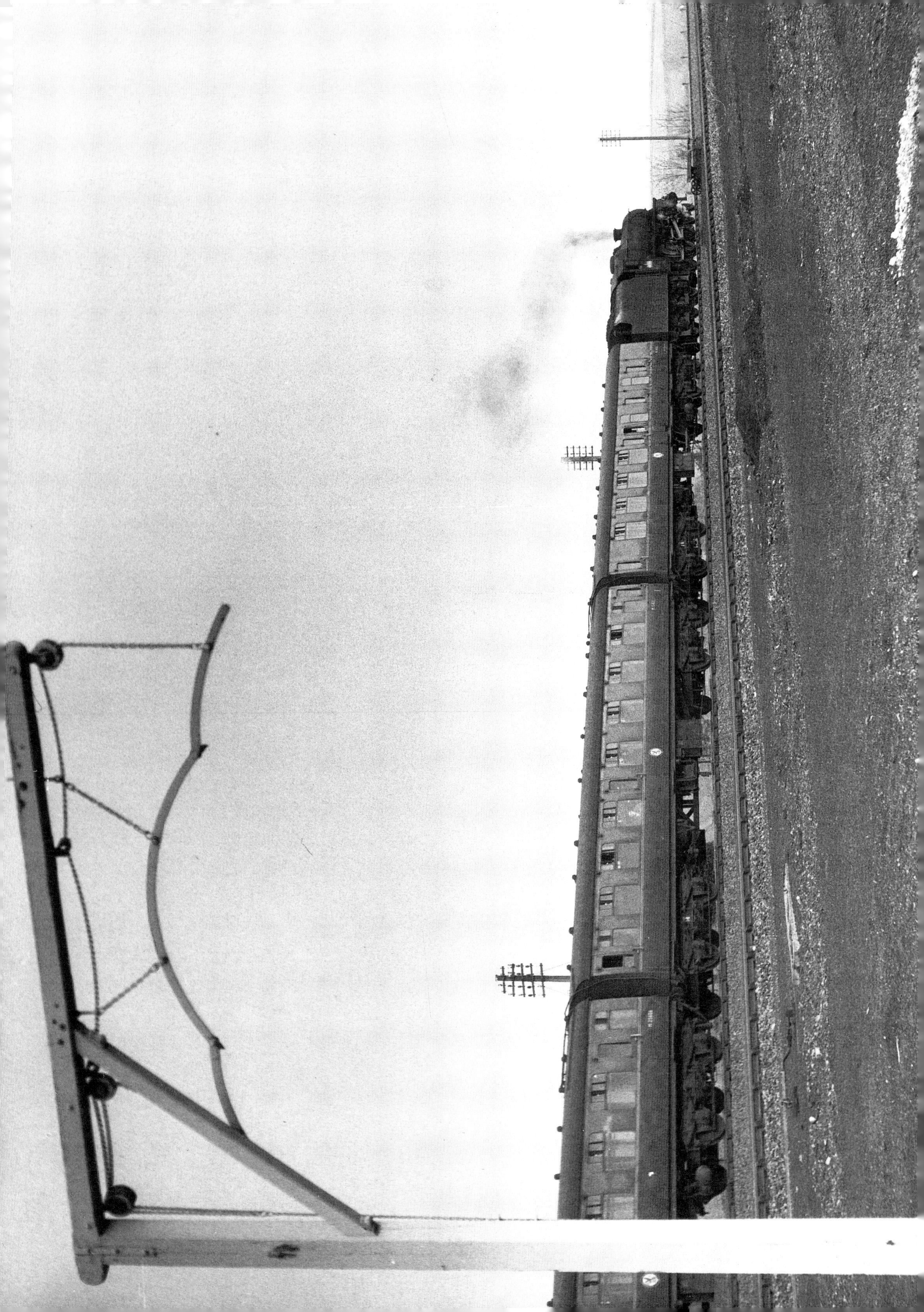

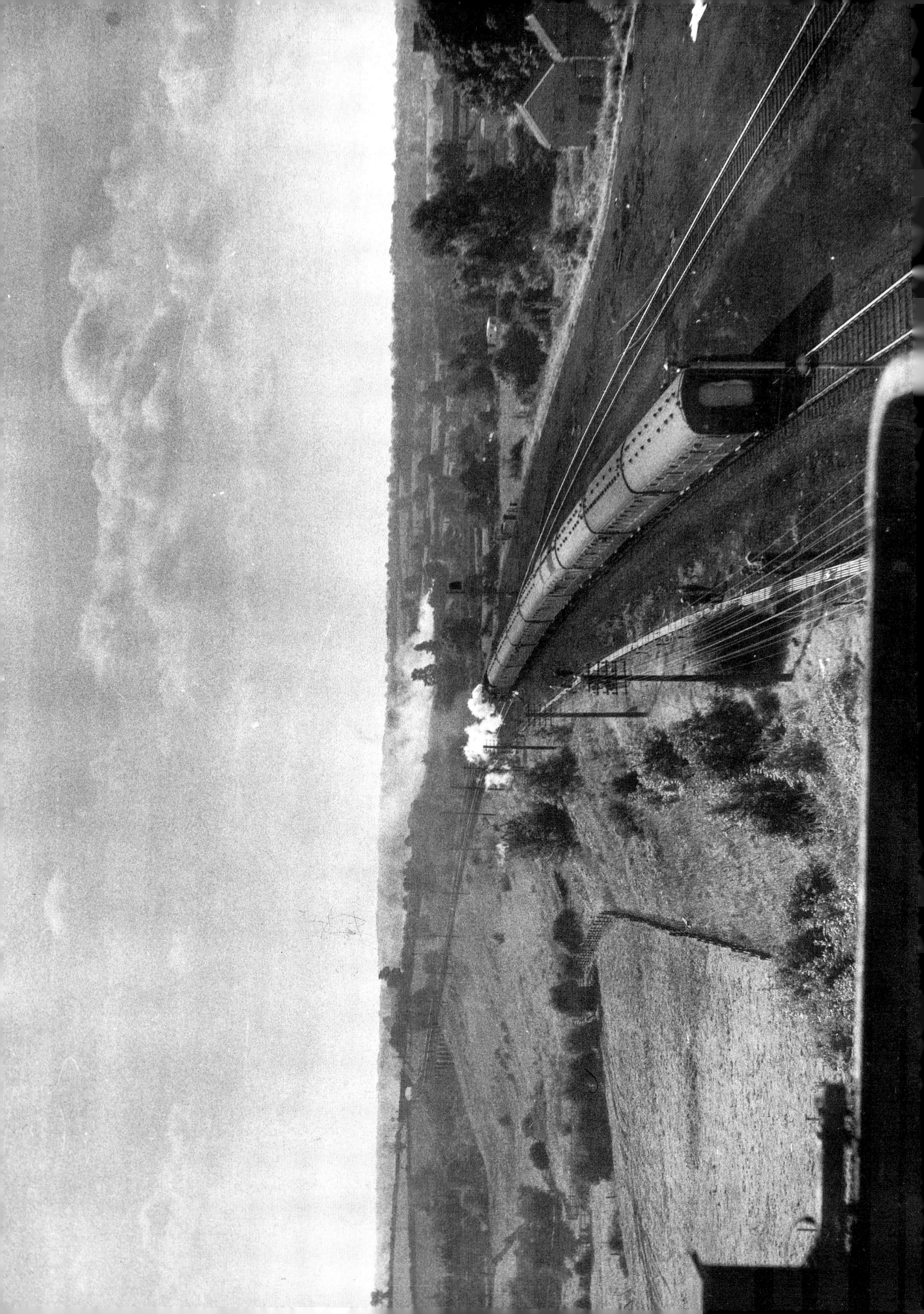

233. The 8.15 am up semi-fast from Nottingham to Marylebone was strengthened to eight coaches on the last day of the service on Saturday, September 3rd 1966. Stanier Class 5 No 44872 was late and struggling as it left Brackley for Aylesbury where it failed and was removed from the train which eventually arrived in Marylebone behind a Class 24 diesel. This shot of No 44872's departure from Brackley was taken from the top of the station water tower. 3.9.66

234. The big 'Royal Scots' were not employed specifically on the semi-fast trains for which they were grossly overpowered. A more appropriate duty was the haulage of the heavy overnight sleepers that were temporarily diverted to Marylebone during the electrification and modernisation of Euston station. However, even on these trains they did not always cover themselves with glory and failures were not uncommon. Here, in a deplorable condition No 46163 stands under the Rossmore Road bridge at Marylebone ready to leave with the 11.45pm sleeper to Manchester.

235. No 46163's crew that night were Leicester driver George Evinson and his fireman John Barrow who both nearly needed retinal treatment after a flashbulb was discharged in their faces at rather close range.

Special traffic.
236. Pigeon Special. Another lucrative traffic to desert the railway was that provided by the racing pigeon fraternity which would sometimes book and fill a whole train with baskets of birds which would be taken to a distant venue where they would be released by station staff at an arranged time. A Doncaster B1 No 61329 stands in Banbury station with a return pigeon special from South Yorkshire.

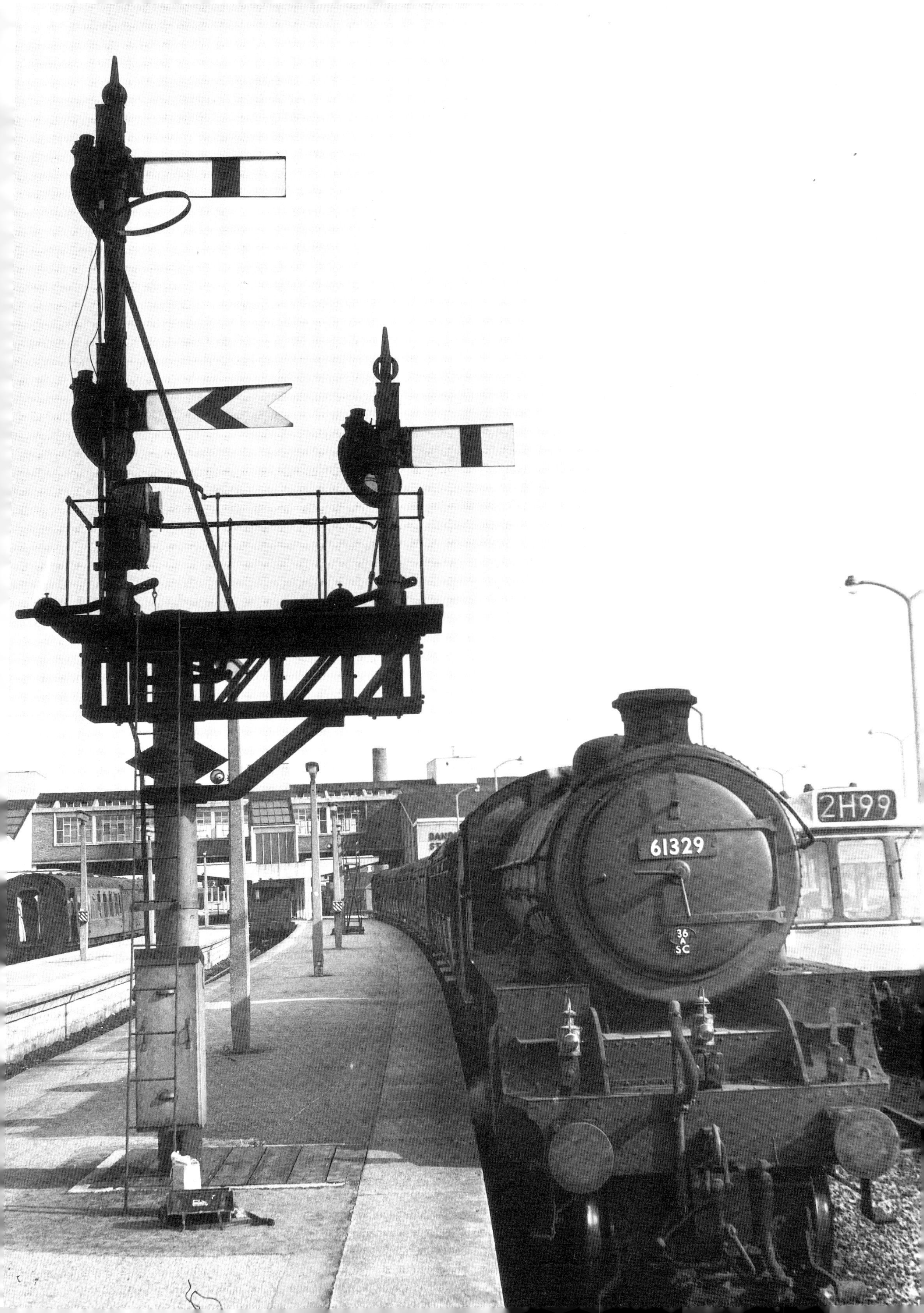
61329
2H99

237. In 1961 Leicester City football club reached the cup final and a number of Wembley specials were run over both the Midland and Great Central routes. Following the take-over by the London Midland Region and the withdrawal of the expresses the number of big engines worthy of such a prestigious duty on the Great Central line had shrunk to just one V2. A temporary injection of 'loaned' engines was therefore made in the shape of 'Royal Scots' and rebuilt 'Patriot' 4-6-0s. After a vigorous application of spit and polish they made a fine spectacle.

In this photograph rebuilt 'Patriot' No 45532 'Illustrious' pulls out over the West Bridge viaduct at Leicester with the last of the specials for London, which was 3 feet-<!--illegible-->

238. Another rebuilt 'Patriot' No 45540 'Sir Robert Turnbull' was used as a reserve to cover any failure and was therefore not accorded such generous attention with the cleaning rags. While the procession of specials set out from Leicester Central No 45540 was kept in the engine siding beside the station where Passed Fireman Ron Cassie had charge of it. 'You're not going to take a photograph of this thing are you?' was his reaction to my preparations with the camera. No 45540 was later given a trip to Banbury on the York-Bournemouth. 6.5.61.

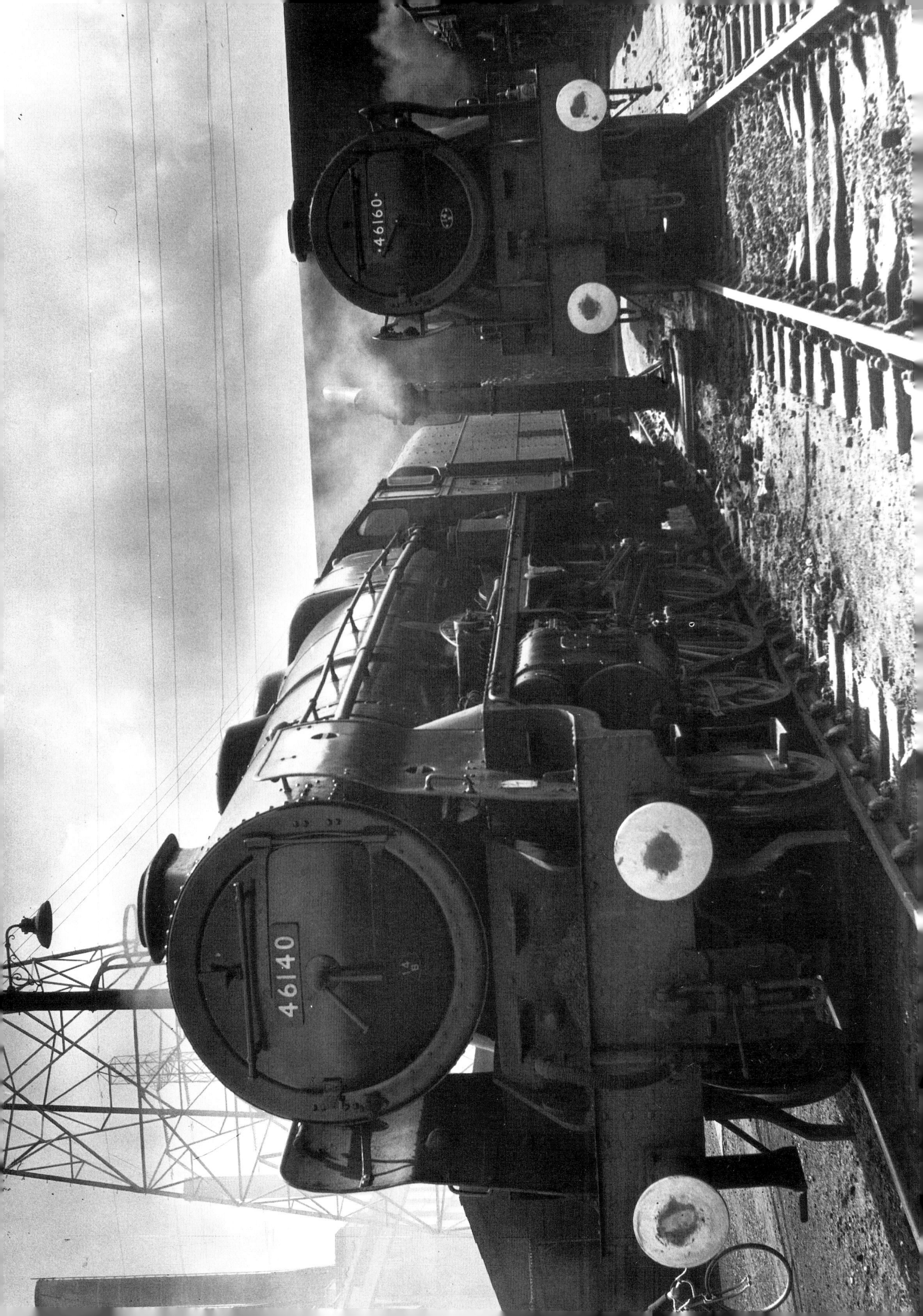
46140
46160

Scots' Nos 46140 'The King's Royal Rifle Corps' and 46160 'Queen Victoria's Rifleman' are still in showman's condition apart from the removal of some silver paint from their buffers. 7.5.61.

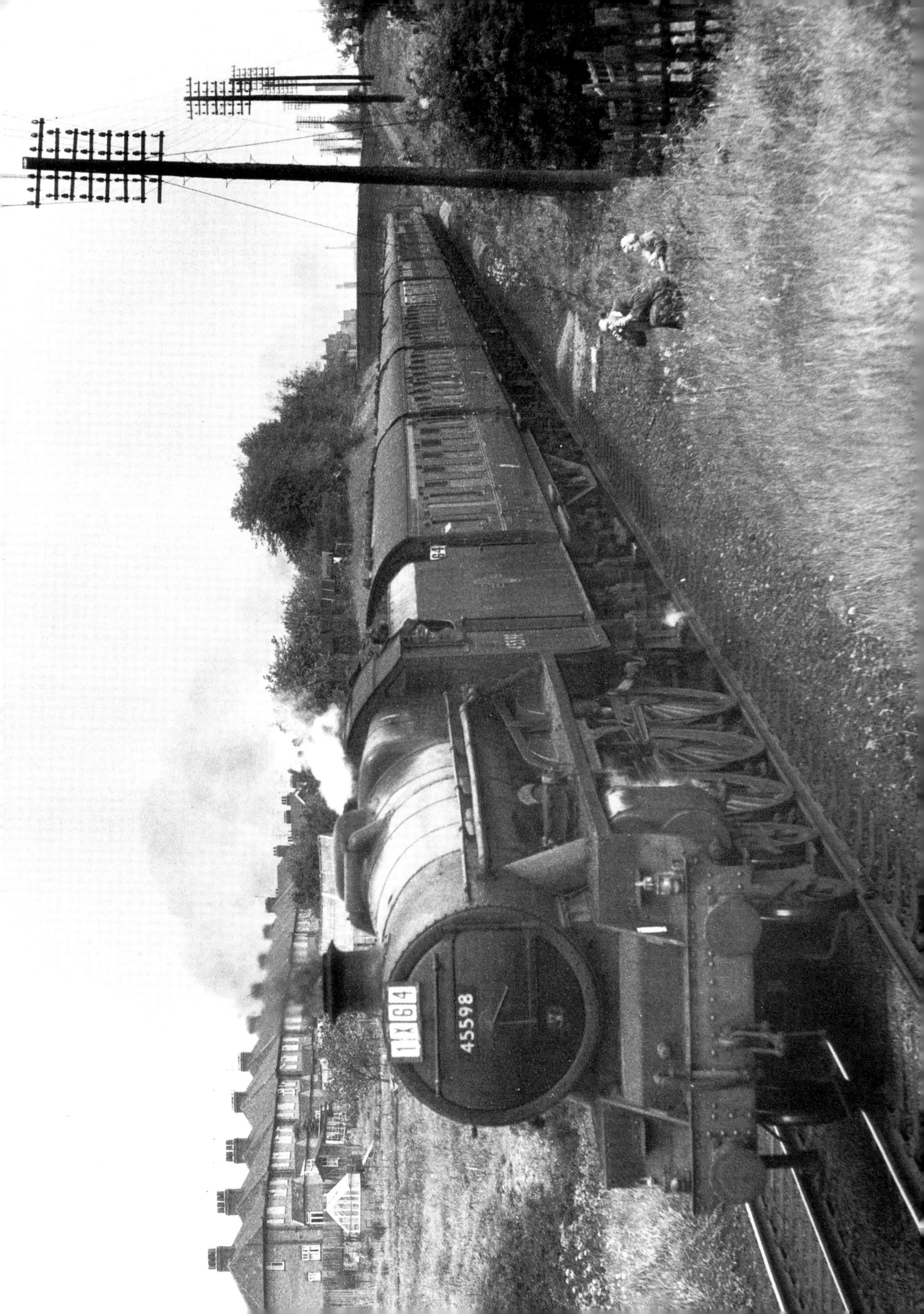
45598

241. ...'ceremonial' steam locomotives meant scraping the barrel. In the event some remnants of the London Midland 'Jubilee' class 4-6-0s were taken out of store and dusted down for the occasion. One of them was No 45598 'Basutoland' which worked a First Class only special to Wembley Hill at 11.45 am from Leicester Central. It is seen near Rowley Fields on its way out of Leicester. 25.5.63.

242. Later the same day a return Football special bound for Sheffield passes Shawell headed by English Electric Type 3 diesel No D 8015.

243. An unscheduled Saturday six coach special hauled by a Crewe Class 5 No 44714 hurries past Aylestone Fields on its way up the Great Central main line on 8th

244. Works Outing 1957. A Colwick B1 No 61088 sets out from Leicester Central with a special train to London organised for employees of the Bentley Engineering Company which was a long-established local firm manufacturing high quality machines for the hosiery industry including the famous 'Komet' range of knitters. As with so much manufacturing industry in Leicester

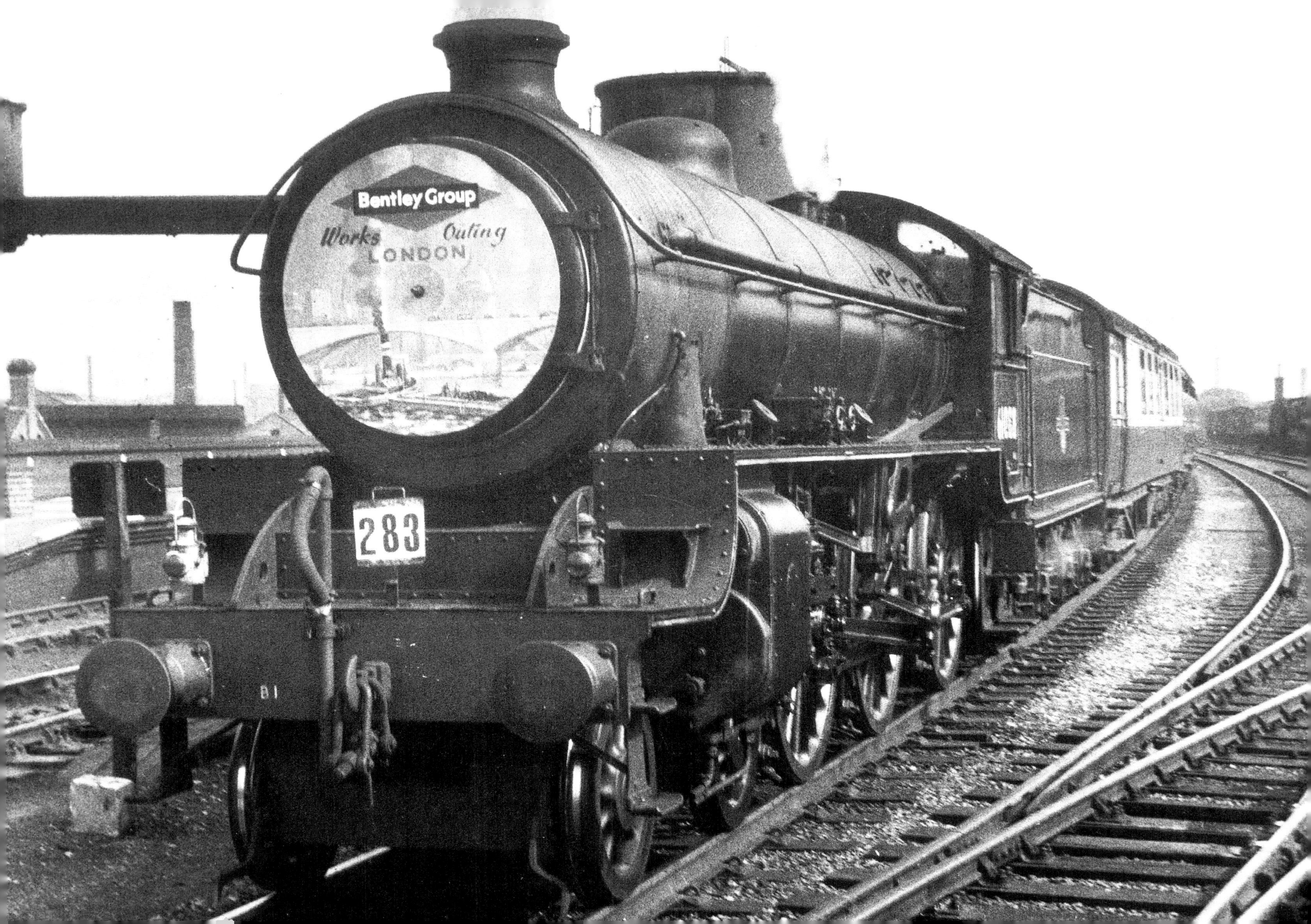
Bentley Group
Works Outing
LONDON
283
B1

245. Another Wembley special from Nottingham passes Whetstone on 25th May 1963 with Stanier Class 5 No 45334 in charge.

Enthusiast Specials.
246. Alan Pegler's recently restored A3 No 4472 'Flying Scotsman' passes Weekday Cross Junction at Nottingham with a Railway Preservation Society special to Marylebone in June 1963.

SIMMONS
EMBROIDERER
WHELDON
GREAT CENTRAL
No
4472
DONCASTER

247. Another Great Central line farewell special that was worked by 'Flying Scotsman' was the SLS/MLS rail tour from Manchester to London via High Wycombe on April 18th 1964. In this photograph No 4472 arrives at Leicester South Goods and stops for a crew change, water and a brake inspection.

248. Earlier in the month on April 7th a rail tour from Paddington to Doncaster brought Western Region 'Castle' No 7029 'Clun Castle' to Leicester Central where it changed engines with 'Royal Scot' No 46143 'The South Staffordshire Regiment' which was given a clean for the occasion. The 'Scot' is seen climbing away from Leicester past Beaumont Leys on its way north. The local Locomotive Society Page B-----

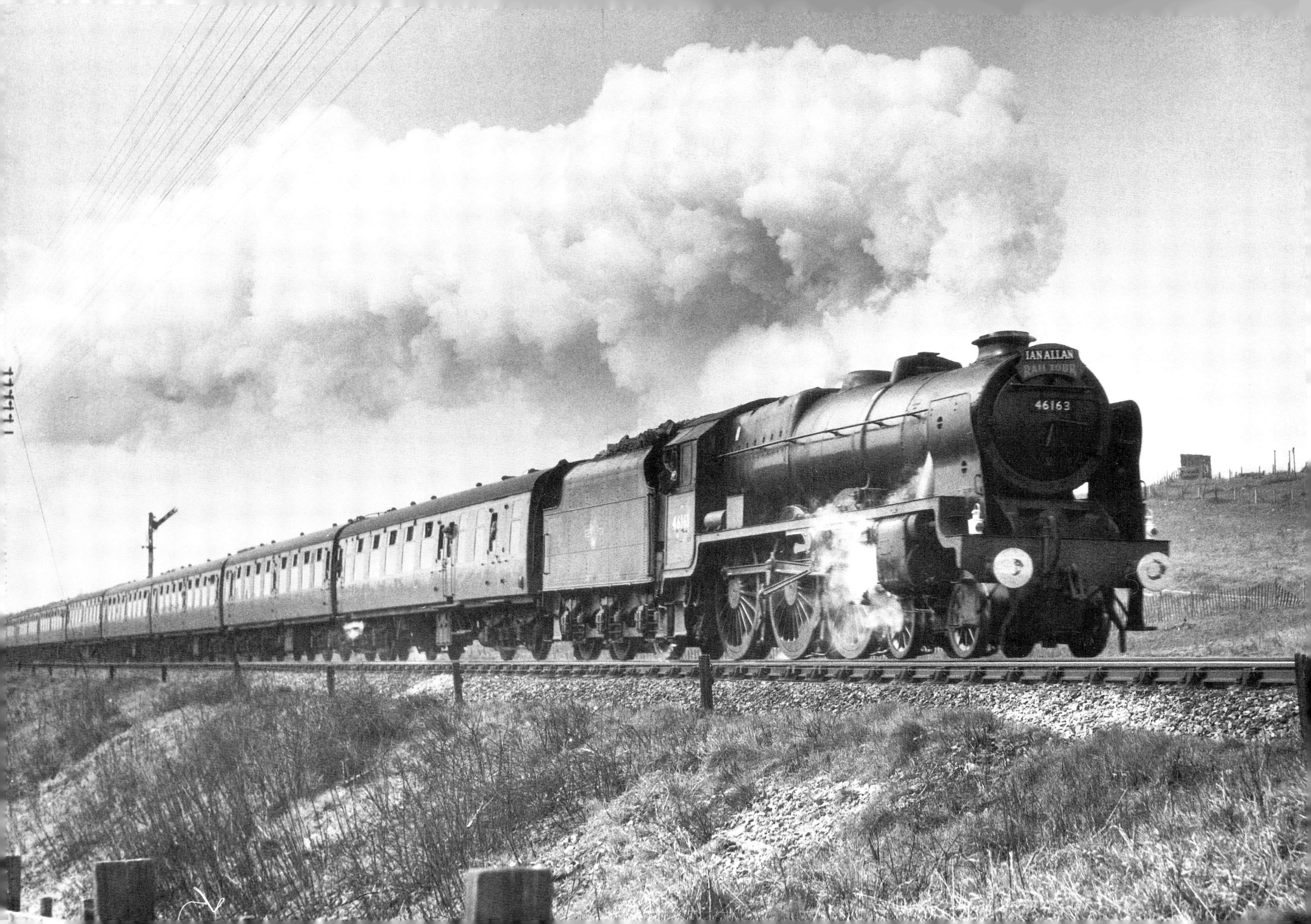
IAN ALLAN
46163

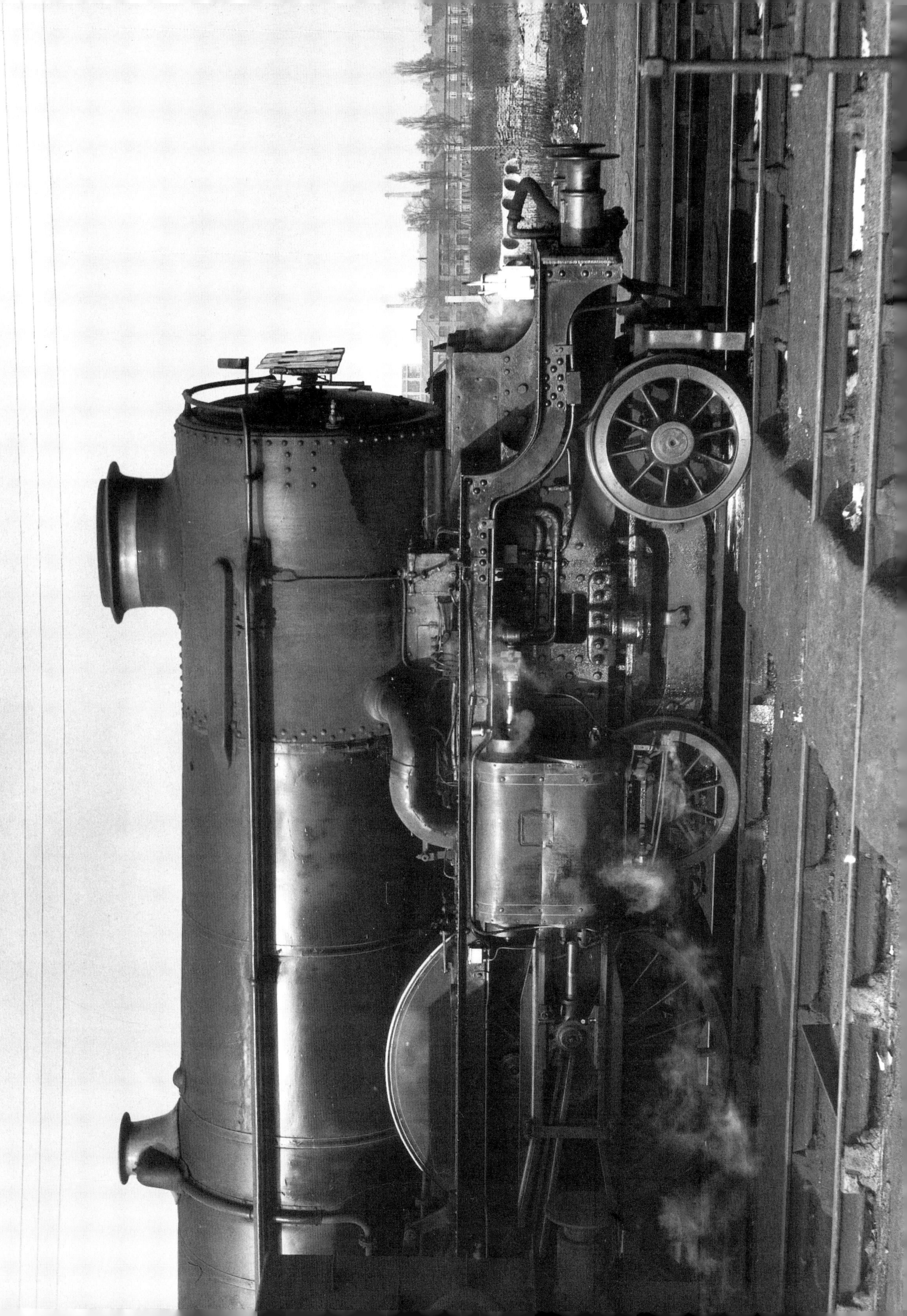

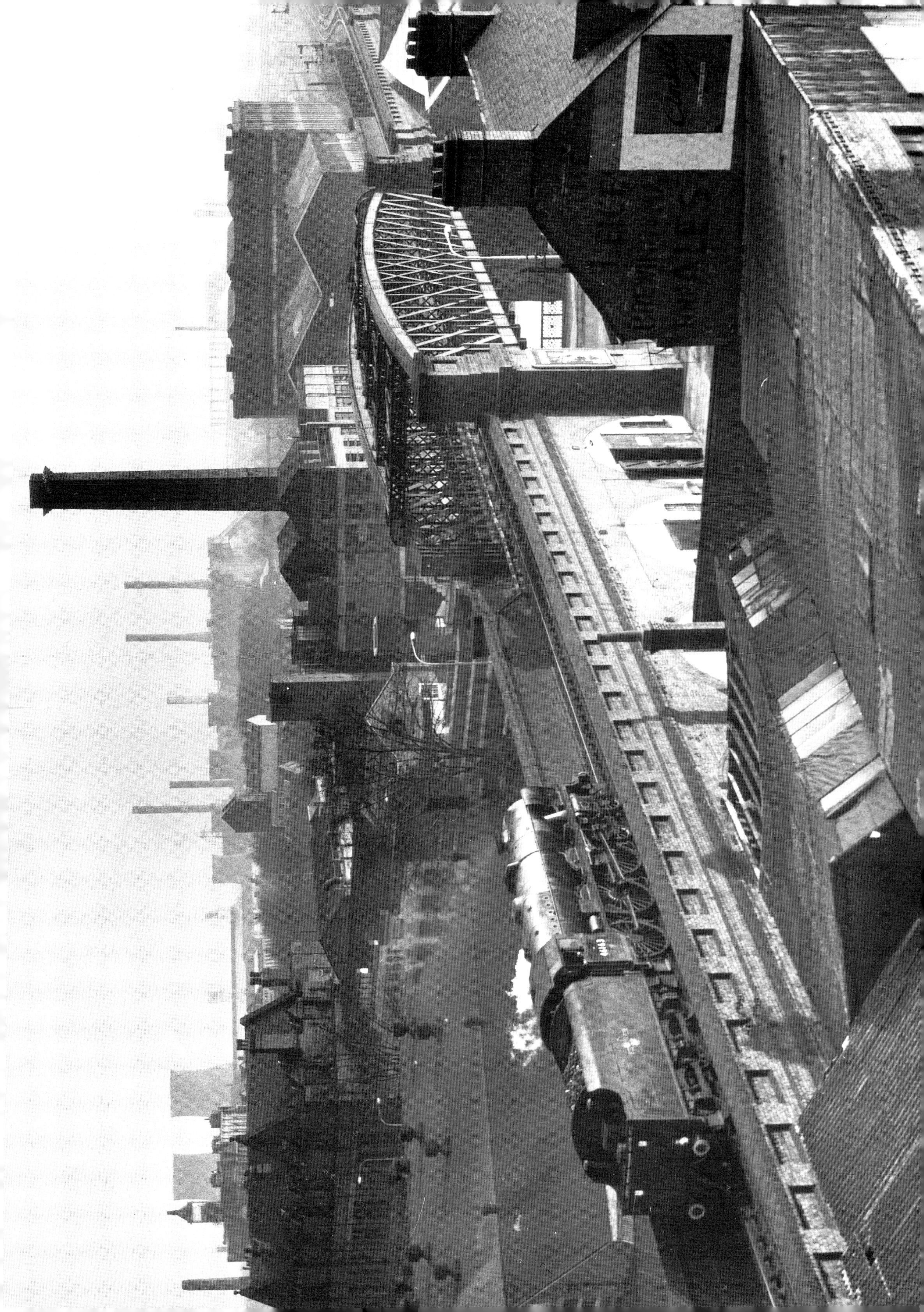

**Previous pages.
249.** Having relinquished its train at the station No 7029 'Clun Castle' retired to Leicester Central shed to await its return journey and to fill its tender with some Nottinghamshire coal. 7.4.64.

250. After its return from Doncaster with the return special 'Royal Scot' No 46143 drifts over the Leicester viaduct on its way to the shed. 7.4.64.

251 & 252. On 12th October 1963 The Locomotive Club of Great Britain ran a special over the southern end of the Great Central as far as Woodford where the train reversed and took the Stratford and Midland Junction line to Stratford on Avon as part of a circular route. The train was double headed and the engines employed were the preserved L&SWR T9 4-4-0 No 120 and a Southern Region Maunsell N Class Mogul No 31790. They were photographed at Woodford shed after their arrival where they were turned and serviced.

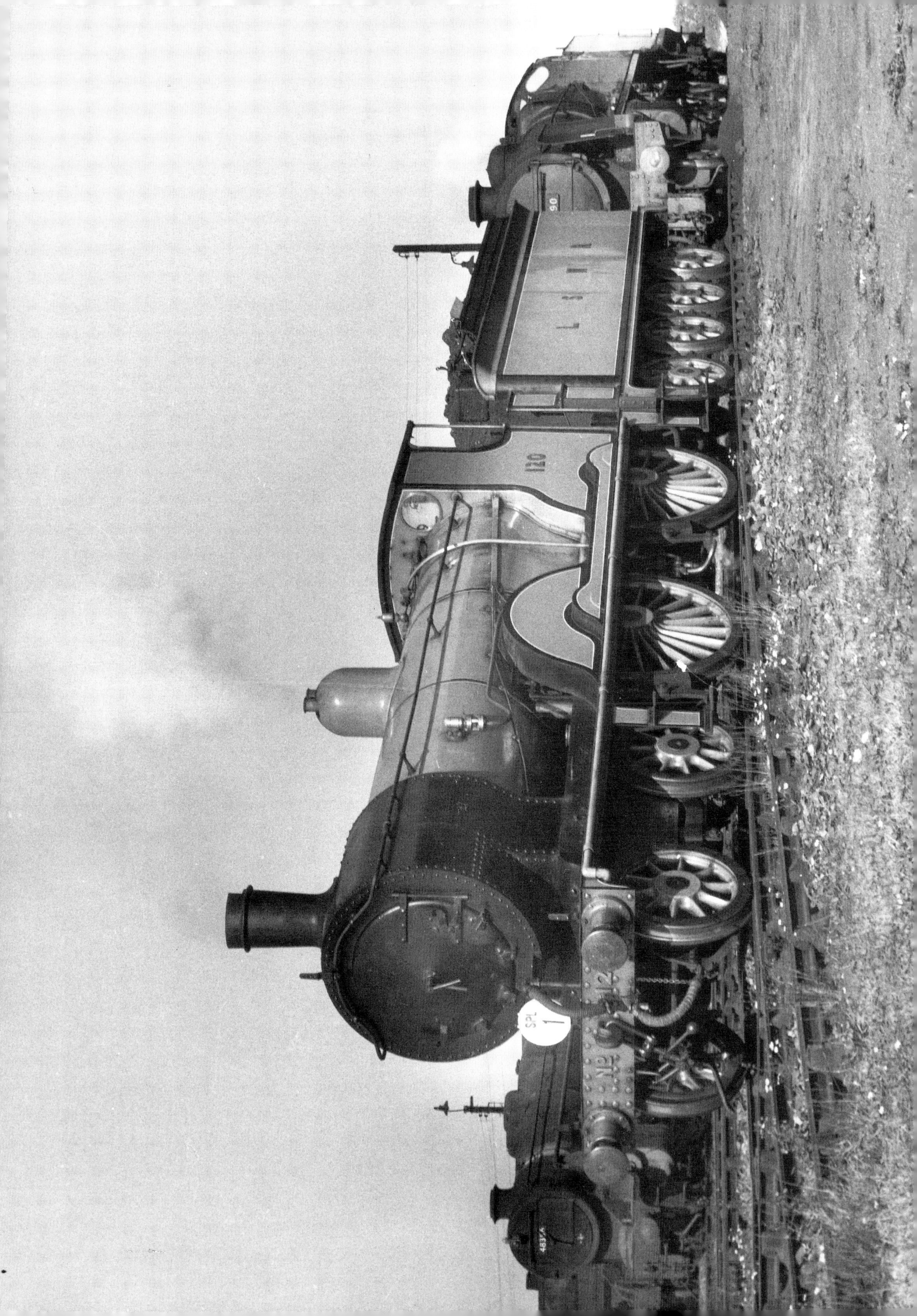

253. The train was taken on to Stratford and Gloucester by two Western Region engines, Mogul No 6368 and Collett 0-6-0 No 2242 set out from Woodford

254. Another interesting special was the annual 'East Midlander' run by the R.C.T.S. On 13th May 1962 it travelled from Nottingham Victoria to Darlington and was exceptional for its use of Southern Region 'Schools' class 4-4-0 No 30925 'Cheltenham' as partner to an aged Midland 2P 4-4-0 No 40646. The Southern engine travelled down light engine on the evening of May 11th complete with a Southern Region inspector, the

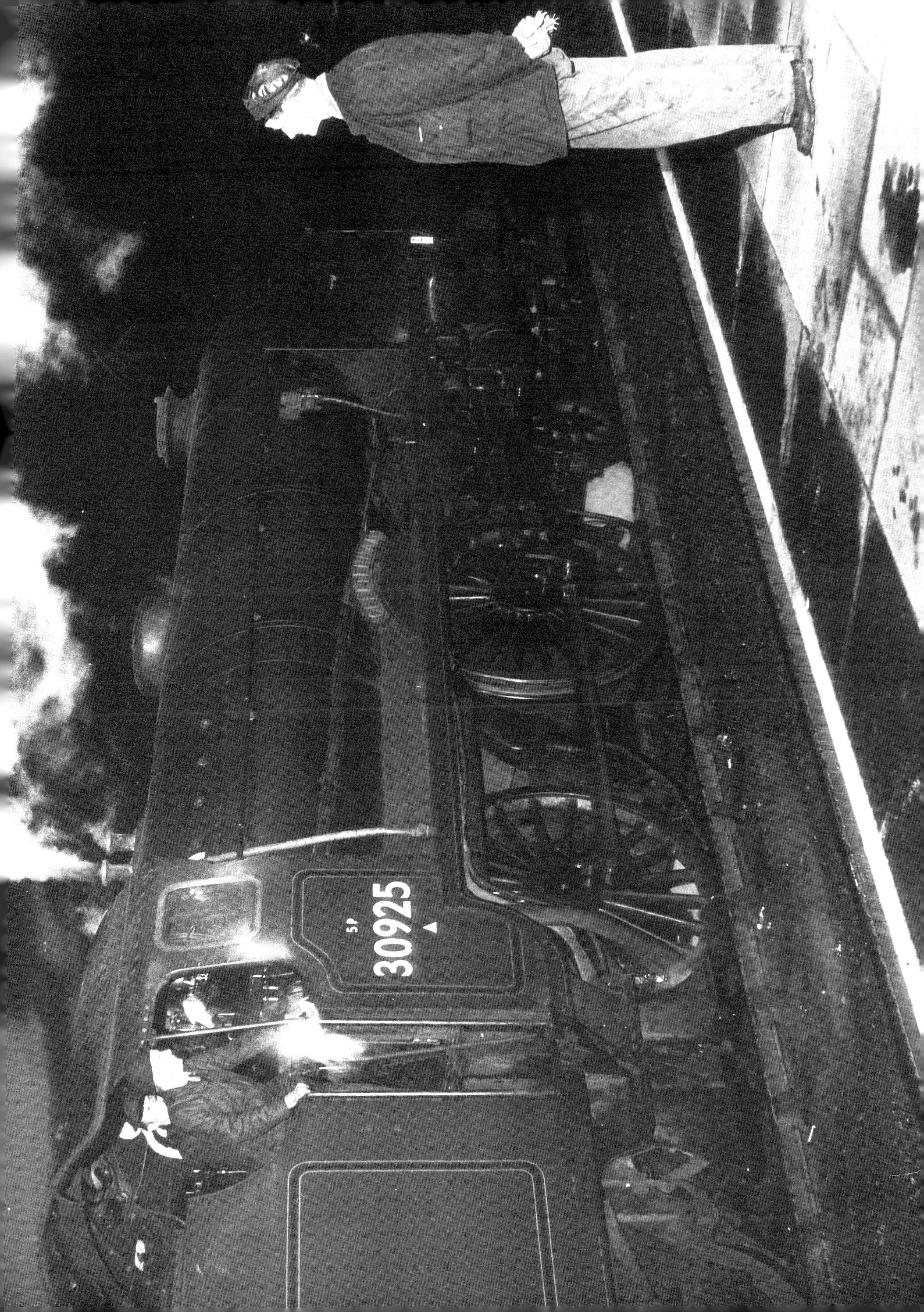
5P
30925

255. On the morning of May 13th 1962 the two 4-4-0s draw a captive audience as they wait at the head of their

256. One of two open-flash shots taken of the two engines in the dark after their arrival back at Nottingham Victoria. As the leading engine the Southern loco had the brake and therefore also dictated the running. The speeds of over 80 mph on the way

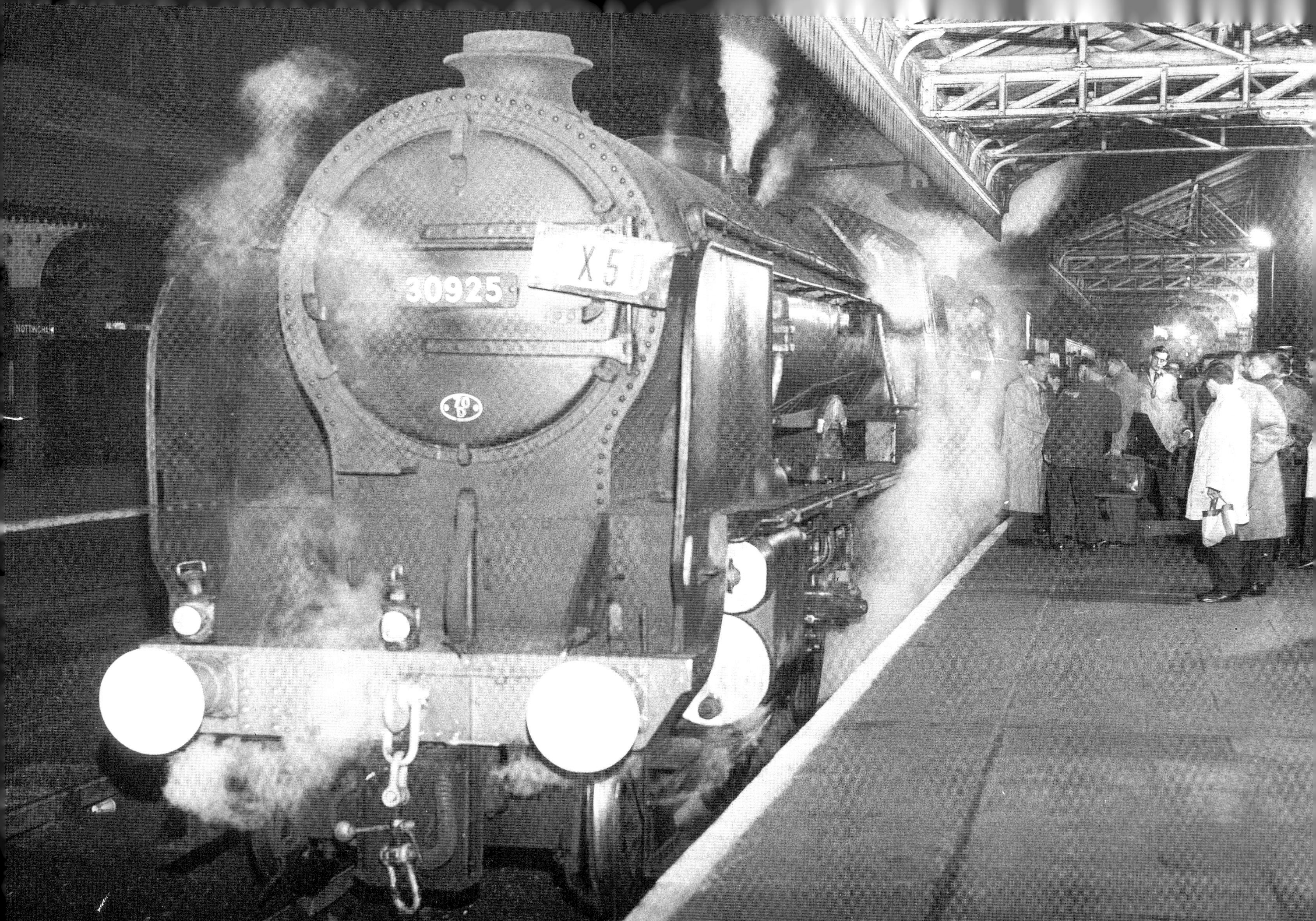
30925
X 50

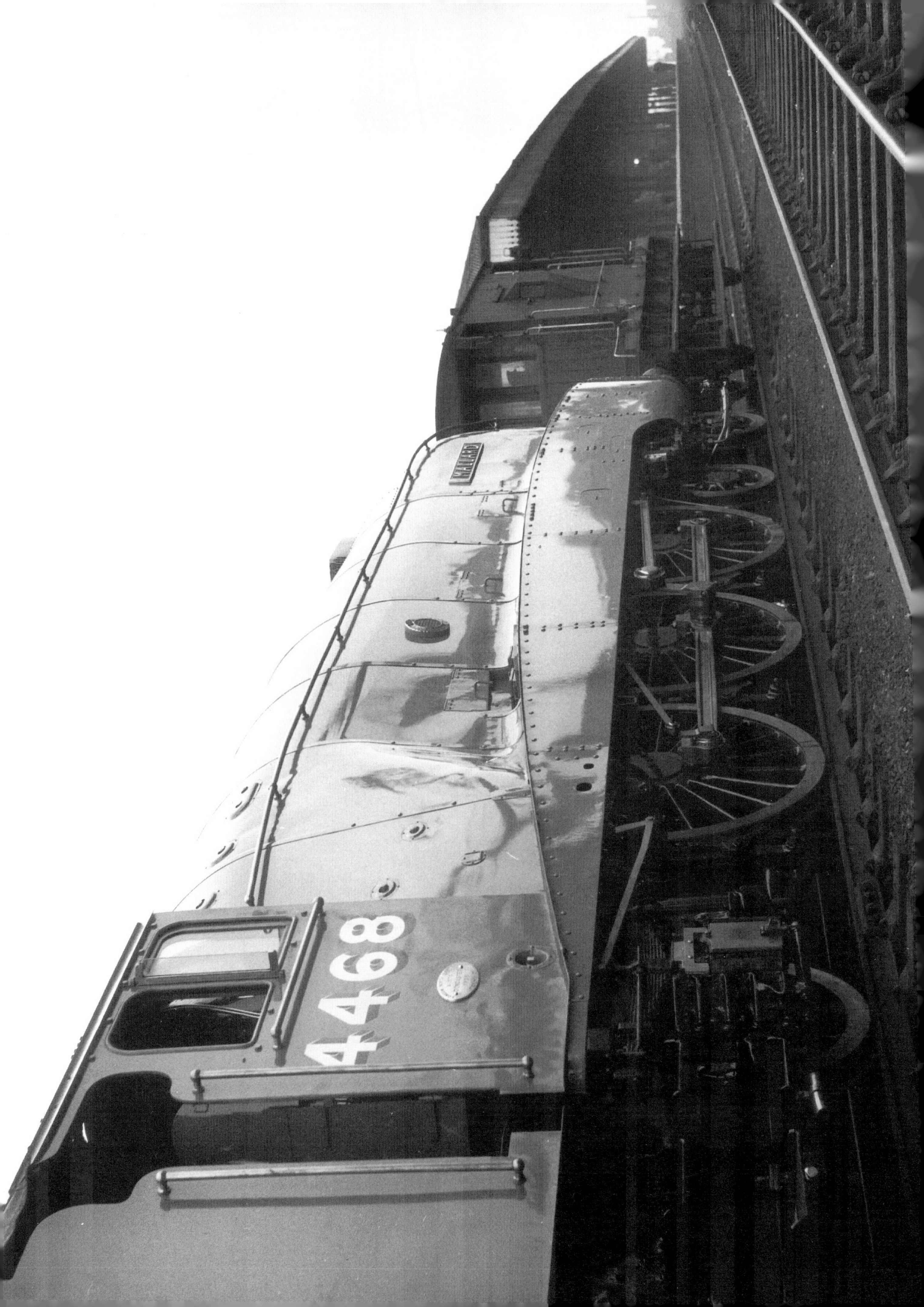
MALLARD
4468

Clapham bound. The world speed record holder, *Sir Nigel Gresley*, is hauled delicately and 'dead' up the Great Central on its journey from Doncaster works to Clapham Tranport Museum. It pauses at Leicester Central for its bearings to be checked for any overheating. 25.2.64.

3rd 1966 a diesel service continued to operate between Rugby Central and Arkwright Street, Nottingham. It lingered until 3rd May 1969 when the line was abandoned completely. The 16.20 from Rugby Central to Nottingham runs onto the 'birdcage' bridge over the West Coast main line at Rugby.

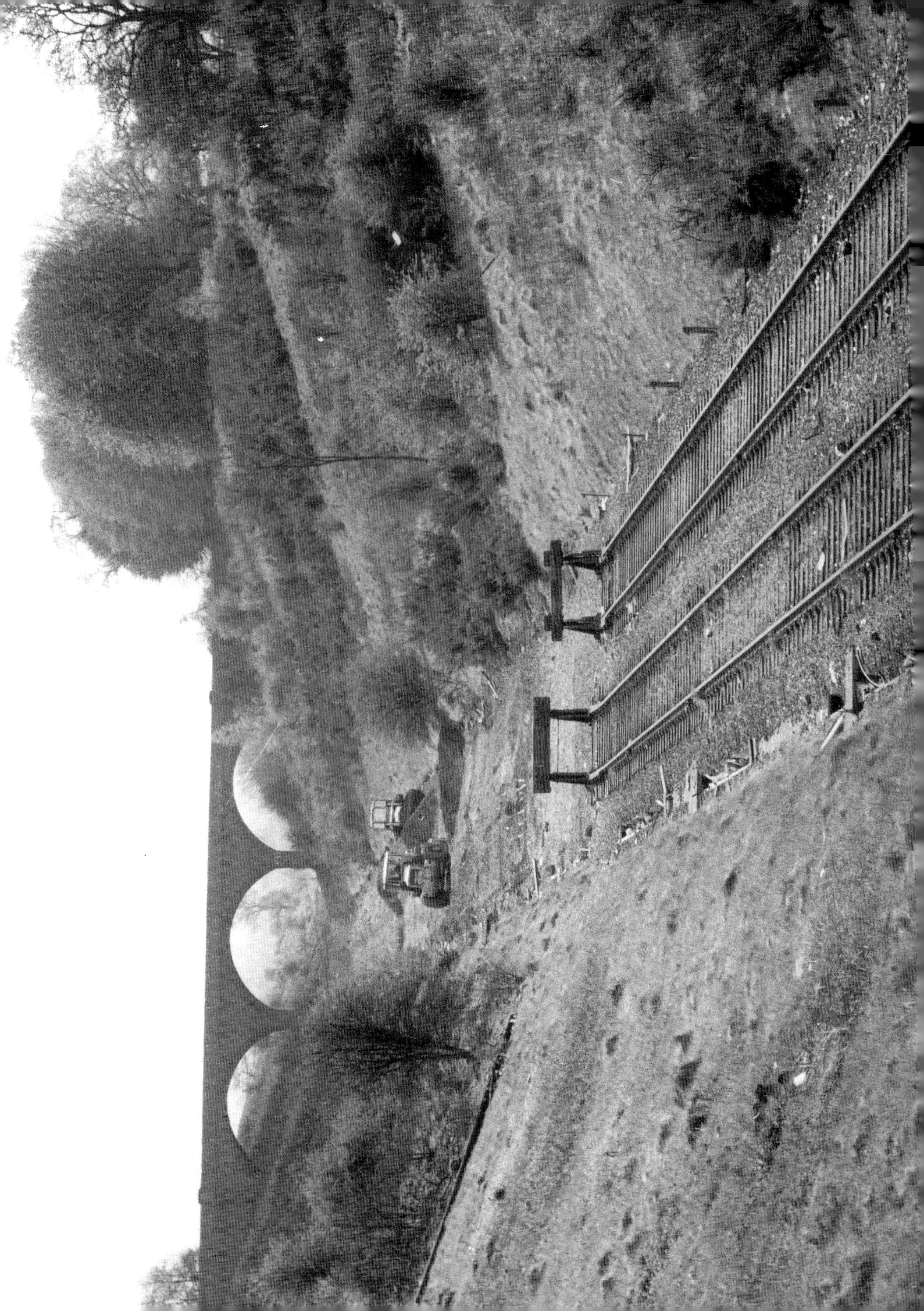

Destruction and dereliction.

259. Rugby. Stop blocks and ballast removal in the Dunsmore cutting in November 1966. The haste with which the track was removed south of Rugby after the closure of the through route in 1966 made it seem almost an act of triumph and it confirmed the underlying desperation and hostility with which the rundown of the Great Central was effected.

260. Brackley viaduct demolition. The fine blue brick structure of Brackley viaduct was destroyed by blasting in 1978. Initially 18 piers were blown leaving two at the northern end to be demolished as a separate operation. This photograph was taken at the actual moment of blasting when the shock wave of the explosion was being transmitted around the area of the viaduct. The 'blanket' laid over the point of rupture to contain any flying debris has been blown several feet into the air while the detonation can be seen to have lifted the whole arch from its pier.

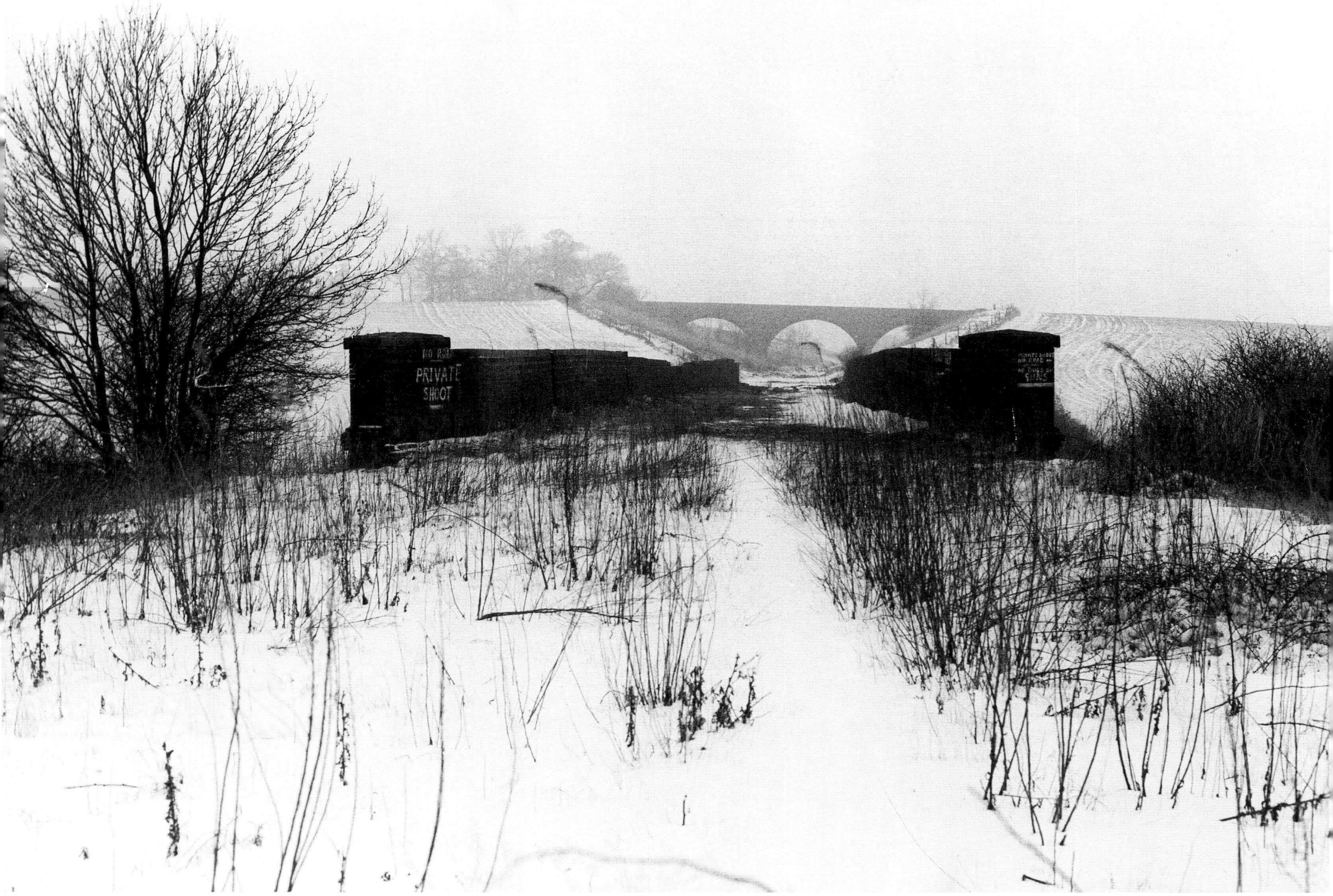

262. Leicester North viaduct. Breach over the River Soar.

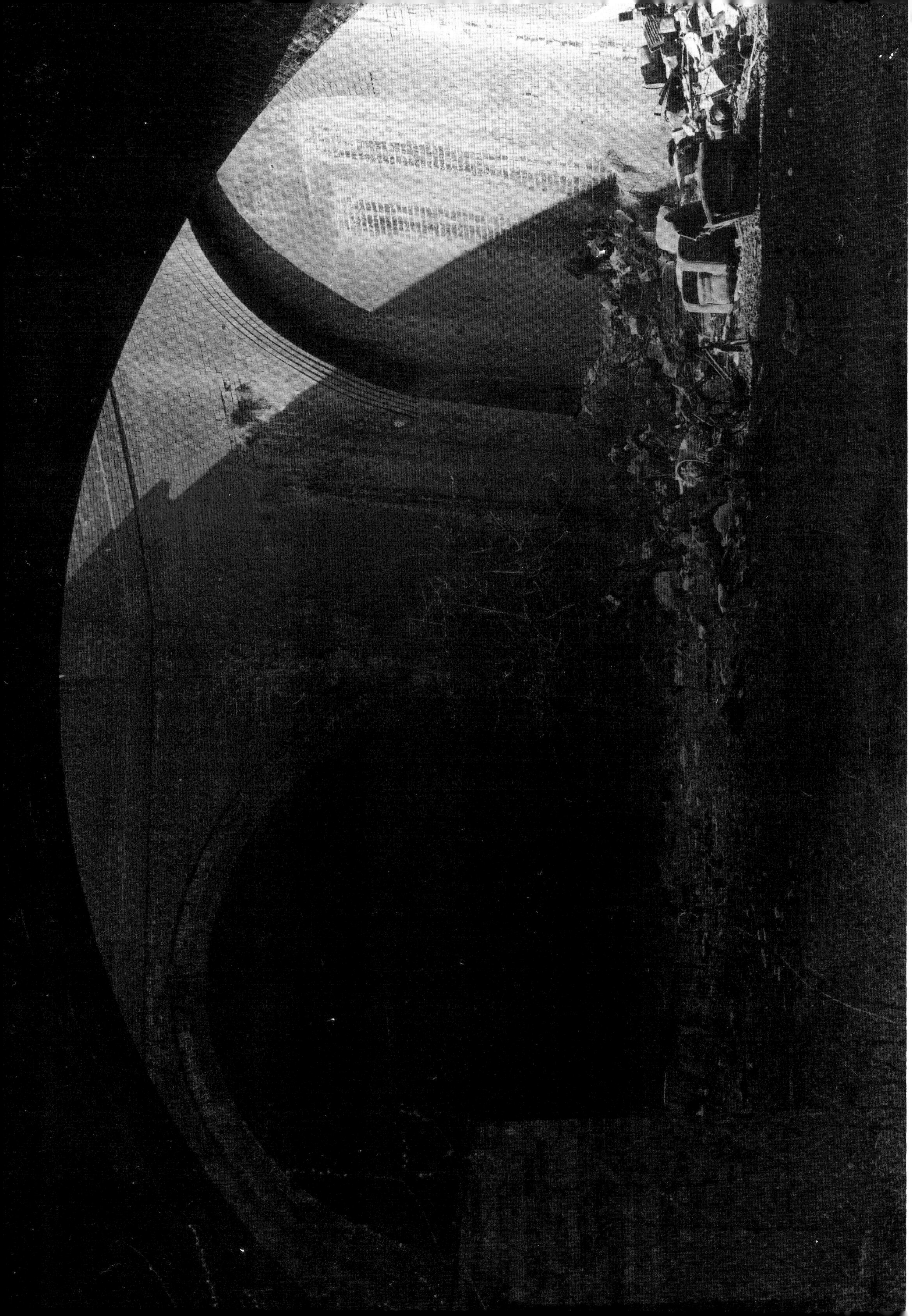

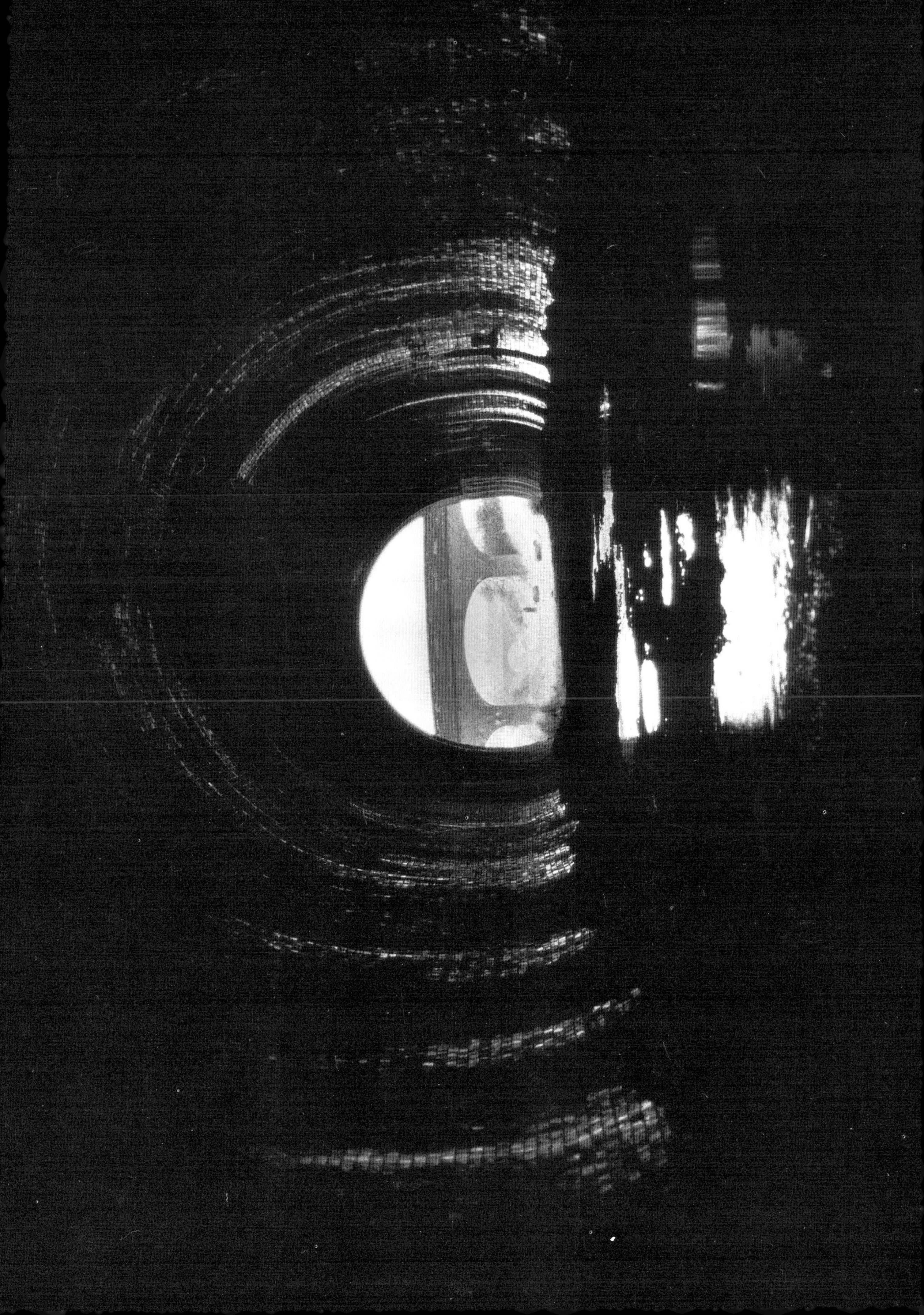

265

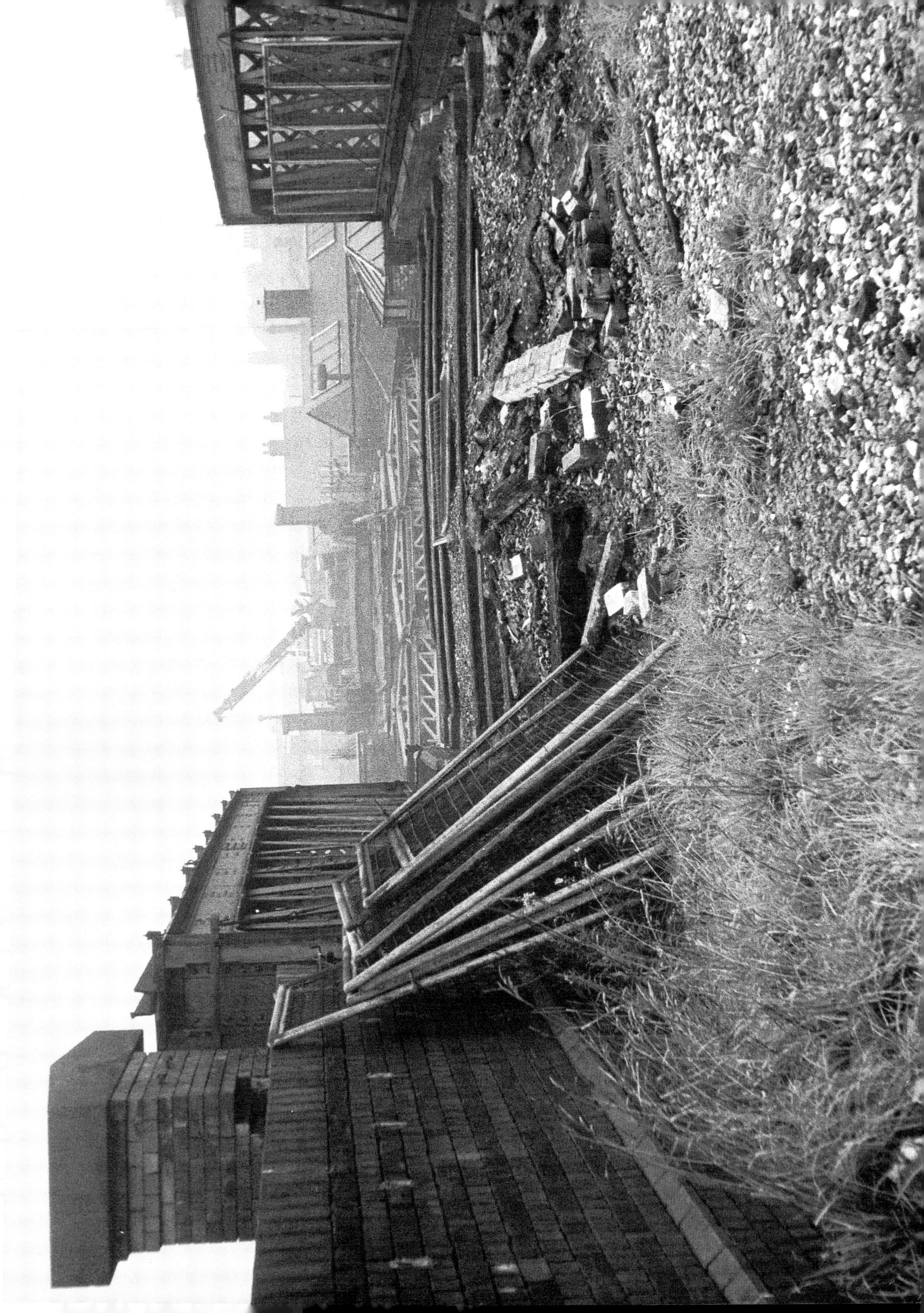

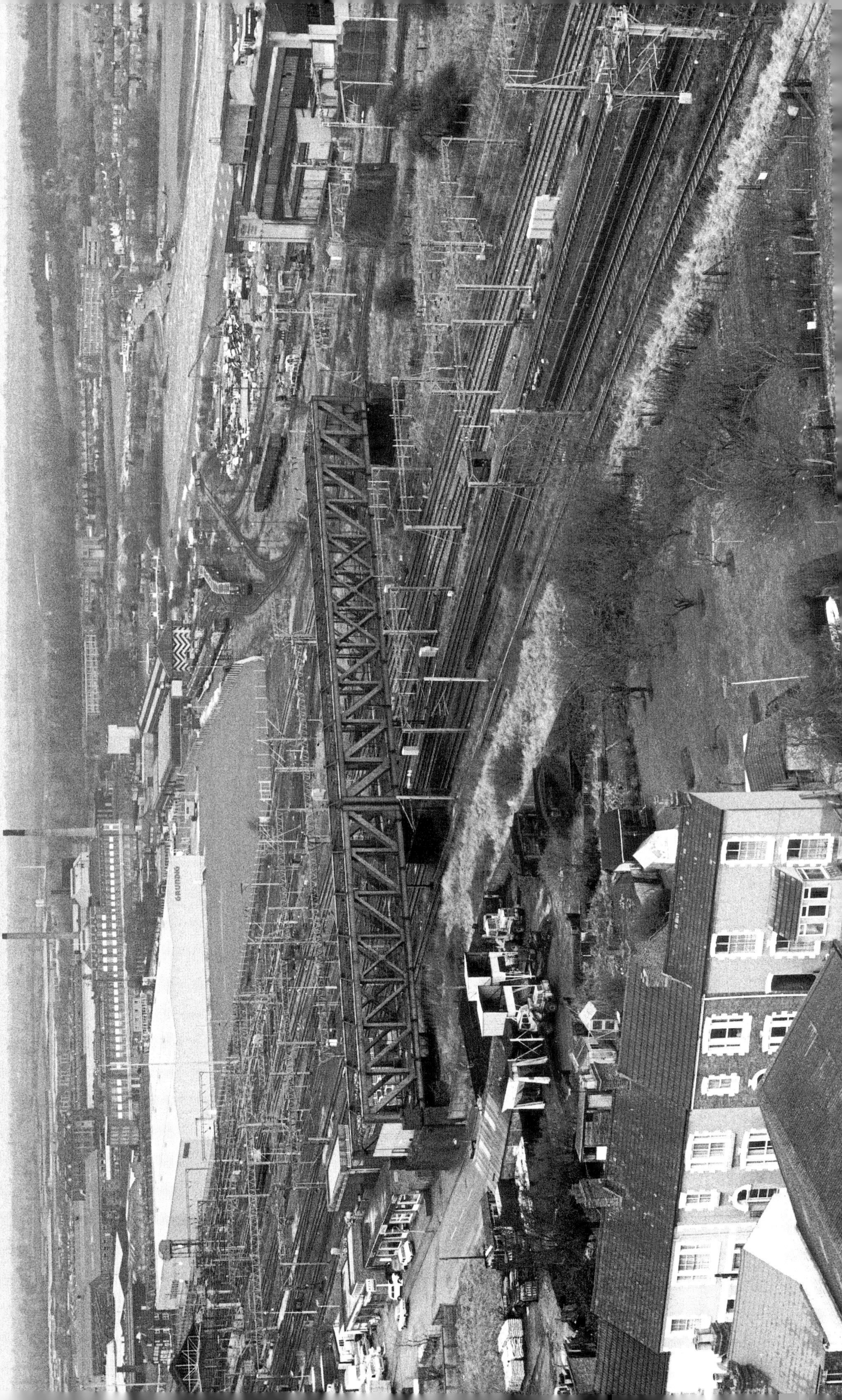
GRUNDIG

Sir John Betjeman once sat in the booking hall and refused to get his tickets.

'birdcage' bridge over the electrified West Coast main line.

269. The Holmewood-Tibshelf Trail which for most of its length follows the filled-in course of the Great Central. The houses of Pilsley are spread along the skyline and the

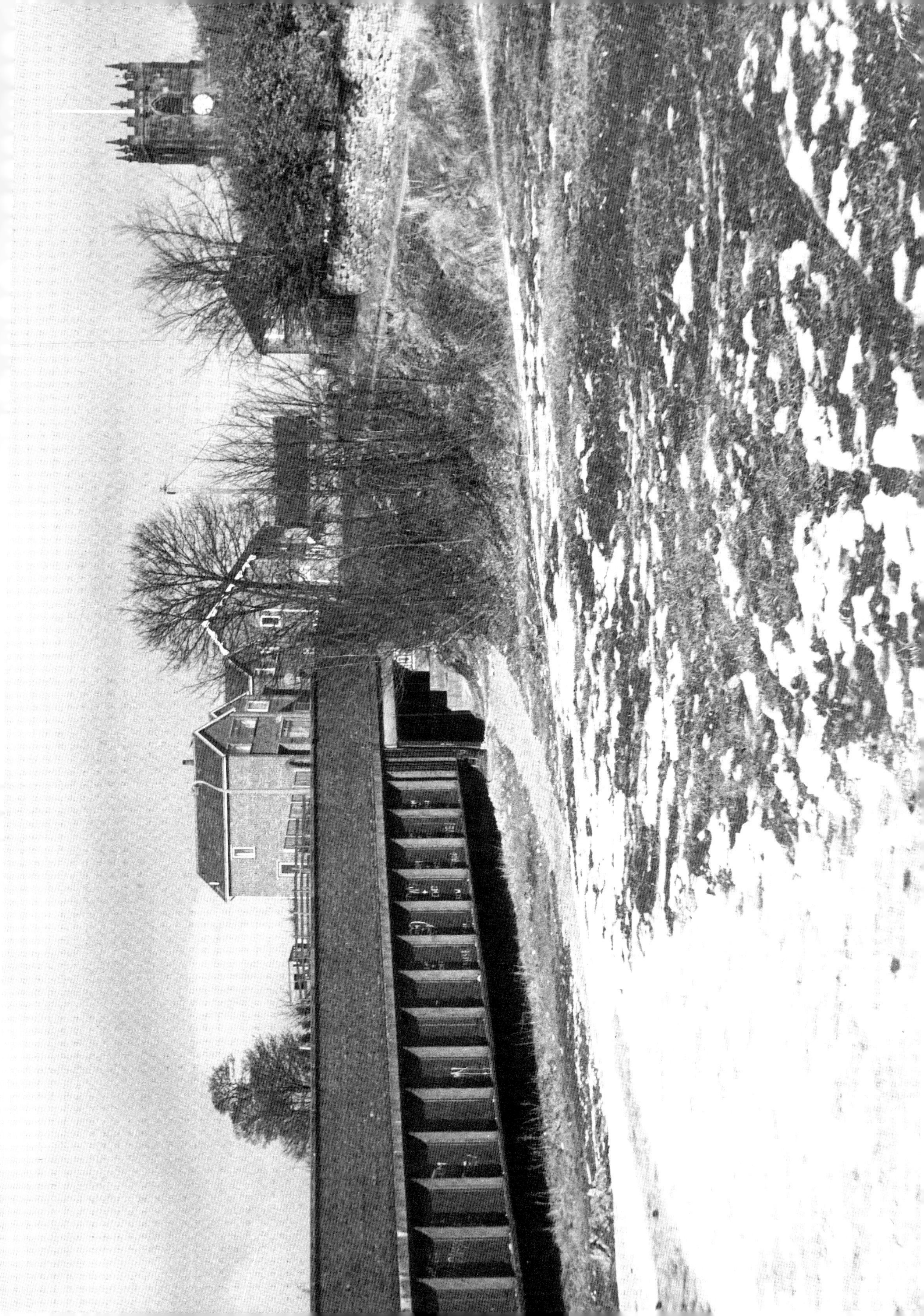

271. Holmewood where a dual carriageway road replaces the railway while beyond are the spoil tips of Williamthorpe colliery which cover the abandoned railway. The pit

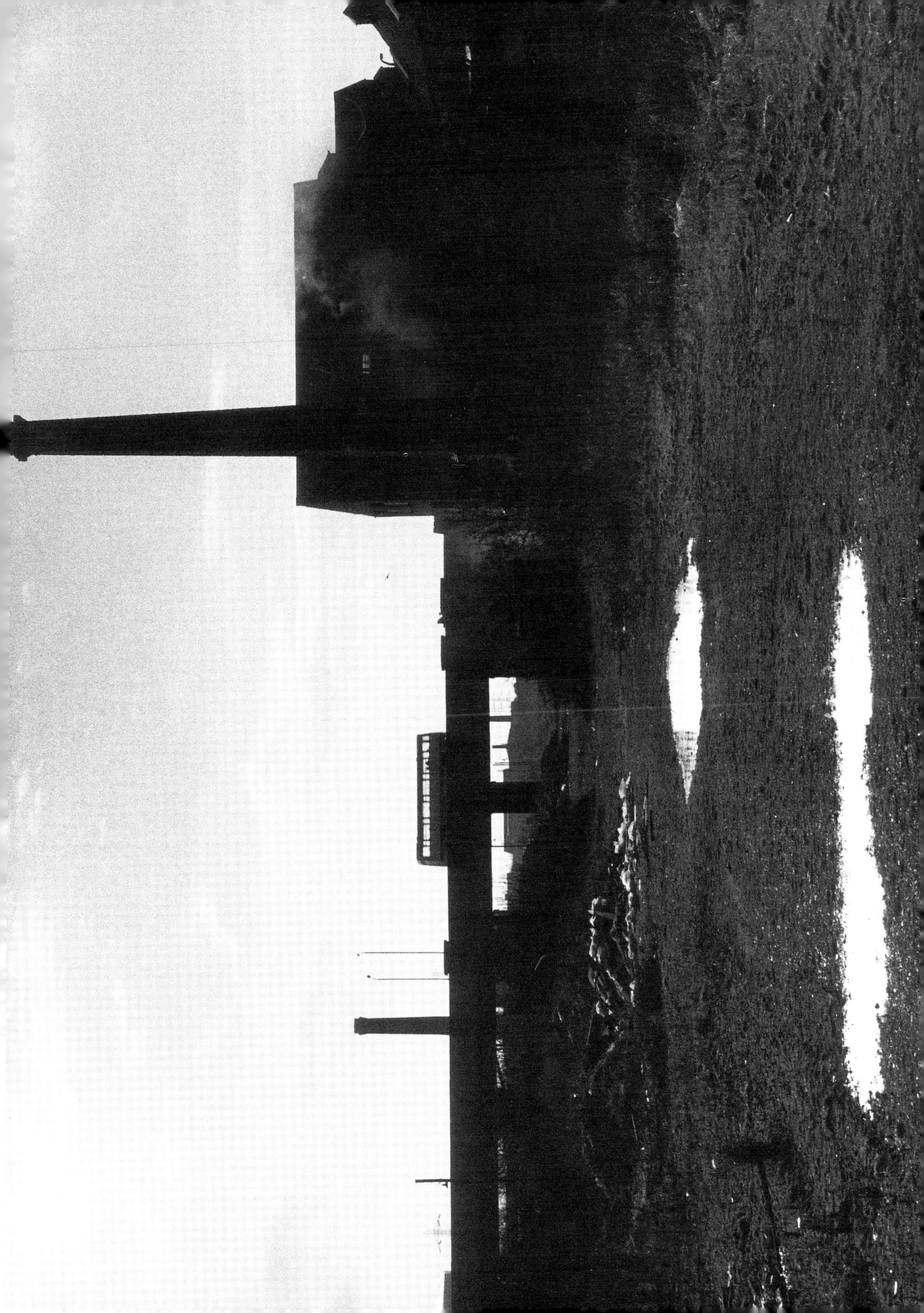

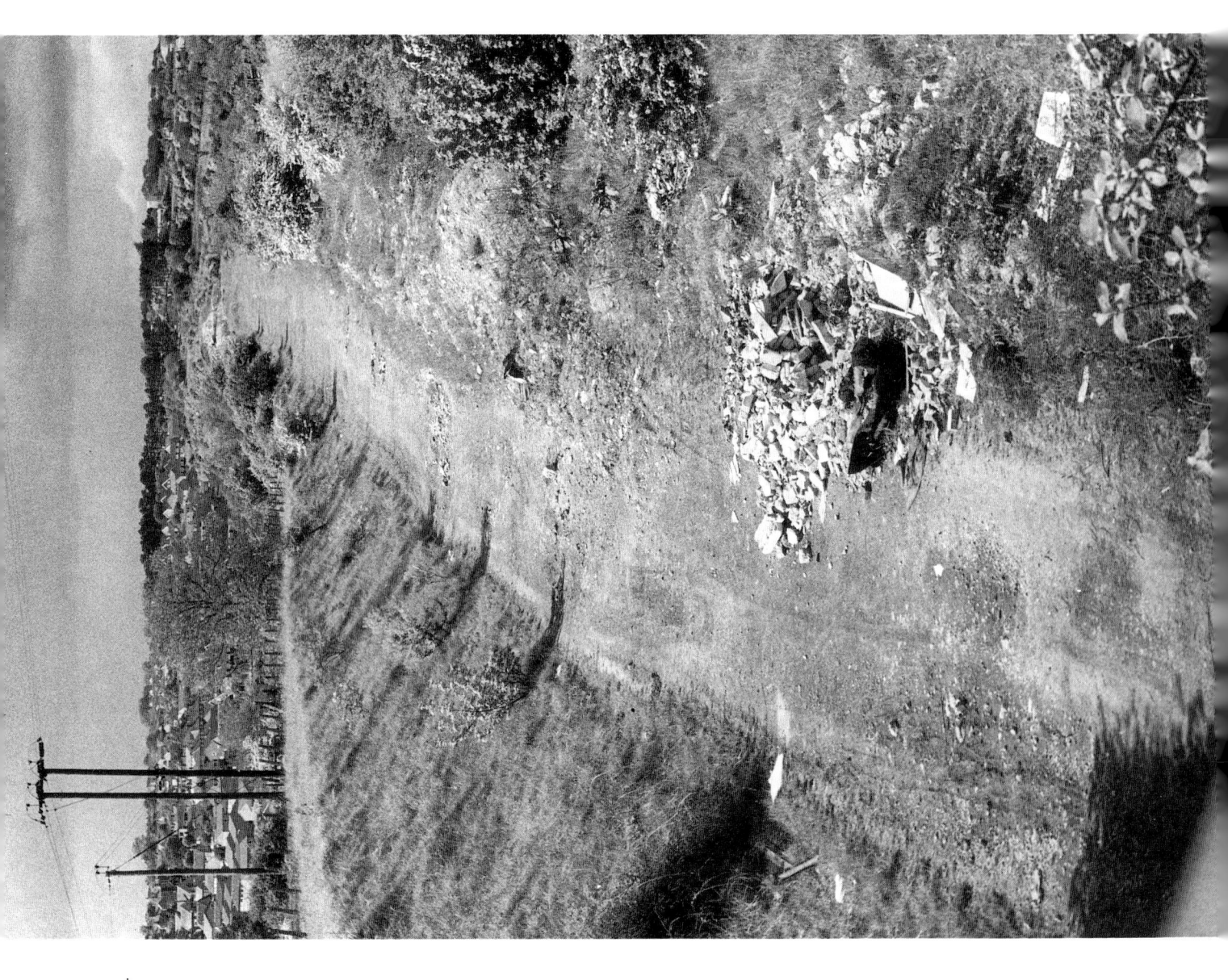

273. Brackley. Trackbed but no viaduct. Looking north from the Buckingham road.

274. Leicester. Memory heap on the site of the Leicester Central carriage sheds. Luggage rack netting, light fittings and upholstery.

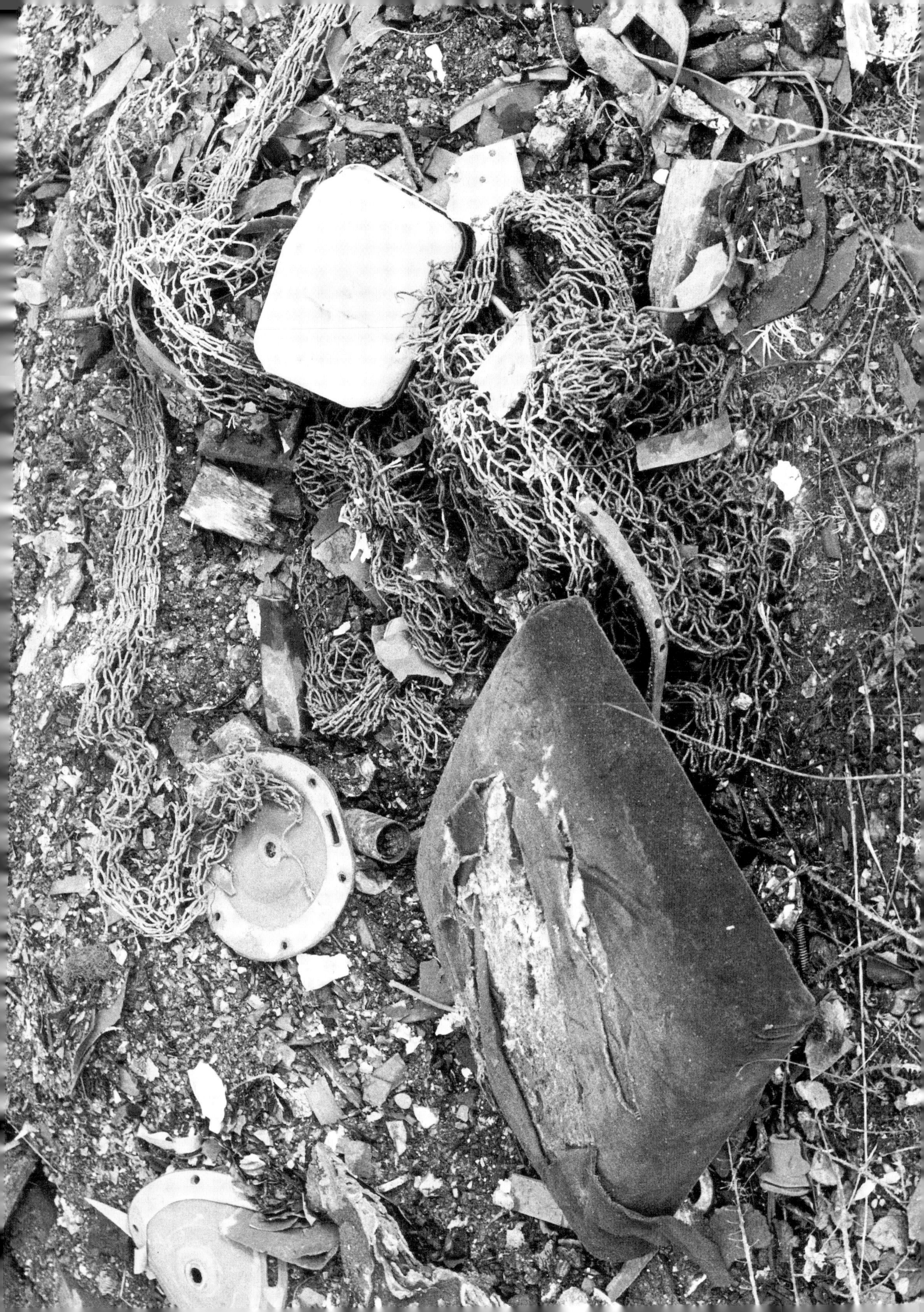

NATIONAL UNION OF RAILWAYMEN
WOODFORD
BRANCH.
LABOUR'S
"YOU HAVE NOTHING TO LOSE BUT YOUR CHAINS; YOU HAVE A WORLD

Parish Church Woodford Halse 1. 13.6.76

telegraph pole insulators is given an airing. 13.6.76

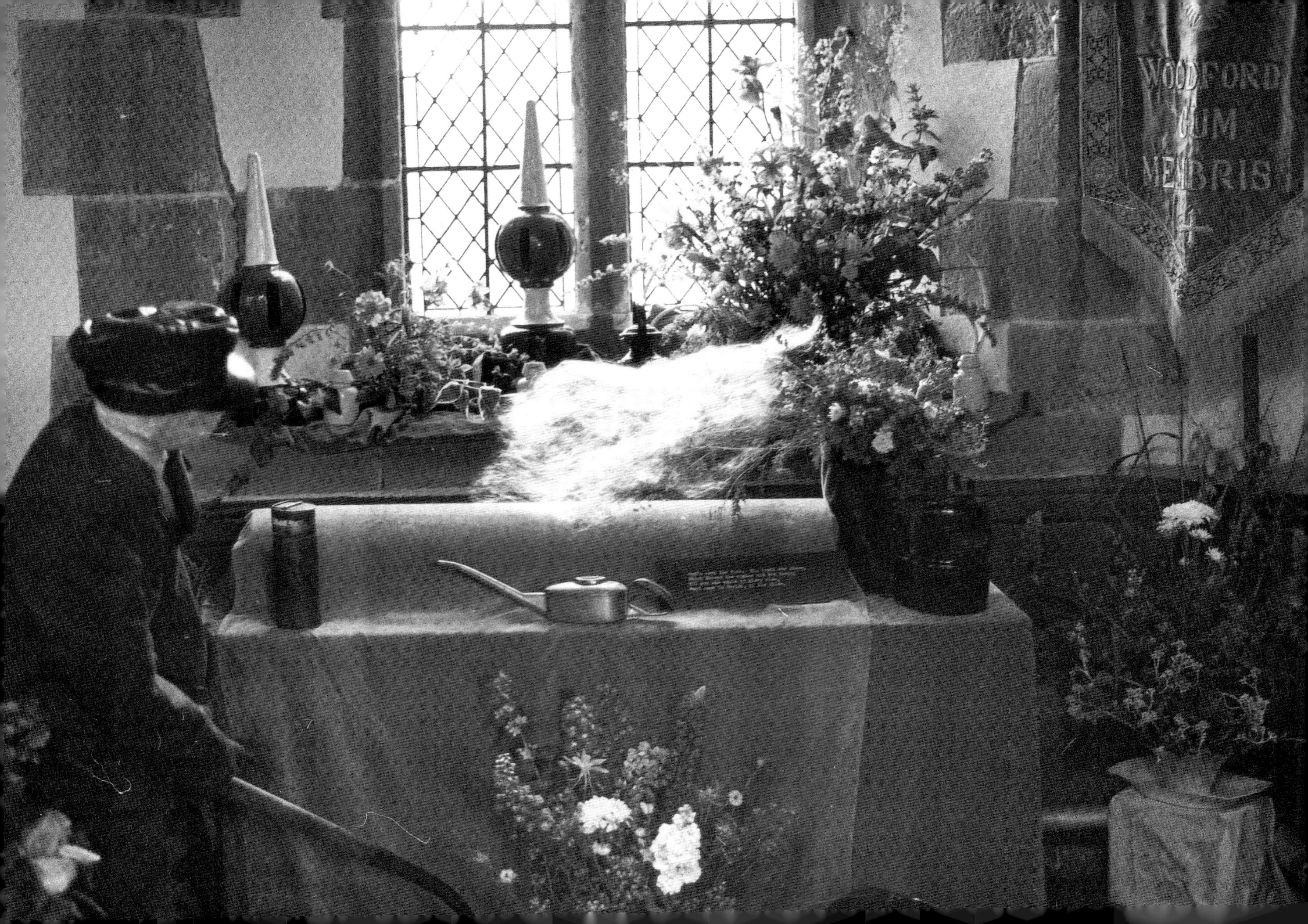
WOODFORD
CUM
MEMBRIS

217. Window sill flower collection and summer flower arrangement (detail). Parish Church, Woodford Halse 2. 13.6.76.

Parish Church, Woodford Halse 3. 13.6.76.

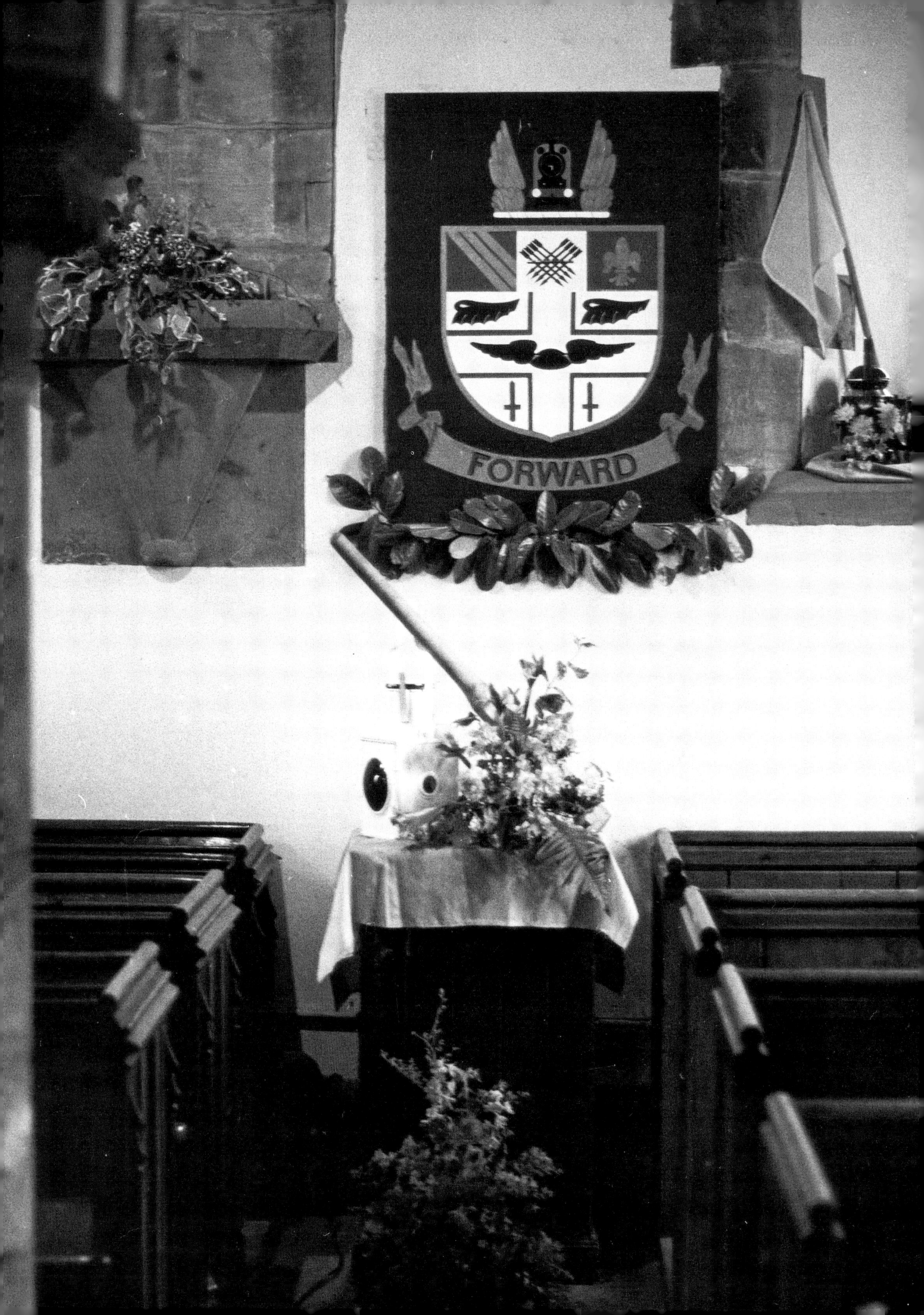
FORWARD

279. Lamps, guard's flag, Great Central coat of arms, leaf and floral decorations- St. Mary's Parish Church, Woodford Halse. 13.6.76.

280. Former Passed Fireman Derek Thornton reads the first lesson. Morning service St. Mary's Parish church, Woodford Halse. 13.6.76.

281. Rescue Operation 1. The Buckinghamshire Railway Centre at Quainton Rd., north of Aylesbury. Metropolitan Railway Class C 0-4-4 tank No 1.

282. Rescue Operation 2. The Great Central Railway (1976) PLC's headquarters at Loughborough Central station with former Robinson 'Director' 4-4-0 No 506 'Butler Henderson' in Platform 1 with a 'Royal Mail' special.

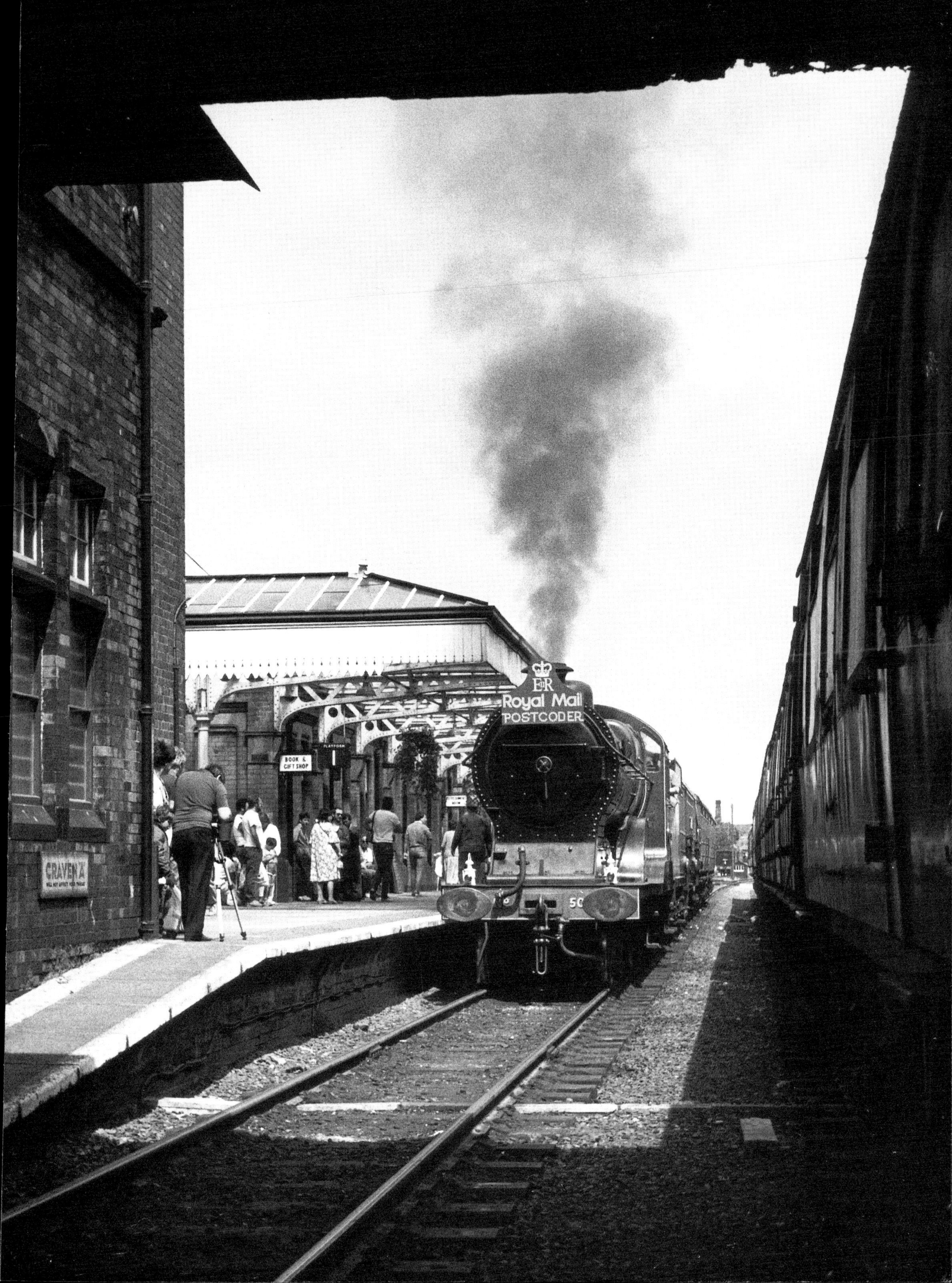
Royal Mail
POSTCODER
BOOK &
GIFT SHOP
CRAVEN "A"

283. Driver Durrington (retired) departs. Aged 85, Albert strikes off to tend and cultivate his two allotment gardens.

397. EAST. BANK. Rd
SHEFFIELD 2
YORKS
9/1/64

Dear Sir

Many thanks for the photographs you kindly sent me. All who have see them think they are wonderfull. I must apologise for my late reply due to being away in London in short kiddy, I fancy Jenny Woods photos on to him now he lbs asked me to worry to you his sincere thanks and best wishes. Our depot now is completely dieselled, though we have three turns where we relieve Mexborough crew on steam engine last week Lincoln and Boston depots closed to steam, so we must now turn down to progress and try and content ourselves my fireman and I enjoyed your company greatly and hope some day to meet you again.

Wishing you all the best for the future.

Yours sincerely
Ernest Wilson

Dear Colin.

Many thanks for the photo's, they are good in detail if not so sharp as you would have liked. I will see that George gets one of them.

Yes I am getting on well with Don we've had a few rough trips with the Black 5s but we now have 879 on the road again. 911 is out of the works. I believe he came back with two or three hot boxes. We should have had him out the newspaper last week but he blew the middle piston gland out and they tell us that a firebox seam has gone, what a show just coming out of the works.!

Hope to be seeing you around soon.

Yours sincerely,
Jack

P.S.
Find enclosed 4/- for photos